BORROWINGS IN INFORMAL AMERICAN ENGLISH

What do "bimbo," "glitch," "savvy," and "shtick" all have in common? They are all expressions used in informal American English that have been taken from other languages. This pioneering book provides a comprehensive description of borrowings in informal American English, based on a large database of citations from thousands of contemporary sources, including the press, film, and TV. It presents the United States as a linguistic "melting pot," with words from a diverse range of languages now frequently appearing in the lexicon. It examines these borrowings from various perspectives, including discussions of terms, donors, types, changes, functions, and themes. It also features an alphabetical glossary of 1,200 representative expressions, defined and illustrated by 5,500 usage examples, providing an insightful and practical resource for readers. Combining scholarship with readability, this book is a fascinating storehouse of information for students and researchers in linguistics as well as anyone interested in lexical variation in contemporary English.

DR. MAŁGORZATA KOWALCZYK is a sociolinguist specializing in lexical variation and its description. Her numerous book publications include *Black Lexicon* (2012) and *The Dictionary of Spanish Loanwords in American Slang* (2015).

Earlier titles not listed are also available

BORROWINGS IN INFORMAL AMERICAN ENGLISH

MAŁGORZATA KOWALCZYK

CAMBRIDGE
UNIVERSITY PRESS

Shaftesbury Road, Cambridge CB2 8EA, United Kingdom

One Liberty Plaza, 20th Floor, New York, NY 10006, USA

477 Williamstown Road, Port Melbourne, VIC 3207, Australia

314–321, 3rd Floor, Plot 3, Splendor Forum, Jasola District Centre,
New Delhi – 110025, India

103 Penang Road, #05–06/07, Visioncrest Commercial, Singapore 238467

Cambridge University Press is part of Cambridge University Press & Assessment,
a department of the University of Cambridge.

We share the University's mission to contribute to society through the pursuit of
education, learning and research at the highest international levels of excellence.

www.cambridge.org
Information on this title: www.cambridge.org/9781009346870

DOI: 10.1017/9781009346917

First published 2023

A catalogue record for this publication is available from the British Library.

A Cataloging-in-Publication data record for this book is available from the Library of Congress

ISBN 978-1-009-34687-0 Hardback

Contents

Acknowledgments

I am grateful to Professor Maciej Widawski of the Department of English Linguistics at WSB University in Gdańsk, a fellow sociolinguist and lexicographer, for his tremendous support for the project; his books on slang have been an inspiration for me since my undergraduate studies, and I have been lucky to work with him on several scholarly projects. I also wish to thank several people who have been helpful to and supportive of me in my academic endeavors, including this work: Professor John Rickford of the Department of Linguistics at Stanford University; Professor Elżbieta Mańczak-Wohlfeld of the Institute of English at the Jagiellonian University in Cracow; Professors Jillian Castillo-Speed and Wei Chi Poon of the Department of Ethnic Studies Library at the University of California–Berkeley; Director Leilani Freund of George Smathers Library at the University of Florida in Gainesville; Director Pamela Gillespie of Morris Cohen Library at the City University of New York; Associate University Librarians Dani Brecher Cook and Tamara Rhodes of Theodor Geisel Library at the University of California–San Diego, and Visiting Scholars Advisor Belén Flores of the Department of Linguistics at the University of California–Berkeley. At Cambridge University Press, I would like to thank Senior Commissioning Editor Helen Barton, and Professor Merja Kytö, editor of the Studies in English Language series, for their generous support and continued interest in my project resulting in the publication of this book; Rachel Goodyear for her superb copyediting; and Isabel Collins, Stephanie Taylor, and Reshma Xavier for their excellent management of the production of the book.

The lexical material used in this book was verified and expanded using library resources at the following academic institutions: Arizona State University (Tempe, AZ), City University of New York (New York, NY), Columbia University (New York, NY), Florida State University (Tallahassee, FL), Harvard University (Cambridge, MA), Princeton University (Princeton, NJ), San Francisco State University (San Francisco, CA), Simon Fraser

University (Vancouver, BC), Stanford University (Stanford, CA), Tulane University (New Orleans, LA), University of Alabama (Tuscaloosa, AL), University of Arizona (Tucson, AZ), University of California (Berkeley, CA), University of California (Los Angeles, CA), University of California (San Diego, CA), University of California (Santa Barbara, CA), University of Florida (Gainesville, FL), University of Miami (Coral Gables, FL), University of Mississippi (Oxford, MS), University of New Mexico (Albuquerque, NM), University of North Florida (Jacksonville, FL), University of Ottawa (Ottawa, ON), University of Washington (Seattle, WA), University of Wisconsin (Madison, WI), and Yale University (New Haven, CT) as well as New York Public Library (New York, NY) and the Library of Congress (Washington, DC). Due acknowledgment is given.

Abbreviations

This book generally eschews abbreviations in the main text, but the following grammatical and bibliographical abbreviations appear in the Glossary:

Grammar

adj.	adjective
adv.	adverb
excl.	exclamation
n.	noun
num.	numeral
phr.	phrase
pron.	pronoun
sent.	sentence
v.	verb

References

AS   Angus Stevenson, *Oxford Dictionary of English* (Oxford University Press, 2010)

JG   Jonathon Green, *Green's Dictionary of Slang* (Chambers Harrap, 2010)

KC   Barbara Kipfer and Robert L. Chapman, *Dictionary of American Slang* (HarperCollins, 2007)

TD   Tom Dalzell, *The Routledge Dictionary of Modern American Slang and Unconventional English* (Routledge, 2009 and 2018)

Introduction

This book documents and describes lexical borrowings in informal American English, an interesting and expanding part of the vernacular vocabulary of American English. Their popularity is hardly surprising given the growing social, cultural, and political **importance** of ethnic minorities, which in 2021 constituted almost 40 percent of the entire population of the United States (see US Census Bureau Online); they are also firmly entrenched in the fabric of American speech reflecting the immigrant character of the country symbolized by the concept of "the melting pot" (Mauk and Oakland [1995] 2005: 8). Although seen as the bailiwick of immigrants or their descendants, these expressions are no longer limited in use to their speech, and – as evidenced in this book by the sheer bulk of citations from diverse contemporary US sources – they have grown increasingly common among larger segments of American society. The popularity of informal borrowings also stems from the spreading ubiquity of informal language featuring prominently in social media, press, film, television, and literature and occurring in more communicative situations than ever (see Ayto 1999: vii). Moreover, informal lexicon – jointly composed of slang and colloquialism – takes up at least 20 percent of all vocabulary known by the average American (see estimates by Lighter 1994: xxxvi; Widawski and Kowalczyk 2012: 200), while slang itself is considered to be a distinctively American phenomenon (Coleman 2014: 12), strongly rooted in the oral tradition and sociocultural context of the country. Finally, the frequent use of informal borrowings in mass media and popular culture contributes to their popularity and increases their circulation nationwide.

Despite the growing importance of this type of vocabulary, **publications** on borrowings in informal American English have been scarce. First of all, borrowings are often considered a marginal or "negligible" part of informal lexicon, especially its slang component (see, for instance, Eble 1996: 75), a repeated and uninformed claim which this book aims to disprove. Second of all, while there are several academic papers loosely connected with the subject, they are either narrowed in scope to individual languages or focused on select aspects of informal borrowings; general dictionaries on slang and colloquialism, while often including borrowings, are necessarily limited to lexicographic presentation and understandably lack any detailed linguistic analysis; finally, there are no book-length monographs designed specifically to address the issue (see Chapter 1 for details). As a result, there has been a growing need for an informative resource book which would offer a systematic and comprehensive description of this type of lexicon, especially in an educational context.

By addressing specifically borrowings in informal American English, this book attempts to fulfill this need. Importantly, instead of focusing on theoretical aspects or sociohistorical context, it has a chiefly descriptive and educational **orientation**. While both *informal* and *borrowing* are thoroughly defined and characterized in the book (see Chapters 2 and 4), for the sake of this introduction let us briefly define the two concepts. First of all, in this book both of these terms refer to language and not any other aspect of human life. *Informal* refers to a type of vocabulary which is stylistically "lower" than the standard language and "below" the formal and neutral registers on the formality scale (Widawski 2015: 9), while *borrowing* is generally defined as an expression "borrowed" or "taken" from one language to another (Stevenson 2010: 199). Fused together, these two terms refer broadly to a subset of lexicon composed of foreign-origin expressions transplanted into an informal lexicon of American English. Such expressions are used mainly by immigrant and ethnic minorities in the United States but have also become assimilated into general informal American English (Allen 1993: 6) and are widely known by Americans regardless of their ethnicity.

The aim of this book is primarily the documentation and description of informal borrowings. Accordingly, the methodological **foundations** of this project stem from documentary and descriptive linguistics as well as sociolinguistics (see, for instance, Kipfer 1984, Thorne 1990, Llamas et al. 2007, Sakel and Everett 2012, or Mallinson et al. 2013), particularly slang lexicography. Such a multidisciplinary approach relies strongly on the collection of authentic lexical material in the form of a large lexical database of contextual examples, which then serves as the basis for analysis. The assumption has been to gain as much exposure to informal borrowings as possible and to record their usage in natural contexts from diverse contemporary sources. To that end, citations have been collected from such sources as film, television, magazines, literature, the Internet, and utterances by native speakers. The material was collected through extensive fieldwork in the United States in recent years, and research at academic institutions such as Stanford University, the University of California at Berkeley, the University of Arizona, the University of Florida, and the City University of New York. The methods used in data collection and database creation were varied but largely conventional: data was recorded in the form of written notes or Dictaphone recordings which were systematically entered into the database. The Internet was used extensively, and a sizable portion of citations was taken directly from online sources. The result of the project was a database of several thousand citations, which was the basis for this book. A detailed description of methodology is given in Chapter 1, while a complete list of sources is given under Sources at the end of the book.

The description of borrowings in informal American English is multi-leveled and is clearly indicated in the organization of this book's **contents**. The first two chapters are introductory in character. Chapter 1, "Foundations," focuses on an overview of research on the subject and the methodological characteristics of this project involving its scope, collection, and description of data. Chapter 2, "Terms," outlines the fundamental linguistic nomenclature including the titular "borrowing" and "informal language" as well as terms which are related or confused with these terms. Chapter 3, "Donors," identifies the language donors that have contributed to borrowings in informal American English, including both major donors, such as Spanish and Yiddish, and lesser ones. Chapter 4, "Types," views informal borrowings from diverse typological levels such as borrowed material, part of speech, assimilation, modification, frequency, or register. Chapter 5, "Changes," analyzes various lexical changes the informal borrowings have undergone when adapted into the linguistic system of American English, including phonological, orthographical, morphological, semantic, grammatical, and stylistic changes. Chapter 6, "Functions," discusses the motives for using informal borrowings and presents their referential, social, psychological, rhetorical, and cultural functions, including the phenomenon of linguistic appropriation. Chapter 7, "Themes," provides an overview of the main lexical fields of informal borrowings, grouped into three superordinate fields: core, culture-specific, and miscellaneous. All in all, the assumption is that rather than focusing on borrowings representing a single theme or taken from a single language, such multileveled linguistic description of informal borrowings from numerous languages is much more informative and useful, and lends itself to a holistic treatment of the subject matter in and of itself.

An integral part of the book is the Glossary, forming over half of the book. Aside from serving as a quick **reference**, its main purpose is to document and define the entire collection of borrowings in informal American English, many of which have been featured as illustrations in the main text of this book. The glossary lists 1,200 entries. Each entry contains grammatical identification, usage labels, a definition in standard English, a quick bibliographical reference, two contextual examples with clearly identified sources and dates, as well as dating and etymological information. Because of its large size and in-depth description, it can easily stand as a dictionary in its own right.

Finally, it should be noted that while this book is aimed primarily at linguists, teachers, and students of linguistics, it is written in a manner which is hopefully also suited to a general **readership**. Aside from its primary orientation, it is intended to have a fairly practical quality as well. This can be seen in the multileveled but straightforward organization of its contents, including chapter outlines and summaries, in its illustratory use of citational examples in the main text, as well as in the utilitarian character of the Glossary and the extensive Index. The book also avoids jargon and excessive linguistic nomenclature, although it explains such terms when needed.

CHAPTER I

Foundations

Chapter Outline

The presentation of borrowings in informal American English should be preceded by an explanation of the foundations of this project. While the essence of this book is documenting and describing informal borrowings rather than proposing a linguistic theory of the phenomenon per se, an introduction explaining the scholarly background is in order. Accordingly, the first of the two introductory chapters, this chapter overviews the **state of research** on borrowings and informal English and explains the main **research methodologies** involved in this project, in particular related to its scope, the collection of data, and the format of description. The linguistic terminology involving informal language and borrowings is presented in the next chapter.

1.1 Background

The state of research on informal borrowings in the English language is somewhat striking. There is, no doubt, a massive bulk of literature on borrowings and a modest but growing number of publications on informal language, especially slang. However, informal language is virtually nonexistent in the former, while borrowings are largely left out in the latter. More strikingly, when one combines these two themes into one, it turns out that despite the growing importance of informal borrowings, publications on the subject remain scarce. There are no monographic books written specifically on borrowings in informal English, be they American, British, or any other, while the very few academic papers are too narrow in scope or size, being limited to borrowings from individual languages or restricted to select aspects. The following paragraphs provide an overview of the status quo.

Let us start with borrowing. First, there is a plethora of book publications on general description of the English language where borrowings are at least acknowledged as an important part of the lexicon, even if their coverage is limited to just a few pages. Many of them highlight the importance of lexical borrowings in the development and enrichment of the English vocabulary, often emphasizing their sociolinguistic influence. A cursory selection of such **general linguistic books** may include Algeo and Pyles ([1964] 2005: 271–294), Yule ([1985] 2014: 51–52), McArthur (1992: 141–145), Crystal ([1995] 1999: 124–127), Stockwell and Minkova (2001: 30–46), Gramley and Pätzold (2004: 28–33), Steinmetz and Kipfer (2006: 301–328), and Pearce (2007: 25–26), but of course there are many more.

Next, there exists a long-standing, rich, and diversified literature in English on the **theory of borrowings**. One may choose from various works. Traditionally, perhaps the best starting point is the seminal essay by Haugen (1950) which proposes the most-cited typology of lexical borrowings, and the equally seminal book by Weinreich ([1953] 1968) which addresses various aspects of borrowings, particularly interference. Thomason and Kaufman (1988), Winford (2003), and Matras (2009) all discuss borrowings within a larger framework of contact linguistics, with notable themes including borrowability and integration. Other important contributions by Field (2002) and Wohlgemuth (2009) offer panoramic outlines of academic work written on diverse theoretical aspects of borrowing, including borrowability. Kuźniak (2009) offers an entirely novel and somewhat unorthodox approach to the subject, by presenting a typological model involving metaphorical comparison between borrowings and astrophysical concepts. Durkin (2014), another definitive must-read, is principally devoted to outlining the history of borrowings in the English language across the ages, including American English. Finally, Poplack (2018) views borrowings from the perspective of variationist linguistics, with particular emphasis on bilingual communities. All of the above are seminal and edifying texts that are essential for any study of borrowings. Yet – it must be emphasized – none of them analyzes borrowings in the context of informal language.

Similarly, **language-specific works on borrowings** in American English – usually in the form of dictionaries and glossaries – contain at best scant references to informal language or fail to identify it as such. As for **Spanish**, the most important source of informal borrowings in American English, Fought's book (2003) on Chicano English, mentions borrowings in informal English only in passing while Bentley (1973) and Schultz (2018) focus on standard borrowings. Murray (in Rodríguez González 1996) does concern informal borrowings, but his essay-sized work is limited in scope (drugs) and description (mere listing of defined expressions). Probably the only sizable exploration of Spanish borrowings in informal English is Widawski and Kowalczyk (2015), a dictionary based on real-life usage material with clearly identified sources. As for **Yiddish**, Rosten ([1968] 1996), Hoffman and Freedman (1983), and Bluestein (1998) all document a large number of borrowings but lump together standard and informal ones, without any labels to differentiate between them. Widawski (2012), aside from a comprehensive introduction, offers a sizable glossary containing both standard and informal borrowings but with helpful labeling. As for **German**, Knapp (2005) lists very few informal borrowings, fails to list informal senses of expressions, and interprets Yiddish borrowings as German ones while Pfeffer and Cannon (2010) list no informal borrowings at all. As for **other languages**, Urdang and Abate (1988) record borrowings from various languages, mostly foreignisms, some of which are informal but not identified as such. Similarly, Adeleye et al. (1999) list foreignisms, largely erudite expressions borrowed from Latin, Greek, or French, none of which are informal.

Another matter is literature concerned with the opposite direction of borrowing, namely **from English into other languages**. Given the international status of English and its global influence on other languages, there exists a massive number of publications on the subject, so there are, for instance, various collections and discussions of English borrowings in German, Japanese, Polish, and Spanish. A good instantiation of these is the dictionary of English borrowings in European languages edited by Görlach (2001) as well as its companion volume listing a bibliography of the lexical influence of English on these languages (Görlach 2002); another example may be the dictionary of English borrowings in Polish by Mańczak-Wohlfeld (2010) or the dictionary of English borrowings in informal Polish by Kowalczyk and Widawski (2019b). However, these and similar works are outside the framework of this book, which describes borrowings *from* other languages *into* English, and not the other way around.

In contrast to borrowing, the treatment of informal language in **general literature on linguistics** has until recently been scarce. This informal subset of lexicon – especially slang, an important and vibrant component of it – has generally been relegated to the margins of scholarly discussion and treated at best as a curiosity or colorful deviation from standard English rather than an autonomous phenomenon worthy of academic study. While informal language does appear in numerous general books on the English language or English linguistics, they mention it largely in passing as, for instance, is the case with Algeo and Pyles ([1964] 2005: 221),

Yule ([1985] 2014: 259–260), Gramley and Pätzold (2004: 11–12), Pearce (2007: 37, 169–170), or Fromkin et al. (2014: 319–320). With the exception of a chapter in Mencken (1919: 304–312), now a highly dated and naive outline, the very few books which devote more space to slang and colloquialism are McArthur (1992: 940–943), a compact introduction in the form of an encyclopedic entry; Eble (in Finegan and Rickford 2004: 375–386), another compact yet informative introduction addressing the main characteristics including the differentiation between slang and similar types of lexicon; and Lighter (in Algeo 2001: 219–253), the most extensive introduction to the subject in a book on general English, especially valuable for its outline of the history of slang scholarship and figurative devices used in slang.

Informal language, including slang and colloquialism, is also surprisingly seldom discussed in **general literature on sociolinguistics** – the subfield of linguistics concerned with the social aspects of language – where one would expect it to be featured prominently. This is probably because, on the one hand, most contemporary sociolinguistic studies are largely concerned with either phonological and morphosyntactical levels of description rather than the strictly lexical; on the other hand, they also tend to be focused more on geographical or ethnic variations of language rather than on sociostylistic ones. Consequently, there is at best a mere mention of informal lexicon in such sociolinguistic classics as Fishman (1970), Labov ([1972] 1991), Trudgill ([1974] 2000: 83), Fasold (1984), Wardhaugh (1986), Romaine ([1994] 2000), Stockwell (2002), Chambers et al. ([2002] 2004), Chambers (2003: 188–189), and Llamas et al. (2007: 229) or in more recent publications such as Meyerhoff (2011), Tagliamonte (2012), Holmes (2013: 176–178), Bell (2014: 151–152), or Poplack (2018), to name just a few.

Luckily, there is a modestly growing number of **monographs on informal lexicon**, nearly all devoted to slang. One should perhaps start with Partridge (1933), the first book-length discussion on general slang ever published, although flawed with imprecise dating and etymology, and treating American slang rather cursorily. Although it deals with student slang, Eble (1996) contains many theoretical issues which can be extrapolated to American slang in general; interestingly, while it discusses borrowings, these are described as a "negligible source of slang," a claim which this book unquestionably disproves. Adams (2009) discusses in detail only a few select themes pertaining to slang and fails to even mention borrowing. Coleman (2012) is an all-round must-read introduction to slang but devotes little space to the description of borrowings. Garcarz (2013) concerns African American hip-hop slang; it does not include borrowings per se, but it discusses at length the mechanism of appropriation of African American slang into general English, which may be considered a form of borrowing. Coleman (2014) presents a collection of diverse academic papers on slang, with some discussion of the influence of English slang on other languages but not vice versa. Widawski ([2015] 2019) describes African American slang but most of its contents can be extrapolated to a larger context to describe slang in general; his presentation of forms, meanings, themes, and functions is one of the best scholarly treatments of slang ever written; it contains some discussion on borrowings, but it is restricted to those in African American slang. Green (2015) describes the historical development of slang but somehow fails to contain any discussion of borrowings, which feature prominently in other books by this esteemed author, for instance in his voluminous dictionary (Green 2010). Another book by Green (2016) is a short introduction to the subject but, despite its all-inclusive character, it surprisingly fails to mention borrowings.

A good source of knowledge on informal American English has traditionally been **introductions to slang dictionaries**. This is primarily because, by their very function and design, they are often compact, informative, and readable. Sometimes they can be extensive and, much like book chapters, provide a more detailed discussion. Also, in contrast to academic texts written by theoretical linguists, they offer a picture of slang from the point of view of practitioners whose main occupation has been collecting and documenting lexicon. Such a practical, hands-on perspective is highly valuable. Let us start with Wentworth and Flexner's classic lexicographic work ([1960] 1975) which includes a seminal essay on slang with an invaluable description of wordbuilding and coinage mechanisms. Its direct successor, Chapman (1986), also includes an informative essay on slang, focused on the psychological motives behind its use. Perhaps the best introduction ever written is Lighter (1994), which presents an extensive overview of slang, addressing its definition, characteristics, sociocultural and historical context, and comparison between slang and similar types of lexis. Written by one of the foremost slang lexicographers, this is a classic and unquestionably seminal text.

Finally, one should mention **slang dictionaries**. While there are virtually no dictionaries of slang borrowings, borrowings are often found in general slang dictionaries. American lexicography abounds in them, so the selection was difficult and necessarily subjective. Wentworth and Flexner ([1960] 1975), considered to be the first modern dictionary of American slang, contains numerous borrowings from various languages, with entries amply supported by citational evidence. Chapman (1986) – subsequently updated and published as Chapman and Kipfer (1995) and Kipfer and Chapman (2007) – is a direct continuation of Wentworth and Flexner and also lists a vast number of borrowings from diverse languages, clearly identified by relevant labels; according to my estimate, it contains some 600 entries that are borrowings (excluding borrowings from African American Vernacular English). Spears (1990), a popular dictionary aimed at non-native speakers of English, lacks both dating and sources of its examples, which diminishes its scholarly merit; while it does contain some borrowings, these are rarely identified as such. Lighter (1994 and 1997) stands out as the most authoritative and scholarly treatment of American slang, including borrowings; sadly, the dictionary remains unfinished and only covers letters from A to O. Finally, Dalzell ([2009] 2018) is another important contribution to American slang lexicography; it contains numerous borrowings, yet many are surprisingly devoid of labels which makes it somewhat difficult to assess their number. According to my estimate, the dictionary contains some 400 entries that are borrowings from foreign languages.

1.2   Scope

The scope of the present research is reflected by the title of this book. Essentially, the most fundamental criterion was that all the lexical material in this study had to be identified as *borrowings in informal American English* (see the definition and discussion of these terms in the next chapter). Still, there were a few finer **distinctions used to determine the scope** of lexical data to be searched, included, and analyzed. These are presented below.

First, all expressions in this study had to be identified as *informal*. In other words, the focus was not on all borrowings but only those which are informal – that is, the expressions which are stylistically lower than standard English and below the formal and neutral registers on the formality scale. At the same time, *informal* is a superordinate term which encompasses both slang and colloquialism, so expressions included in this book represent both slang and colloquial borrowings. See Chapter 2 for a detailed description of the formality scale as well as the terms *informal*, *slang*, and *colloquialism*.

A follow-up criterion was that the expressions also had to be *American English*. Put differently, the focus was not on all informal expressions used in English-speaking countries or communities – such as Australia or

Britain – but only on those used in American English. The label *American* is sometimes used in sociolinguistics to include both US and Canadian usage, and thus is synonymous with the label *North American* (see Widawski and Kowalczyk 2011, for instance), perhaps because of the wealth of shared lexicon used in both countries. In this case, *American* refers principally to US usage, a decision motivated by the somewhat different language borrowing patterns in both varieties – for instance, Canadian English has far more borrowings from French but lacks many borrowings from Spanish.

Equally important was that the expressions discussed in this study be *borrowings*. In other words, the focus was not on simply any informal expressions – for instance, those created from native lexical material by morphological processes of lengthening and shortening or by semantic processes of figuration or shifting – but only those which were the result of importation from other languages, and in lesser cases substitutions. In general, all types of borrowings were included – such as loanwords, loan translations, semantic loans, or loan blends – although the focus was on loanwords, the most prototypical and fundamental type.

A follow-up criterion was that expressions be borrowed from foreign languages. This seemingly obvious qualification is especially important since borrowings may also be understood as expressions taken from other varieties of English, such as dialects or ethnolects. Such is the case with lexical contributions from African American Vernacular English (AAVE), in itself an important source of American slang (see Smitherman 2000, Widawski and Kowalczyk 2012, or Widawski [2015] 2019). However, AAVE is treated here – as in much of mainstream linguistics nowadays – as a variety of English rather than a separate language. Hence, contributions from AAVE or similar varieties of English were not included in this book.

However, determining an exact origin of informal expressions – especially the slang component – is not always possible because of their chiefly oral and often changeable nature, so some reservation is in order. Many slang lexicographers such as Dalzell ([2009] 2018) even deliberately omit information on origin in their dictionaries, claiming it is sometimes "a matter of guesswork," while even renowned researchers of borrowings such as Görlach (2001: xix) admit that "it is impossible to state with any degree of precision why some items are included and others are not." This extends to informal borrowings, too, since there are certain borderline expressions whose origin is unclear or debatable, for instance those from Yiddish and German. All in all, in this study a compromise was attempted and the few borderline expressions were given the benefit of the doubt.

Representativeness was another notable criterion for inclusion in this study. To all intents and purposes, informal borrowings had to be either commonly known and used by the majority of Americans or typically identified and highly popular with minorities whose languages served as the basis for these expressions. In other words, the focus was both on expressions in wide general circulation and those highly popular among select groups. With this in mind, informal borrowings were collected from general American sources as well as those restricted to minority groups. In both cases, the reliance on authentic, real-world examples in the form of citations was instrumental in ensuring the representativeness of expressions.

Currency was another important criterion. The emphasis was on present-day informal borrowings rather than historical or ephemeral ones. Exceptions included the so-called passive expressions (see Lighter 1994: xiii) – that is, commonly known but no longer in popular use. The insistence on current citations from contemporary sources was meant to guarantee such currency: the majority of sources are less than a decade old. Still, ensuring currency was not always easy because of the changeability of informal language and slang in particular (see Green 2002: 27). On the other hand, one should bear in mind that not all slang changes quickly; for instance, a comparison of successive editions of *Dictionary of American Slang* (1960, 1975, 1986, 1995, 2007) shows that many entries remain the same.

1.3   Collection

As indicated earlier, this study takes as its basis the authentic material collected in the form of a sizable citations database from diverse contemporary American sources, an approach commonly used in documentary linguistics, particularly in slang lexicography (see, for instance, Wentworth and Flexner [1960] 1975, Chapman 1986, Thorne 1990, Lighter 1994, Kipfer and Chapman 2007, or Green 2010). The aim of such a database was to get as much exposure to informal borrowings as possible and to record their usage in natural contexts to ensure a representative basis for research. The following is an overview of the main types of sources and methods used in collecting the lexical material.

The database of informal borrowings was devised to include an extensive number of diverse and contemporary sources. In essence, informal borrowings were sought where they are used. With this in mind, the focus was on specialized sources with a sizable amount of informal borrowings, for example dialog from television series *Seinfeld* and *The Sopranos*, films *El Cantante* and *Price Above Rubies*, articles from the *Jewish Daily Forward* and the *Miami New Times* newspapers, web pages such as Latin Life and Soy Chicano, and fiction by David Montejano and Ralph Flores; conversations with users of borrowings, such as minority students at the University of California at Los Angeles or the University of Miami, were also valuable sources of data. Additionally, general or nonspecialized sources were also considered to determine the influence of borrowings on informal American English in general and to assess the degree of their assimilation; these included television series such as *Modern Family* and *The Simpsons*, newspapers such as the *Los Angeles Times* and the *Washington Post*, magazines such as *Cosmopolitan* and *People*, and social media such as Facebook and Twitter.

Let us present the **main types of sources** in more detail. Spoken utterances – the most natural source of any informal language including informal borrowings – were also of the utmost importance in this study. Often spontaneous and devoid of any censorship, they usually contain what is called *primary slang* (see Kipfer and Chapman 2007: x), which is slang used by its coiners within their subgroups, particularly for the purpose of internal solidarity or group allegiance. Utterances collected by Latino student volunteers, for instance at the University of Florida or the University of Arizona, or those from monologues such as the Old Jews Telling Jokes web page, are good instantiations of this source of data used in this project.

Films were another important source of informal borrowings. This is because film dialogs are often highly stylized, written with meticulous care to convey authenticity and ensure representativeness of the specific language used by fictional characters in their life context. While they essentially contain what is called *secondary slang* (see Kipfer and Chapman 2007: x) or slang used by those other than its coiners, they are meant to serve de facto as primary slang. Hence they are usually selected with great care to ensure authenticity. A good example of this type of source are films depicting the life and experience of ethnic minorities in America, such as *La Bamba* and *Price Above Rubies*.

A similar type of source used in this study was television shows, especially television series. Also in this instance, their dialog lists are often meticulously stylized to most accurately represent the authentic language characteristic of the presented social, cultural, economic, or ethnic context, so this is an excellent source of informal borrowings. Representative examples of this type of source include the series *Fresh Off the Boat* and *Orange Is the New Black*.

Informal borrowings can also be found in plenitude in the press – newspapers and magazines – in both print and online forms. The cornerstone source for many lexicographers, the press offers invaluable and almost limitless material for lexical study. Informal borrowings appear here either indirectly as stylization or as direct quotation from authentic utterances. At the same time, the press is the great disperser of informal language, especially its slang component – and in the United States has been at least since Prohibition (see Lighter 1994: xxxii) – which is even truer with regard to online press: thousands of informal expressions have been disseminated in this way and thus made to resonate more powerfully in American society. Examples of this type of source include the *Huffington Post* and *USA Today*.

A similar type of source is social media, especially blogs. They are especially valuable because many of them tend to instantly pick up sociocultural trends and verbal novelties – including informal borrowings – and popularize them on a large, often global, scale. Also, because of their often anonymous nature and lack of censorship, social media pages tend to contain data that is very authentic, yet sometimes offensive, vulgar, or politically incorrect as well. Examples of such sources include *Blogspot* or *Twitter*.

Finally, literature is sometimes a valuable source of informal borrowings as well. Much as with dialogs in films and television shows, works of fiction feature carefully stylized expressions, aimed at achieving authenticity, put in the mouths of their characters. More significantly, these works often represent the authentic experiences of their authors coming from social or ethnic minority backgrounds, thus their use of informal borrowings reflects the abovementioned primary slang. Examples of this type of source may be works by *David Montejano* and *Jackie Mason*.

While the selection was sometimes subjective, every effort was made to collect data from sources reflecting nationwide and mainstream usage. In sum, over 1,700 different sources were used from the press, the Internet, literature, music, film, television, and conversation. A complete list of sources of the expressions used in this book is presented at the end. All in all, the breadth of sources can be extremely telling in and of itself.

Let us now talk about the **methods of data collection**. These were chiefly conventional (see Kipfer 1984: 32–35, Thorne 1990: vi, Sakel and Everett 2012: 99–138), and involved a combination of methods. The reading, listening, and watching procedures were extensive and represent hundreds of hours of analyzing text, sound, and images. Below is an overview of the main types of methods.

Taking written notes was the single most pervasive method of collecting data. This traditional data-collection technique has been used extensively as a fundamental and universal method by most documentary linguists, especially sociolinguists and lexicographers. It also remains the single most important method in collecting informal lexicon, especially because of its applicability in capturing its figurative character which tends to be inadequately captured by other methods such as using language corpora (see below). Its main advantage is that it produces individually selected material in the form of citations, practically ready for inclusion in the database and for linguistic analysis. It was also used in this study: written notes, often spontaneously made when talking, listening, or watching, were systematically entered into the computer database. Numerous citations in this study were recorded in this way.

Making recordings was another traditional technique that was used extensively. This technique has been used especially in field and documentary linguistics to capture spoken language. It is also widely used in collecting informal lexicon, especially its slang subset (Thorne 2009: x). However, it has two flaws: it requires access to native speakers and should require their consent, and often involves the so-called observer's paradox (Wardhaugh 1986: 19) where participants, who know they are being recorded, tend to sound unnatural; it also produces material which only partially includes informal lexicon and must subsequently be filtered. Still, this is a highly useful method and was used extensively in this study. Data was recorded in the form of Dictaphone recordings, which allowed replaying of the material several times to ensure accuracy, and was then systematically entered into the database.

Using volunteers to collect data was another method. This is another traditional yet rarely used technique of data collection. It requires the active participation of volunteers who themselves conduct fieldwork and gather language data. Frequently, they are themselves the coiners and users of informal expressions, so this is an ideal method for collecting the lexicon used by social, occupational, or ethnic groups, for instance students (see Munro 1989: 1–3 or Eble 1996: 4–7). Its main advantage is the quality of the collected material, usually defined or annotated. It was also used in this study.

Direct input or importation of lexical data from web pages was another method. This is an increasingly popular method, similar to taking notes. Essentially, citations containing expressions interesting to researchers are copied directly from Internet pages to computer memory. Especially useful is input from social media containing much informal lexicon which, as observed by Coleman (2012: 276), may otherwise be left out in books or traditional journalism in paper form, for instance because of their vulgar or offensive character. Equally serviceable are news aggregators such as Google News, which allow access to the newest and most popular expressions (see Thorne 2009: x and Kowalczyk 2011); searching them also allows one to assess the relative popularity of expressions as well as their timeline. This method was also used in collecting informal borrowings, and a sizable portion of citations was copied directly from online sources.

Finally, large searchable language corpora like the American National Corpus were also used, although with caution. They still have rather marginal applicability to the study of informal lexicon because of its largely figurative nature, which is still difficult to be satisfactorily processed by computers. As observed by Stefanowitsch and Gries (2007: 1–4), "extracting metaphors and metonymies from corpora is difficult [...] for the simple reason that conceptual mappings are not linked to particular linguistic forms." Put differently, the search engines of such corpora simply cannot distinguish between the literal and figurative meanings of informal expressions, including informal borrowings; for instance, a search for the word *hombrecitos*, which in slang means "hallucinogenic mushrooms," would return thousands of usage examples (or concordances) with its literal meaning, "little people" or "children"; similarly a search for the slang meaning of *tortilla eater* "Mexican" would return literal examples referring simply to "someone who eats tortillas." Accordingly, the results of corpora searches – which may run into hundreds of thousands of concordances – have to be individually checked for figurative senses of words. However, when the form of informal expressions is somehow different – either as a result of coinage or morphological manipulation of an already existing expression – corpora can be extremely useful in checking their meanings, establishing the relative frequency of occurrence, or attesting to their existence. For instance, checking corpora for *mama-san* "East Asian child or young woman" or *shleppable* "one that can be carried" reveal much about these expressions and contexts in which they are used.

With regard to **numbers**, there were over 12,000 citations including informal borrowings collected in the original database. Not all of them were equally applicable for this book: some of them were better for illustrating the meaning and function of borrowings while others only served for corroboration or validation purposes. With this in mind, approximately half of this number was selected as material for illustration of patterns of borrowings and their description, and is presented in the book as follows: about 700 citations are located in the main text while a further 5,500 citations are featured in the Glossary. The Glossary itself is composed of approximately 1,200 entries excerpted from these citations. A detailed description of the Glossary is given further below.

1.4 Description

This book is essentially descriptive in character. Accordingly, the emphasis is on observation of informal borrowings in actual use leading to generalizations, rather than formulating theory first and checking it against the actual language use later. Moreover, while occasional references are made to the "external description" of borrowings – the social, cultural, and historical context in which they are used – the book is less concerned with them, focusing instead on the "internal description," that is, linguistic description per se (see Fisiak 2000: 8 for further clarification of the two approaches). In this, the book joins the sociolinguistic and descriptive tradition of writing about informal lexicon – especially its slang component – seen in such works as Eble (1996), Coleman (2012), or Green (2016), but of course is focused specifically on informal borrowings.

With description coming to the fore, much space is devoted to the presentation, explanation, interpretation, and illustration of language data. The format of description is designed to be extensive, covering a wide range of themes which allow an examination of informal borrowings from various linguistic perspectives. Essentially, the purpose is to answer the following **main questions**: how are informal borrowings defined, what languages do they come from, how are they classified, how are they formed, how do they convey meaning, how are they modified, why are they used, and what they are about?

To achieve such a panoramic perspective, several **levels of description** are employed. On the typological level, the book presents an extensive classification of informal borrowings according to various criteria such as donor language, borrowed material, part of speech, degree of assimilation, degree of modification, frequency of usage, and register. On the modification level, the book describes the main processes by which informal borrowings are changed, such as phonological, orthographical, morphological, semantic, grammatical, and stylistic changes; the biggest two levels, however, are morphological and semantic modification. With regard to the former, the book describes the main processes by which informal borrowings are changed, such as lengthening, shortening, blending, corruption, and application of proper names as borrowings; with regard to the latter, the book presents the processes of figuration in informal borrowings such as metaphor or metonymy and analyzes the main semantic shifting processes such as generalization, specialization, melioration, and pejoration, as well as conversion. On the pragmatic level, the book analyzes the referential, social, psychological, rhetorical, and cultural functions of informal borrowings. Finally, on the thematic level, the book describes their most productive themes, including the core, culture-specific, and miscellaneous themes.

The **Glossary of informal borrowings** is an integral part of the description. It serves as a quick reference, providing definitions of informal borrowings and complementing examples featured in the main text. In terms of size, the Glossary is extensive in that it includes approximately 1,200 of the most representative expressions, all excerpted from the above-mentioned lexical database; because of its size and description, it could easily stand as a dictionary in its own right. In terms of description, it offers a comprehensive entry format composed of several microstructural elements: headword, abbreviated grammatical identification, source-language label, usage label, standard English equivalent or definition, additional reference information, and citational examples, each preceded by the date and name of its source. This layout was partially modeled on slang dictionaries by Lighter (1994 and 1997) and Green (2010), which in turn were themselves modeled on the *Oxford English Dictionary* (1989) and rely heavily on citational material with dating and sources.

The equivalents and definitions are the result of standard lexicographic procedures, which involved analyzing the meaning of each expression in various contextual examples from the database, verifying them with native speakers, and cross-checking them with several reference books which consistently mark borrowings, including a sizable general English dictionary edited by Angus Stevenson, the *Oxford Dictionary of English* (2010), and three comprehensive dictionaries of general slang: Barbara Kipfer and Robert Chapman's *Dictionary of American Slang* (2007), Tom Dalzell's *Routledge Dictionary of Modern American Slang and Unconventional English* (2009), and Jonathon Green's *Green's Slang Dictionary* (2010). References to these works – labeled AS, KC, TD, and JG respectively – which also serve as acknowledgments, can be found at the end of Glossary definitions. Naturally, the equivalents and definitions are not meant to cover all of the semantic senses and may vary according to geographical, generational, or social context. Aside from the above reference books, etymology and dating of the expressions were additionally verified with several specialist dictionaries including Douglas Harper's *Online Etymological Dictionary*, *Etymonline* (2000), Adrian Room's *Cassell Dictionary of Word Histories* (2000), and John Simpson and Edmund Weiner's *Oxford English*

Dictionary (1989). Naturally, both dating and etymology are subject to correction where better evidence is found. Also, one should make a reservation here: dating may sometimes be dissimilar from the general public's association of a particular expression with a particular period; for instance, *ganja* "marijuana" is usually associated with the 1960s and 1970s but actually debuted in the 1850s. However, language historians must rely on dating rather than public perception, and such an attitude is also exhibited in this book, including the Glossary.

Usage examples – used extensively throughout the entire book – constitute the fundamental part of the description. There are 6,200 examples in the book: 700 located in the main text and a further 5,500 featured in the Glossary. They serve several important functions: they form the basis for linguistic observation; they illustrate particular linguistic patterns within informal borrowings; they support the definitions or standard English synonyms; they add idiomatic nuance to the meaning of expressions; they show the social, cultural, and ethnic context in which they are used; and they attest to the very existence of these expressions. Additionally, they contribute to a better understanding of both informal lexicon and borrowing.

1.5 Format

The **layout conventions** regarding examples are fairly straightforward and self-explanatory, but some general information may be in order. Examples in the form of citations are clearly distinguished from the main text of the book, being grouped in separate paragraphs and set in italics. Each example contains an informal borrowing set in boldface, followed by its standard English equivalent or definition in brackets; source and date information follow each example. This organization is modeled on the format devised and implemented by Widawski ([2015] 2019), which seems optimal for describing and illustrating this type of lexicon.

The **organization of the Glossary** follows a more extensive format. The entries are given in alphabetical order. Homonymic entry expressions – those belonging to different parts of speech – are treated as separate entries, following one another. Polysemic entry expressions – those having two or more meanings – are located under one entry with their meanings set apart by Arabic numerals. Finally, lexicalized compounds and phrases are treated as separate entries and located under the first letter of the first word. Each entry has the following elements: headword (that is, entry expression), abbreviated grammatical identification, source-language label, usage label (if applicable), standard English equivalent or definition, additional reference information, two citational examples, each preceded by the date and name of its source, and etymological information with dating.

In most cases, etymologies list one donor language; however, in a few rare cases of the so-called shared etymology, two languages are given. Also, in the case of the so-called pseudo-borrowings, the label *pseudo* precedes the donor language which they imitate. Since this book identifies primarily the so-called immediate source borrowings, etymological information goes back to the direct donor language; in certain cases, however, the etymology goes further back and lists an indirect (or previous) donor language as well.

In the case of nonalphabetic donor languages, namely those which use a writing system different from the Roman (Latin) script, romanization reflecting English respelling is given; every effort has been made to use the standardized respelling reflecting the romanization tradition of a particular language – for instance, the respelling of Mandarin Chinese uses Pinyin, Japanese uses Hepburn, while that of Yiddish uses YIVO spelling. Abbreviations used in the Glossary are listed at the beginning of this book.

Chapter Summary

Informal borrowings constitute an increasingly important linguistic phenomenon, yet they remain surprisingly underrepresented in the literature on both borrowings and informal language. There are no book-length monographs written specifically on the subject; academic papers are usually limited to borrowings from individual languages or restricted to their select aspects; dictionaries on slang and colloquialism, while often including borrowings, understandably lack any detailed linguistic analysis. This book is to remedy the situation. As for its **scope**, it attempts to cover most representative and current expressions identified as lexical borrowings in the informal subset of *American English*, and not any other. As for the **data collection**, the lexical material comes from a sizable citations database from diverse contemporary sources including spoken utterances, films and television shows, newspapers and magazines, social media, and literature. The methods used in data collection include notetaking, audio recording, direct importation from web pages, as well as using volunteers and searchable language corpora. As for **description**, much space is devoted to the presentation, explanation, interpretation, and illustration of language data; the **format** of description is designed to be extensive, covering a wide range of themes which allows an examination of informal borrowings on various levels such as typological, morphological, semantic, pragmatic, or thematic. Usage examples are the fundamental part of the description: they form the basis for linguistic observation, illustrate particular linguistic patterns, support the definitions, show the social, cultural, and ethnic context in which they are used, and also attest to the very existence of these expressions. An integral part of the description is the **Glossary**, serving as a quick reference, providing definitions of informal borrowings and supplementing examples featured in the main text.

CHAPTER 2

Terms

Chapter Outline

This chapter is a continuation of the introductory part of this book. It outlines the fundamental **linguistic terminology** applicable to the studies of informal borrowings. First, it provides an array of definitions of both terms – *borrowing* and *informal* – which allows one to view these phenomena from different perspectives. Second, it catalogs and defines several related terms which complement the above two, are partially synonymous with them, or tend to be confused with them. Additional terms are explained, where necessary, as the description of informal borrowings unfolds in the following chapters.

2.1   Borrowing

Borrowing (or **linguistic borrowing**, to differentiate it from any other, e.g. artistic or financial) is possibly one of the most commonly known terms for the type of lexis resulting from language contact. It is also relatively unambiguous: At its simplest, it straightforwardly refers to "a word taken from another language" (Stevenson 2010: 199); the language from which such a word has been taken being called the donor language, and the one into which it has been taken being called the recipient (or target) language. Similar definitions abound – with slight modifications including the substitution of the word *taken* with other synonyms such as *acquired* (Katamba 2005: 140), *adopted* (Katamba 2005: 137), *borrowed* (Widawski 2015: 54), *entered* (Smallman and Brown 2015: 121), *imitated* (Winford 2003: 42), *imported* (Katamba 2005: 137), *incorporated* (Malmkjaer 2009: 242), *integrated* (Spolsky [1998] 2007: 121), *replicated* (Durkin (2014: 3), or *reproduced* (Haugen 1950: 212), while *word* may be substituted with *element* (Polański 1993: 616), *item* (Winford 2003: 42), *linguistic form* (Crystal [1980] 1991: 41), *pattern* (Haugen 1950: 212), or *word or phrase* (Graddol et al. 1996: 33) – but the essence is the same.

Borrowing is also the most inclusive term, in a number of respects. First, as noted above, it may go beyond words and refer also to phrases (Steinmetz and Kipfer 2006: 303), as in *in loco parentis* or *raison d'être*, for example. In that, borrowing has a certain advantage over the term **loanword**, which by definition should refer solely to words and thus should exclude phrases (see Section 2.2). Second, borrowing may have an even more inclusive scope and may refer to other elements of lexicon, smaller than words (such as affixes, e.g. *exo-* or *uber-*) or larger than them (such as catchphrases or formulaic expressions, e.g. *cherchez la femme* or *dura lex sed lex*). Third, the broadest scope of the term means that it may also refer to reproduction not only on a morphological (or lexical) level but also on other levels (see Crystal [1980] 1991: 41), such as syntactical (e.g. the French-based word-order in *Air Canada*), phonological (e.g. the French-based pronunciation of *restaurant*), or orthographical (e.g. the German-based spelling *of Blitzkrieg*). This creates some ambiguity in the otherwise fairly unambiguous term. While it is normally assumed that the term refers to the lexical level, some scholars add the modifier *lexical* in front of the term, thereby yielding **lexical borrowing**.

But borrowing can be even more inclusive in scope, as it can refer to a broader spectrum of contact-induced lexical phenomena. A classical definition of borrowing by Haugen (1950: 212) is rather broad: "the attempted reproduction in one language of patterns previously found in another." Accordingly, borrowing may be understood not only as the reproduction (either complete or partial) of words or phrases but also as the reproduction of foreign structures by lexical elements of the native language as well as the reproduction of meanings. Hence one can talk about **loanwords** (e.g. *kamikaze* or *toque*), **loan hybrids** (e.g. *Southern belle* or *ubersexy*), **loan translations** (e.g. *bottom line* or *brainwash*), and **semantic loans** (e.g. *by* or *landsman*). No wonder many scholars such as Winford (2005), Mańczak-Wohlfeld (2006), or Görlach (2003) consider it to be a superordinate category, de facto encompassing all other terms (see Section 2.2).

Naturally, while the above instances of the broad scope of borrowing are considered advantageous, they may also point to the opposite: a certain imprecision of the term. For, one may argue, while its semantic scope covers all the abovementioned phenomena, in each instance a precise term is needed. There are some other drawbacks of the term as well.

Borrowing may also refer to the process rather than its result. Durkin (2014: 3) defines borrowing as "a process in which one language replicates a linguistic feature from another language, either wholly or partly." Some scholars make a clear distinction between the two; for example, Algeo and Pyles ([1964] 2005: 271) state that "the process is known as borrowing, and the word thus borrowed is a loanword." Still, this distinction seems less categorical, and more and more scholars incorporate both meanings into their definitions, making them more inclusive. For instance, McArthur defines borrowing as both "taking a word or phrase from one language into another and the item so taken" (McArthur 1992: 141), while Haspelmath and Tadmoor (2009: 36) define borrowing "as a word that at some point in the history of a language entered its lexicon as a result of borrowing (or transfer, or copying)."

While the term borrowing is universally known and commonly used, some scholars point out that it sounds somewhat awkward. It is based on a rather peculiar metaphor since, as observed by Crystal ([1995] 1999: 126), the name implies that the word "borrowed" from a language will someday be given back, although in reality it never left it. Haugen (1950: 211–212), who first noted it, considers this implied metaphor absurd, "since the borrowing takes place without the lender's consent or even awareness, and the borrower is under no obligation to repay the loan. One might as well call it stealing, were it not that the owner is deprived of nothing and feels no urge to recover his goods." What is more, because of this metaphor, the term may also suggest ephemerality (Mesthrie 2001: 433), which simply is not the case (incidentally, the same can be said about the term **loanword** which originated in the same metaphor). In an attempt to remedy this, several more or less felicitous synonyms have been proposed, including **transfer** or **transference** (see Clyne 2004) or **copying** (see Johanson 2002) or **incorporation** (Akmajian 2001: 573), none of them as popular as borrowing.

Having said all this, the term borrowing – although far from perfect – is probably the most commonly known and thus universal expression, and "has been firmly entrenched in linguistics" (Durkin 2014: 3). Also, as observed by Wohlgemuth (2009: 52), Steinmetz and Kipfer (2006: 303), and Haugen himself (1950: 211–212), no apter term has yet been invented.

2.2   Related Terms

There have been several terms proposed to name language phenomena which are related to borrowing. They are presented below, starting with the most and ending with the least related. Accordingly, the former involves terms focused primarily on lexical phenomena, directly pertinent to informal borrowings. The latter involves terms applied in a broader contact language context, indirectly related to the subject matter of this book, which nevertheless may shed extra light on our characterization of informal borrowings.

To this day, the key terms applied in the study of borrowing stem largely from the classic terminology proposed by Haugen (1950) and his influential twofold division based on importation and substitution. He described borrowings as being either the result of **morphemic importation**, that is, transferring or "importing" a lexical item (or its part) from one language to another; or the result of **morphemic substitution**, that is, transferring or "substituting" the meaning of a lexical item from one language by using native elements of another (note that the terms importation and substitution can also function as the results of these processes). On the basis of this distinction, one can distinguish two elementary types of borrowings: **loanwords**, which show morphemic importation without substitution, and **loanshifts**, which show morphemic substitution without importation. In practice, this translates into a few important types of borrowings. Let us characterize them in more detail.

Loanword (alternatively labeled **borrowing proper**, **lexical borrowing**, or **lexical importation**) is considered to be the most common alternative term for borrowing and is used more or less interchangeably with it. For Steinmetz and Kipfer (2006: 303), "a loanword is the same as a borrowed word," hence, the same as lexical borrowing. Still, as mentioned above, there are subtle differences in that loanword essentially refers to a borrowed word rather than phrase, although again in common usage its semantic scope is more inclusive. Its abbreviated synonym, **loan**, is perceived as better than loanword since it avoids being limited to words and may extend to phrases or even other layers of language. Crystal ([1980] 1991: 205) defines it as "a linguistic unit (usually a lexical item) which has come to be used in a language or dialect other than the one where it originated." Yet it is scarcely used. To illustrate the term, here are some examples of well-known loanwords which have enriched the English language, all of them standard: *aardvark, bazaar, boomerang, café, chinook, ennui, kindergarten, latte, quesadilla, menorah, sari, soprano, toque, trek,* and *vodka.*

The second most noticeable type of borrowing is **loan translation** (alternatively labeled **loan shift**, **calque**, **morphological calque**, or **structural borrowing**), fundamentally dissimilar from loanword. This is because in loan translation, "a word is not borrowed whole, but its parts are translated separately and a new word formed" (Crystal 2005: 225). In other words, it involves translation of the element (or elements) of the foreign language rather than taking or copying it (or them) into the native language, or, in Haugen's terminology, it shows substitution without importation. Examples of this type of borrowing are *flea market* "bazaar for selling or bartering merchandise," literally translated from French *marché aux puces*, or *paper tiger* "person or thing that appears threatening but is ineffectual," literally translated from Chinese *zhǐ lǎohǔ*.

Loanblend (alternatively termed **hybrid loan** or simply **hybrid**) is another term often encountered when talking about borrowing. As succinctly defined by Steinmetz and Kipfer (2006: 304), "this is a word made up of elements from two different languages," which one can extend also to a phrase. Put differently, only part of a loanblend – either a word or phrase – is borrowed, while the remaining part is made of a native element. Examples of loanblends include *kinderwhore* "young woman whose dress suggests both youthful innocence and sexual abandon," which is composed half of German *kinder* "children" and half of English *whore* "prostitute," or *mushu pork* "dish of stir-fried pork with scrambled eggs, sesame, and black mushrooms," composed of Chinese *mushu* "scrambled eggs" and English *pork*.

Another category of borrowings which could be added to the above types is **semantic loan** (alternatively labeled **semantic calque**, **loan meaning**, or **neosemantism**). It refers to a native word to which a new meaning was added, transferred from a foreign word with a similar morphological structure. Put differently, in order for a semantic loan to be possible, there must exist two morphologically similar words in both languages, and the meaning of one is then extended. This makes a semantic loan a relatively rare type of borrowing, especially in the context of two distantly related languages. Some semantic loans are results of mistranslation and are never accepted, being treated as so-called **false friends**, or words similar in shape but different in meaning. Examples of semantic loans include *canton* "apartment or house" and *carnal* "close male friend," which borrowed their meanings from the identical-looking Spanish words.

Yet another type of borrowing, **foreign word** refers to a word taken from another language which has not yet been adapted (or integrated) in the recipient language's system. The lack of integration can be manifested by foreign spelling, morphology, or, as emphasized by Kuźniak (2009: 95), phonology. As such, they are still perceived as foreign, and because of this foreignness they are contrasted with borrowings proper, which show various degrees of adaptation. However, the distinction is sometimes lost, and Graddol et al. (1996: 33) define borrowing as "a word or phrase that 'feels' to you as though it is foreign," that is, more of a foreignism. Foreign words also serve different functions: As observed by McArthur (1992: 409), "foreign expressions in English (as opposed to loanwords proper) are generally used for special effect, for 'local color,' or to demonstrate special knowledge. In print, they typically appear in italics and are usually glossed." A term similar in meaning is **foreignism**, yet its semantic scope is larger since it can refer to language units larger than words, such as phrases. Relevant examples include *bon vivant* "someone who has a sociable and luxurious lifestyle," *joie de vivre* "exuberant enjoyment of life," or *Schadenfreude* "pleasure derived from another person's misfortune."

Finally, **citation** is quintessentially a synonym of foreignism (and foreign word). Mańczak-Wohlfeld (2006: 49) defines citations as "expressions which are unknown to many readers, yet introduced by journalists to attract readers' attention," and places them as the least assimilated type of borrowings in the three-tiered scale (the other two being assimilated borrowings and nonassimilated but frequently used borrowings). Rodríguez González (1996: 73), who also calls such borrowings citations, explains that they are used "as if they were meant to reproduce an expression in its original context."

2.3   Additional Terms

There is a number of terms that are used in a broader context of language contact. As such, they are only indirectly related to the subject matter of this book, which, to all intents and purposes, is the documentation and description of informal borrowings.

However, there is one particular term that needs clarification, since it is often confused with borrowing: **code-switching**. This is the alternation between two languages in the same discourse, sometimes even within the same sentence (an instance of such alternation being sometimes referred to as a **code switch**). Crystal defines it as "the use by a speaker of more than one language, dialect or variety during a conversation" ([1995] 1999: 449). As observed by Haspelmath and Tadmoor (2009: 40), in code-switching the alternation between the two languages is not conventionalized, although there may be some grammatical restrictions (see Muysken 2000). In other words, users of code-switching produce mixed utterances including elements of both languages at various times.

On the other hand, borrowing (or loanword) is an expression which can be conventionally used as part of the language in that it is established; it also usually shows various kinds of adaptation, whereas code-switching usually does not. Haspelmath and Tadmoor (2009: 36) say that "borrowings are established by definition; code-switching, by contrast, is defined as the use of an element from another language in speech 'for the once'." Grosjean (1982: 308) further explains the difference: "a code-switch can be of any length (a word, a phrase, a sentence) and is a complete shift to the other language, whereas borrowing is a word or short expression that is adapted to the language being spoken." An example of code-switching may be these three sentences: *Oy vey, stop your kvetching! You've found the Yiddish Slang Dictionary to help you shmooze or kibitz. Be warned though, this website contains some words not fit for your bubbe* (yiddishslangdictionary.com), alternating between elements of English and Yiddish; this particular code-switching being called Yinglish.

Interestingly, code-switching may occur between two languages or the mixed variety, such as dialect or ethnolect (Spolsky [1998] 2007: 49), since "code" may refer to a language or a variety or style of a language (McArthur 1992: 228). Hence one may call it **sociolectal code-switching**, in that one may apply the concept to slang, which in itself involves code-switching because it assumes inserting slang expressions in place of standard ones within the same discourse, something we may call substitutionability (see definitions of slang by Lighter and Widawski on the following pages); that is, it assumes alternation between two language varieties. Still, the use of slang for standard expressions is something different from the use of slang borrowings (which remain borrowings and thus differ from code-switching).

Additionally, one may also encounter the term **code-mixing**, similar in scope to code-switching. However, there is a slight difference between the two: As observed by McArthur (1992: 228), "the term 'code-mixing' emphasizes hybridization," that is, a change in linguistic structure, while "the term 'code-switching' emphasizes movement from one language to another," that is, change in linguistic performance. Still, many scholars use these two terms interchangeably.

The middle case between borrowing and code-switching is the so-called **nonce borrowing**, an unestablished (not conventionalized) borrowing used spontaneously. As noted by Myers-Scotton (1993), many loanwords start out as singly occurring code switches that gradually become conventionalized. Much like with **nonce word** – a type of neologism created for a single occasion – this type of borrowing is difficult to tackle because of its fleeting character. A serviceable example of a nonce borrowing might be *o'taco* "taco filled with traditional Irish ingredients such as potatoes and cabbage," recently invented by the US comedian of Irish descent Conan O'Brien on his late-night talk show.

2.4 Informal

The term **informal** is commonly perceived as straightforward and thus used extensively and broadly, especially in the context of language education (see, for instance, Neufeldt 1999: 1–2). It is also a serviceable umbrella term with unquestionably the broadest sense of application, covering diverse types of language which are simply not formal. Yet, precisely because of this inclusiveness, in certain contexts and applications the term may appear too vague, so finer terminological distinctions are necessary; this pertains especially to slang and colloquialism but also involves several other more or less related terms (see discussion below). Moreover, informal may refer to various levels of language (Pearce 2007: 69), such as phonological, syntactical, orthographical, and so on. So, for instance, the pronunciation *anyhoo* (for *anyhow*) is considered informal, as is the syntax in the sentence *What can I do you for?* or the spelling *drive-thru*. In most cases, however, the label "informal" refers to the lexical level, and it is in this sense that it is used in the book. All these reservations aside, there is no better general term for this type of language.

One of the most fundamental ways to define informal language – including informal vocabulary – is to contrast it with **formal**. For, at its simplest, informal language is essentially the one which is not formal. But what exactly is formal? This type of language is often defined as "suitable for official or serious situations" (Rundell 2002: 556), "elevated and impersonal" (McArthur 1992: 410), "careful" (Spolsky [1998] 2007: 32), or "characterized by more elaborate, conservative and technical vocabulary" (Stevenson 2010: 687). With these characterizations in mind, informal could be defined as a casual, familiar, plain, and personal language which is suitable for unofficial or everyday situations (similar definitions abound – with a variety of qualifying adjectives including *intimate* and *familiar* [Crystal [1980] 1991: 140] or *casual, simple, private* [Pearce 2007: 69] – but the essence is the same). This definition encapsulates much of the meaning of the term, but there are still finer distinctions which need to be addressed.

A good idea of what informal means can be inferred from looking at the formality continuum in language. This is often referred to as the **formality**

scale and includes **levels of formality**, also called formal registers or styles. The simplest scale, as evoked by Crystal ([1995] 1999: 452), essentially consists of two levels: formal ("language use relating to situations that are socially careful or correct") and informal ("or otherwise"), which are also referred to as high and low registers respectively (Polański 1993: 522). Such a dichotomic division, although basic, is useful and employed extensively in language education: Authors and educators use appropriate labels "formal" and "informal" to mark specific vocabulary items and signal to the learner the range of their stylistic usage; examples of such practice include didactic dictionaries, for instance the *Cambridge Advanced Learner's Dictionary* (2013) or *Oxford Advanced Learner's Dictionary* (2020). A larger scale introduces one more level, dividing the lexicon into three: formal, neutral (or casual), and informal (see Swan 2003: 216 or Garcarz 2013: 109), where "neutral" refers to whatever is not marked as formal or informal. Such a scale is highly useful in explaining the stylistic layers of the lexicon. Naturally, languages differ in stylistic aspects, and a formality scale for Japanese, for instance, would be more complex (Wardhaugh 1986: 270); still, probably all languages make some kind of distinction relating to the level of formality (Spolsky [1998] 2007: 32).

Let us make an important terminological distinction here. One of the foremost authorities on informal American English, Jonathan Lighter, has observed that informal lexicon can be divided into slang and colloquialism (1994: xv), an assertion now widely accepted by most linguists specializing in informal English, for instance Eble, Coleman, Green, or Widawski. Accordingly, one can modify the above scale by including two subcategories: colloquialism and slang. Thus, such a modified scale would encompass four levels: the highest or formal is reserved for official situations; the middle one is neutral or commonly used in most everyday situations; the lower one is colloquial and, although also used in many everyday situations, largely used among friends or colleagues in more intimate situations; finally, the lowest level is slang which is deliberately informal, outwardly emotional, markedly extreme, and used especially by social or ethnic groups. These levels could be illustrated by comparing the following synonyms: *male* (formal), *man* (neutral), *guy* (colloquial), and *dude* (slang); another example may be *regurgitate* (formal), *vomit* (neutral), *throw up* (colloquial), and *shoot one's cookies* (slang).

According to the above scale, let us repeat, *informal* encompasses both slang and colloquialism, and is thus a superordinate term. Put differently, slang and colloquialism are always informal, although they differ in their semantic scopes (see the definitions of slang and colloquialism below). In relation to slang, then, one may say that all slang is informal, but not all that is informal is slang, and the same can be said about the relationship between colloquialism and informal language. Interestingly, lexicographers sometimes name their works *dictionaries of slang and colloquialisms* (or *colloquial expressions*) (see Spears 1990, for instance), which is meant to be synonymous with *dictionaries of informal expressions*. That being said, it is worth mentioning that in some countries – for instance, in Poland or Germany – linguistic tradition scarcely makes any distinction between slang and colloquialism, both falling into the single category of informal language.

The above informality scale is useful for putting things in context, but defining colloquialism and slang is in order. The first and "less informal" part of informal lexicon, **colloquialism** is easier to explain. Stevenson (2010: 342) defines it as a "word or phrase that is not formal or literary and is used in ordinary or familiar conversation," while Widawski ([2015] 2019: 9) calls it an "informal expression more common in conversation than in formal writing, usually conveying the feel of casual naturalness." Further characterization is offered by Lighter (1994: xv) who describes colloquialism as "an expression more typical of the unstilted voice of daily conversation, and of a writing intended to convey such a voice, than it is of formal, carefully edited prose" and Coleman (2012: 13) who adds a very telling comment: "by speaking in colloquial English, we indicate that we are warm, friendly, approachable individuals who want to connect with other human beings on a personal level." Note that the above descriptions of the term colloquialism are similar to those of informal language yet add the feel of familiar friendliness and casual naturalness. Examples of colloquialisms, beside the abovementioned *guy* "man" and *throw up* "to vomit," include *crazy* "foolish," *pretty* "very," or *mess up* "to ruin or make messy."

But in linguistic usage the term colloquial also has another sense, synonymous with "vernacular" or plain and natural "language spoken by the ordinary people" (Stevenson 2010: 1974). For this reason, colloquial often features in titles of books on everyday language, for instance in the Routledge series of coursebooks for language learners exemplified by such titles as *Colloquial Chinese* (Kan Qian 2021) or *Colloquial Dutch* (Donaldson 2016). Naturally, these titles may be misleading in that rather than presenting colloquial language per se – in the sense "part of informal language" – such books present ordinary language, largely devoid of any informality.

While colloquialism is a part of informal lexicon that is relatively easy to define and understand, **slang** requires a more exhaustive explanation. This is because it is commonly misunderstood and notoriously misrepresented. For instance, the respected *Merriam-Webster Dictionary*'s online edition (2016) defines slang as either "language peculiar to a particular group or an informal nonstandard vocabulary composed typically of coinages, arbitrarily changed words, and extravagant, forced, or facetious figures of speech." This definition leaves much to be desired since slang may not necessarily be peculiar to a particular group, it is something a little different from nonstandard expressions, and it is rarely composed of coinages. To give another example, according to the equally respected *Concise Oxford Dictionary of Linguistics* by Matthews (2007), slang is "used especially of vocabulary specific, e.g., to a particular generation of younger speakers; also, as in ordinary usage, specific to a group or profession." There are two things wrong in this definition: Slang is not necessarily specific to a particular generation of younger speakers nor does it have to be specific to a group or profession. Similar vague characterizations of slang abound.

What is more, since slang lies outside the focus of mainstream sociolinguistics, even trained sociolinguists sometimes fail to capture the nature of slang, offering such astonishingly uninformed characterizations as the one proposed by Spolsky ([1998] 2007: 125): "slang [is] a kind of jargon marked by its rejection of formal rules." This is clearly wrong (see the difference between slang and jargon on the following pages; see Chapter 5 for formal rules including morphological and semantic ones). To give another example, here is a definition proposed by Van Herk (2012: 210): "slang [is] words that are new to a language, or old words or phrases with new meanings," which is a very vague thing to say and completely fails to capture the nature of slang (see the informality, missing from this definition, as the key component of slang on the following pages).

Indeed, slang is commonly perceived as difficult to define and characterize. As Adams says, "slang is what it is. You'll know it when you hear it" (2009: 49). This difficulty is largely ascribed to its fleeting character and alleged vagueness. Consequently, definitions of slang are plentiful. Also, as observed by Coleman (2012: 12–17), slang has been used to refer to various types of language, often in a discordant way. While most linguists studying slang agree that it is "the most informal type of language," they tend to stress one aspect or another of slang (Chapman 1986: x). Let us briefly summarize some of the main approaches to slang. For most scholars, for instance Ayto and Simpson (1992: v), Lighter (1994: xi), or Widawski ([2015] 2019: 8), slang is primarily a lexical phenomenon, serving as a colorful alternative vocabulary to standard expressions. Still for many others, for instance Eble (1996: 11) or Dalzell (2010: 1–8), slang is mostly a sociological phenomenon, inherently linked with its social context and used primarily as a marker of group identification, which is encapsulated in the often quoted maxim, "The raison d'être of slang is social" (Eble 1996: 120). For other scholars, such as Dumas and Lighter (1978: 5–17) or Thorne (1990: iii), slang is a rhetorical phenomenon, stylistically below standard language, used deliberately for desired stylistic effects such as lowering the formality of communication. For yet other scholars, such as Chapman (1986: xii–xiv), slang is essentially a psychological phenomenon, with its roots in the unconscious self, serving as a therapeutic means of expressing emotions. Finally, some scholars, such as Coleman (2012: 26–116) or Green (2015: 1, 1994: v), see slang as a diachronic (or historical) phenomenon, the ever-changing type of language labeled "lexis in motion" where its changes are often compared to changes in standard language over time in its historical development, except in slang these happen at a much more rapid pace.

All of the above qualities and characterizations are correct, yet each of them emphasizes a particular approach stemming from a particular point of view. Leaving such partial, emphasis-oriented characterizations of slang aside, let us cite here two more inclusive definitions which attempt to describe slang in a more holistic manner. Perhaps one of the best such definitions of slang is the one by Lighter (1994: xi–xii) who elegantly outlined its diverse characteristics in the following way:

> Slang in an informal, nonstandard, nontechnical vocabulary composed chiefly of novel-sounding synonyms for standard words and phrases [. . .]. It turns up especially in the derisive speech of youthful, raffish, or undignified persons or groups; and partly owing to this and partly because of the unconventional images slang often evokes, the use of slang often carries with it striking overtones of irreverence, especially for idealized values and attitudes within prevailing culture. Often too, the use of slang suggests, as standard speech cannot, an intimate familiarity with the referential object or idea [. . .]. The use of slang undermines the dignity of verbal exchange and charges discourse with an unrefined and often aggressive informality. It pops the balloon of pretense; there is also very often a raw vitality in slang, a ribald sense of humor and a flip of self-confidence; there is also very often locker-room crudity and toughness, a tawdry sensibility.

Another extensive and inclusive definition of slang, which integrates most of the above aspects, is the one proposed by Widawski (2015: 8) who synthesized it as follows:

> Slang is a highly informal and unconventional type of vocabulary. It is perceived as deeply expressive, attractively catchy, and deliberately undignified. It consists of standard expressions modified in some way or appended with new meanings, and sometimes of entirely novel expressions. Slang is coined chiefly by members of social, occupational or ethnic groups which are typically separate from mainstream society, yet it is often adopted by larger social segments. It is employed in place of standard expressions to convey some extra information of a psychological, social or rhetorical nature. It thus provides alternative, highly informal synonyms for referents already named in the language, but sometimes gives names for referents for which there are no standard expressions, or which have yet to be named.

Examples of slang include the abovementioned *dude* "man" and *shoot one's cookies* "to vomit." However, to illustrate the term more fully and show a whole range of its applications, let us present more examples: with regard to form, *babelicious* "sexually attractive" (created by the lexical modification of a standard expression), *cow* "despicable woman" (created by the figurative modification of a standard expression), *barf* "to vomit" (created out of nothing); with regard to users, *homeboy* "someone from the same neighborhood" (group-restricted), *ammo* "ammunition" (originally group-restricted but adopted by larger social segments); with regard to functions, *white trash* "poor white people, esp. from the Southern US" (used to convey extra sociocultural information), *my ass* "I don't believe it" (used to convey extra psychological information), *and shit* "and other things" (used to convey extra rhetorical information); with regard to themes, *funbags* "female breasts" (referring to the human body), *shtup* "to have sex" (referring to human sexuality), *booze* "alcoholic drink" (referring to human intoxication), *wigger* "white person who assumes the behavior or values of African American culture" (referring to human categorization); with regard to use, *loaded* "drunk" (providing alternative synonyms for things already named in the language), *egosurf* "to search the Internet for instances of one's own name" (providing alternative synonyms for things for which there are no standard expressions).

Having defined colloquialism and slang, one should perhaps point out the **differences** between these two subsets of informal lexicon. The abovementioned formality scale offers one important distinction: slang is stylistically lower – or more informal – than colloquialism. In other words, while colloquial is informal, slang is very informal. This characterization is helpful but there are some additional distinctions as well. These are perhaps best captured by Lighter (1994: xv) who characterizes colloquialism as "an expression more typical of the unstilted voice of daily conversation, and of a writing intended to convey such a voice, than it is of formal, carefully edited prose," and contrasts it with slang which "carries a greater sense of opposition to 'form' than does the merely colloquial." To continue with the comparison, while colloquialism is casual, mild, and more acceptable, slang is deliberate, extreme, undignified, and rebellious: "for slang to be slangy, it has to startle, amuse, shock" (Bauer 2002: 115). Put differently, colloquialism is used by the laid-back, and slang is used by those with an attitude.

The above distinctions become evident in the diachronic process of change from slang to standard language through the intermediate stage of colloquialism. It works like this: a slang expression may lose its impact and become more acceptable, thus changing into a colloquial expression which, in turn, may itself lose its colloquial qualities, thus changing into a completely standard expression (see Crowther 1999: 494). This is a natural process and sometimes makes it difficult to assess if a given expression is still slang or already a colloquialism. However, even if the above differences are sometimes tonal or blurry, it would be an exaggeration to claim that "one person's slang is another's colloquialism" (Ayto 1998: v).

To complete our presentation of differences between colloquialism and slang, perhaps one more important distinction must be made. It regards the scope of use. Because colloquialism is casual, it is widely acceptable, having a fairly broad range of application in nearly all social situations (except for formal, solemn, or ceremonial ones). In contrast, slang has a more limited range of general application because of its extreme or undignified nature. However, it features more prominently among social groups. When used by these groups, slang often serves various sociocultural functions such as social identity, including in-group solidarity or social distancing: it "is used to fit in and stand out" (Addams 2009: 6); colloquialism, on the other hand, is hardly used for these reasons. See more in Chapter 6.

Naturally, both parts of informal language – colloquialism and slang – in this book refer to American usage. Of course, the phenomenon of informal language is by no means restricted to American English since it features prominently in other varieties of English, such as Australian or South African, and it has for centuries been a feature of British English. Nor is it restricted to English since it is to be found in various languages such as Spanish, French, German, Russian, Arabic, or Chinese: one may even say that it is universal. Yet, it is the informal vocabulary of American English which is probably most prolific and influential: informality – especially slang – has long been considered a hallmark of American English. Kövecses (2000: 236), following Wentworth and Flexner ([1960] 1975: ix), links it with democratic mingling and attributes it to the unrestricted use of various registers in what he calls "style mixing." In that, the role of informality in American English can be compared to the one of borrowings, and the two have greatly invigorated the fabric of American English. American freedom, mobility, urbanization, and democratic society have all helped in the creation and dissemination of informal expressions, much as American immigration – epitomized by the concept of the melting pot – has contributed to the importation and assimilation of borrowings.

2.5 Related Terms

The term *informal* often serves as a grab-bag for a number of linguistic phenomena which, although sometimes similar, mean something else. Neufeldt (1999: 1–22), examining informal language, says this: "in opposition [to formal] stands everything else, including regionalism, slang, colloquial language, neologisms, dialect, archaic and obsolete words, etc." Naturally, such a characterization may be illustratory and exaggerated, but it makes a point. Still, a good notion of what *informal* is can be inferred from contrasting it with similar types of the lexicon which are often confused with it (see an analogous discussion related to slang in Lighter 1994: xiv–xv). These include such terms as nonstandard, substandard, unconventional language, spoken language, lingo, vernacular, sociolect, ethnolect, and jargon. All of them tend to be loosely used as synonyms for informal language, and though they share certain characteristics with it, their respective semantic scopes are to various degrees dissimilar. Let us discuss them below.

Nonstandard language is sometimes used more or less synonymously with informal language. There are notable differences. In its broadest sense, nonstandard exists in opposition to standard, which is understood as language "widely accepted as the usual correct form" (Stevenson 2010: 1737) or "the established speech and writing of educated people" (Steinmetz and Kipfer 2006: 338). Note that the emphasis is on correctness, acceptance, and education, and these three elements often reappear in definitions of standard language. Nonstandard, then, includes expressions which are incorrect, unacceptable, and frowned upon by educated speakers. Put differently, they are considered bad "English" and thus excluded from standard prose, unless done as stylization. They do, however, appear in speech and are often used unknowingly by native speakers. Moreover, some scholars restrict the scope of the term to grammar: Pearce (2007: 126) claims it refers to "any grammatical structure or word which is not recognized as part of a 'standard' variety"; in that, nonstandard is synonymous with ungrammatical. Examples of such expressions include *ain't* "am not, are not, or is not," *ain't got* "do not have or does not have," *irregardless* "regardless," and *might could* "might or could."

Substandard language is similar to nonstandard and often used interchangeably with it (see Munro 1989: 3). However, it is a more stigmatizing and pejorative label since it suggests language or an expression which is below the standard. Substandard is normally applied in an educational context to expressions and usages that have become "shibboleths as presumed markers of ignorance and illiteracy" (Lighter 1994: xv). This term connotes that users of such expressions are too unintelligent to understand or use the corresponding standard form. For the above reasons, it is nowadays rarely used by sociolinguists and descriptive linguists.

Unconventional language is fairly self-explanatory. It broadly refers to language which is deliberately unorthodox and somehow departs from the established conventions, yet it is not necessarily nonstandard or substandard. In that, it resembles slang, which sometimes plays with the established language conventions (although rarely violates them), and perhaps for this reason it often features in titles of slang dictionaries, as in *The Routledge Dictionary of Modern American Slang and Unconventional English* (2009), or is part of slang definitions (see Widawski's definition above). Still, strictly speaking, this is not a linguistic term. Examples of unconventional – and at the same time slang – expressions include *infanticipating* "expecting a baby" or *overstand* "to understand completely or have a profound knowledge"; other serviceable examples include expressions which use unconventional spelling meant to represent African American English pronunciation, for instance *bidness* "business," *brutha* "fellow African American man," or *sista* "fellow African American woman."

Spoken language is sometimes equated with informal language. This is understandable since informal language has always been largely oral in nature. However, while spoken language can and often does involve informal expressions, not all of it is informal; for instance, a spoken sermon may contain no informal expressions at all; similarly a speech by a member of Congress. Also, while informal language is a principally spoken phenomenon, not all of it must actually be spoken, and because of the revolution in mobile communication, nowadays much informal language exists as text and abounds in social media, television series, independent journalism, and so on. One should bear these distinctions in mind.

Lingo is sometimes found to be more or less synonymous with informal language. In particular, it is used frequently in journalism as a general omnipurpose word for an unusual language of a particular group of people, such as slang, jargon, or dialect; it may also refer to a hybrid language, especially used in an area where different languages come in contact. However, the term itself is perceived as informal, and thus nontechnical, and is hardly used in scholarly discourse unless for jocular reasons, as in the title of the paper "Digging the Lingo of European Teens" (2001) by Widawski or the book *Spanish Lingo for the Savvy Gringo* (2003) by Reid. More importantly, as observed by McArthur (1992: 605), the term is often dismissive and carries negative connotations as either a "language perceived as strange and unintelligible" or "an unusual way of speaking that is hard to follow." Finally, it is somewhat ambiguous since some linguists equate it with jargon (see Stevenson 2010: 1028).

Vernacular is yet another term sometimes confused with informal language. The term refers to "the language spoken by the ordinary people of a country or region" (Stevenson 2010: 1974). As observed by Pearce (2007: 196), "vernacular forms are typically non-standard, dialectal, colloquial and informal." While such characterization is similar to that of informal language, the term has a larger scope, as visible in African American Vernacular English (AAVE) the lexicon of which is only partially composed of informal expressions (see Kowalczyk and Widawski 2017: 7).

Sociolect (or **social dialect**) is a scholarly term used to refer to "a linguistic variety defined on social (as opposed to regional) grounds, e.g. correlating with a particular social class" (Crystal [1980] 1991: 319). In that, it is similar to slang rather than colloquialism. In fact, slang is often referred to as a sociolect or part of it (see Pearce 2007: 170), possibly because many slang expressions originate among social groups. However, slang may not necessarily have to originate in or be used by particular social or occupational groups; there are numerous slang expressions – those belonging to so-called general or secondary slang (see discussion in Section 1.3) – which are devoid of any social connotations and are commonly used by larger social segments. In other words, sociolect can be applied as a synonym of slang – and by extrapolation of informal language – but only of the one related to specific social groups.

Ethnolect (or **ethnic dialect**), as the name suggests, is rather restricted in its semantic scope when compared with informal language. Pearce (2007: 65) defines it lucidly as "a language variety associated with a particular ethnic group." While informal language may and often does have an ethnic character – the best exemplification here is African American slang – it is a larger phenomenon, including more than just ethnic contributions. On the other hand, ethnolect – to resort again to the speech of African Americans and use African American English as an example – includes more than just informal expressions but other parts of lexicon as well, or even extends over the lexical level, exhibiting phonological and syntactic characteristics too (see Widawski [2015] 2019: 12). Examples of African American ethnolect include *Kwanzaa* "secular festival observed by many African Americans between December 26 to January 1 as a celebration of their heritage and values," *soul food* "food traditionally associated with African Americans of the Southern USA," or *play the dozens* "to tease, especially by provocative rhyming comments in a gamelike manner."

Jargon, a term often confused with informal language – especially with slang – has generated numerous meanings. It is most generally understood as "the technical terms peculiar to specific occupations and professions" (Lighter 1994: xvi); in that, jargon is often codified and has normative character. Crystal ([1995] 1999: 454) offers a similar definition, "the technical language of a special field," but also adds another, "the obscure use of specialized language." And it is in this second meaning related to "the obscure lexicon" that jargon tends to be confused with slang. Still, the two terms are diametrically different. Widawski ([2015] 2019: 9) neatly compares the two: "jargon is a precise and professional nomenclature developed among specialists chiefly to facilitate cooperation. Slang, on the other hand, is a non-technical and lighthearted vocabulary developed among colleagues chiefly for expressiveness or exclusivity." Significantly, as observed by Lighter (1994: xvi), jargon "is essentially standard English that is unfamiliar beyond the limits of those specialized fields for which it provides the recognized standard vocabulary." In that, it is totally different from informal language. Examples of jargon include such medical nomenclature as *emesis* "vomiting," *myopia* "the quality of being nearsighted," or *endoscope* "tube-like instrument inserted into the body to view its internal parts."

2.6 Additional Terms

There are even more terms confused with informal language. These include cant, argot, vulgarism, offensive language, swearword, taboo, euphemism, dysphemism, neologism, nonce word, and possibly dialect. Let us examine them in relation to informal language.

Cant can only partially serve as a synonym of informal language or, specifically, slang. This is because in modern linguistic usage the term is largely applied to the secret slang of the underworld, especially the slang of criminals. In that, it has a rather restricted sense, although sometimes it is used interchangeably with slang in general (see Adams 2009: 8). The association with the slang of criminals gave way to a broader meaning of cant, "language specific to a particular group or profession and regarded with disparagement" (Stevenson 2010: 255) or "the special speech of a group with low social standing" (Crystal 1987: 416), and it still has negative associations which slang does not necessarily have to share. Also, cant is used chiefly in historical contexts to refer to the beginnings of slang as evidenced by the slang of criminals in the sixteenth and seventeenth centuries (see Eble 1996: 11), as employed in the title of Coleman's diachronic study of slang dictionaries, *A History of Cant and Slang Dictionaries* (2005). Examples of cant include *bracelets* "handcuffs," *bull* "prison guard," and *stretch* "period of imprisonment."

The term **argot** appeared in the nineteenth century as a synonym for cant (Adams 2009: 8). In modern English linguistics it is used sporadically and often vaguely: Crystal ([1995] 1999: 449) defines it as "special vocabulary used by a secretive social group," while Pearce (2007: 17) says that it "is sometimes used to describe the slang of a particular group." However, the term is well rooted in the linguistic tradition of several countries and is favored, for instance, in French linguistics (see *Dictionnaire Argot Français* [Hayard 2015]).

To nonlinguists, **vulgarism** is often synonymous with informal language – and specifically slang – so many mistakenly believe that all slang is vulgar. In reality, the relation is one-directional. Vulgarism refers to an impolite or coarse expression which, as noted by Stevenson (2010: 1992), "makes explicit reference to sex or bodily functions" and thus is not accepted in a majority of everyday situations and unaccepted in official or formal situations. Hence, all vulgarisms are slang (but of course, not all informal language is slang). On the other hand, not all slang (or informal language) is vulgar, and there are virtually thousands of expressions which do not violate sociocultural conventions of propriety; by my own estimate, only about one-tenth of slang is vulgar. Examples of vulgarisms – and slang – include *blowjob* "oral stimulation of the penis," *fuckable* "desirable or ready for sex," or *shit* "excrement."

Offensive language is another term occasionally equated with informal language – and again slang – and often confused with vulgarism. Still, there are differences. Although both vulgarism and offensive language are impolite or coarse expressions, the former refers primarily to sex or bodily functions and the latter refers primarily to nationality, race, or religion. Put differently, vulgarisms are meant to shock or disgust, while offensive expressions are meant to offend or denigrate. Again, much like with vulgarism, all offensive language is slang (although note, again, that not all informal language is slang); on the other hand, not all slang (and, of course, informal language) must be offensive. Examples of offensive language include *Jesus Freak* "a fervent evangelical Christian," *kike* "a Jew," or *towel head* "a person who wears a turban, especially an Arab."

Swearword can be defined as "an offensive word, used especially as an expression of anger" (Stevenson 2010: 1796). In that, swearwords are types of offensive language (see above). They are also similar to vulgarisms in their relationship with informal language and slang: by analogy, one can say that all swearwords are slang but at the same time not all slang is vulgar. Examples of swearwords include *blow me* "I hold you in contempt or I am not afraid of you," *holy crap* "I am surprised or annoyed," or *fuck me* "I am surprised" (important note: the accent falls on *me*).

Taboo, often discussed in relation to informal language and specifically slang, refers to a subject that is forbidden or disapproved of because it is considered socially unacceptable, such as sex, scatology, race, or religion. Such social taboos are exemplified by taboo expressions, "linguistic forms whose use is avoided in a society" (Crystal ([1995] 1999: 459). Because of the irreverent nature of slang, taboo is often linked with slang. Garcarz considers taboo expressions to be an important component of slang (2013: 131), while Spolsky ([1998] 2007: 36) explains that "slang regularly transgresses social norms, making free use of taboo expressions." However, a given subject may be treated as taboo but its linguistic exponent – taboo expressions – may not necessarily be vulgar. Finally, although a sizable portion of slang refers to taboo subjects, not all slang is about them. Examples of taboo expressions include *buttfuck* "to have anal sex," *Aunt Flo* "menstruation," or *Jesus H. Christ* "I am shocked."

Euphemism is similar to taboo in its relation to informal language. Nature abhors a vacuum, and the avoidance of taboo expressions produces euphemisms. Steinmetz and Kipfer (2006: 111) define a euphemism as "a mild or acceptable word or phrase used to replace a harsh or unacceptable one," and indeed such expressions are often used to replace slang epithets or exclamations. However, not all euphemisms are informal, and they can occur in language of all levels of formality, for instance, in literary or official language. Conversely, while there is a plethora of informal euphemisms, not all informal language is euphemistic. Examples of euphemisms include *meet one's maker* "to die," *powder one's nose* "to go to the bathroom to urinate or defecate," and *wax the dolphin* "(of a man) to masturbate."

Dysphemism has much more in common with informal language and slang than euphemism. This is because dysphemism, by definition, is a "negative or derogatory expression that is used to replace a neutral one" (Steinmetz and Kipfer 2006: 111); its variant is **cacophemism**, which refers to a cruel or offensive dysphemism (McArthur 1992: 328). In fact, slang is often dysphemistic (or cacophemistic) in nature, and there are numerous derogatory slang synonyms for neutral standard expressions. Having said this, while dysphemisms abound in informal language, not all of it is composed of them. Examples of dysphemisms include *cunt* "woman," *loony bin* "mental hospital," and *pukehole* "the mouth."

Neologism, too, has a confusing relationship with informal language and slang. Neologisms are usually understood as recently coined expressions or, as Ayto put it, "newly minted lexicon" (1999: iii). Slang is similar to neologism because it frequently involves novelty and spontaneous creation. Also, if we extend the definition of neologism to "the creation of a new word out of existing elements" (Crystal [1995] 1999: 455), either by morphological or semantic manipulation, then all slang at some point is neological. Examples of neologisms include *chocoholic* "someone addicted to chocolate," *mankini* "bikini for men," or *whoredom* "profession of a prostitute." However, there are many neologisms which may not necessarily be informal or slang, as evidenced by the following expressions created in recent times: *Brexit, eating disorder, download, webinar*. Also, as noted by Widawski ([2015] 2019: 11), "many slang words have been around for centuries, clearly having lost their novel value yet remaining slang all the same."

Nonce word (or **occasionalism**), a term similar to neologism, is "a word which comes into existence to serve a temporary purpose and then vanishes" (Pearce 2007: 125). Steinmetz and Kipfer (2006: 227) refer to such expressions as "words serving a need of the moment." Put differently, some fleeting neologisms are quickly forgotten or remain a mere oddity, thus turning into nonce words. Informal language and slang can also be created spontaneously for a particular occasion yet, in aggregate, they are longer lasting. For instance, most scatological vocabulary in the English language is several centuries old and continues to be used as slang. Nonce words, in turn, live a life among only a few individuals and for a limited time. Some of the more recent examples of nonce words include *Trumpesque* "resembling or characteristic of Donald Trump," *Kavanaughty* "referring to beer-partying nature of the future US Supreme Court Judge Brett Kavanaugh," or *feel the Bern* "to support Senator Bernie Sanders for the US President during the 2016 presidential election."

Finally, **dialect** is sometimes confused with informal language and slang, especially in its wider sense (see below). In its fundamental meaning, dialect refers to a regional variety of language, as in US Southern dialect or Canadian Newfoundland dialect. Dialect expressions are chiefly oral in nature and often lower in prestige than the standard, and that is why they tend to be considered informal or nonstandard. Although slang is not geographically restricted, it is often regional and – just like standard vocabulary – some expressions are associated with a particular area (see Eble 1996: 19). The differences can be seen in national varieties of English: consider, for instance *double-double* "coffee with two sugars and two creamers," *loonie* "dollar coin," or *Timmy's* "Tim Horton's fast-food restaurant," all from Canadian slang. Yet, slang is not a dialect. As observed by Lighter (1994: xiii), "people who speak the same dialect necessarily share a similar regional or cultural background, but a shared slang is more likely to suggest mutually held antiestablishment attitudes, especially a sharpened disdain for convention or pretense." In that respect, slang is more social. However, dialect may correlate with slang when it is used in its wider sense of "a form of language," extended to cover differences not only according to region but also according to class and occupation (McArthur 1992: 289–290); thus, we may have, for instance, regional dialect, social dialect, class dialect, occupational dialect, urban dialect, and rural dialect. Examples of dialect – in its basic, geographical sense – include the following expressions used in the Southern USA: *chitlins* "dish made from boiled and stewed intestines of a pig," *reckon* "to think," and *y'all* "you (in plural)."

Chapter Summary

Informal **borrowings** are defined as expressions taken from a foreign language and used in informal American English. They conform to the traditional typology of borrowings and include such **main types** as loan-words, loan translations, and semantic loans, but there are other finer distinctions, such as loanblends or foreignisms, much as there are certain **terms** often confused with borrowings, such as code switches or nonce borrowings. **Informal language**, in turn, refers to a type of vocabulary which is stylistically "lower" than the standard language and "below" the formal and neutral registers on the formality scale. It includes two subsets: **colloquialism**, which is composed of moderately informal and casual expressions, and **slang**, which is composed of highly informal and unconventional expressions, perceived as very expressive, deliberately undignified, and strongly linked with a sociocultural context. Again, there are several similar **terms** to account for this type of lexicon, such as nonstandard, jargon, or neologism, but their semantic scopes are different.

CHAPTER 3

Donors

Chapter Outline

The self-explanatory division of borrowings **by language** (or **by language origin**) is a traditional and perhaps the most fundamental way to analyze this type of lexicon. It also works for borrowings in informal American English. In other words, informal borrowings can be distinguished on the etymological basis of the languages they came from, technically called **donor languages** (or **donors**) and alternatively called **source languages**. Such classification is used in this chapter.

Two issues require explanation here. First, following a traditional approach, this book identifies primarily **immediate source borrowings**: expressions borrowed directly from one donor language which themselves had been borrowed from another donor language (see Haspelmath and Tadmoor 2009: 16). For instance, the immediate source of the borrowing *spiel* "a persuasive or eloquent talk" or "an advertising monologue or salesperson's speech intended to attract customers" is Yiddish because this word was introduced and popularized in the USA by Jewish immigrants and their descendants, although the Yiddish word itself naturally has a Germanic origin and comes from the Middle German *Spiel*; for similar reasons, *chutzpah* "arrogance or insolence" or "bravery and courage" and *tochus* "buttocks" are identified here as coming from Yiddish, their immediate source, although their ultimate origin is Hebrew. That being said, there are some borderline cases which will be discussed later in this chapter.

Second, the majority of borrowings are associated with a **single donor language**; that is, they can be clearly demonstrated to have come from a single language. Still, some informal borrowings are associated with **two donor languages** or more because tracing them to a single language would prove difficult or impossible, as is often the case with expressions borrowed from Yiddish and German (see Sections 3.2 and 3.3).

Again, in most cases, single donor languages can be identified. Accordingly, the following paragraphs present the main languages which have contributed to informal American English. They are presented in decreasing order of importance, reflected by a combination of the number of borrowings found in the database with their relative frequency of occurrence, and illustrated by representative samples of citational examples.

3.1   Spanish

Spanish has contributed greatly to the lexicon of American English. Given the size and influence of the Latin American minority in the United States, it is no surprise that expressions taken from Spanish constitute the most sizable and an ever-expanding part of informal borrowings, constituting a little less than half of all, which comes down to around 500 expressions, a massive number. They also have a long history in informal American English, for some entered it as early as the eighteenth century during the forging of the nation, others appeared in the nineteenth during the Mexican War, and the largest part arrived in the latter part of the twentieth century with mass immigration from Latin American countries, particularly Mexico. However, one should make one reservation: many expressions found in the database are restricted in use to Latin Americans and thus not universally used by the majority of Americans who may otherwise perceive them as foreignisms (see Section 4.3). Here is a representative sample of such borrowings:

> I showed his picture to the **alambristas** [= Mexicans illegally present in the US (Spanish)] there, but no one had seen him (San Diego Reader, 2001)
>
> I gotta spend a little quality time with the **mamacita** [= woman, especially a young and attractive one (Spanish)] (Ant Bully, film, 2006)
>
> Yanks vacationing south-of-the-border face a fate far worse than **turistas** [= diarrhea, especially as contracted in a foreign country (Spanish)] (Variety magazine, 2006)
>
> **Viejo** [= old man (Spanish)], you know she ain't gonna pay you, right? (Washington Heights, film, 2003)

Within this largest group of borrowings one can distinguish three main types based on the variety of Spanish they came from. Unquestionably, the majority of Spanish borrowings in informal American English come from **Mexican Spanish**, which is not surprising since Mexican Americans are the largest subgroup of Latin Americans in the United States. While this group is diverse and changing, its core has traditionally been composed of lower socioeconomic classes (see Agius Vallejo 2012: 6–7) and younger people (Fought 2003: 11–12), both of which tend to use more informal language – especially its slang subset – than others. Also, a number of expressions come directly from **caló**, a type of Spanish street slang popular among Mexican Americans, and a sizable number of borrowings refers to the criminal underworld. Here are a few examples of such expressions:

> Some **cholos** [= *young and tough Mexican Americans (Spanish)*] *here were involved in gangs, but not many* (New York Times, 2013)
>
> *The firm handshake is the hallmark of the older generation and* **chúntaros** [= *Mexican nationals, especially if poor (Spanish)*] (Phoenix New Times, 2014)
>
> *The Mexican Mafia, known as the* **Eme** [= *Mexican Mafia (Spanish)*], *imposed new rules on Southern California Latino street gangs* (Los Angeles Times, 2008)
>
> *He is just some* **Tejano** [= *Texan of Mexican origin or descent (Spanish)*] *with a lot of questions I don't have to answer* (Lone Star, film, 1996)

The second group of Spanish borrowings are those from **Puerto Rican Spanish**. Many of these expressions are associated with the New York City metropolitan area, where the majority of Puerto Ricans on the mainland have lived following large waves of migration in the middle of the twentieth century. Large urban areas are considered the birthing ground for coining and using informal language – especially its slang component – so it is not surprising to find slang borrowings from Puerto Rican Spanish. Consider the following examples:

> *I feel compelled to add that I am from Long Island and yes, there are quite a few* **Juans** [= *persons from Puerto Rico (Spanish)*] *here* (Baby Center, 2010)
>
> *In the spoken word, the* **Nuyoricans** [= *Puerto Rican, especially one living in New York City (Spanish)*], *or Puerto Rican New Yorkers, embraced identity and culture* (New York Times, 2002)
>
> *My daughter's boyfriend, who's* [sic] *family is from* **PR** (= *Puerto Rico (Spanish)*)), *took us to Barrachina for drinks* (Yelp, 2014)
>
> *You know a few* **PR's** [= *Puerto Ricans (Spanish)*] *and you generalize about all PR's* (Topix, 2012)

The third group of Spanish borrowings are those from **Cuban Spanish**. Associated with Cubans who flocked to Florida after the Cuban Revolution in the 1960s, they are much less numerous compared with borrowings from Mexican or Puerto Rican Spanish, possibly because most Cuban Americans come from educated middle classes (Winn 2006: 602), which tend to use fewer informal expressions. Also, one will find very few expressions referring to the criminal underworld. Here are some representative examples of such expressions:

> *I'm in love with a* **chonga** [= *working-class, sexualized, and aggressive young woman (Spanish)*] (Miami New Times, 2010)

*Jay, can you grab me a brew, **porfa** [= please (Spanish)]?* (Urban Dictionary, 2005)

Que cool [= how excellent (Spanish)]! *I'm going to add you as a friend* (YouTube, 2014)

*As savvy muchachos know, it is the number one show on commercial television, and **que nice** [= how nice (Spanish)]!* (*Miami New Times*, 2003)

3.2   Yiddish

Yiddish, once the main language of the European Jews, is the second most important source after Spanish and has contributed hundreds of borrowings to informal American English. In terms of sheer numbers, Yiddish borrowings (or Yiddishisms) constitute roughly one-third of all borrowings, which comes down to a hefty 350 or so expressions. Most of these expressions appeared in American English at the turn of the twentieth century when millions of Jews immigrated to the United States to escape the growing antisemitism in Europe. They assimilated quickly, and as a result few people today can speak Yiddish. Yet many Yiddishisms prevailed and are a vibrant element of the lexicon of American English; their popularity reflects the importance of Jews as a powerful socioeconomic group in American society, visible especially in the worlds of business and entertainment. Here are a few examples:

*Pull this embarrassing **dreck** [= something worthless or of inferior quality (Yiddish)] off the Internet!* (*Philadelphia City Paper*, 2010)

*You see, that's the **schlemiel** [= stupid, awkward, and clumsy person who is also unlucky (Yiddish)] I've got for a brother* (*Sixty Six*, film, 2006)

*They are perfectly fine selling their **schlock** [= something that has no value, especially shoddy or inferior merchandise (Yiddish)] to the public* (*Los Angeles Times*, 2010)

*That's not the only reason why we think he's a **schmuck** [= despicable person (Yiddish)]* (*LA Weekly*, 2013)

Interestingly, because of the composite nature of Yiddish lexicon (see Kowalczyk 2010: 14), one can distinguish three groups of Yiddishisms: Yiddish-German borrowings (or Germanic Yiddishisms), Yiddish-Hebrew borrowings (Hebraic Yiddishisms), and Yiddish-Slavic borrowings (Slavic Yiddishisms). Each group exhibits certain noticeable linguistic characteristics, outlined below.

Yiddish-German borrowings in informal American English are Yiddish expressions which themselves came into Yiddish from

German. They constitute the main stock of Yiddish vocabulary – as much as two-thirds of the entire lexicon (Stevens et al. 2002: 4) – and are highly diversified thematically (Geller 1994: 81). Borrowings from this group are most numerous and tend to be most easily assimilated, a fact attributed to their Germanic form. Consider the following examples:

> Some **gelt** *[= money (Yiddish)] could probably persuade them to take on the assignment from the high bidder* (*New York Post*, 2014)
>
> *While you* **nosh** *[= eat (Yiddish)], check out the striking museum-quality art hanging on the walls* (*Atlanta Journal Constitution*, 2016)
>
> *You wouldn't believe it, but I used to be a* **shtarker** *[= physically strong person, especially if muscular (Yiddish)], a strong guy* (*New York Times*, 2014)
>
> *What about the cover with the scantily clad,* **zaftig** *[= curvaceous (Yiddish)] women?* (*Chicago Magazine*, 2016)

Yiddish-Hebrew borrowings are expressions which entered Yiddish from Hebrew. They are the second most numerous part of Yiddish lexicon, accounting for about one-sixth (Stevens et al. 2002: 4). They refer primarily to traditional Jewish and religious life (Geller 1994: 81). In contrast to the previous group, they are much less numerous and are not easily assimilated. Still, their popularity in informal American English stems from their exotic form. Here are a few representative examples:

> *This has been a male turf and Hillary Clinton has got the* **chutzpah** *[= bravery or courage (Yiddish)]* (*Time* magazine, 2016)
>
> *The mayor referred to Mr. Lehman, who was Jewish, as a* **ganef** *[= thief (Yiddish)]* (*New York Times*, 2015)
>
> *No fear if you don't have in-laws who've mastered the matzo, or even if you're just a* **goy** *[= non-Jew (Yiddish)] who wants a taste of this tradition* (*Santa Barbara Independent*, 2016)
>
> *Twerk till your* **tokus** *[= buttocks (Yiddish)] can't take no more, girl!* (Perez Hilton, 2014)

Finally, **Yiddish-Slavic borrowings** are expressions which entered Yiddish from Slavic languages such as Polish, Russian, Ukrainian, Belarusian, or Czech. They constitute about one-sixth (Stevens et al. 2002: 4) of the entire Yiddish lexicon. They are the least numerous in informal American English, most likely because of their Slavic form which is difficult to spell or pronounce for Americans. Still, because of the very form, such expressions are considered exotic and often humorous (see Kowalczyk 2010: 16). They are also perceived to convey "a special sense of Yiddishness or Jewish flavor" (Wex 2005: 25), possibly because they refer to everyday mundane activities, and are especially serviceable in expressing emotions (Geller 1994: 81). Consider the following:

> When I see something beautiful, a piece of music or a painting, it gets me in the **kishkes** [= deepest emotional experience or consciousness (Yiddish)] (News, MTV-TV program, 2016)
>
> He's a classic British comic type, the **nebbish** [= weak, timid, ineffectual, or pitiful person (Yiddish)] who endures constant humiliation (New York Times, 2012)
>
> A bookshelf isn't just functional; it can also be utilized to display art and small **tchotchkes** [= plaything or trinket (Yiddish)] (Seattle Times, 2016)
>
> I never had to pay the **vigorish** [= interest on a loan or debt, profits of a bookmaker, usurer, or criminal conspirator (Yiddish)] he demands (Goodfellas, film, 1990)

3.3   Other Key Donors

German is the third most important source language that has contributed to borrowings in informal American English, although German borrowings are far less numerous than those from Spanish or Yiddish, constituting some ninety expressions. Most of them represent the oldest stock of informal borrowings dating back to the eighteenth century. Another sizable group comes from World War I and World War II, brought by the American soldiers who fought in Europe. Although German influence has waned since then, these old expressions are still relatively numerous and continue to be known and used, a fact attributed to their Germanic form which facilitated their assimilation into English. Here are a few examples:

> You must be getting quite a lot of **flak** [= severe criticism (German)] on that, right? (Scream 2, film, 1997)
>
> The A/C compressor is **kaput** [= out of order, inoperative, or useless (German)], there's a dent in the hood, and the dash is cracked (Jalopnik, 2015)
>
> I won't sit on my **keister** [= buttocks (German)] and watch them get rich (A Walk to Remember, film, 2002)
>
> Tattoos are strictly **verboten** [= forbidden (German)], sorry! (Bring It On, film, 2000)

When discussing borrowings from German, one needs to address the problematic issue of "shared etymology" with Yiddish, a phenomenon also found in certain borrowings from Yiddish or

Slavic languages (see Section 3.4). That is to say, a handful of borrowings may have entered American English via either German or Yiddish, or both. In such cases, clear-cut etymology is difficult and debatable. Luckily, there are just a few such borderline cases, most typically involving suffix words *fest* and *meister* used to create numerous compounds:

> *That's the attitude* **admeisters** *[= specialists in advertising (perhaps German)] are banking on* (Businessweek, 1997)
>
> *I do not encourage having a* **boozefest** *[= drinking party (perhaps German)] every night of the week* (Daily Nebraskan, 2013)
>
> *Sullivan is arguably the most prominent gay* **opinionmeister** *[= opinion-maker or expert (perhaps German)] in the business* (Questia, 2012)
>
> *It will conclude with a* **songfest** *[= song festival or singing session (perhaps German)] and gala this weekend* (Atlanta Journal Constitution, 2014)

Italian is the fourth source language of informal borrowings in American English and contributed about sixty borrowings in total. Associated with Italian immigrant communities in places like New York City, most of these expressions came to informal American English with the waves of Italian immigration to the United States at the turn of the twentieth century. Many, although not all, of them are stereotypically connected with the language of the underworld and organized crime, heavily present in southern Italy, from where most immigrants originated. Consider the following expressions:

> *Let's be clear, 'cause being clear will save us both a lot of* **agita** *[= feeling of agitation or anxiety (Italian)]* (Dexter, Showtime-TV series, 2008)
>
> *Eventually, he reached the rank of* **capo** *[= head of a local unit of the Mafia (Italian)] inside the Carlotta crime family* (Smokin' Aces, film, 2007)
>
> *No more monkey business, Al.* **Finito** *[= that is the end (Italian)]* (Boardwalk Empire, HBO-TV series, 2010)
>
> *I just hired us a* **numero uno** *[= the best person (Italian)]* (Tune in Tomorrow, film, 1990)

Much like Italian, **French** has contributed surprisingly few expressions – about fifty in total – to informal American English, given its linguistic and cultural importance, on the one hand, and the shared history of the French in North America, on the other. Perhaps the reason is the long aversion of the Americans toward the French; perhaps it is the nature of the language, which is considered too elegant, posh, or upper-class to be interesting to users of informal language, especially its slang component. That said, here are a few expressions which are well known and highly popular among the American public:

> Selena showed off her sexy **gams** [= legs (French)] in a daring black gown with a very high slit at Annabel's in London (Hollywood Life, 2015)

> Everybody claiming to be a **mack** [= pimp (French)], you got to go through something before you become that (San Francisco Chronicle, 2006)

> Prices are correspondingly higher than your average bottle of **plonk** [= cheap or inferior wine (French)], but then again, this wine is built for savoring and sipping (Portland Mercury, 2015)

> There are plenty of **tres** [= very (French)] sophisticated Mensa society folks who fear to fly (Susan Cushman, 2018)

While French may be too posh for informal language, there are a handful of pseudo-French borrowings which have been coined specifically for a humorously posh effect. These borderline case borrowings are especially popular among students (see Eble 1996: 79) who appreciate their jocular character. Here is a handful of such playful creations:

> If he leaves, he's going to want **boo-koo** [= very much or a lot of (French)] money (Miami New Times, 2008)

> I'm curious whether it is antique or **junque** [= old and discarded things, junk (French)] (Creators Syndicate, 2018)

> It was an attempt to inveigle him into the subtleties of the **parley-voo** [= the French language (French)] (Baltimore Sun, 2008)

> When I encounter an unknown **shittoir** [= toilet (French)], I press buttons before getting down to business (Tribe Magazine, 2006)

Japanese is a language so diametrically different from English in terms of linguistic structure – such as phonology, morphology, syntax, or writing – that it is hardly surprising that it has contributed little to informal American English: about thirty expressions (which is nearly the same as Chinese, discussed below). The first borrowings date back to the mid-nineteenth century and originated among Japanese immigrants in Los Angeles and San Francisco, but the majority come from World War II and the Korean War (see Kowalczyk 2016: 163). Still, there are a few expressions which have caught on since these two wars and remain popular in usage. Consider the following:

> Hello, who's the **honcho** [= important person, especially a chief (Japanese)] here? (O Brother, Where Art Thou? film, 2000)

> I could have gone for a **kamikaze** [= reckless and self-destructive (Japanese)] move, but that wouldn't have made sense (Los Angeles Times, 2014)

*I may have glossed over the details with you boys just a **skosh** [= a little (Japanese)] (Two and a Half Men, CBS-TV series, 2005)*

*You'll be in the army and shooting other Japanese, or end up being sent home in a **wooden kimono** [= coffin (Japanese)] (Come See the Paradise, film, 1991)*

Chinese, much like Japanese, has contributed little to informal American English; some two dozen expressions come from Chinese. The first borrowings date back to the mid-nineteenth century and originated among Chinese immigrants in New York City and San Francisco, but the majority come from the Korean War and the Cold War era (see Kowalczyk 2016: 158). Interestingly, they prominently feature loan translations, typically associated with the Cold War. The following selection illustrates both:

*"Republicans have brains, Democrats are **brainwashed** [= submitted to a forcible indoctrination (Chinese)]," says farm equipment dealer Chris Jenkins (Time, 2016)*

*Can we please try to get a little less **gung-ho** [= zealous, committed, enthusiastic (Chinese)] in our coverage? (Baltimore Sun, 2021)*

*Some are free, others require a fee, all are worth a **look-see** [= look or inspection (Chinese)] (Los Angeles Times, 2014)*

*Mark Cuban called Donald Trump a **paper tiger** [= person or thing that appears threatening but is ineffectual (Chinese)] (Sports Illustrated, 2015)*

Aside from the above borrowings from **Mandarin Chinese**, there are several borrowings taken from **Cantonese**, a variety of the language used most frequently by Chinese immigrants in the United States. Here are some serviceable examples:

***Chop chop** [= quickly or instantly (Chinese)]! Don't hesitate to open up prime garden real estate (Providence Journal, 2016)*

*Between takes, Ermey is spending some time eating **chow** [= food (Chinese)] and chatting with Marines (Military Times, 2017)*

*Russell is an ex-con with pop-star aspirations and a **yen** [= intense craving (Chinese)] for underage female runaways (Austin Chronicle, 2016)*

*The steady rise in the number of home office users **yenning** [= having an intense craving (Chinese)] for superior performance at an affordable price has led to this (Tech Gadgets, 2010)*

Dutch has contributed a number of expressions which date back to as early as the seventeenth and eighteenth centuries. While they may not be numerous – and constitute some twenty borrowings in informal American English – they are still used today and are completely assimilated. See the following selection:

*I don't want any thirty-second **nookie** [= sexual intercourse (Dutch)] (Obsessed, film, 2009)*

*Oh, that's all **poppycock** [= nonsense (Dutch)]. I don't know where that came from (Guitar World Magazine, 2016)*

*The surgeon turned out to be a **quack** [= incompetent or fraudulent doctor (Dutch)] (Ed Wood, film, 1994)*

*He'd flip if he knew I was **snooping** [= prying (Dutch)] in his car (Sacramento Bee, 2016)*

3.4   Lesser Donors

Borrowings from other languages are less discernible in informal American English, each having contributed less than a dozen or so expressions on average. Still, some of these expressions are often encountered. Let us present them below.

Classical languages, Greek and Latin, have contributed few borrowings to informal American English. This is possibly because most borrowings from these languages are considered to have an erudite, learned, or "official" tinge, and they feature prominently in formal communication such as legal or medical English. The above qualities are simply less appreciated in informal language – especially its slang component – which favors informality, crudeness, irreverence, and shock value. If Greek and Latin are used as sources for informal borrowings, they tend to have a playful or mocking pseudo-intellectual character. Additionally, they are often hybrid loans, with one element borrowed and the other native. Consider these examples from **Greek**:

*It includes such **factoids** [= presumed facts of dubious validity (Greek)] as "Smoking can decrease penis size by up to a centimeter" (New York Times, 2014)*

*Americans admire the **mega** [= extremely (Greek)] rich and don't resent them (Spartanburg Herald Journal, 2015)*

*Highlights include "**Pornorama** [= spectacular display or instance of pornography (Greek)]," a marathon showing of porn films (Metro, 2010)*

*New rules, **waitrons** [= waiters or waitresses (Greek)]! If I can't read it, I can't make it! (Kitchen Confidential, Fox-TV series, 2005)*

And here are a very few relevant examples of informal borrowings from **Latin**:

*Amy Schumer has a few great **ad libs** [= spontaneous speeches or performances (Latin)] of her own (Slate Magazine, 2015)*

*The vaccine will be distributed **free gratis** [= without charge (Latin)] (Deadwood, HBO-TV series, 2004)*

*Dismiss it as **hocus-pocus** [= trickery (Latin)] if you wish, but if you're interested in peeking into the future, you might want to pay attention (Tampa Bay Times, 2019)*

Well, then. **Semper fi** *[= greetings to a fellow Marine (Latin)], brother. What outfit were you? (Prison Break,* Fox-TV series, 2007)

Slavic languages likewise have not generally contributed many expressions to informal American English. This can be explained by their form, perceived as too foreign or difficult for the average American to be used informally. The only two languages which contributed a handful of expressions are, *ex aequo*, Russian and Polish. The former is largely limited to the world of politics and the Cold War. See the following examples from **Russia**:

> *Voters aren't interested in electing a former CIA* **apparatchik** *[= official or staff member in a large organization (Russian)] (Townhall,* 2016)
>
> *We probably don't need to worry that much about going to war with the* **Ivans** *[= Russians (Russian)] (Wired,* 2012)
>
> *Does Russia have* **kompromat** *[= compromising information collected for use in blackmailing or discrediting someone, esp. for a political purpose (Russian)] on Trump? (News,* CNN-TV program, 2018)
>
> *It may be attainable with some of the* **Russkies** *[= Russians or persons of Russian descent (Russian)] out for doping (Maple Ridge Times,* 2016)

Borrowings from **Polish** are also fewer in number and less assimilated, except for the third example below, which displays a relatively high frequency of use:

> *I'm up for any challenge from my old buddy Doug Topolski, who's going to be freezing his* **dupa** *[= buttocks (Polish)] off up there on the Island pretty soon (Detroit News,* 2021)
>
> *Don't forget to put a rubber on his* **kielbasa** *[= penis, especially if big (Polish)]!* (Michelle Kane, 2007)
>
> *Why was the Kosciuszko Bridge named after a* **Polack** *[= Pole or a person of Polish descent (Polish)]? (Angels in America,* HBO-TV series, 2005)
>
> *I got a few* **Polskis** *[= Poles or persons of Polish descent (Polish)] who might be able to help you* (Twitter, 2013)

Still, the importance of Slavic borrowings is greater than it may appear. While this book considers only immediate source borrowings, there are a sizable number of Yiddish borrowings in informal American English which themselves were taken from Slavic languages, some of them with a borderline status. (See notes on immediate source borrowings in the Chapter Outline and on two donor languages in Section 3.5.)

Arabic has also contributed few expressions to informal American English, which again may be explained by their form, perceived as too foreign or difficult to be used informally. Most of them are the product of language contacts in recent decades and have to do with American military engagement in the Middle East. They also seem to be on the rise, possibly because of the growing Muslim population in the United States. See the following examples:

> *You're a good guy,* **habibi** *[= darling (Arabic)]. I just don't know what to do* (*You Don't Mess with the Zohan*, film, 2008)
>
> *The* **haji** *[= Arab (Arabic)] wants us all in so he can blow us up* (*American Sniper*, film, 2014)
>
> *Taking a road trip to Florida is probably a* **halal** *[= approved or acceptable (Arabic)] thing to do* (Reddit, 2015)
>
> *The CIA estimates that seven out of every ten times the* **muj** *[= Muslim guerilla fighter engaged in a holy war (Arabic)] fires a Stinger, a Soviet chopper or a plane falls out of the sky* (*Charlie Wilson's War*, film, 2007)

Finally, there are two **African languages** whose traces can be found in informal African American English. These languages are Wolof and Mandinka, both used in western Africa. Interestingly, there are very few expressions in informal African American English which can be traced back to the languages of Africa since most of the lexicon of African American English is based on English. The following are the **Wolof** borrowings found in the database:

> *"Look at me. These are* **hip** *[= fashionable or popular (Wolof)]?" "No, try these on"* (*That Thing You Do*, film, 1996)
>
> *There was nothing left for* **hipsters** *[= people who want to be fashionable or popular (Wolof)] to do* (*Williamsburg Observer*, 2013)
>
> *I ain't trying to* **jive** *[= deceive or mislead (Wolof)] you, Jim* (*Requiem for a Dream*, film, 2000)
>
> *Got a quarter for the* **juke** *[= coin-operated record player in a bar (Wolof)]? I want to play a song. Got a quarter?* (*U-Turn*, film, 1997)

And here are the very few borrowings from **Mandinka** which can be found in the database; note that some are loan translations:

> *I'm tryin' to* **jazz** *[= have sex with (Mandinka)] his wife* (James David Horan, 1991)
>
> *One wall has been covered with a very* **jazzy** *[= lively, stimulating, or exciting (Mandinka)] wallpaper he designed* (*New York Times*, 2008)

*Them motherfuckers ain't here to buy no **Mandingos** [= strong and big-built African American men (Mandinka)]. They's here for the girl (Django Unchained, film, 2012)*

*Now that I want to **slap some skin** [= slap hands in greeting or congratulation (Mandinka)], Brandi ain't even down for it (Boyz n the Hood, film, 1991)*

Although, to all intents and purposes, this book is about borrowings from foreign languages in informal American English, one should perhaps mention the influence of **African American Vernacular**. Its status is debatable: most linguists consider it a form of English spoken by descendants of enslaved Africans in the present-day United States; still some linguists consider it a separate language (see discussion in Widawski [2015] 2019: 4). In this book the former viewpoint has been adopted; hence borrowings from African American Vernacular have not been taken into account (with the notable exception of those coming from African languages and spread through African American English; see above). However, the degree of borrowing from informal African American English into "general" informal American English and its sociocultural influence is massive (see Smitherman 2000), so it deserves at least a mention here. Consider a handful of examples:

*He has a **cool** [= excellent] car. He gets all the girls. He's also the smartest guy in the room (Columbian, 2011)*

*Chicks **dig** [= like] it when you compare your feelings for them to a dependency on opioids (Las Vegas Review-Journal, 2014)*

*Emma Stone is talented and gorgeous, so how could anyone **diss** [= disrespect, especially by belittling] her? (Hollywood Life, 2015)*

*Anna Duggar followed the rules that were imposed on her **from the get-go** [= from the very beginning] (USA Today, 2015)*

Finally, there are languages whose contributions to informal American English are limited to one or two borrowings. These are chiefly languages that are dissimilar to English in terms of their linguistic structure or spoken in geographical places that are very distant from the United States. Let us present a relevant sample of such expressions:

*Jens goes to begin a new life in the **boondocks** [= remote or isolated regions (Tagalog)] of upstate New York (New York Times, 2014)*

*You do that one more time, and you're **in big kimchi** [= in serious trouble (Korean)] (Facebook, 2015)*

*Janie, what happened? We used to be **pals** [= friends, especially close ones (Romany)] (American Beauty, film, 1999)*

*He was taking 13–14 prescription drugs per day and described feeling "**zombied out**" [= made him look like a zombie (Kikongo)] (News, Fox-TV program, 2018)*

3.5   Other Considerations

So far, single donor languages have been identified as sources of borrowings in informal American English. However, it is also possible that expressions may have involved **two donor languages** at the same time. In other words, one element is taken from one donor language while the other is taken from another. Some examples of such borrowings have already been featured above, but here are more of them to illustrate this interesting phenomenon. Curiously, nearly all of them are based on Yiddish and usually have a jocular character:

*It's **deja nu** [= feeling of repetition or recurrence of the present situation, especially when an instant action is required (French and Yiddish)] for Dion all over again (Words on Words, 2011)*

*How typical is this behavior, at least among **dopeniks** [= drug addicts (Dutch and Yiddish)]? (Straight Dope, 2008)*

*I think it's a complete waste of money, a big **schmoozefest** [= idle or gossipy conversation session (Yiddish and German)] (News, CTV-TV program, 2016)*

*My experience with these affairs is that the accused **uber-gonif** [= super thief (German and Yiddish)] tells everyone who will listen that the charges are bogus (New York Times, 2008)*

Chapter Summary

Borrowings in informal American English come from various languages. Unsurprisingly, Spanish has contributed the most expressions, accounting for almost half of the entire database; nearly all come from Mexican **Spanish**, with a handful of expressions borrowed from Puerto Rican and Cuban varieties. Borrowings from **Yiddish** are the second most frequent group, constituting one-third of the entire database; within these, Germanic Yiddishisms are most frequent, followed by Hebraic and Slavic ones. Other key language donors to informal American English are **German**, **Italian**, and **French**, followed by Japanese, Chinese, and Dutch. Lesser donors – languages which have contributed considerably fewer borrowings – include Slavic languages, Russian and Polish, followed by Arabic and two African languages, Wolof and Mandinka.

Surprisingly, contributions from other languages – such as Hindi, Korean, Portuguese, Tagalog, or Vietnamese – feature in numbers that seem marginal given the sizable number of speakers of these languages in the United States; also surprising is the lack of any borrowings from such languages as Norwegian or Armenian, once spoken by large diasporas in the country. Interestingly, some expressions are a result of borrowing from not just one but **two donor languages**, typically involving Yiddish plus another language; other borrowings have a shared origin, as in the case of several expressions from German and Yiddish; still others are the result of **pseudo-borrowing**, a playful imitation of a foreign language specifically for a humorous effect. In general, findings corroborate the common perception that the top contributor of borrowings in informal American is Spanish, but they also reveal that the second position unquestionably goes to Yiddish, whose impact on informal American English is pronounced.

CHAPTER 4

Types

Chapter Outline

While the typology of informal borrowings by donor languages is perhaps the most obvious and fundamental, it is certainly not the only one possible. Various **typological classifications** of borrowings have been proposed, including those by Bloomfield (1933), Haugen (1950), Weinreich ([1953] 1968), Fisiak (1961), Mańczak-Wohlfeld (1995 and 2006), Katamba (2005), Field (2002), Zuckerman (2003), Myers-Scotton (2006), Wohlgemuth (2009), Kuźniak (2009), Matras (2009), and many others. Each of them on its own presents a valuable theoretical framework for classifying borrowings, but none of them is particularly followed nor challenged throughout this book whose function – let us stress this again – is quintessentially to document and describe rather than theorize and hypothesize.

This being said, the book does offer a typological description of borrowings, and a highly extensive one at that. Aside from the donor typology described in the previous chapter, informal borrowings can be classified on **various levels** according to the following parameters: type of borrowed material, part of speech, degree of assimilation, degree of modification, relative frequency of use, and register; these are all described in the following pages. Additionally, further typological criteria can be considered such as the changes and functions of informal borrowings; these are discussed in Chapters 5 and 6. All in all, such a multifaceted classification permits a panoramic view of informal borrowings from diverse linguistic viewpoints and lends itself to a better understanding of them.

4.1   By Borrowed Material

Let us start our presentation with the classification according to **borrowed material**, or borrowed element, for lack of any better expression. This is one of the most fundamental typological distinctions, stemming from classic works by Haugen (1950) and Fisiak (1961), and appears to be one of the most frequently utilized categorizations of borrowings, if not synonymous with the typology of borrowings. In essence, it involves the division of borrowings into *what* has been borrowed: the entire foreign expression, a translation of it, part of it, or its meaning. Accordingly, four main types can be distinguished: loanwords, loan translations, loanblends, and semantic borrowings. All these also feature in informal borrowings, as demonstrated below.

Loanwords (or **loanwords proper**) are entire expressions borrowed together with their form and meaning (Geller 1994: 100). This is one of the most prototypical and frequent types of borrowings. In informal American English, this is the largest category, constituting over two-thirds of all the expressions found in the database. It is also a highly inclusive category in that it comprises both expressions with usage limited to ethnic groups or their culture and those increasingly used outside these groups by larger social segments. Interestingly, most loanwords are found among expressions borrowed from Spanish, Japanese, and French, which means that expressions from these languages – possibly because of their non-Germanic provenience – are statistically less likely to be combined with English words to form loanblends and tend to be borrowed as a whole. Here is a sample of representative examples:

> *It looks like you fell off the bus in the wrong part of town,* **amigo** *[= man (Spanish)]* (*Men in Black*, film, 1997)
>
> *He wrote horrible things about it in that* **farkakte** *[= despicable or accursed (Yiddish)] newspaper of his* (*Marvelous Mrs. Maisel*, Amazon-TV series, 2022)
>
> *You can't argue with him, he's the* **honcho** *[= important person, especially a chief (Japanese)] around here* (*Late Show with David Letterman*, CBS-TV series, 2010)
>
> *Sleeping naked helps your* **huevos** *[= testicles (Spanish)] at a cool 95 to 96 degrees, which is the perfect range for healthy sperm* (*Maxim*, 2018)

Loanblends, expressions created by simultaneously borrowing elements of foreign expressions and using them together with native elements (Fernandez 1983: 16), belong to the second most frequent type of our classification, constituting one-third of all expressions. In other words, they involve a combination of foreign and native elements, most typically used as a compound or phrase. They are extremely popular in informal American English, perhaps because they introduce a foreign element which fills the so-called lexical gap in English or brings with it an element of attractive freshness, but they also bring the familiarity of native elements to the mix. Interestingly, most loanblends are found among expressions borrowed from German, Dutch, and Yiddish, which means that expressions from these languages – possibly because of their Germanic provenience – are statistically most easily blended with English words. The following examples illustrate this point:

> *Madoff was a **big macher** [= very important, influential, and well-connected person (Yiddish)] outside prison (Wall Street Journal, 2010)*
>
> *Her husband is a **bimbo** [= attractive and hedonistic young man, especially if also stupid (Italian)] who enjoys his obnoxious wife's fat paycheck (Us Weekly, 2016)*
>
> *She dresses like a **kinderwhore** [= young woman whose dress suggests both youthful innocence and sexual abandon (German)] (Tumblr, 2015)*
>
> *I had our pilot tell him the plane was **on the fritz** [= broken or malfunctioning (German)] (Casino, film, 1995)*

Loan translations, renditions of foreign lexical structures by means of native lexical elements (Polański 1993: 255), are the third type in this classification. Put differently, these are borrowings created by literally translating foreign expressions into English. Such expressions are also used in informal American English where they are so strongly ingrained in the system that most users consider them typically American, devoid of any foreignness. They are relatively infrequent in our database: there are about fifty such expressions. Interestingly, most loan translations are found among expressions borrowed from Chinese and Yiddish. See the following citational corroboration:

> *The guards tried to **brainwash** [= submit to a forcible indoctrination (Chinese)] starving soldiers to get them to sign propaganda documents (Wichita Eagle, 2022)*
>
> *You guys **get lost** [= leave me alone (Yiddish)]. I don't want to see you (Léon, film, 1994)*
>
> *Hey, Ray, you are fantastic! **Give me some skin** [= slap hands with me in greeting or congratulation (Mandinka)] (Ray, film, 2004)*
>
> *Iran is a **paper tiger** [= thing that appears threatening but is ineffectual (Chinese)], postmodern threat (New York Times, 2010)*

Semantic borrowings are the last type in this classification. Treated as a type of neologism (Witalisz 2007: 24), these originate when already existing native expressions are appended with new meanings taken from foreign expressions whose forms are similar. In other words, it is only the meaning that is borrowed (Algeo 1991: 4). As indicated before, such borrowings are possible only in cases where the donor language expression is similar in form to the native expression. For this reason, they are rather marginal. The same goes for informal borrowings, of which there are fewer than a dozen expressions. Here are a few examples found in the database:

> *There is only my list, in my **canton** [= apartment or house (Spanish)], on my conditions (*Grimm,* NBC-TV series, 2012)*
>
> *Democrats look to Marco Rubio to **corral** [= acquire, secure, or find (Spanish)] votes for top Hispanic White House nominee (*Miami Herald,* 2012)*
>
> *Their **landsman** [= someone who comes from the same hometown or country (Yiddish)] Harry Tarowsky bought into the partnership in April 1917 (*Katz's Delicatessen Online,* 2012)*
>
> *The U.S. has sought multiple times to **liquidate** [= kill, especially by violent means (Russian)] him, but he has evaded all assassination attempts (*National Review,* 2017)*

4.2 By Part of Speech

Borrowed expressions can belong to various grammatical categories and can be classified by **parts of speech**. Traditionally, these parts fall into two main categories: content words, such as nouns, verbs, adjectives, and adverbs, and function words (also labeled grammatical words), such as prepositions or pronouns. Most typically, in terms of distribution, the former are more borrowable than the latter (see Haspelmath and Tadmoor 2009: 59–61), while within content words nouns tend to be borrowed more (see Mańczak-Wohlfeld 2010: 11), followed by verbs and adjectives and adverbs. Likewise, borrowings in informal American English exhibit similar patterns of distribution: most are composed of content words and there are very few grammatical expressions such as informal prepositions or pronouns. Yet, the part-of-speech distribution is slightly different: although nouns are the most numerous, they are followed by adjectives and verbs in more or less equal numbers, then followed by exclamations and adverbs; other parts of speech are marginally represented. Let us examine these in more detail.

Nouns are unequivocally the most frequent part of speech among informal borrowings, constituting a hefty well over two-thirds of the entire database, or some 800 expressions. This is most likely because in informal language, much like in standard, people have more need to name things than to name actions or qualities. Also, because of the functional shift in English, there is a tendency for nouns to modify other nouns in an adjectival function without any change in form, and a tendency for nouns to be changed into verbs, again without any change in form, which is also evident in borrowings (see shifting in Section 5.4); nouns are simply more convertible – and thus more functional – than any other part of speech. Here is a handful of relevant examples:

> At first, Mia didn't know what the **hoopla** [= unnecessary fuss or commotion (French)] was until she got to middle school (Milwaukee Journal Sentinel, 2018)
>
> I'd make myself a **shiv** [= knife or knife-like weapon (Romany)] (Bones, Fox-TV series, 2012)
>
> Such a **tsimmes** [= great outrage, fuss, or complaining (Yiddish)] over nothing! (Dallas Observer, 2012)
>
> Have you seen my **wiener** [= penis (German)]? (There's Something About Mary, film, 1998)

The second most frequently found part of speech is **adjectives**, although they are still much less numerous than nouns, constituting one-tenth of the entire database, or some 120 expressions. In that, informal borrowings are similar to the distribution found in "general" informal vocabulary but dissimilar to that found in noninformal borrowings, where the second position is occupied by verbs (see Mańczak-Wohlfeld 2010: 11). This position can be explained by the extraordinary productivity of descriptive terms in informal American English – especially the slang component – and particularly for qualities that are often polarized into positive or negative; the process often leads to heavy synonymity called overlexicalization (see Halliday 1978: 165–166), especially in adjectives. See the following:

> You could belong to a fraternity of rich and powerful men in the **bizarro** [= strange or bizarre (Spanish)] world (Buffy the Vampire Slayer, WB-TV series, 1997)
>
> The music is automatically added to playlists no matter how **drecky** [= worthless or of inferior quality (Yiddish)] it is (Examiner, 2010)
>
> Maybe it's the **haimish** [= homelike and cozy (Yiddish)] atmosphere it cultivates (New York Press, 2011)
>
> Well, I'd have to say that this one is **ichiban** [= excellent (Japanese)] (Twicsy, 2011)

Verbs come in third in this classification: there are about ninety such expressions among all borrowings in informal American English, almost *ex aequo* with exclamations. This is again in line with the above distributive tendencies regarding informal language – and unlike noninformal borrowings where verbs come second – and is likely motivated by the same reasons: people have less need to name actions than they have to name things or qualities. Here are a few relevant examples:

> *We're all **fatmouthing** [= talking too much (Mandinka)] here (Washington Post, 2010)*
>
> *Judge Steven Rhodes will either approve or **nix** [= refuse, reject, or veto (German)] the city's plan (Los Angeles Times, 2014)*
>
> *"You didn't tell Dad?" "Not yet. He's gonna **plotz** [= lose emotional control and burst with emotion (Yiddish)]" (Meet the Fockers, film, 2004)*
>
> *Right now is our chance to **vamoose** [= leave or depart, especially hastily (Spanish)] (Scooby-Doo and the Goblin King, film, 2008)*

The next notable category is **exclamations**, which are surprisingly common among informal borrowings: there are ninety such expressions in the entire database. One possible explanation is that they are usually invariant in terms of form and highly emotionally loaded in terms of meaning, which makes them particularly handy to use in everyday communication as well as easy to borrow and disseminate. Here is a representative sample:

> *Give me all of that shit! **Andale** [= get moving or hurry up (Spanish)], nigga! Move! (Wrong Side of Town, film, 2010)*
>
> *Ay **carajo** [= I am irritated (Spanish)], stop whining already! (Miami New Times, 2014)*
>
> *"It must be true. I read it in the New York Times." "**Feh** [= I am disgusted (Yiddish)]! What does the Times know?" (National Review, 2008)*
>
> *It's done. Go and enjoy your life. **Sayonara** [= goodbye (Japanese)]! (True Stories, film, 1986)*

The last sizable category is **phrases**. There are fifty such expressions in our database. While technically they can represent various parts of speech – functioning as extended nouns (noun phrases), verbs (verb phrases), adjectives (adjectival phrases), or adverbs (adverbial phrases) – they can be and are often considered to be a separate grammatical category. Interestingly, nearly all of them are either loanblends (or hybrid loans), in that a borrowed word is incorporated into a native phrase, or they are loan translations, in that elements of the phrase are the result of word-for-word translation (see more in **phraseology** in Section 5.3). Consider the following examples:

> *That creep is always **giving me shpilkes** [= is making me nervous or anxious (Yiddish)] (UCLA Student, 2016)*
>
> *If this happens again, we're going to be **in deep kimchi** [= in serious trouble (Korean)] with the next pandemic (Honolulu Civil Beat, 2021)*

> *Harold assumed his watch was simply **on the fritz** [= broken or malfunctioning (German)] (Stranger Than Fiction, film, 2006)*
>
> *He doesn't remember how much he sold it for, but he knows he **took a bath** [= went bankrupt or lost a lot of money (Yiddish)] on it (Los Angeles Times, 2017)*

Other parts of speech are represented in scant numbers. Accordingly, much like in the case of noninformal borrowings, **adverbs** constitute a margin of informal borrowings, totaling a little over a dozen of expressions. Here are a few notable examples:

> *It could make even him a **bissel** [= a little (Yiddish)] cool (New York Magazine, 2012)*
>
> *We were **mega** [= extremely (Greek)] surprised when he started braiding an intern's hair (News, MTV-TV program, 2014)*
>
> *Chandler would become eligible to be a free agent and sign for **mondo** [= a lot of (Spanish)] dollars (Los Angeles Magazine, 2001)*
>
> *Your complete honesty will be **mucho** [= extremely (Spanish)] appreciated (Hard Candy, film, 2005)*

As for function words, **affixes** can be borrowed, too. Pearce (2007: 25) calls them **structural borrowings** and defines them as "borrowed bound morphemes which are combined with native lexical items to form new English words." Although extremely rare, such borrowings can also be found in informal American English. A good instance is the German prefix *uber* which is highly functional and can be attached to nouns, adjectives, and also verbs:

> *The company has dreamed up an **uber**cool [= totally superior or excellent (German)] way to promote its signature summer item (New York Daily News, 2014)*
>
> *If you are ever uncomfortable with how happy you are feeling, you can read my memoir about my **uber**-fucked up [= totally dysfunctional (German)] family (Movie Pilot, 2015)*
>
> *We share a love of **uber**-sexy [= totally sexy (German)] alpha male characters that also double as eye candy (USA Today, 2013)*
>
> *LOL, I **uber**-understand [= totally understand (German)]. Let's leave it as it is, then (Wikipedia, 2015)*

Pronouns, likewise, are decidedly rare among informal borrowings. There are practically only two expressions found in our database that belong in this category:

> *Behold the work of Albert Einstein, a professor once, like **moi** [= me (French)] (Transformers: Revenge of the Fallen, film, 2009)*

The collection features Miss Piggy's notable quotes and phrases such as "Who **Moi** *[= me (French)]? (Los Angeles Times,* 2016)*

*"You, Ferret, this ain't Roots, man!" "**Que** [= what (Spanish)]?" (Crank: High Voltage,* film, 2009)*

*"Do you think it was weird Enrique has this oyster on his wall?" "**Que** [= what (Spanish)]?" (Snowfall,* FX-TV series, 2017)*

The same goes for **prepositions** which have a decidedly marginal role in both borrowings and informal American English. Here is what has been found in our database:

*The way to stop it is not to go all wobbly-kneed **a la** [= in the style of, manner of (French)] Tillerson this week (New York Times,* 2017)*

*Look, third place is fine **by** [= as far as concerns (Yiddish)] me (USA Today,* 2011)*

*All of a sudden, she's left **sans** [= without (French)] money, sans direction (Wall Street Journal,* 2014)*

4.3 By Assimilation

Borrowings are often can also be classified according to the degree of **assimilation** (also labeled **integration**) in the recipient language. Put differently, some borrowings are highly integrated into the native system – to the degree that they are perceived as belonging to native word stock – while others are perceived as outwardly foreign. Usually, there are intermediate stages of gradation regarding assimilation. While, as observed by McArthur (1992: 410), "it is difficult to specify precisely where the 'properly' foreign begins: all the [borrowed] items are foreign, but some are more foreign than others," classification by assimilation can still be a useful way of describing borrowings.

Various typologies of gradation have been proposed, such as those by Thomason and Kaufman (1988: 40), Mańczak-Wohlfeld (2006: 49), or Görlach (2003: 29). The classification presented by McArthur (1992: 623), itself borrowed from the German linguistic tradition (see Von Polenz 1967: 65–80), distinguishes three such stages: unassimilated, partially assimilated, and fully assimilated borrowings, which are sometimes described by their respective German counterparts: *Gastwörter, Fremdwörter,* and *Lehnwörter.* This, in reverse order, roughly corresponds to another useful gradation of borrowings proposed by Mańczak-Wohlfeld (2006: 49). Note that such classification is necessarily based on perception, so the assignment of expressions into these categories may be impressionistic rather than absolute. Let us discuss them in relation to our subject matter.

Unassimilated borrowings (or *Gastwörter*) are expressions taken from one language to another in unchanged graphic and phonological form, and thus perceived as foreign elements. From this point of view, they can be considered synonymous with **foreign words** or **foreign-isms** (Kuźniak 2009: 95). In Mańczak-Wohlfeld's (2006: 49) classifi-cation, this type would correspond to Category Three: **citations** "which are unknown to many readers, yet introduced by journalists to attract readers' attention." Generally speaking, unassimilated bor-rowings in informal American English have a limited scope and are largely restricted to immigrant and minority subcultures, such as those of Jewish Americans, Hispanic Americans, or Italian Americans. Put differently, they are not very well known to – let alone used by – the average user of informal American English. If they happen to be used in general sources such as the national media, they are largely used for stylization. Such borrowings are not numerous in our database and constitute perhaps one-tenth of all entries (note that this is a mere approximation: as mentioned above, assimilation is largely a matter of perception and establishing a precise number proves difficult due to the relative vagueness of their status). This is because the primary emphasis was on the collection of well-known expressions in wide circulation. Still, a sizable number of unassimilated yet culturally important borrowings were also included. Some of them are presented below:

> The central character is an **ausgespielt** [= exhausted or worn-out (German)] freelance journalist (DVX User, 2015)
>
> "His dad is really a gangster?" "**Capo di tutti capi** [= the senior figure in the Mafia (Italian)]!" (Sopranos, HBO-TV series, 2006)
>
> **Coño** [= I am surprised (Spanish)], he even has a private chauffeur! (Before Night Falls, film, 2000)
>
> **Hijo de puta** [= despicable man (Spanish)]! It's McClane again! (Die Hard 2, film, 1990)

Partially assimilated borrowings (or *Fremdwörter*) represent the in-between stage in the assimilation of borrowings in that they are perceived as both somewhat foreign and somewhat familiar; their intermediate status results in them sometimes being spelled with quotation marks. This type would correspond to Mańczak-Wohlfeld's (2006: 49) Category Two: "non-assimilated but frequently occurring borrowings." Such borrowings feature prominently in informal American English and are much more universal than the previous category. While they may still be associated with a given immigrant group or ethnic minority, they are often known to larger social segments of American society, regardless of their national or ethnic origin. See the following citational corroboration:

> *Start tomorrow morning, they're gonna see a fucking **blitz** [= sudden and heavy attack (German)] (Ides of March, film, 2011)*
>
> *The only things I know run in my family are a lot of "**chutzpah**" [= arrogance or insolence (Yiddish)] and the ability to sleep for ten years (House, M.D., Fox-TV series, 2004)*
>
> *The fact that she has **cojones** [= courage or audacity (Spanish)] is a good thing, but that's all she's got (Baltimore Sun, 2011)*
>
> *I'm a **gringo** [= white person from an English-speaking country (Spanish)] who lives and works in Mexico (Dallas Observer, 2012)*

Finally, **fully assimilated borrowings** (or ***Lehnwörter***) are expressions which have been assimilated to such a high degree that they are commonly no longer identified as foreign elements, or as Katamba (2006: 144–145) puts it, became "fully nativized." In other words, "they are treated exactly like English words" (Stockwell and Minkova 2001: 166). This type would correspond to Mańczak-Wohlfeld's (2006: 49) Category One, defined plainly as "assimilated lexical items in the target lexicon." Such borrowings are numerous in informal American English – and constitute approximately one-half of expressions in our database – and most Americans are not aware of their foreign provenience, considering them to be Americanisms. Such is the case with the following examples:

> *I don't wanna be perceived as a **bimbo** [= attractive and hedonistic young woman, especially if also stupid (Italian)] (Ugly Truth, film, 2009)*
>
> *Girls this age are **dumb** [= stupid (German)] but give them a few years and they'll wise up (Stranger Things, Netflix-TV series, 2016)*
>
> *Some believe it was Tommy Lasorda doing a favor for his **pal** [= friend, especially a close one (Romany)], Vince (New York Daily News, 2016)*
>
> *He spends all of his allowance on **reefer** [= marijuana (Spanish)] (Half Baked, film, 1998)*

Assimilation usually corresponds to modification: borrowings assimilated into the recipient language usually undergo modification in form or meaning (see the next chapter). However, this does not necessarily have to be the case: some borrowings may be totally accepted in the receiving language without undergoing any change at all. Consider these examples:

> *They'd dug up Spitzer's personal medical history and found evidence he was **loco** [= crazy or insane (Spanish)] (OC Weekly, 2018)*

*The surgeon was skillful, and Medicare was happy to pay **mucho** [= much (Spanish)] dollars to fix mom's hip* (Huffington Post, 2014)

*Entrepreneurs and **politicos** [= politicians, especially unscrupulous (Spanish)] dominate this year's list* (Forbes, 2016)

*I meant to pick up some **vino** [= wine, especially cheap (Italian)] on my way, but I blew it* (Scent of a Woman, film, 1992)

4.4   By Modification

Borrowings can also be classified according to the degree of **modification** (also labeled **alteration** or **adaptation**) in the receiving language. The source words of borrowings often feature peculiar linguistic properties – phonological, orthographic, morphological, semantic – in the donor language that do not fit into the linguistic system of the recipient language, such as gender marking or vowel nasality. In such instances, borrowings undergo changes to make them fit better into the recipient language. As observed by Haspelmath and Tadmoor (2009: 16), "borrowing a word often entails a certain modification of the source word, required for the integration of the word into the recipient language." They introduce three categories which they say are impressionistic rather than absolute: "unintegrated," "intermediate," and "highly integrated." Note that these could be somewhat misleading in that they de facto refer to the degree of assimilation (in usage) rather than modification (in form or meaning). Instead, let us suggest three labels which perhaps more aptly refer to the subject matter: unmodified, intermediate, and highly modified.

Unmodified borrowings are those which retain significant peculiarities of the donor language with regard to form or, put differently, involve no change in spelling, pronunciation, or grammar. As such, they are instantly recognizable as non-native elements by most Americans. They are relatively the most frequent in our database, constituting nearly half of all expressions. Consider the following examples:

*Your mother was a **loca** [= crazy woman (Spanish)] when it came to love. It almost killed her* (Junot Díaz, 2007)

*He gets offended when someone calls him a **negrito** [= black-skinned male (Spanish)]* (YouTube, 2011)

*Discussing our sex life is **verboten** [= forbidden (German)]?* (Everybody Loves Raymond, CBS-TV series, 2000)

*Is that the reason Mexican food is not allowed when her **viejo** [= husband (Spanish)] is home?* (Blogspot, 2014)

Partly modified borrowings, as the name suggests, constitute the intermediate category in this typology. They are less numerous than unmodified borrowings. Such borrowings involve only minor changes in spelling or pronunciation, as corroborated by these examples:

> *They have taught him that a **bissel** [= little bit (Yiddish)] cream cheese is just a light schmear* (*Wall Street Journal*, 2013)
>
> *Maybe White's not so **dumb** [= stupid (German)] after all* (*L.A. Confidential*, film, 1997)
>
> *Anna is a **hausfrau** [= woman whose primary interests are keeping house and raising children (German)] with a blond banker husband and two little blond boys* (*USA Today*, 2015)
>
> *The plane's totaled. **Kaput** [= out of order, inoperative, or useless (German)]* (*Madagascar 3*, film, 2012)

Finally, **highly modified borrowings** are those which, as Haspelmath and Tadmoor put it, "have no structural properties that betray their foreign origin" (2009: 16). In other words, they became modified to conform to the orthographic, phonological, or morphological system of the receiving language, often to a degree where they are regarded as perfectly native creations. Such borrowings are the least frequent in our database, constituting approximately one-fourth of all expressions. Here is the relevant citational corroboration:

> *Me and him are going to whack you in the **labonza** [= stomach (Italian)]!* (*Simpsons*, Fox-TV series, 2001)
>
> *Droves of **pickaninnies** [= black children (Spanish)] romp in the streets* (*Los Angeles Times*, 2021)
>
> *The cop took all my **reefers** [= marijuana cigarettes (Spanish)]* (*Contract*, film, 2006)
>
> *You're not going to have your mommies here to wipe your **tushies** [= buttocks (Yiddish)]* (*Kindergarten Cop*, film, 1990)

So far the presentation has involved modification in form, but informal borrowings can also be modified in meaning, especially via the processes of figuration (see Chapter 5 for details). The simplest distinction can be between expressions that retained their original meaning and those that changed their meaning. Let us present some representative examples of the former:

> *Everyone has eaten, and the bus is leaving. **Ciao** [= goodbye (Italian)]!* (*New York Times*, 2012)
>
> *"What is all the yelling about?" "Just your mother's normal **kvetching** [= complaining or grumbling (Yiddish)]"* (*Love, Wedding, Marriage*, film, 2011)

*He's a **mayate** [= black person (Spanish)] in the wrong neighborhood* (*Snowfall*, FX-TV series, 2017)

*Gilbert can smell money from across town. He came to help you spend that **plata** [= money (Spanish)]* (*Bound by Honor*, film, 1993)

The second type involves borrowings which changed their meaning in informal American English. The change can sometimes be extreme, and unrecognizable to someone unfamiliar with informal American English, especially its slang subset. Consider the following examples:

*They were dysfunctional **desperados** [= degenerate gamblers (Spanish)] usually associated with the gambling scene in the early '60s* (*Las Vegas Review-Journal*, 2014)

*Early puzzles can be solved with a bit of mental **jiu-jitsu** [= something involving dexterity and flexibility, especially a particular technique (Japanese)]* (US Gamer, 2016)

*"License?" "Relax, the van's **kosher** [= legal (Yiddish)]!"* (*Man Who Knew Too Little*, film, 1997)

***Shmeck** [= heroin (Yiddish)] is an old term still used by "old dope fiends"* (Monique Layton, 2010)

Note that the above classification has involved the degree of modification only and focused on the form and meaning of the expressions. However, several finer distinctions can be made. See Chapter 5 for a description of modification involving phonological, orthographical, morphological, semantic, grammatical, and stylistic changes.

4.5   By Frequency

Borrowings can also be divided according to their **frequency of usage** (or **frequency of occurrence**). Some borrowings are highly popular and commonly used, while others are used at best marginally. Again, various classifications have been proposed; for instance, Haspelmath and Tadmoor (2009: 15) divide borrowings into such self-explanatory categories as "very common," "fairly common," or "not common." In this study, a similar three-tiered scale is proposed: frequent borrowings which enjoy a high frequency or wide circulation; passive borrowings which display a medium frequency or moderate circulation; and restricted borrowings which show a relatively low frequency or limited circulation.

Of course, this and similar classifications are necessarily somewhat impressionistic rather than absolute and thus should be interpreted with a grain of salt. This is because of the assumption that the frequency of occurrence of informal borrowings in the database more or less translates into their frequency in real life. While the number of occurrences of a given borrowing in our database does give an idea of how frequently it is used, relying on statistics can be misleading with regard to informal American English, especially its slang component; for instance, as observed by Widawski ([2015] 2019: 15–16), statistics-based "corpus linguistics still has a rather marginal applicability to the study of slang due to slang's largely figurative nature, as yet impossible for computers to process adequately; the search engines of electronic corpora simply cannot differentiate between the literal and figurative meanings of expressions." This goes double for informal borrowings, which are often mistaken for native expressions in their native languages rather than borrowings in the receiving language, that is, English. Still, there is no better way and, with some degree of approximation, one can distinguish the difference in frequency of usage.

This being said, the first category in our classification comprises **frequent borrowings** (or frequently used borrowings). This is a sizable group, constituting a little less than half of all expressions in the database. They are usually borrowings that are highly assimilated in the system, are perceived as native, and are used on a regular basis in everyday situations. Statistically, the majority of such borrowings come from Dutch and German, possibly because most expressions from these two languages have been functioning in informal American English for a long time; their Germanic provenience also makes for their ease in adaptation and use. However, other languages are also represented. Here is a modest selection:

> *With lots of makeup, overdone hairdos, and too much jewelry, one can quickly look like a **bimbo** [= attractive and hedonistic young woman, especially if also stupid (Italian)] (Vogue, 2016)*
>
> *We were out in the **boondocks** [= remote or isolated region (Tagalog)] with no electronics. All of our time was screen-free (Princeton Union Eagle, 2016)*
>
> *We told him to **get lost** [= leave us alone (Yiddish)], to get out (Waco Tribune-Herald, 2016)*
>
> *"How's your **tush** [= buttocks (Yiddish)]?" "Fine. How are your boobs?" (Two and a Half Men, CBS-TV series, 2010)*

Passive borrowings (or passively known borrowings) are those which are known to most users of informal American English but are nevertheless not used by them on a regular basis. In other words, they are used analogously to what may be called "passive slang" (see Lighter 1994: xiii). Standing in between the more frequent and less frequent expressions, they constitute a small fraction of all expressions in the database. Here is a selection of relevant examples of borrowings of this kind:

> *You've got to have some **cojones** [= courage (Spanish)] to do that (New York Magazine, 2016)*
>
> *I spent a shitload of **dinero** [= money (Spanish)] here, and I expect to nut (Internship, film, 2013)*
>
> *"Anything to declare?" "No sir. **Nada** [= nothing (Spanish)]" (Dallas Buyers Club, film, 2013)*
>
> *I'm just some **schmo** [= average or mediocre person (Yiddish)] in LA sitting at my CPU (New York Times, 2007)*

Finally, there are **restricted borrowings** (or culture-specific borrowings): those which are largely restricted to use by ethnic groups in the United States. If ever used by outsiders, they serve the purpose of stylization rather than true identification: writers often resort to them to achieve the desired stylization effect, as do politicians who may, for instance, seek to secure the votes of ethnic minorities in elections. Still, they do feature prominently in our database, constituting a little less than half of all expressions, most found in those from Yiddish and Spanish. This means that they enjoy a high degree of frequency despite being largely restricted in use to ethnic groups. Consider the following examples:

> *Both Trump and Sanders have discussed America's **farkakte** [= despicable or accursed (Yiddish)] campaign finance system (Detroit Free Press, 2016)*
>
> *"Suzie, that boy is no good for you." "**Pero like** [= however (Spanish)], he's super-hot" (Miami Herald, 2014)*
>
> ***Que onda** [= hello (Spanish)], brother! How are you? (Southland, NBC-TV series, 2010)*
>
> *I was on the phone with my mother, and she can be such a **yenta** [= gossipy and annoying person, especially a woman (Yiddish)] (Nanny, CBS-TV series, 1993)*

4.6 By Register

Dividing borrowings by **register** may seem surprising at first since all borrowings discussed here belong to informal register (or style). However, since the informal register is composed of two subsets – slang and colloquialism – such a classification makes perfect sense. Let us repeat that slang is stylistically lower – or more informal – than colloquialism. In other words, while colloquialism is informal, slang is very informal.

Slang borrowings are the most common in our database, accounting for at least three-fourths of all expressions. They exhibit all the characteristics of slang (see Chapter 2), are often group-restricted, usually emotionally loaded, and sometimes offensive and vulgar. Consider the following citational corroboration:

> *You're turning into a **cabron** [= contemptible man, especially if also stupid and brutish (Spanish)] (Mambo Kings, film, 1992)*
>
> *I thought your all-expense paid **fuckfest** [= prolonged sex session, especially an orgy (German)] was just for the weekend (Queer As Folk, Showtime-TV series, 2001)*
>
> *Don't call me **pocho** [= Mexican American who emulates behavior or values of the non-Hispanic majority (Spanish)] (Narcos: Mexico, Netflix-TV series, 2018)*
>
> *It takes two to **schtup** [= have sex (Yiddish)] while you can go tango alone (Gail Parent, 1990)*

Colloquial borrowings constitute the rest of the expressions in our database and are visibly less frequent. They also exhibit the features of colloquialism (see Chapter 2), are less deliberate and extreme, more casual and universally known, and accepted in many more social situations. See the following:

> *Miriam worked in a **bodega** [= grocery store, especially Puerto Rican in New York City (Spanish)], a neighborhood grocery store about the size of a small garage (Los Angeles Times, 1997)*
>
> *My father's my best friend, my swimming **guru** [= influential or popular expert (Hindi)] (Life of Pi, film, 2012)*
>
> *The border is **numero uno** [= the most important thing (Italian)] in Texas (Dallas News, 2018)*
>
> *It sounds like you're pretty hot. I bet you got a great **tush** [= buttocks (Yiddish)] (Contract, film, 2006)*

4.7 By Impact

Finally, borrowings in informal American English can also be classified according to the level of **impact**. Roughly synonymous with a "shocking effect," the impact refers to Chapman's (1986: xxxiii) classification of slang dictionary entries "considered to have strong social or emotional impact." In practice, this category includes two parameters: offensiveness and vulgarity. Both are important in discussing informal language, especially its slang component. This is because of often repeated negative stereotypes which equate slang with offensive or vulgar language. In reality, only a fragment of slang lexicon can be characterized as such, since most slang is neither vulgar nor offensive; the same is even truer with regard to informal language in general, most colloquialisms being neither offensive nor vulgar. These observations are also consistent with our findings regarding informal borrowings. That being said, informal borrowings still can be classified according to these two parameters.

Vulgar expressions can be encountered among informal borrowings. They refer essentially to sex, body parts, and functions, and are meant to shock or disgust. They can be gradable, meaning that some are more vulgar than others. Various classifications have been proposed, but let us suggest a three-tiered scale, based on that of Kowalczyk and Widawski (2017: 15). Accordingly, those informal borrowings with the strongest impact are labeled **vulgar**: they make direct and rude reference to a taboo subject and are generally avoided in polite discourse. They are relatively rare in our database and are only a fraction. Consider the following examples:

> *I hope you have insurance, Jack.* ***Adios motherfucker!*** *[= goodbye (Spanish)]* (*Lost Highway*, film, 1997)
>
> *It's that late?* ***Chinga!*** *[= I am surprised (Spanish)]* (*UNF Student*, 2015)
>
> *I put it in her* ***coño*** *[= vagina (Spanish)] and had sex!* (Fiction Press, 2011)
>
> *I'm one of you, you* ***dumbfucks*** *[= stupid people (German)]* (*Against the Wall*, film, 1994)

Next on the scale are **potentially vulgar expressions** which are perceptibly less vulgar than the previous category. They are also a little more frequent in our database. Still, they should be used with caution. See the following:

> *You need to go and find an airhead with big* ***casabas*** *[= woman's breasts, especially if large (Turkish)]* (Reddit, 2020)
>
> *We stole it from this* ***dumb-ass*** *[= stupid (German)] cop* (*Hangover*, film, 2009)
>
> *Don't forget to put a rubber on his* ***kielbasa*** *[= penis, especially if big (Polish)]!* (Michelle Kane, 2007)
>
> *Sometimes couples sneak up here for some hot* ***nookie*** *[= sexual intercourse (Dutch)]* (*Dante's Peak*, film, 1997)

Finally, **non-vulgar expressions** are those that are completely neutral in terms of vulgarity. They constitute the overwhelming majority of informal borrowings in our database. Here is a relevant sample:

> *His wife is the* ***big kahuna*** *[= important person, especially a chief (Hawaiian)] here* (*Christmas Cottage*, film, 2008)
>
> *He never even called. Not once.* ***Go figure*** *[= imagine this (Yiddish)]!* (*Amazing Spider-Man*, film, 2012)
>
> *He's believable and more* ***simpatico*** *[= nice or affable (Spanish)]* (*San Francisco Examiner*, 2015)
>
> *But no one said, "it's* ***verboten*** *[= forbidden (German)], don't do it."* (*New York Times*, 2016)

The second impact parameter consists of offensive expressions. These are also found among informal borrowings. In contrast to vulgarisms, they refer primarily to nationality, race, or religion, and are meant to offend or denigrate. Interestingly, this sometimes makes for a paradoxical case, since such expressions are borrowed from languages spoken by people whom these expressions are meant to denigrate. Again, a similar three-tiered scale can be applied, with those with the strongest impact being labeled **offensive** (or **very offensive**, as labeled in the Glossary). These, again, constitute a fraction of expressions in the database. Here is a citational corroboration:

> The **Polacks** [= Poles or persons of Polish descent (Polish)] would speak in their native tongue and either start or finish all their sentences with the word "kurwa" (*Seattle Weekly*, 2009)

> I never thought I'd say this on American soil, but the **Russki** [= Russian or person of Russian descent (Russian)]'s right (*Madagascar 3*, film, 2012)

> Okay, **taco breath** [= Mexican or person of Mexican descent], swim south back to Mexico! (MMA Weekly, 2013)

> I was frequently called a "**yid**" [= Jew (Yiddish)] by other students, and regularly called a "f-ing yid" (*Forward*, 2016)

Potentially offensive expressions (or simply **offensive**, as labeled in the Glossary) have a perceptibly lower impact in terms of offensiveness than the previous category. They are also more frequent in our database, constituting one-tenth of all entries. Still, they should always be used with caution. Here are a few representative examples:

> Sometimes I like to speak Spanish at work just to mess with all the **blancos** [= white persons (Spanish)] in the office (Twitter, 2014)

> Danny, you're rich. You're pretty much **boojie** [= upper-middle-class persons (French)] (*Education of Charlie Banks*, film, 2009)

> Find a nice Jewish girl and don't live it up with the **shikses** [= non-Jewish woman, especially a young and attractive one (Yiddish)] (*New York Times*, 2010)

> "Did you see the look on her face?" "**Speedy Gonzales** [= man who ejaculates prematurely (Spanish)]!" (*Smallville*, WB-TV series, 2003)

Finally, **non-offensive expressions** are those that are completely neutral in terms of offensiveness. Again, these are the majority of informal borrowings in our database. Consider this relevant sample:

> Conceived from **chisme** [= gossip or rumors (Spanish)], these stories are revelatory (*Austin American-Statesman*, 2015)

> Go ahead, **fress** [= eat, especially heartily, quickly, or noisily (Yiddish)] a bissel! Try it, you'll like it (*New York Times*, 1998)

We're to be **liquidated** *[= killed, especially by violent means (Russian)]?* (*Dogma*, film, 1999)

Alright, **yalla** *[= hurry up (Arabic)] man! Let's eat!* (*Bordering on Bad Behavior*, film, 2014)

Chapter Summary

Borrowings in informal American English can be classified according to a few main criteria. As for typology **by borrowed material**, one can distinguish loanwords (or borrowings proper), which are the most frequent in the database, followed by loanblends and loan translations, with semantic loans having a marginal occurrence; while, understandably, most loanwords come from Spanish, loanblends come largely from German, Dutch, and Yiddish, while loan translations come from Chinese and Yiddish. As for typology **by part of speech**, the majority of expressions are nouns, followed by adjectives and verbs, which is consistent with the part-of-speech distribution patterns found in noninformal borrowings; however, exclamations are surprisingly frequent while phrases, adverbs, affixes, pronouns, and prepositions feature in scant numbers. As for typology **by assimilation**, one can distinguish partially assimilated borrowings, which are most frequent, followed *ex aequo* by fully assimilated and unassimilated expressions; all of these types come from a variety of languages without any particular one constituting a majority. As for typology **by modification**, unmodified borrowings are the most frequent in the database, followed by partly modified and highly modified ones; again, all of these types come from various languages without any particular one standing out. As for typology **by frequency**, one can distinguish frequently used borrowings and restricted borrowings, followed by passive borrowings; expressions from Dutch and German feature prominently in the first group, those from Yiddish and Spanish in the second, without any particular language dominating the third. As for typology **by register**, most borrowings in informal American English are slang, the rest being colloquialisms; aside from Spanish and Yiddish, there are no other distinctive donor languages among those two types. Finally, as for typology **by impact**, non-vulgar borrowings constitute the majority of all expressions, with vulgar and potentially vulgar ones featuring in marginal numbers; a similar correlation is to be found among non-offensive, offensive, and potentially offensive expressions.

CHAPTER 5

Changes

Chapter Outline

Borrowing usually involves the importation of an entire expression from one language to another without any change in form, and in the popular understanding these are considered prototypical borrowings. However, in the process of adaptation, some borrowings undergo **changes** (or **modifications** or **transformations**), especially in their forms and meanings. The former is usually conditioned by the need to conform to the linguistic rules of the recipient language, while the latter usually involves semantic modifications or extension of meanings due to various reasons, which is essentially done through figuration and accompanied by shifting. However, the modifications go beyond the form and meaning, and may involve other **levels** as well. Accordingly, one can talk about phonological, morphological, semantic, grammatical, and stylistic changes. The same is applicable to borrowings in informal American English.

5.1 Phonological

Phonological changes are those involving the pronunciation of borrowings. Simply put, this normally happens when expressions borrowed from the donor language include sounds that have no immediate equivalents in the recipient language; in such cases, a proxy or approximate sound must be used instead to conform to the phonological rules of the recipient language. Phonological changes involve all major sound types such as vowels, diphthongs, and consonants, but also word stress or accentuation, all exhibiting varying degrees of modification. While the nature and confines of this book preclude any systematic phonological analysis – this is, after all, a book on vocabulary and not on pronunciation – some general tendencies involving sound changes in informal borrowings can be observed. They are presented on the following pages.

One category of phonological changes involves the **vowels** and **diphthongs** (or **double vowels**) of informal borrowings which have been modified in American English. Various degrees of modification are possible, from mild to extreme. As a rule, because of this modification, such borrowings tend to be used by larger social segments of American society, or the so-called general public, rather than immigrant or minority groups whose members often prefer to use the original form in their native languages, especially if they speak them fluently. Consider the following examples:

> He was acting like a **fagola** [= gay man (from Yiddish "feygl" or "feygele")] (Hollywood Reporter, 2015)
>
> I can't wait for our first shore leave so I can get me some fucking **poontang** [= woman considered as a sex object (from French "putain")] (South Park, film, 1999)
>
> They can be elusive and have a tendency to **vamoose** [= leave or depart, especially hastily (from Spanish "vamos")] quickly once spotted (Military Times, 2016)
>
> Staffers began to question the source of his **yen** [= intense craving (from Chinese "yuàn")] (New York Post, 2015)

Aside from vowels and diphthongs, informal borrowings may also be modified by changes in their **consonants**. Various degrees of modification are possible as there are various consonants incompatible with those found in the phonological inventory of American English; one particular instance is the Spanish consonant /ñ/ – featured in numerous informal borrowings – which is often rendered as /n/ in English, especially by those speakers who do not know Spanish. Here is the relevant citational corroboration:

> Kidnapping, robbery and drug-dealing were just a few of the sins he and his **companeros** [= companions, especially in illegal activity (from Spanish "compañeros")] committed (Lively Arts, 2014)
>
> He's waiting for me to quit **futzing** [= wasting time doing nothing (from Yiddish "fartsn")] and get some work done (Motley Fool, 2012)
>
> He's a big **macher** [= very important, influential, and well-connected person, especially involved in shady dealings (from Yiddish "makher")] in the music business (Examiner, 2011)
>
> We had them toss a grenade into a bathroom and blow a guy to **smithereens** [= small pieces or fragments (from Irish Gaelic "smidrins")] (Washington Post, 2016)

The changes may be more complex and involve the modification of a vowel and consonant at the same time. Consider the relevant selection of examples:

> Those same **boojies** [= upper-middle-class people (from French "bourgeois")] were madly in love with the Clintons before the arrival of Obama (Black Agenda Report, 2008)

*Why does the U.S. Navy get all that money and we get **bupkis** [= nothing or an absurdly meager amount (from Yiddish "bobkes")]? (InformationWeek, 2013)*

*This time a bad cold and a **schnozzle** [= the nose, especially if very long or big (from Yiddish "shnoytsl")] full of snot are not the reasons (Village Voice, 2006)*

*She's good looking, you saw that **tokus** [= buttocks (from Yiddish "tokhes")] (House, M.D., Fox-TV series, 2004)*

However, sometimes the change in pronunciation is not visible in spelling. In other words, borrowings may retain their original spelling but they are pronounced according to the rules of American English; one recurring example is the Spanish vowel /o/ – featured in numerous informal borrowings – which in English is often rendered as diphthong /ou/, especially by those speakers who do not know Spanish. Again, this tendency is mainly true for the general public since speakers from ethnic minority or immigrant communities usually prefer to retain the original pronunciation, especially if they are fluent in the donor language. See the following:

*You two **femmes** [= (in a homosexual relationship) the person who plays the passive, "feminine" role (from French "femme")] can talk about it next year at your little slumber party (Superbad, film, 2007)*

*Is it **kosher** [= legitimate, legal, or lawful (from Yiddish "kosher")] to demolish the existing building? (Brooklyn Daily Eagle, 2018)*

*Ex-Mexican president trolls Donald Trump on Twitter, says he's **loco** [= crazy (from Spanish "loco")] (Houston Chronicle, 2017)*

*Many **gringos** [= white people from an English-speaking country (from Spanish "gringo")] seem to like the dry, cylindrical Mexican tamales (Detroit Metro News, 2014)*

Finally, **word stress** (or **accentuation**) can also be modified. This is especially evident in the case of borrowings from syllable-timed languages (like Spanish, French, and Italian where there is no word accentuation per se) which acquire the word stress according to the phonological rules of American English (which is stress-timed and requires accentuation in bi- or polysyllabic words). See the following examples:

*Kardashian revealed she was **au naturel** [= naked (from French "au naturel")] at the time she received her first phone call from Trump (Hollywood Gossip, 2018)*

*Here there is work, just not for the **indocumentados** [= immigrant without legalized stay and without the necessary documents (from Spanish "indocumentados")] (New York Times, 2013)*

*If our local DA chooses not to prosecute or pursue charges against the **influyentes** [= important people, especially in a drug ring (from Spanish "influyente")], are we screwed? (Blogspot, 2012)*

*He finished fifth in Iowa with 0.9 percent of the vote and said **sayonara** [= goodbye (Japanese)] that night* (Daily Beast, 2015)

5.2   Orthographical

Orthographical changes are those which involve modification of the spelling of the borrowed expressions. The written form of informal borrowings is often respelled, usually in order to conform to the rules of American English but also for other reasons. These are discussed below.

The simplest yet most discernible changes involve special characters or diacritical marks which had been used in the donor language but became lost in the American English spelling. Two notable instances featured in numerous informal borrowings are the Spanish acute accent over vowels resulting in /á, é, i, ó, ú/ and the tilde in /ñ/, which are all often left out in the American English spelling, especially by those speakers who do not know Spanish. Again, this is not absolute, and some borrowings retain their diacritics, especially if used by people who know the donor language and make the effort to use the original form. Consider the following expressions:

*You are a **huevon** [= lazy person, especially if also stupid (from Spanish "huevón")] as we say in South Dallas* (Yahoo Answers, 2007)

*They'll do whatever it takes to get the sexy **mamis** [= woman, especially, an attractive one (from Spanish "mamí")] moving* (Miami New Times, 2014)

***Omerta** [= code of silence, especially the one used by members of the Italian Mafia (from Italian "omertà")] has never taken deep root in the media-entertainment industrial complex* (Hollywood Reporter, 2017)

*Then a mysterious stranger crosses their path, and shit gets properly surreal and **tres** [= extremely (from French "très")] fucked up* (Rolling Stone, 2021)

However, the changes can sometimes be so extreme that such respelled expressions are hardly recognizable as borrowings. Here is a selection of relevant examples:

*I'm watching people **sashay** [= walk in a casual way (from French "chassé")]* (Treme, HBO-TV series, 2010)

*Light has worked a **slew** [= large number (from Irish Gaelic "sluagh")] of jobs in newspapers* (San Diego Union-Tribune, 2016)

*I did a little **snooping** [= prying (from Dutch "snoep")] and here's everything to know about it* (Marie Claire, 2018)

*Save the **spiel** [= persuasive or eloquent talk (from Yiddish "shpil")]. The lady in your waiting room convinced me you weren't worth my time* (Nip/Tuck, FX-TV series, 2003)

The orthographic modification can sometimes be startling. This is usually in the case of informal borrowings transplanted into American English from nonalphabetic languages – using writing systems other than Roman (Latin) script – since there is no one-to-one relationship between these systems. Such writing systems include Chinese characters, Japanese or Korean syllabaries, Yiddish (or Hebrew) script, Arabic script, or Devanagari (Hindi) script, to name a few major ones. While standardized systems of transcription exist that reflect the romanization tradition of a particular language, such systems were mostly unknown to the users of borrowings – such as soldiers or immigrants – who had to cope with transcribing these expressions themselves and came up with unorthodox spellings. Here is a handful of examples:

> *The doormat? Pretty* **chintzy** *[= cheap or inferior but showy (from Hindi "chiṃṭ")], huh? Considering the money she makes (Seinfeld,* NBC-TV series, 1996)

> *We slept in the high,* **cushy** *[= comfortable, providing comfort (from Hindi "khush")] bed (Houston Chronicle, 2015)*

> *Other fonts displayed "***tofu*** [= an empty box shown in place of undisplayed character in computer encoding (from Chinese 'dòufǔ')]" for this character* (Math Works, 2016)

> *Andy lives a schizophrenic existence, working at the center of the couture world, while dressing like a* **zhlub** *[= sloppy, slovenly, or poorly dressed person (from Yiddish "zshlob")] (San Francisco Chronicle, 2006)*

Occasionally, there is a considerable degree of variation in spelling, resulting in numerous variants of the same borrowing. This is often caused by several dialectal forms used in the source language, all of which were borrowed into informal American English. A good example is Yiddish, which used to be composed of four main dialects: Western (used in Germany and Austria), Northeastern (used in Lithuania and Latvia), Central (used in Poland, the Czech Republic, Slovakia, and Hungary), and Southeastern (used in Ukraine and Romania) (see Wex 2005: 47), each distinct in pronunciation. As a result of Jewish immigration to the United States, numerous Yiddish borrowings that came into American English reflect these dialectal differences (see Widawski 2012: 72). Consider these variants of the informal borrowing *tokhes* "the buttocks":

> *Inevitably, Neil Simon will flop on his* **toches** *but it appears less and less likely to happen in our lifetime* (Hollywood Reporter, 2018)

> *I achieved all my success on my own ability. I didn't pop a pill, I didn't stick a syringe in my* **tokhes** *(MMA Junkie, 2013)*

*Points for Pai for highlighting what a pain in the **tuchis** robocalls have become* (*Fairfield Daily Republic*, 2018)

*Johnson slipped on a banana peel and fell backward to the hardwood on his **tuchus** with just a minute remaining in the first quarter* (ESPN, 2018)

5.3   Morphological

Changes in the form of borrowings often go beyond mere spelling. Borrowings may also feature manipulation in their form by means of adding or removing lexical material. This is similar to creating new expressions in English from already existing native vocabulary, except in this case the sources of this vocabulary happen to be foreign. Such **morphological changes** are usually the result of several **wordbuilding processes** which may be collectively categorized into two main superordinate groups: lengthening and shortening, to which one can also add a few minor categories (Algeo 1991: 3–14). All of these are discernible in borrowings in informal American English, although with varying degrees of change and occurrence in our database. This extensive section presents these processes and their effects in detail.

Lengthening is one of the most frequent processes of morphological change in English. It is an umbrella term which encompasses such productive morphological processes as compounding and affixation, and may include phraseology as well. All of these share a common feature: the form of a word becomes lengthened. All of them have also been used to modify the form of borrowings imported into informal American English.

Compounding (also termed **composition**) is the most common process of word-formation in English (Algeo 1991: 7). In the simplest terms, compounds are words that are made of two elements which are words themselves (Pearce 2007: 39). Compounds are characterized by unstable spelling conventions since one may come across the two elements spelled together, separately, or hyphenated. They are also characterized by relative freedom of combination, since the two elements may come from various parts of speech in various order. As such, compounding is a frequent mechanism allowing manipulation in the form of borrowed expressions in informal American English. Typically, one element of a compound is a borrowing while the other is a native word, thus rendering them hybrid loans (discussed in Chapter 2), but there are other combinations as well. Consider the following examples:

*What do we expect? A promise that you won't try this kind of **bunco game** [= swindle (Spanish)] again?* (*San Diego Union-Tribune*, 2015)

> You all come out for some piping **hot tacos** [= sexually attractive women, especially of Hispanic origin (Spanish)] (*InSecurity*, CBC-TV series, 2011)
>
> He also had to create a **splatterfest** [= event when a lot of people die, especially one depicted in a movie (German)], one requiring around 25,000 liters of blood (*Houston Press*, 2013)
>
> That's just a **juke joint** [= bar with a coin-operated record player (Wolof)], man, where everybody hangs out (*Snow on Tha Bluff*, film, 2012)

However, sometimes both elements of a compound are borrowed: one is taken from one donor language, while the other is taken from another. Such "double borrowings," involving two donor languages, are occasionally found in informal American English. Nearly all of them are based on Yiddish and usually have a jocular character. Consider the following corroboration:

> He could be viewed as a **schlockmeister** [= someone making or selling something that has no value (Yiddish and German)] lowering standards for an inarticulate public (*Newsweek*, 2015)
>
> Lowe and Trump engaged in a bit of a **schmoozefest** [= idle or gossipy conversation session (Yiddish and German)] (*Washington Scene*, 2011)
>
> The fairy godmother transforms her into a **taco belle** [= Latin American woman, especially if attractive (Spanish)] (*New York Daily News*, 1997)
>
> My experience with these affairs is that the accused **uber-gonif** [= super thief (German and Yiddish)] tells everyone who will listen that the charges are bogus (*New York Times*, 2008)

Interestingly, certain borrowings retain the **original word order** found in their donor languages. Typically, this happens in case of borrowings which take the form of postmodified nouns, a common practice in Romance languages such as Spanish, Portuguese, Italian, and French. Here is a selection of illustrative expressions:

> Carlitos grew up to be more of a problem than a **bato loco** [= crazy person, especially of Latin American descent (Spanish)] (*My Family*, film, 1995)
>
> This **chica blanca** [= white woman, especially a young one (Spanish)] is pretty great (Instagram, 2014)
>
> I was so conflicted. "Conflicted" is the **word du jour** [= currently popular word (French)] (*America's Sweethearts*, film, 2001)
>
> What happens if you smoke **yerba buena** [= marijuana (Spanish)]? (*Okay* magazine, 2014)

In informal American English, borrowings can also be modified by adding native **affix words** to them and changing them into compounds. These are highly productive words used to form compound combinations with other words, in a manner similar to affixes. Several dozen such affix words may be discerned in informal American English (see Wentworth and Flexner [1960] 1975: 596–655), of which two are exceptionally productive in combination with borrowings. The first one is *head* meaning "someone associated with what is indicated by the preceding word." It also serves as a mechanism for creating ethnic or racial slurs based on the other compound element associated with a given ethnic or racial group. Consider the following examples:

> *Artie, what is that **dopehead** [= drug addict or user (Dutch)] doing? (Godzilla, film, 1998)*
>
> *God, we are the fools! **Dumbheads** [= stupid people (German)]! (3rd Rock from the Sun, NBC-TV series, 1998)*
>
> *The **krautheads** [= Germans (German)] hold the town and it's being bombed (Military, 2015)*
> *I'll take care of you later, **taco head** [= Mexican or person of Mexican descent (Spanish)]! (Retroactive, film, 1997)*

The second affix word is *eater*, "someone of a particular nationality or ethnicity signaled by the preceding word, which is usually the name of a traditional or stereotypical food associated with that nation or ethnicity." Again, it is often used for the creation of ethnic or racial slurs. See the following:

> *An unknown man from the army opened fire on fifteen unsuspecting **frijole eaters** [= Mexicans (Spanish)] (Planet Ice, 2002)*
>
> *We are still in Germany keeping the **kraut eaters** [= Germans (German)] from killing each other (Topix, 2011)*
>
> *Some French Quebecers even agreed to rent from these **spaghetti-eaters** [= Italians or people of Italian descent (Italian)] (Montreal Gazette, 2012)*
>
> *Andreopoulos shouted racial insults at Vargas. He called him a **tortilla-eater** [= Mexican (Spanish)] (Los Angeles Times, 1991)*

The reverse is also possible: there are a few borrowed affix words that are extremely productive and serve to coin dozens of compounds based on English words (Widawski 2011: 441). The first one is the German-origin word *fest* which indicates "a long, extreme, or unrestrained activity involving what is indicated by the preceding word." Here is a representative sample of expressions formed in this way:

> *In this novel, six friends gather one night for a **boozefest** [= drinking party (German)] at a Manhattan loft (Sex and the City, HBO-TV series, 1998)*
>
> *Wall Street honcho seeks two horny gal pals for an East Hampton **fuck-fest** [= prolonged sex session, especially an orgy (German)] at my summer house (Sex and the City, HBO-TV series, 1998)*

*This **gabfest** [= idle or gossipy conversation session (German)] is meant to give President Bush a chance to show his more intellectual side (New York Times, 2004)*

*The songwriter is notably irascible, but this **songfest** [= song festival (German)] should leave him tickled (Hartford Courant, 2007)*

The other affix word is *meister* and means "a specialist or expert in what is indicated by the preceding word." It also comes from German, although due to language similarities it is sometimes regarded as a Yiddish affix word. Consider the following selection of examples:

*Bloomberg Markets magazine today profiles internal GE **dealmeister** [= skillful negotiator or a specialist in making deals (German)] Pam Daley (Wall Street Journal, 2007)*

*Many a **hypemeister** [= specialist in publicity or public relations, especially insincere (German)] will offer you dramatic scenarios that revolve around Garnett (News, CBS-TV program, 2010)*

*The New York Times **opinionmeister** [= opinion-maker or expert (German)] gives him a glowing recommendation for veep (Time, 2008)*

*He and **rapmeister** [= skillful performer of rap songs (German)] Russell Simmons came up with the idea for a slick hip-hop magazine (Chicago Tribune, 1998)*

Affixation is another process of lengthening which is employed in the modification of borrowings in informal American English. Native word elements such as **prefixes**, **suffixes**, or **infixes** can be added to borrowed words, thus modifying their meanings but also signaling growing assimilation in the English language. In informal American English several dozen such affixes can be used, much like in standard English. Let us mention here two which are among the most frequent: the suffix *-y*, used to shift the grammatical category into an adjective, and the suffix *-er*, used to mean an agent or doer of an action or activity. Here is a selection of examples, the first batch with the *-y* suffix:

*It's a cloddish, harmlessly **drecky** [= nonsensical (Yiddish)] comedy from the Sandler factory of crude mush (Entertainment Weekly, 2012)*

*For some, it's the **glitzy** [= flashy or showy (Yiddish)] stores of New York and Paris (News, CNN-TV program, 2013)*

*I put red on it and it looked very **jazzy** [= lively, stimulating, or exciting (Mandinka)] (Hair Dye Forum, 2011)*

*I grew up drinking good pilsners and boks, just because my fam is very **krauty** [= German (German)] (Beer Advocate, 2013)*

And the second one with the -er suffix:

> I would end up like a delinquent **doper** [= illegal drug user (Dutch)], like you? (*Another Day in Paradise*, film, 1999)
>
> I'm a **kveller** [= someone who is proudly happy, especially because of an achievement of a child (Yiddish)], obviously! (*New York Times*, 2007)
>
> A Woody Allen-type nebbish, Lenny is a **kvetcher** [= chronic complainer or grumbler]; he frets about his age, his baldness, and his parents (*Wall Street Journal*, 2010)
>
> He always had confidence and was a **schmoozer** [= someone who talks persuasively, especially by using flattery (Yiddish)] (Huffington Post, 2012)

Again, the reverse is also possible: borrowed affixes can be attached to native English words which, interestingly, can be either informal English or standard English. Here is the citational corroboration of such expressions found in our database:

> You can kiss your **mega**bucks [= a lot of money (Greek)] goodbye (*Game Plan*, film, 2007)
>
> Health**niks** [= people obsessed with health, especially healthy diet (Yiddish)] were working out at gyms, jogging or taking walks (*South Florida Sun Sentinel*, 2011)
>
> Here's a fact**oid** [= presumed fact of dubious validity (Greek)]to share at your next cocktail party (*Seattle Center*, 2012)
>
> "Who the hell is this guy?" "Mike Chadway. He's an **uber**-moron" [= total moron (German)] (*Ugly Truth*, film, 2009)

Certain foreign affixes are highly productive in informal American English. Notable is the *el-* element or *el- -o* construction. Although the *el* element is usually not linked with the following word, it may in fact be considered a kind of prefix, reinforced by the suffix *-o*, and thereby forming a **circumfix** (or **confix**). This combination is used to form countless pseudo-Spanish expressions, and the association is usually humorous or ironic but can sometimes be regarded as offensive to Latin Americans. See the following corroboration:

> Splurge on the upgrade options because the basic packages tend to be very **el cheapo** [= cheap (Spanish)] (Lonely Planet, 2007)
>
> I believe the odds of Leinart doing an **el floppo** [= failure (Spanish)] are greater (Arizona Sports Fans, 2008)
>
> If the Jets were hoping for an **el foldo** [= failure (Spanish)] from Oakland, it's not happening (*New York Times*, 2006)
>
> When I smoke a cigar, one of my cheap **el stinkos** [= cheap and strong cigars], my wife cries (*Orlando Sentinel*, 1998)

To be clear, the above pseudo-Spanish construction involving the *el* prefix is not to be confused with the *el* retaining its original function as the definite article, featured in several informal borrowings. In other words, the *el* is part of many Spanish expressions taken together with their preceding articles. Note, however, that in some cases, the *el* may be dropped. See the following:

> *So what brings you girls to* **el barrio** *[= Spanish Harlem (Spanish)]?* (*Carlito's Way: Rise to Power*, film, 2005)

> *I need some* **el diablito** *[= mixture of marijuana, cocaine, heroin, and phencyclidine (Spanish)]. I can pay* (Lolly Dream, 2010)

> *Zidane is still the greatest, he's* **el magnifico** *[= excellent (Spanish)]!* (*Body Building*, 2006)

> *Possibly the rain last night kept some people at home, but the track was* **el primo** *[= the best (Spanish)]* (Houston Motocross, 2005)

In like manner, the *la* article forms part of numerous expressions taken from Spanish. This, too, may sometimes be dropped. Here is a representative selection of examples:

> *It's known for folks suffering from* **la cruda** *[= hangover (Spanish)]* (*San Diego Reader*, 2015)

> *I don't want to be in the* **La Eme** *[= the Mexican mafia (Spanish)] any more* (*American Me*, film, 1992)

> *You're fucking up, Jimmy! You want to go back to* **la pinta** *[= prison (Spanish)]?* (*My Family*, film, 1995)

> **La Raza** *[= advocacy group for Latin Americans (Spanish)] did indeed attack McCain on immigration* (*News*, ABC-TV program, 2008)

Two frequently encountered suffixes come from Slavic languages – Russian and Polish – although many words created with them may have entered English via Yiddish and are thus treated as Yiddishisms. The first one is *-nik* (alternatively also *-chik* or *-ik*) and denotes a "person associated with what is indicated in the root word, especially an enthusiast or connoisseur." It usually has a slightly jocular connotation, sometimes outwardly sarcastic (Kowalczyk 2010: 19). See the following:

> *He is sixty-five, a New York* **allrightnik** *[= someone who has succeeded financially, especially an affluent Jewish immigrant (Yiddish)] who has made it big in real estate* (*New York Times*, 2012)

> *They're hanging around the campus being busy-beavers and* **do-goodniks** *[= well-intentioned, selfless, or altruistic person (Yiddish)] without pay* (Chronicle of Higher Education, 2011)

> *Obama is a textbook* **Facebooknik** *[= someone addicted to Facebook, a social networking service and website (Yiddish)]* (*Forbes*, 2008)

*Many people, like me, are slobs in one domain but **neatniks** [= people obsessed with cleanliness and neatness (Yiddish)] in the others (Chicago Tribune, 2007)*

The other suffix is *-ski* (alternatively spelled *-sky*). While it serves an identical function and has similar connotations as *-nik*, it may also refer to things and "denote a specimen or example of something indicated by a root word." Consider the following examples:

*On my right, a pair of fellows chatted over a **brewski** [= beer (Yiddish)] (Seattle Weekly, 2013)*

*If I'm interrupting, please tell me. I hate to be a **buttinsky** [= someone who habitually interferes with someone else's affairs (Yiddish)] (Tune in Tomorrow, film, 1990)*

*"Toy Story 3" is a **flopski** [= failure (Yiddish)] in Russia (Los Angeles Times, 2010)*

*I drop a **sawski** [= ten-dollar bill (Yiddish)] in the collection plate (Daily Kos, 2006)*

As for **infixes**, there is just one found in our database. It is the Yiddish *-schm-* (alternatively spelled *-shm-*) and is very productive: it serves to form seemingly countless expressions based on reduplication, or doubling of the word or its element. It has derisive and sarcastic connotations (Soukhanov and Flexner 1997: 20). Here is a handful of representative examples:

*We'll have the party at our place, we don't need their fancy-**shm**ancy [= overly elegant, ornate, or sophisticated (Yiddish)] shit (Out Cold, film, 2001)*

*Health-**shm**ealth [= health seen as overrated (Yiddish)], pass me another slice! (Blogspot, 2012)*

*"It's love, I tell you. Love!" "Love-**shm**ove [= love seen as overrated (Yiddish)]. It doesn't matter" (Mulan II, film, 2005)*

*Eh, money-**shm**oney [= money seen as overrated (Yiddish)], it comes and goes. It's all about the loooove! (Twitter, 2014)*

Phraseology, the creation of strings of words in a fixed order forming a conceptual entity, is perceptibly less frequent among methods of modifying borrowings in informal American English. Still, one can distinguish a few notable types. The most frequent are **verb phrases** centered around the verbs which serve as extended verbs (see Widawski [2015] 2019: 36–37). Typically, the verb is a native English element, while the rest of the phrase is borrowed. See the following:

*My dad looked kind of ashen and ready to **blow** his **burritos** [= vomit (Spanish)] (YouTube, 2014)*

*I'm about to **go jihad on his ass** [= attack someone forcibly and mercilessly (Arabic)]* (Reddit, 2014)

*When he discussed Hillary's loss to Barack Obama in the 2008 election, Donald said she **got schlonged** [= got defeated or victimized (Yiddish)]* (Hollywood Life, 2015)

*He no doubt would prefer the classier knicknack, but why **make a tsimmes** [= create a great outrage, fuss, or complain (Yiddish)] over it?* (New York Magazine, 1991)

There are other possible **phrase combinations** as well. These include phrases serving as extended nouns, extended adjectives, or extended adverbs. Here is a representative sample of such borrowings:

*You get in that water when it is 20 degrees outside, you are **in big kimchi** [= in serious trouble]* (Georgia Outside News, 2014)

*I'm **on shpilkes** [= nervous or anxious (Yiddish)]. No son of mine is being married in a church* (Confessions of an American Bride, film, 2005)

*When your PC is **on the fritz** [= broken or malfunctioning (German)], who you gonna call?* (New York Times, 2005)

*If we sent these kids to war, you'd have sick calls **out the ying yang** [= to the extreme, to excess (Chinese)]* (Los Angeles Times, 1997)

In informal American English, borrowed verbs can also be modified by adding various English particles to form **phrasal verbs**, which are idiomatic phrases consisting of a verb and another element, typically either an adverb or a preposition (Stevenson 2010: 1339), often called particles. The resulting verbs function in a way similar to standard phrasal verbs, but the combinations are sometimes completely unexpected or idiomatic. Here is some citational corroboration:

*Promise me that you'll **dummy up** [= be quiet (German)] about this* (Sopranos, HBO-TV series, 2001)

*Don't worry, I got some ideas on how you can **jazz** it **up** [= make it lively, stimulating, or exciting (Mandinka)]* (Family Guy, Fox-TV series, 2012)

*Sandler will dress as a woman and **klutz around** [= behave in a stupid way (Yiddish)]* (Huffington Post, 2013)

*If you just want to **pal around** [= associate or socialize (Romany)], call us* (Angel, WB-TV series, 2000)

Occasionally, the verb can be followed by two particles. Consider the following examples:

*You don't **futz around with** [= provoke or play with (Yiddish)] Uncle Sam* (Wall Street Journal, 2013)

*Fans will be able to **putz around with** [= tamper or meddle (Yiddish)] the customization* (Examiner, 2011)

*Doesn't Michaelson **pal around with** [= associate or socialize (Romany)] a Ryan from "C" Company? (Saving Private Ryan, film, 1998)*

Of course, phrasal verbs can change into **phrasal nouns**, where the verb and particle complex becomes nominalized. Such creations are usually hyphenated or spelled as one word. Although they can theoretically be formed out of any phrasal verb, these are rare in our database. Here are the only two examples:

*So who's picking up the tab on this little **chow-down** [= act of eating (Chinese)]? (Entourage, HBO-TV series, 2006)*

*The first month of college was an epic **futzup** [= confusion (Yiddish)] (NYC Student, 2012)*

Informal borrowings can also be modified to form **binomials** (or **binomial phrases**). These are fixed-order two-part phrases linked with a conjunction – usually *and* – and function as formulaic expressions (McArthur 1992: 128). Again, they are rare; see the following:

*There will be plenty of snacks to nosh on, so we'll **ess and fress** [= eat, especially heartily, quickly, or noisily (Yiddish)] (Yahoo, 2011)*

*I can't tell you how many black people were **juking and jiving** [= dancing in a boisterous fashion (Wolof)] to his latest album (Lipstick Alley, 2013)*

*Suzanne opted to take drastic action by packing up the whole **kit and caboodle** [= everything entirely (Dutch)] and relocating to the Canadian bush for nine months (Los Angeles Times, 2016)*

*He showed up early, **schmoozed and cruised** [= mingle socially, and especially converse idly or gossip (Yiddish)] for a few minutes, and then hastily decamped (Los Angeles Weekly, 2002)*

Longer phrases can also be found among borrowings in informal American English. These are longer strings of words in a more or less fixed order which are borderline sentences. They often function as proverbs, slogans, or clichés and telegraphically convey information (Titelman 1996: ix), and they are often considered formulaic expressions. Most such expressions in our database are loan translations from Yiddish and are strongly linked with Jewish oral cultural traditions but there are also a few from Mandinka and Wolof; some have a hybrid structure. Consider these examples:

*The Brief: **Deja Vu All Over Again** [= a feeling of repetition or recurrence of the present situation (French)] (Texas Tribune, 2014)*

*"I will give you the money back." "**I should live so long** [= I should live long to see something so unrealistic (Yiddish)]!" (Texas Tribune, 2014)*

When my mom left my dad, I accepted it. **That's the way the cookie crumbles** *[= such is life (Yiddish)]* (*Scream 2*, film, 1997)

"Hey, jefe. **What's cooking** *[= what is going on (Yiddish)]?" "I don't know"* (*War*, film, 2007)

Shortening (alternatively labeled **abbreviation**) is the other main morphological process of forming new words out of already existing words in English. Much like lengthening, it is an umbrella term which encompasses several morphological processes such as clipping, initialism, and acronymy. Nearly all of these, with varying degrees of frequency, can be used to modify expressions borrowed from donor languages into informal American English.

Clipping is the most frequent process of shortening. As the name suggests, it involves "clipping" or cutting off part of a word. Clipping is very common in informal English, which has a tendency to aim at the shortest possible mode of expression, while short word forms are attributes of informal and spoken language (see Eble 1996: 35). For these reasons, clipping is also frequently used to modify borrowed words. Two types of clipping can be discerned, the first being **back clipping** where the end of a word is clipped:

What do you see, **compa** *[= close friend (Spanish)]?* (*Beverly Hills Chihuahua*, film, 2008)

That's a **fin** *[= five-dollar bill (Yiddish)] you owe me* (*Slight Case of Murder*, film, 1999)

She's got a great set of **gams** *[= legs, especially a woman's legs (French)]* (*Awkward*, MTV-TV series, 2014)

He's not paying any **vig** *[= interest on a loan or debt, profits of a bookmaker, usurer, or criminal conspirator (Russian)] on any of it* (*Chicago Tribune*, 2008)

The second type is **front clipping**, where the beginning of a word is clipped, as shown in these expressions:

"This here's my woman." "That **chacha** *[= woman (Spanish)] will do you no good"* (*Black Snake Woman*, film, 2006)

Not all cholos and **chucos** *[= young and tough Mexican American (Spanish)] are criminals* (Yahoo Groups, 2007)

Fucking **Ricans** *[= Puerto Ricans (Spanish)] think they know everything* (*Departed*, film, 2006)

He was bragging about having his big **yang** *[= penis (Chinese)]* (UCB student, 2013)

Interestingly, in informal American English borrowed compounds and phrases can also be clipped, forming **clipped compounds** and **clipped**

phrases, respectively. The same goes for informal borrowings, as corroborated by the following:

> *Who are you trying to get crazy with,* **ese** *[= fellow Mexican male (Spanish)]?*
> (*Zoolander*, film, 2001)

> *Same old shit. I am going to sulk now.* **Hasta** *[= goodbye (Spanish)], dudes*
> (Diary Land, 2004)

> **Luego** *[= goodbye (Spanish)]! I'll see you in the morning, okay?* (UCB student,
> 2013)

> *Major* **mazels** *[= congratulations (Yiddish)] to them on this landmark occasion!*
> (Miami Online, 2018)

Initialisms are much less frequent. As the name suggests, these are words created from the first letters of strings of two or more words read out as a sequence of separate letters (McArthur 1992: 520). Although there are no absolute spelling conventions here, they are normally spelled in capital letters and separated by periods. Here are a few examples of such expressions found in our database:

> *Hope you have a great b'day! I wish I could be there to drink* **AMFs** *[= strong,*
> *multi-liquor cocktails including vodka, rum, tequila, gin, blue Curaçao, sour*
> *mix, and 7-Up or ginger ale (Spanish)] with you!* (iPhoneogram, 2014)

> *Many* **PR's** *[= Puerto Ricans (Spanish)] receive federal assistance* (Trip
> Advisor, 2007)

> *I plan to still keep my apartment in* **TJ** *[= Tijuana, Mexico (Spanish)]* (*San*
> *Diego Downtown News*, 2015)

> *He's the worst* **T.L.** *[= insincere flatterer, sycophant (Spanish)] you ever saw!*
> (Leo Rosten, 1996)

Surprisingly, the third type of shortening, **acronyms**, are not represented in our database. Acronyms are words created from the first letters of strings of two or more words read out as one single word (Lieber 2010: 53) and normally spelled without capital letters and periods. Their lack of occurrence among borrowings in informal American English may be caused by their rather obtuse and cryptic character which impedes quick understanding, although there need to be more in-depth studies to support this hypothesis.

Blending (also called **amalgamation** or **fusion**) stands in between lengthening and shortening. In simplest terms, **blends** (alternatively termed **portmanteau words**) are words that were formed by joining parts of two other words and combining their meanings (Stevenson 2010: 178). Put differently, two words are fused together with a simultaneous clipping of some part or parts of one or both of them. Very often it is the middle part of such a newly created compound that is clipped. Blending also features among borrowings in informal American English, where it is appreciated for its attention-grabbing, eye-catching, and ultimately jocular form; some also attest to the great creativity of their coiners. Consider the following:

> *How do I become a member of the **cliterati** [= influential women, especially lesbian or feminist writers (Italian)]?* (Twitter, 2016)
>
> *A man I had worked with at the Center Theater happened to be directing the **jubilesta** [= festive jubilee (Spanish)]* (Soap Opera Network, 2011)
>
> *It feels good to be a **Nuyorican** [= Puerto Rican, especially one living in New York City (Spanish)] holding up a trombone instead of a tray* (El Cantante, film, 2006)
>
> *It implies that the ABC **schlockudrama** [= movie or television play that has no value, is shoddy or inferior (Yiddish)] doesn't meet high standards either* (Daily Kos, 2006)

Corruption is another morphological process of altering the form of expressions. Corruption (alternatively labeled **respelling**) involves deliberate misspelling of an expression (Widawski [2015] 2019: 61). Corruption is also used in borrowings in informal American English, and there are many expressions involving foreign elements. The changes in form often feature facetious or sensational respelling. Here is a handful of relevant examples:

> *Collectibles coyly referred to as **junque** [= old and discarded things (French)] are scattered throughout the region* (Daily Press, 1990)
>
> *So y'all just **parlaying** [= speaking or talking (French)] up in here, huh?* (Friday, film, 1995)
>
> *We should build the wall for the **spics** [= Spanish-speaking persons (Spanish)] are scattered throughout the region* (Ray Donovan, Showtime-TV series 2016)
>
> *We're on to our second bottle of red **veeno** [= wine, especially cheap (Spanish)]* (Instagram, 2016)

A special category in corruption involves **pseudo-borrowings** (or **imitative borrowings**), expressions that are loosely or vaguely coined on the basis of foreign words. Most typically, such expressions are phonetic or graphic imitations of foreign expressions, with the accompanying addition of certain word elements or reordering of syllables, all aimed at a playful or jocular effect; however, because of their often mocking or parodic character, some may also be perceived as offensive to native speakers of their donor languages. While expressions of this kind are comparatively rare in our database, some have caught on. Here are a few examples:

> *"I'll be back Thursday." "Till then, **au reservoir** [= good-bye (pseudo-French)]"* (Deuce, HBO-TV series, 2017)

*We're gonna raise the money to get you out of this **fox paw** [= embarrassing mistake (French)] (Married with Children, Fox-TV series, 1992)*

*I should say "**hasty banana** [= goodbye (pseudo-Spanish)]!" Good night, all! (Washington Post, 2007)*

*"Can you bring the car around?" "Yeah, I'll drive it around." "**Mercy buckets** [= thank you (pseudo-French)]!" (Northern Exposure, CBS-TV series, 1993)*

Informal borrowings are sometimes altered to such a high degree that they give way to **folk etymology** (or **popular etymology**), a popular but mistaken account of the origin of a word or phrase (Stevenson 2010: 679). Put differently, because of the changes in their form, some informal borrowings are mistakenly thought to have been borrowed from a different language or are regarded as a native element rather than a borrowing. An example of the former is *poontang* "woman considered as a sex object," which in popular perception seems to have been borrowed from an Asian or African language but in reality comes from the French *putain* "prostitute" and was popularized by the French-speaking population in the New Orleans area. An example of the latter is *tush* "buttocks," which is commonly thought to be a native English word yet comes from Yiddish and, ultimately, Hebrew. There are a few more such instances found in our database. Here is a handful of such easily misidentified expressions:

*We've got a lot of **old cockers** [= old men, especially despicable (Yiddish)] out there who wanted to hear a ball game (New York Magazine, 1992)*

*You poke the **poon** [= woman considered as a sex object], she marries the next guy she dates after you (Good Luck Chuck, film, 2007)*

*He liked a **reefer** [= marijuana cigarette (Spanish)], he smoked a heck of a lot (Fargo, FX-TV series, 2017)*

*When an ogre in the bush grabs a lady by the **tush** [= buttocks (Yiddish)], that's bad (Shrek, film, 2001)*

Borrowed **proper names** – which can be treated as a form of borrowings or foreign expressions (see Kuźniak 2009: 145–149) – can also be modified in informal American English. They are modified with various degrees of modification and often appended with new meanings. This category includes two main types: eponyms and toponyms.

Eponyms are "new words based on names" (Stockwell and Minkova 2001: 15), often in the sense of "family names or first names" (Pearce 2007: 64). When they are foreign eponyms – or words made from foreign names – with a new meaning, they function as borrowings. A typical pattern of change consists of borrowing names associated with a given nation or country and adding a native element, often carrying particular characteristics; the results look like family names or pseudo-family names:

> *I felt that same specter of death that I felt in Vietnam, but this time, death was coming in the form of a virus, not* **Charlie Cong** *[= members of Viet Cong (Vietnamese)]* (Iowa City Press-Citizen, 2020)
>
> *At least I'm still ahead of* **Joe Schmo** *[= undistinguished and average person, especially unfortunate (Yiddish)] in the net income category* (Chicago Tribune, 2012)
>
> *Terrorism drops as our* **Johnny Jihads** *[= militant, antiwestern Muslims (Arabic)] trade their bomb suitcases for bomb pops* (American Dad, Fox-TV series, 2012)
>
> *Slow down,* **Speedy Gonzales** *[= person who is very fast (Spanish)]* (Say It Isn't So, film, 2001)

The second type is **toponyms** (or **placenames**), which constitute a vibrant part of informal American English (see Widawski and Kowalczyk 2011). Toponyms do not really have a semantic denotation: although they refer to individual locations, they do not really "mean" anything, and even their reference potential is typically restricted to precisely one item only (Schneider 2007: 79). However, when appended with a native element carrying additional information, they become regular – lexicalized – expressions in informal American English. Consider the following examples based on foreign toponyms:

> **Ho Chi Minh's Revenge** *[= diarrhea (Vietnamese)]! Well, I must have ate or drank something my body did not like* (Blogspot, 2010)
>
> *The prices here are nothing compared to what you can pay for a place in* **Hongcouver** *[= Vancouver (Chinese)]* (Calgary Sun, 2014)
>
> *Many Vietnamese women sold glasses of "***Saigon tea** *[= illegal alcohol (Vietnamese)]" to lonely U.S. grunts* (New Republic, 2020)
>
> *The kid here has dysentery. The* **Viet shits** *[= diarrhea (Vietnamese)]. If you don't want him dead, you better do something* (Tripod, 2015)

5.4   Semantic

Informal borrowings in American English can also be modified in meaning and display **semantic changes**. In other words, some imported borrowings may become semantically modified and acquire new meanings in informal American English (note that it is sometimes impossible to establish definitively if such changes have occurred after importation or before it). Semantic changes normally involve two main processes: figuration, which makes use of metaphor, metonymy, and related figures of speech; and semantic shifting, which includes generalization, specialization, melioration, and pejoration (see

McArthur 1992: 403 and 913); the former are often accompanied by the latter. Both figuration and shifting feature prominently in informal borrowings and account for about one-third of all expressions.

Figuration is an important mechanism of change in the meaning of words. Although associated with literary language, it strongly features in everyday language (see Lakoff and Johnson 1980: ix) and is also a powerful tool in creating novel meanings in informal American English. Figuration involves an expression gaining further, nonliteral meanings, specifically through such devices as metaphor and metonymy. These two figurative devices can often be discerned in borrowings which came into informal American English, where they are used to change or modify their original meaning.

Metaphor is "the application of a word or phrase to someone or something that is not meant literally but to make a comparison" (Soukhanov 1999: 1188). Importantly, metaphor uses an analogy between things that are fundamentally dissimilar, so the effect is often startling, as shown in some of the examples below. Borrowings that came into informal American English can also be changed in this way with regard to their original meanings. See the following:

> *He would freak out if someone called him a **burrito** [= anyone of Latin American descent (Spanish)]* (Big Brother Network, 2017)
>
> *Would it be **kosher** [= approved or acceptable (Yiddish)] to make a joke about Sasha holding hands with a pedophile?* (*Los Angeles Times*, 2009)
>
> *He's a real **ninja** [= tough person (Japanese)], you don't wanna mess with him* (UCB student, 2014)
>
> ***Noshing** [= practicing oral sex, especially fellatio (Yiddish)] is okay, but I want the real thing* (UNF student, 2015)

Metonymy is another common vehicle of semantic change. It is "a figure of speech in which a word or phrase is replaced by another with which it is associated in some way" (Pearce 2007: 114). Put differently, it compares things that are related, unlike metaphor where they are fundamentally dissimilar. A type of metonymy is **synecdoche** where this relationship is very specific: a part is meant to represent the whole or vice versa (Stevenson 2010: 1804). Many borrowings in informal American English can also be the result of such changes. Here is a representative selection of examples:

> *Two **azuls** [= police officers (Spanish)] were stopping motorists and checking their ID's* (ASU student, 2013)
>
> *More recent historians have credited him with being a master of political **jiu jitsu** [= something involving dexterity and flexibility, especially a particular technique (Japanese)]* (*Entertainment Weekly*, 2013)

I seem to recall he was a bit of a **schlong** *[= despicable person, especially an idiot (Yiddish)]* (*Like It Is*, film, 1998)

He'll make me hear another disgusting joke. He's such a **schmuck** *[= despicable person (Yiddish)]* (*What Women Want*, film, 2000)

Figuration is often accompanied by **semantic shifting**, an established mechanism of change in the meaning of words. It involves such semantic processes as generalization, specialization, melioration, and pejoration (Stockwell and Minkova 2001: 156–160). Although associated with the historical change of word meanings over a long time, in informal language these processes operate faster and account for numerous new meanings (see Widawski 2013). Borrowings in informal American English can also feature semantic shifting, and all of the four processes can be discernible.

Generalization (also termed **broadening** or **extension**) widens the meaning of a word (McArthur 1992: 433); put differently, the new meaning of a word becomes broader or more inclusive than the original meaning. There are numerous instances of such shifts in our database of informal borrowings. Consider the following examples:

*Is it "***halal** *[= approved or acceptable (Arabic)]" to take Saudi money and sell them U.S. arms to kill their neighbors and oppress their people?* (*Arab American News*, 2018)

Shove the disc into the **kishkes** *[= inner workings or the inside (Yiddish)] of the DVD, and make us all watch it* (*Tablet Magazine*, 2012)

Would it be **kosher** *[= approved or acceptable (Yiddish)] if I prayed for a little help?* (*Switch*, film, 1991)

I didn't watch this because I was just too darn cheap to spring or a few more **shekels** *[= money] a month for Showtime* (*Baltimore Sun*, 2012)

The opposite of generalization, **specialization** (or **narrowing**) narrows or reduces the meaning of a word (Steinmetz and Kipfer 2006: 145); the new meaning becomes less general or less inclusive than the original meaning. Here is a representative selection of borrowings which underwent such a change:

I had a small **bolsa** *[= bag of narcotics (Spanish)] for fifty pesos, that's less than $4* (International Cannagraphic, 2009)

I bet you secretly fantasize about bedding a **Mandingo** *[= strong and big-built African American man (Mandinka)] since Bob isn't getting it done* (TMZ, 2015)

Here he comes. He's gonna **plotz** *[= lose emotional control, to burst with emotion, especially with anger, irritation, or frustration (Yiddish)] when he sees us* (*Angel*, WB-TV series, 1999)

*My Uncle Cesar is a **veterano** [= experienced, respected gang member (Spanish)]. Out the game, but still got his name (Boondock Saints II, film, 2009)*

While the above two processes involve the scope of meaning, the next two involve the association or connotation in meaning. The first, **amelioration** (also termed **melioration** or **elevation**), improves the meaning of a word (see McArthur 1992: 649); put differently, the new meaning of a word becomes more favorable or positive than the original meaning. Many borrowings in informal American English have become modified in this way. See the following:

*It takes **chutzpah** [= courage (Yiddish)] to attempt all this (Atlanta Journal-Constitution, 2013)*

*I really didn't think you'd have the **huevos** [= courage (Spanish)] for this (American Pie Presents: Beta House, film, 2007)*

*They were looking for a "**rabbi** [= benefactor or sponsor (Yiddish)]," they said, someone who knew about network TV (New Yorker, 2016)*

*I wouldn't have the **schmooze** [= ability to talk persuasively (Yiddish)] and confidence to be a salesman (Lonely Planet, 2012)*

The opposite of melioration, **pejoration** (also termed **degradation** or **degeneration**) depreciates the meaning of a word; the new meaning of a word becomes less favorable or more negative – or even taboo – than the original meaning (Soukhanov 1999: 1392). There are numerous instances of such a semantic shift in our database. Here is a representative selection of borrowings that underwent pejoration:

*It's regardless of whether you do the girl in the **casa** [= brothel (Spanish)] or your hotel, and then the girl negotiates her price with you (International Sex Guide, 2004)*

*Agnew hurled insults at minorities and opponents, calling a reporter a "fat Jap" and referring to Poles as "**Polacks** [= Poles or people of Polish descent (Polish)]" (Milwaukee Journal Sentinel, 2016)*

*Police found $100,000 worth of **shmeck** [= heroin (Yiddish)] in his house (Blogger, 2012)*

*It might be a little weird to have his mom talking about his **wiener** [= penis (German)] on primetime television (Cinema Blend, 2018)*

5.5   Grammatical

Modification of borrowings in informal American English may also involve **grammatical changes**. A process involving the change of grammatical category – part of speech – without a change of form is called

conversion (also termed **zero derivation**) (McArthur 1992: 263). For instance, nouns can be changed into verbs or adjectives, and the other way around. Importantly, conversion is possible in analytical languages like English but virtually impossible in other types, such as inflectional languages like Polish; when imported into English, however, borrowings become assimilated and may theoretically undergo conversion regardless of the type of source language.

Conversion is common in informal language and can also be found among informal borrowings, where numerous borrowed expressions have been changed in this way. This usually attests to a high degree of their assimilation. Here are a few examples of **adjectivization**, the change of a given part of speech into an adjective, which is most common:

> *We went out one night, I got a little **borracho** [= drunk (Spanish)] (Silver City, film, 2004)*
>
> *When will we see the end to this **carajo** [= despicable (Spanish)] communist regime in Cuba? (Nancy Asencio, 2011)*
>
> *You know, this movie is very **pendejo** [= perverted (Spanish)] (Prime Wire, 2014)*
>
> *Did she say that I'm a lazy-ass **schlock** [= having no value, shoddy or inferior (Yiddish)] jingle writer? (Two and a Half Men, CBS-TV series, 2003)*

The second most widely used process of conversion is **verbification**, or changing a part of speech into a verb. As aptly put in a well-known maxim, "there is no noun that cannot be verbed," this process is pervasive in informal language, including informal borrowings. Here is a handful of representative examples:

> *People were **chowing** [= eating (Chinese)] and guzzling to their hearts' content at this event (Miami New Times, 2013)*
>
> *The prick who **finked** [= informed (German)] on Anne Frank was never discovered and persecuted (News, KQED-TV program, 2016)*
>
> *It is **honchoed** [= led or directed (Japanese)] by his former campaign manager Nick Baldick (Time, 2007)*
>
> *The officials **nixed** [= refused, rejected, or vetoed (Yiddish)] the idea of separate entrances (Los Angeles Times, 2014)*

The third and least productive process is **nominalization**, or changing a part of speech into a noun. Consider the following citational corroboration from our database:

*If you filtered all the **glitz** [= flashiness or showiness (Yiddish)] out of Miami, you'd get Naples, Florida (Naples News, 2010)*

*Bring me some rope and I'll tie it around that **jodido** [= contemptible person (Spanish)] (Ralph M. Flores, 2004)*

*She gets the last word, she's also something of a **kvetch** [= chronic complainer or grumbler (Yiddish)] (New York Times, 2007)*

*I know Odenton may be a bit of a **schlep** [= long, slow, or difficult journey (Yiddish)] from your place, but the flavors make it worth the journey (Baltimore Sun, 2008)*

Although this process usually involves a change from one part of speech to another, sometimes the product of zero derivation applied to one expression may involve several parts of speech. This is the case with the following:

*Mary agrees his **ad lib** [= spontaneous speech or performance (Latin)] was effective (Tumblr, 2015)*

*Who knows what you'll do? Make it up as you go along. **Ad-lib** [= speak or perform spontaneously (Latin)]! Improvise! (Madagascar, film, 2005)*

*I talked **ad-lib** [= spontaneously (Latin)] about driving into Manhattan (Connecticut Magazine, 2015)*

*It was a very **ad-lib** [= spoken or performed spontaneously (Latin)] show (Inspirational Stories, 2015)*

5.6   Stylistic

Informal borrowings can also be analyzed by **changes in register** (or **changes in style**). This may seem surprising at first, since all borrowings discussed here belong in the informal register (or style). However, they can also be classified according to the register of the original expression in the donor language. In other words, before a given expression was borrowed into informal American English, it had led its own life in a given language and belonged to a given register, not necessarily informal. It would be interesting to determine how they changed.

But first, let us recall the concept of **register**. It has been variously defined, but in sociolinguistics and stylistics it is synonymous with the **level of formality**. Stevenson provides a more thorough definition, "a variety of language or a level of usage, as determined by degree of formality and choice of vocabulary, pronunciation, and syntax, according to the communicative purpose, social context, and standing of the user"

(Stevenson 2010: 1495). This understanding of register is also used in informal language studies – especially slang – where one often resorts to the formality scale. Typically, it consists of four main registers: slang, colloquial, neutral, and formal (see Chapter 2 for more detail), the first two belonging to informal register and the last two belonging to standard register. In the case of informal language, there is a general mechanism of formation and change, as described by slang scholars (see, for instance, Coleman 2012: 31–32). Essentially, two main scenarios of register change can be observed: downward movement (or shift) involving standard expressions turning into slang and, conversely, upward movement (or shift) involving slang becoming standard, usually via the intermediate stage of colloquialism.

Similar mechanisms of change can be discerned in informal borrowings. The most common pattern is **from informal to informal** register. Put differently, an informal expression in the donor language in the process of borrowing remains on the same stylistic level and becomes an informal expression in American English, sometimes with a change in meaning. In terms of numbers, this is the most frequent type of borrowings. Consider the following examples:

> *Quit acting like a **cabron** [= despicable man, especially if also stupid and brutish (Spanish)] (Stanford Daily, 2015)*
>
> *We got **flak** [= anti-aircraft fire (German)] everywhere! (Pearl Harbor, film, 2001)*
>
> *The danger of ads like these is that they can quickly descend into **schmaltz** [= excessive sentimentality (Yiddish)] (Ad Week, 2011)*
>
> *You really had to be there to fully appreciate what all the **tzimmes** [= great outrage, fuss, or complaining, especially over trivial matter (Yiddish)] was all about (Harvard Magazine, 2013)*

Borrowings may also shift **from neutral to informal** register. In other words, an expression belonging to a neutral register in the donor language in the process of borrowing becomes an informal expression in American English. Again, such a change sometimes involves a change in meaning. Here is a selection of examples which illustrate this:

> *There is no officially recognized list of them, which is fine **by** (= as far as concerns [Yiddish]) me (Inside Higher Ed, 2016)*
>
> *This is the guy who is **gung-ho** [= zealous, committed, enthusiastic (Chinese)] for all these deals (Mother Jones, 2016)*
>
> *It's going to be a **mega** [= very large (Greek)] party. It will be fun to see them (USA Today, 2016)*

*Jokes about **Polacks** [= Poles or persons of Polish descent (Polish)] have always been tasteless and silly (Burlington Times News, 2013)*

Finally, borrowings may also shift **from formal to informal** register. That is to say, an expression belonging to a formal register in the donor language in the process of borrowing becomes an informal expression in American English. This process is extremely rare, both in informal borrowings and in informal language in general. Here are just a few examples found in our database:

*Why sit in the dark while the **goys** [= non-Jews (Yiddish)] have all the fun? (Huffington Post, 2015)*

*Republican political **guru** [= influential or popular expert (Hindi)] Karol Rove used the issue against Democrats (New York Times, 2015)*

*I figure when the detail's over, I go back to straight narcotics. Try to get over to Dawson's shift, find a new **rabbi** [= benefactor or sponsor (Yiddish)] (Wire, HBO-TV series, 2013)*

*Do you think his **ying-yang** [= penis (Chinese)] is big? (Lesbian Vampire Killers, film, 2009)*

Chapter Summary

Borrowings in informal American English are often subject to various modifications. **Phonological changes** involve the modification of their pronunciation to conform to the phonological rules of American English; various changes can be observed in the original vowels, diphthongs, consonants, or accentuation, but particularly recurring is the change of /ñ/ into /n/ in borrowings from Spanish as well as that of /o/ into /ou/. **Orthographical changes** involve modification of the spelling of borrowed expressions; again, two notable instances are the Spanish acute accent over vowels resulting in /á, é, i, ó, ú/ and the tilde in /ñ/ which are often left out in spelling; the most startling changes concern borrowings from nonalphabetic languages like Chinese, Japanese, Korean, or Hindi, but also Dutch, Portuguese, or Irish Gaelic; finally, variation in spelling of informal borrowings sometimes reflects regional differences in their donor languages, which is especially visible in the case of Yiddish. **Morphological changes** involve modification in the form of informal borrowings by means of adding or removing lexical material via standard wordbuilding processes; these are lengthening, which includes compounding, affixation, and phraseology; shortening, which includes clipping and initialisms (with acronyms notably absent); and other wordbuilding processes such as blending or corruption. **Semantic changes** involve modification in the meaning of informal borrowings by means of the processes of figuration and accompanying semantic shifting. Figuration, which accounts for one-third of all expressions, involves metaphor, metonymy, and several other processes; notable is the use of allusion, specific to immigrant culture and experience. Semantic shifting is extensive as well, and involves generalization, specialization, melioration, and pejoration. **Grammatical changes** involve modification or conversion in the part of speech of informal borrowings; adjectivization and verbification are most common, with nominalization and a few other processes being rare; such grammatical conversion usually attests to a high degree of assimilation of borrowed expressions. Finally, **register** or **stylistic changes** involve modification (or lack thereof) in the original register of informal borrowings which may shift their stylistic status in American English; while most informal borrowings exhibit no such change and retain their informal status in American English, some reveal two notable patterns: from neutral to informal and, in rare cases, from formal to informal.

CHAPTER 6

Functions

Chapter Outline

Borrowings in informal American English can also be described according to the **functions** they serve. In other words, they can be viewed according to why people use them. Culpeper ([1997] 2005: 36) neatly summarizes the reasons for using borrowings in general: "borrowing is facilitated by languages coming into contact; changes in the environment, including cultural changes, creating a need for new vocabulary; and speakers wanting to use the vocabulary of a prestigious language to improve, for example, their social status." Interestingly, only some of these reasons are applicable to informal borrowings; for instance, they are not used because of their prestige, simply because informal language – especially slang – is the least prestigious type of language. Importantly, they are more often used for other reasons. The following breakdown into their functional categories will help explain them.

Language functions have long been of interest to linguists and philosophers, and have prompted various classifications (see, for instance, the classical functional taxonomies by Bühler 1934 or Jakobson 1960). The most fundamental function is obviously a referential one, which – simply put – is used to name things. However, informal borrowings can serve a number of other functions as well. These may be very peculiar to and result from sociolinguistic parameters such as the social, cultural, or ethnic context in which these borrowings are used; but they may also result from the peculiar applications of informal language, especially its slang component. The **functional classification** presented below incorporates both. It is partially based on the typology proposed by Widawski (2012) and Kowalczyk (2015), including five main functions: referential, social, psychological, rhetorical, and cultural.

6.1 Referential

The **referential function** (also termed **denotative** or **informational**) in language essentially refers to naming things, people, states, actions, or qualities. In other words, "it focuses on conveying information about the world" (Pearce 2007: 72). This is the most fundamental of language functions, and informal borrowings are also primarily used for this reason. Consider the following random examples taken from our database:

> *Lucky was regularly injecting something called "**bam** [= amphetamine (Spanish)]," an amphetamine-like stimulant* (*Washington Post*, 1994)

> *Can't you see our mother's completely **gaga** [= crazy or irrational, especially as a result of old age or excitement (French)]?* (*Eye of the Storm*, film, 2011)

> *She fell hard for a less than handsome gringo with plenty of **plata** [= money (Spanish)]* (*Planet Love*, 2013)

> *They are hanging out in their driveways in their **ranflas** [= cars with a lowered suspension or otherwise customized (Spanish)] kicking loud-ass music* (GTA Forums, 2013)

Borrowings can be further divided according to the **effect** they have on the recipient language. Haspelmath and Tadmoor (2009: 16) explain this in the following way: "when a word is borrowed it has an effect on the lexicon of the recipient language. It may replace an earlier word of roughly the same meaning, or simply be added to the lexicon where no earlier word with that meaning existed, or it may coexist with an earlier word of roughly the same meaning." And they add three functional categories: "insertion," "coexistence," and "replacement," which correspond with three rather self-explanatory functions: enriching, diversifying, and replacing ones. All three can be used in combination with the referential function but also with several other functions described in this chapter.

The **enriching function** involves borrowings that are simply new additions to the lexicon where no earlier expressions with that meaning existed. As observed by Widawski (2013: 69), the enriching function refers to a situation when the standard lexicon turns out to be insufficient to name or express certain concepts taken from other languages. In other words, such borrowings are used to fill what is called the lexical gap – itself often a strong motivation for borrowing (see Pearce 2007: 108) – and provide expressions for things for which there is no standard term. They correspond to "insertion borrowings" in Haspelmath's classification, but one could label them simply as **enriching borrowings** (or **neological borrowings**) in that they enrich the lexicon and bring novelty to it. For that reason, they can hardly be replaced by a synonym and require a longer string of words to accurately render their meaning. There are many such expressions found in our database. The following selection illustrates this:

> *Good thing both of your parents like **bukkake** [= sex act in which several men ejaculate on a woman or another man (Japanese)]* (Cinema Blend, 2016)
>
> *I love the **gringa tacos** [= tacos in a white flour tortilla with gyros-like pork filling (Spanish)] and cold beers!* (Trip Advisor, 2013)
>
> *For Spring 2016, the Saint Laurent designer continued his exploration of grunge with a collection aimed at **kinderwhores** [= young women whose dress suggests both youthful innocence and sexual abandon (German)]* (Fashion Spot, 2016)
>
> *My parents were relieved, not to mention filled with **naches** [= joy and pride because of one's kids (Yiddish)]* (Harvard Gazette, 2014)

The **diversifying function** pertains to borrowings that coexist with earlier expressions of the same or similar meaning. Languages often borrow foreign expressions that are synonymous with native expressions because such borrowings are perceived to have attractive novel qualities of exotic freshness; they are borrowed "out of love of a new term" (Gramley and Pätzold 2004: 33). Such expressions correspond to "coexistence borrowings" in Haspelmath's classification, but one could refer to them simply as **diversifying borrowings** (or **synonymous borrowings**) since they are diversifying and synonymous additions to the native word stock. In informal language – especially slang – they are even more important because of its prevalent overlexicalization or high productivity of synonyms for certain contexts (see Kowalczyk 2015: 46). Borrowings in informal American English belonging to this group are the most numerous. Here are a few examples of such borrowings:

> *They pay a visit to demonstrate just how uninhabitable and **disgusto** [= disgusting (Spanish)] it is* (Houston Chronicle, 2013)
>
> *The argument to spend your extra **mazuma** [= money (Yiddish)] for the ever-amazing 911 Carrera looks more threadbare by the day* (Autoblog, 2013)
>
> *If the day shifts to an overwhelming swelter, you don't want to start **schvitzing** [= sweating (Yiddish)] like a fat kid at a summer camp* (Maxim, 2016)
>
> *Now grab a glass of **vino** [= wine, especially cheap (Italian)] and get started!* (People Magazine, 2016)

Finally, one can also talk about the **replacement function**, which involves borrowings that come to be used instead of earlier expressions with the same meaning. Put differently, such borrowings become more popular than native expressions and may ultimately replace them altogether. They correspond to **replacement borrowings** in Haspelmath's classification, but one might just as well call them "cannibal borrowings." Borrowings in informal American English belonging to this group are comparatively rare, yet some are used very frequently. Consider the following examples:

> *It's like Jews who've spent a lot of time with **goys** [non-Jews (Yiddish)] (Esquire, 2015)*
>
> *She is a new-age **guru** [= influential or popular expert (Hindi)] who runs a partnering seminar for singles (International Business Times, 2016)*
>
> *It's a small restaurant chain out of Memphis that touts their **jumbo** [= very big in size (Kongo)] burgers (Tennessean, 2016)*
>
> *He was always fascinated by all that **macho** [= aggressively masculine (Spanish)] mobster bullshit (Starsky and Hutch, film, 2004)*

6.2 Social

Borrowings in informal American English – especially in slang – are often used in the **social function** (or **group-identification function**). This is because one of the main uses of slang is to communicate social status. Called "the expression of identity" (Crystal 2005: 466), slang helps to compartmentalize specific groups or subcultures within society and to identify their members. In like manner, informal borrowings in American English can also be used in this way, and the social reasons for using them include group solidarity, social distancing, and social rebellion.

Group solidarity is the first reason for using informal borrowings, especially slang. Spolsky ([1998] 2007: 50) calls slang "a powerful mechanism for signaling social attitudes or claiming group membership or solidarity." Slang functions within social and ethnic groups to validate and enhance this solidarity. The same can be said about borrowings, and the "solidarity" function of slang and borrowing reinforce each other: slang borrowings used in this function can serve to identify and classify fellow members of social or ethnic groups, usually viewed in positive terms:

> *It is dedicated to social empowerment of **Chicanas** [= Mexican or Mexican American women (Spanish)] through higher education (Los Angeles Times, 2003)*
>
> *If you think Bob Arun was rooting for his **landsman** [= someone who comes from the same hometown or country (Yiddish)], Foreman, you ain't seen nothing yet (Examiner, 2010)*
>
> *White cops lynch a member of the **pachucos** [= Mexican American gang members (Spanish)] who took the rap for the murders (Entertainment Weekly, 2020)*
>
> *Nobody'll kick us out of this joint. They're **Tejanos** [= Texans of Mexican origin or descent (Spanish)], like us (Selena, film, 1997)*

However, informal borrowings can also be used to label social or ethnic groups which one despises or dissociates from, which one may call **social distancing**. Members of these groups are treated as outsiders and usually viewed in negative terms:

> *These instructions were probably translated by some **gringo** [= white person from an English-speaking country (Spanish)]* (*Space Cowboys*, film, 2000)
>
> *You can promise me that you are not **maricón** [= gay man (Spanish)]?* (*Eastern Promises*, film, 2007)
>
> *Look, it's a new ghost writer he needs, not another goddamn **politico** [= politician, especially unscrupulous (Spanish)]* (*Ghost Writer*, film, 2010)
>
> *He's a **tío taco** [= Mexican American who emulates behavior or values of the non-Hispanic majority (Spanish)]. There, I've said it* (Democratic Underground, 2005)

Finally, there is **social rebellion**: informal borrowings are sometimes used to rebel against the established authority and to distance oneself from it, which is linked with the rebellious and nonconformist nature of slang. While slang can be "used to fit in," it can also be "used to stand out" Adams (2009: 6). The main users of slang borrowings in this function are obviously criminals but also people who have unorthodox lifestyles outside the mainstream of society, such as sex workers, drug addicts, and perhaps also feminists as well as members of the gay and lesbian community (see Widawski 2008: 284). Consider the following examples:

> *They put together the list of **dedos** [= police informants (Spanish)]* (*Collateral*, film, 2004)
>
> *Hey, ese, if you want to shoot, you need a **fuete** [= hypodermic needle (Spanish)]* (ASU student, 2013)
>
> *Kober is a **hausfrau** [= woman whose primary interests are keeping house and raising children (German)] who gaily encounters the counterculture* (*New York Magazine*, 2009)
>
> *I talked with the girls and their **macks** [= pimps (French)] who worked on Second Avenue* (Melvin Lasky, 2011)

6.3   Psychological

The **psychological function** (or **expressive function**) involves principally the expression of emotions. As observed by numerous linguists (see, for instance, Chapman 1986: xii–xiii or Widawski and Kowalczyk 2012b: 32), informal language – and slang in particular – is a powerful and effective means to express emotions, and the same goes for borrowings. While standard vocabulary is sometimes insufficient to express emotions with the desired degree of intensity, informal lexicon serves as an excellent vehicle for verbalizing various emotional states and reactions, such as anger or surprise. Accordingly, the psychological reasons for using informal borrowings include the said expression of emotions, humor, and toughness.

Many informal borrowings in American English are used in this function. Typically, they assume the form of **exclamations** or interjections (see Kowalczyk 2014). Most commonly, they refer to anger, which can be illustrated by the following:

> **Caramba** [= I am irritated or angered (Spanish)]! I missed it again! (*Adventures of Tintin*, film, 1991)
>
> "**Coño** [= I am irritated or angered (Spanish)]! You said ten!" "Oh, I'm sorry" (*Grindhouse*, film, 2007)
>
> Oh **marone** [= I am irritated (Italian)]! How many times do I have to tell you? (UCLA student, 2014)
>
> Just look at this! **Puta madre** [= I am irritated or angered (Spanish)]! What the fuck is this? (Facebook, 2013)

The second most frequent emotion is surprise. Here is a selection of representative examples:

> Oh! **Caramba** [= I am surprised and excited (Spanish)]! What an honor to have you come to see me! (Rómulo Gallegos, 2012)
>
> You're pregnant? **Hot chihuahua** [= I am surprised and excited (Spanish)]! (UCLA student, 2019)
>
> Your family is Italian, too? **Mamma mia** [= I am surprised (Italian)]! (UCLA student, 2014)
>
> **Oy** [= I am surprised (Yiddish)], Hymie, that is very good! (Old Jews Telling Jokes, 2010)

Equally frequently, informal borrowings in American English may also assume the form of **epithets**, be they adjectives, nouns, or phrases. These can be negative, with various degrees of offensiveness and vulgarity. See these examples:

> Ron, your long dissertation about what liberals believe is total **caca** [= nonsense (Spanish)] (*Tulsa World*, 2013)
>
> You called me "**pendejo**" [= stupid or obnoxious person (Spanish)], you fuck! (*Running Scared*, film, 2006)
>
> These **pinche** [= despicable (Spanish)] cops across the street hassled me, man! (*Walkout*, film, 2006)
>
> You're a **schmuck** [= despicable person (Yiddish)] for not wearing a mask (*Vanity Fair*, 2021)

But they may also be positive. Consider the following citational corroboration:

> *She was **en fuego** [= excellent (Spanish)], it was pretty amazing (Cornell Daily Sun, 2001)*
>
> *You were such a **hot tamale** [= sexually attractive woman of Hispanic origin (Spanish)], I couldn't control myself (Choke, film, 2008)*
>
> *He's very **simpatico** [= nice or sympathetic (Spanish)], a nice guy (New Yorker, 2014)*
>
> *Today, some might consider her to be **zaftig** [= pleasantly curvaceous (Yiddish)] (My Best Friend's Girl, film, 2008)*

Used in this function, informal borrowings are often an effective means of expressing **humor**, itself a frequent feature of informal language and – especially – its slang component. In so doing, they often mask the awkwardness connected with taboo topics such as the human body and its physiology, sex and sexuality, illness and death, which in themselves constitute the main lexical fields of slang. In other words, they serve "as protective language that disguises unpleasant reality" (Algeo and Pyles [1964] 2005: 221). They also allow escape from the clichéd and worn-out standard expressions and help introduce a positive atmosphere in otherwise bland reality. See the following examples:

> *I'd like to put my chorizo in her **empanada** [= vagina (Spanish)] (Huddle, 2010)*
>
> *He had to spend the whole day to sort things out due to the reappearance of the **Gringo Gallop** [= diarrhea suffered by tourists in Mexico or Latin America] (Blogspot, 2006)*
>
> *The guy drank too much tequila and **tossed his tacos** [= vomited (Spanish)] (UCLA student, 2013)*
>
> *Harrison Ford had a bad case of the **touristas** [= diarrhea, especially as contracted in a foreign country (Spanish)] (Film Wise, 2003)*

Expressing **toughness** is another psychological reason for using informal borrowings. Again, this is especially true with regard to slang borrowings. Slang is often characterized as having "locker-room crudity and toughness" (Lighter 1994: xii), and the natural reflections of toughness are vulgarisms which, to paraphrase Widawski (2008: 289), by their very nature strengthen the user's image. Put differently, the users of vulgarisms appear tougher than they really are. Here are a few examples:

> ***Coño** [= I am irritated (Spanish)]! If people knew what was going on! (Miami New Times, 2012)*

*Sit down, you fucking **dumbshit** [= stupid person (German)]! (Straw Dogs,*
film, 2011)

*Feels like I had an epic **fuckfest** [= prolonged sex session, especially an orgy*
(German)] with a ghost (Girls, HBO-TV series, 2012)

***Hijo de puta** [= despicable man (Spanish)]! Is it all you got, white boy? (Blue*
Bloods, CBS-TV series, 2012)

Obviously not all informal borrowings are made of vulgarisms, and
toughness can be conveyed by expressions simply associated with the
concept itself. Consider the following selection of representative
examples:

*Being a **chonga** [= working-class, sexualized, and aggressive young woman*
(Spanish)] means I do not have to apologize for my feminism (Latina, 2015)

*Men are still expected to be very **macho** [= aggressively masculine (Spanish)],*
very hypermasculine (Dallas Voice, 2015)

*"Don't be saying shit about my mom or my fucking car, man!" "He a **ninja** [=*
tough person (Japanese)] now!" (8 Mile, film, 2002)

D'Amato learned his lesson during his 1998 re-election campaign when he tried
*to be a **shtarker** [= mentally tough person (Yiddish)] (New York Times,* 2000)

6.4 Rhetorical

Rhetoric is the art of effectively using language to convince or persuade.
Although it is commonly associated with the language of politicians,
lawyers, statesmen, or poets, it is by no means confined to elevated use
and is found in everyday communication. The **rhetorical function**
involves the use of language for desired stylistic effects. When used with
a deliberate purpose (see Allen 1993: 266), informal language can become
an important verbal tool of language manipulation, too. In like manner,
informal borrowings in American English can also be used in this way, and
the rhetorical reasons for using them include informality, conciseness,
forcefulness, wordplay, and small talk.

Informality is the most obvious and inherent function of informal
language. The use of informal expressions in an utterance is often a matter
of intentional and conscious choice and usually lowers its formality,
although in various degrees depending on their type. Accordingly, as
observed by Lighter (1994: xv), informal lexicon can be divided into
colloquialism and slang, the latter situated at the very bottom of the
formality scale (see discussion in Chapter 2). In this context, colloquialism

could be described as informal, while slang is very informal. All this can also be said about informal borrowings, including colloquialisms, which lower the level of formality:

> *I think I know how to **ad-lib** [= speak or perform spontaneously (Latin)]* (*Morning Glory*, film, 2010)

> *It's just great to get the three **amigos** [= male friends (Spanish)] back together again* (*Old Dogs*, film, 2009)

> *Our free cheer service is over as of this moment. **Finito** [= ended or finished (Italian)]* (*Bring It On*, film, 2000)

> *"So you're not a prude?" "**Moi** [= me (French)]? Hey, I'm a very sexy guy"* (*Bones*, Fox-TV series, 2009)

But this can also be said about slang, which lowers the level of formality even more. Consider these examples:

> *She was a **chichona** [= big-breasted woman (Spanish)] and it was hard not to know that, especially when she was wearing a bathing suit* (*Harper's Magazine*, 2008)

> *Is this comparable to the **dumbshits** [= stupid people (German)] who hurt themselves barbecuing?* (Facebook, 2015)

> *People can sniff out **phony-baloney** [= fake or false (Irish Gaelic)] brands from miles away* (*Forbes*, 2018)

> *There were many randy men and women back then, it was one big **shtupfest** [= sexual orgy (Yiddish and German)]* (Free Republic, 2006)

Conciseness (or **conciseness of expression**) is another important rhetorical reason for using informal language and can also be discerned in informal borrowings. Because informal language is largely composed of relatively short words – especially mono- and bi-syllabic ones – it is highly effective in communicating information. Moreover, the brevity of informal borrowings is also attractive as it allows a more forceful way of expressing ideas. Additionally, as observed by Eble (1996: 35), they often "convey a casual and sometimes sardonic attitude toward the subject." In this regard, many informal borrowings are abbreviations, especially clippings. See the following expressions:

> *In my last severe depression, I took **coca** [= cocaine (Spanish)] again* (*Los Angeles Times*, 2011)

> *Like many of his **compas** [= close friends (Spanish)], Castro was moved to support the guerilla cause* (*Los Angeles Times*, 2007)

> *Pass me a **fin** [= five-dollar bill (Yiddish)], I'll pay you back* (*Clueless*, film, 1995)

*How much do you want for that **hooch**? [= low-quality alcohol, especially if illegally produced (Hoochinoo)] (From Dusk till Dawn, film, 1996)*

However, informal borrowings are also used in this function because they communicate more quickly, easily, and personally than do standard words: some ideas often require a series of several standard words, while they can be expressed more economically by one- or two-word informal borrowings. Consider these representative examples:

*Judges will be hearing plenty of evidence from **computerati** [= computer-proficient people, especially programmers (Italian)] about why Apple's technical argument is right (Chicago Tribune, 2016)*

*How did he become a **lobo** [= male who frequents bars alone in the hope of finding a sexual companion (Spanish)]? (Be Careful, film, 2011)*

*My parents bought it, which makes me a **schnorrer** [= beggar or parasitic person, especially if audacious (Yiddish)]? (Marvelous Mrs. Maisel, Amazon-TV series, 2022)*

*A person in possession of a **yiddishe kop** [= Jewish way of thinking, especially being smart (Yiddish)] is someone who looks for a clever way out of problems (New York Times, 2010)*

Forcefulness (or **forcefulness of expression**) is another notable motivation within the rhetorical function. Informal expressions tend to be devoid of diplomacy and sentimentality, and thus often are more direct and expressive than standard expressions (Widawski [2015] 2019: 116). Put differently, people use them to sound more powerful, confident, or emphatic. In this situation, informal borrowings often assume the form of either epithets or exclamations, with varying degrees of vulgarity or offensiveness. See the following:

*Look at y'all standin' here freezin' like **dumb-fucks** [= stupid people (German)]! (8 Mile, film, 2008)*

*You're blaming your mother? What a **farshtinkener** [= despicable (Yiddish)] putz! (Citizen of the Month, 2008)*

***Mierda** [= I am irritated (Spanish)]! There's something wrong (UCLA student, 2019)*

*You're a **puto** [= despicable man (Spanish)] with no huevos (Huffington Post, 2012)*

Borrowings in informal American English are also used for **wordplay**. They are often a result of playful manipulation of language, seen in a sometimes humorous blending of borrowings and English expressions or their parts. This is particularly true with regard to slang which, as observed by Adams (2009: 6), "is used to assert our everyday poetic prowess." Indeed, such experimentation brings informal borrowings closer to poetry and testifies to the great linguistic creativity of their users. Let us have a look at the following citational corroboration:

> *Well, I gotta go get some sleep, so **adios amoebas** [= goodbye (Spanish)]!* (Daily Strength, 2007)
>
> *I'm sorry but it's getting late and I must really go. **Hasta la pasta** [= goodbye (Spanish)], amigos!* (Facebook, 2010)
>
> *He referred to the toilet as **le shittoir** [= toilet (French)], which was very funny* (UCB student, 2013)
>
> *This is what Steven Pinker called the ability to **yidentify** [= be able to spot a fellow Jew in a large group (Yiddish)]* (Tumbler, 2011)

Last but not least, there is **small talk**, which can be described as "polite conversation about unimportant or uncontroversial matters, especially as engaged in on social occasions" (Stevenson 2010: 1863). Borrowings in informal American English are also used in this way: not so much to communicate any specific message as to signal mere communication or a communicative attempt instead. Put differently, they do not contribute much in the form of concrete information per se, but their use serves the purpose of facilitating social interaction, something Polish anthropologist Bronisław Malinowski called **phatic communion** (see Crystal [1995] 1999: 257). Most commonly, they are used to start, maintain, or end a conversation; they also take the form of formulaic terms of address, ice-breakers, topic shifters, or feedback signals. See the following examples:

> *What's goin' on in this house is stayin' here, **comprende** [= do you understand (Spanish)]?* (Spin Magazine, 2016)
>
> *Perhaps he's a tad farshikkert in this video clip, **nu** [= don't you think (Yiddish)]?* (Daily Kos, 2007)
>
> *"**Orale** [= hello (Spanish)], carnalito! Orale!" "Hey, what's up, ese?"* (Bound by Honor, film, 1993)
>
> *"Can we call it a night?" "Good night, **sayonara** [= goodbye (Japanese)]!"* (This Means War, film, 2012)

6.5   Cultural

Borrowings are also used in the **cultural function**. To paraphrase Culpeper ([1997] 2005: 36), they are the product of language contacts but they also result from interactions between cultures. While the military, political, and economic engagement of the United States overseas has created numerous opportunities for borrowing from foreign cultures, much cultural interaction has actually occurred at home. As observed by Crystal (2004: 458), "the amount of borrowing [in a given language] is always influenced by the number of cultures which coexist [. . .]; in a multilingual country, we might expect a greater use of loanwords." Perhaps no other country can relate to this remark better than the United States, which epitomizes the concept of a melting pot, or a multicultural and multilingual society. The popularity of borrowings reflects the social, cultural, and political importance of immigrant ethnic minorities in the country. All this can also be said about informal borrowings; the reasons for using borrowings in this function include expressing cultural identity, cultural crossing, and cultural stylization.

But first let us bring forth the classic distinction between so-called cultural borrowing and intimate borrowing (the third type, dialect borrowing, being irrelevant to this study) proposed by Bloomfield (1933: 444–495). **Cultural borrowing** involves "words that fill gaps in the recipient language's store of words because they stand for objects or concepts new to the language's culture" (Myers-Scotton 2006: 2012) or, in Bloomfield's words, they "show us what one nation taught us." This type of borrowing includes primarily "cultural novelties," is not necessarily one-sided, and does not require intensive contact between speakers of both languages. On the other hand, **intimate borrowing** happens "when two languages are spoken in what is topographically and politically a single community" (Bloomfield 1933: 461) and their speakers come into more intensive contact. This type of borrowing extends to speech forms that go beyond mere cultural novelties and includes various everyday expressions. Interestingly, there is typically a dominant (or more prestigious) language and a less dominant (or less prestigious) one, and the borrowing is usually one-sided: it goes from the former to the latter. Both characterizations can be extrapolated to informal borrowings in American English, albeit with one important reservation: intimate borrowing goes from less dominant languages to a more dominant language, that is, American English. What this means is that borrowing for prestige – an important cultural reason for borrowing in general (Haspelmath and Tadmoor 2009: 58) – is not applicable to informal borrowings. Consequently, there must be other reasons.

Borrowing is often one of the most visible and outward exponents of **cultural identity**, and it is used to signal one's allegiance and sentiments, so that borrowings in informal American English serve as a powerful means of expressing the cultural identity of members of minority groups and immigrants in the USA and their descendants, much like members of social subgroups use slang to signal their social identity. Significantly, when used in this function, such borrowings are often so culture-specific that they may be incomprehensible to those unfamiliar with the immigrant or minority culture (see also Kowalczyk 2015: 47). Consider the following citational evidence:

> *His call for greater restrictions does not keep him from appreciating the good reasons that the **alambristas** [= Mexicans illegally present in the USA (Spanish)] have for moving northward (Tucson Weekly, 1997)*
>
> *The Catskill Mountains were known as the Jewish Alps or the **Borscht Belt** [= region in the Catskill Mountains north of New York City where many predominantly Jewish resort hotels once were found (Yiddish)] (SF Gate, 2016)*
>
> *Poppyseed is one flavor of a new line of **Catholic bagels** [= nontraditional bagels, especially flavored (Yiddish)] that seek to take over the bagel market from the Jews (Daily Kos, 2005)*
>
> *They used to call him **Tío taco** [= Mexican American who emulates behavior or values of the non-Hispanic majority (Spanish)], a sellout (Twitter, 2010)*

While borrowings are used by members of immigrant and ethnic minority groups to express their cultural identity, they can also be used outside of these groups by larger social segments for other reasons. In this instance, there is a transmission of borrowings from one culture to another – in our case, from a minority culture to the dominant "white" American culture. Such transfer is technically called **cultural crossing** and the result of such transfers are called **cross-over expressions** (see Smitherman 2000: 28–33) because they transferred or "crossed over" from one culture to another. Extreme and pervasive crossing often leads to the so-called **appropriation** or extensive borrowing of expressions rooted in a particular culture, which for instance has been happening with African American English (Bucholtz 2011: 76). Many such borrowings functioning in informal American English have become strongly or totally assimilated and are commonly used or understood by the majority of Americans regardless of their ethnic origin. They often use these expressions because of their expressiveness, vividness, or wit; interestingly, they do not use them because of their prestige, an important reason for borrowing in general (see Haspelmath and Tadmoor 2009: 48). Let us have a look at the following citational corroboration found in our database:

> *We have invited many North Korean defectors over the years, but he is the **big enchilada** [= important person, especially a chief (Spanish)] we have always wanted (Los Angeles Times, 2003)*

*Then there's Tom, the money market **maven** [= expert or a connoisseur (Yiddish)], and Perry, the travel agent guy. But no, she wants more (Anything Else, film, 2003)*

*I suggest you get your scrawny asses in here, **pronto** [= immediately or without delay (Spanish)] (Brokeback Mountain, film, 2005)*

*When I do both the yoga and the swim, the **whole megillah** [= anything very long or complicated (Yiddish)] takes about two hours (New York Times, 2011)*

Naturally, another important reason for using cross-over expressions is linguistic and cultural enrichment. No two cultures are the same and so there will always be expressions in one culture that do not have counterparts in another, much as there will be situations when the standard lexicon turns out to be insufficient to name certain concepts taken from other languages (Widawski 2013: 69). In our case, this happens when there is a lack of equivalents from minority culture in the English language. Consider the following expressions which require several words to define them in standard English:

*When I first started shooting heroin they were cutting it with **bonita** [= milk sugar used to dilute heroin (Spanish)], and coke with epsom salts (David T. Courtwright, 2013)*

*He accuses her of opening a hotel for **mojados** [= illegal immigrants to the USA from Mexico, especially those who swim across the Rio Grande (Spanish)] in her backyard (Brooklyn Rail, 2019)*

*Many saw me as a **pocho** [= Mexican American who has assimilated (Spanish)] because I spoke English and lacked fluency in Spanish (LAist, 2021)*

*If his toast lands butter side down, then he is also luckless, he is a **schlemazel** [= unlucky and gullible person, especially a fool (Yiddish)] (New York Times, 1996)*

Finally, one should also distinguish **stylization** (or **imitation**), which in fact stands at the crossroads of the rhetorical, social, and cultural functions. People often consciously imitate others in speech in order to identify with a style or attitude and create their new verbal image. The same can be said about informal borrowing, especially slang which is heavily linked with its sociocultural context. Let us recall the notions of primary and secondary slang (see Kipfer and Chapman 2007: x). The former is used by a group of its coiners in its natural context; the latter, on the other hand, is deliberately used to imitate the primary slang of a particular group outside of its natural context in order to show one's attitude toward that group, either positive or negative. There are numerous informal borrowings that are used much like secondary slang. Here are a few examples:

*What's not to like, **bubbeleh** [= darling (Yiddish)]? Jewish friends have never said no (New York Times, 2009)*

*Luckily, there are plenty of ways to occupy yourself this week that won't cost a lot of **dinero** [= money (Spanish)] (Miami New Times, 2013)*

*Immigration issue largely ignored: Trump vows to deport "bad **hombres** [= men (Spanish)]" (USA Today, 2016)*

*I am watching my weight now that I live in Honolulu. I don't want to get **zaftig** [= curvaceous (Yiddish)] (Huffington Post, 2016)*

Chapter Summary

Borrowings in informal American English are used for several reasons. In the **referential function**, they are used to name things, essentially providing alternative synonyms for things already named in English (synonymous diversification) but also providing names for things yet to be named (neological enrichment). More often, however, informal borrowings are used instead of standard English to communicate additional information that is social, psychological, rhetorical, or cultural in nature. The **social function** involves group solidarity, social distancing, and rebellion; such use of informal borrowings serves especially the purpose of identifying members of immigrant and minority groups. Equally important is the **psychological function** which includes expression of emotions, humor, and toughness; surely, the most prominent usage concerns emotions: informal borrowings provide an extensive repertoire of expressions for a variety of emotional states and actions as well as emotive labels for people or things. The **rhetorical function** includes informality, conciseness, forcefulness, wordplay, and small talk; informality is obviously the most salient characteristic in that the use of informal borrowings always lowers the formality of communication. Finally, the **cultural function** involves expressing cultural identity, cultural crossing, and cultural stylization; while expressing cultural identity is the quintessential reason for using such expressions, cultural crossing and stylization are other notable phenomena accounting for the increasingly common use of this type of lexicon among larger segments of American society, regardless of their ethnic origin or mother tongue. Particularly interesting in the use of informal borrowings is the lack of the prestige function, considered to be one of the prime reasons for using noninformal borrowings.

CHAPTER 7

Themes

Chapter Outline

Our description of borrowings in informal American English should also include the presentation of their **thematic categories**. The lexicon of any language (or its parts) can be divided into such categories, called **lexical fields** (or **semantic fields**). These can be defined as groups, patterns, or frameworks of related words that cover or refer to an aspect of the world (McArthur 1992: 913), and have long been used in lexicography and language teaching. While devising a complete list of lexical fields is impossible, such categorization is very useful. This is because, as observed by Pearce (2007: 165), grouping expressions thematically "can provide an insight into what a linguistic community regards as socially and culturally important: a proliferation of terms within a particular field may suggest that it is of particular significance." But there is more: lexical fields are also linked with the concept of **overlexicalization**, "a proliferation of synonyms or quasi-synonyms for the same entity, concept or activity [. . .], often an indicator of concern with a particular area of meaning," with particular usage in informal language (Pearce 2007: 135). In this way, lexical fields offer valuable insight into what a given language community considers socially and culturally important.

In like manner, viewing borrowings through lexical fields is also important. As Katamba (2005: 140) put it, "the concentration of borrowed words in certain semantic fields reflects the nature of the contact between speech communities. It reflects the areas where new words had to be acquired in order to fill a perceived gap." Lexical fields of noninformal borrowings cover various themes: Haspelmath and Tadmoor (2009: 64) list twenty-four such fields common to borrowings in several languages, the most sizable being religion and belief, clothing and grooming, house, law, social and political relations, agriculture and vegetation, and food and drink.

Informal borrowings in American English can be categorized in a similar manner. However, the thematic distribution of lexical fields in such borrowings is radically different, which is largely due to the thematic specificity of informal expressions, especially slang. While their lexical fields include expressions for a wide variety of themes, certain themes are especially vast and abound in expressions. Accordingly, the lexical fields of informal borrowings can be divided into three main categories: **core fields** which are shared with general informal language, especially its slang component, **culture-specific fields** which are inherent to immigrant experiences, and **miscellaneous fields** which constitute an all-inclusive collection and demonstrate a vast thematic range of informal borrowings, well beyond the first two categories. Core fields include emotive categorization, the human body, human physiology, sex and sexuality, crime and violence, and intoxication by drugs and alcohol; culture-specific fields include immigrant minorities, minority experiences, racism, and white people as well as geography; miscellaneous fields include as many as 150 themes grouped under the following superordinate divisions: the body and its functions; people and society; sustenance and intoxication; articles and substances; money, commerce, and employment; behavior, attitudes, and emotions; thought and communication; arts, entertainment, and media; time and tide; location and movement; abstract qualities and states. All of these will be explored in the following pages.

7.1   Core

Some lexical fields are particularly common among borrowings in informal American English. These mirror the fields used in informal language in general, especially its slang component. As demonstrated by earlier studies (Eble 1996: 50 and Widawski 1997: ix), most slang lexicon has typically revolved around the following themes: the human body, physiology, sexuality, alcohol, drugs, and evaluative categorization, which all are social taboos in mainstream American culture. These can be called **core fields** since they are universally present in the slang of most languages, which may be caused by the fact that they all involve a human element and are close to our nature. Also, the pronounced synonymity and abundance of expressions within these fields imply that standard vocabulary is often insufficient or ineffective. All of these fields feature prominently in borrowings in informal American English and expressions representing these fields constitute over half of all informal borrowings found in our database, which is very telling in and of itself.

Emotive categorization is one of the most important lexical fields in informal language. This is because categorization is often linked with emotions, and verbalizing emotions is one of the most salient characteristics of informal lexicon, especially its slang subset (see Widawski [2015] 2019: 88). Additionally, the proliferation and pronounced synonymity of expressions within this field can again be explained by the abovementioned overlexicalization. This vast theme is also prominent in borrowings in informal American English – constituting a startling one-third of all expressions found in our database – and comprises expressions for all kinds of evaluative categorization: that of people, things, states, actions, and qualities. Interestingly, as evidenced by our database, it is often divided into two opposing groupings: either very positive or very negative expressions. Let us start with the subfield of negative categorization which constitutes some three-fourths of all expressions in this field, interestingly with an exceptionally sizable number of borrowings from Yiddish:

> *I never trusted Charlene, that **bruja** [= contemptible woman thought to have evil influence (Spanish)] (Scooby-Doo and the Monster of Mexico*, film, 2003)
>
> *You offer him a shot, and he turns into a **futz** [= stupid and despicable person, especially older (Yiddish)] (Quantum Leap*, NBC-TV series, 1990)
>
> *That idiot Cantor is a **momzer** [= despicable and untrustworthy person (Yiddish)] and a liar!* (Daily Kos, 2011)
>
> *You owe me $300, **puta** [= despicable woman (Spanish)] (Desperado*, film, 1995)

Some one-fifth of all such negative expressions refer to stupidity and usually take the form of epithets or qualifiers. Here is a representative sample:

> *"Yes" for the looks alone, "no" because he's a **dumb-bell** [= stupid person (German)]* (Celebitchy, 2013)
>
> *Some polls currently show that 63 percent of Americans think he's kind of a **klutz** [= stupid person (Yiddish)] (Chicago Tribune*, 1992)
>
> *I have nothing to prove to a **nitwit** [= stupid person (Dutch)] like you (Cycling Weekly*, 2016)
>
> *These **tontos** [= stupid people (Spanish)] have allowed the opposition to pit them against their only ally (OC Weekly*, 2014)

The other half of expressions within this field falls into the subcategory of positive categorization. These expressions refer to people, things, and qualities viewed as positive, with varying degrees of appreciation. Significantly, a great number of such borrowings come from Spanish. See the following selection of examples:

> ***Mija** [= woman you like (Spanish)], look at me! Nothing about you is pathetic (Grey's Anatomy*, ABC-TV series, 2013)

*I see as many **tushes** [= sexually attractive women (Yiddish)] hanging out here as I do in a more mixed neighborhood* (Yahoo Answers, 2011)

*Tell him I was **numero uno** [= the best person (Italian)] in sales last year* (*Chosen One*, film, 2010)

*We were always good friends. We had this good **simpatico** [= affability (Spanish)] between us* (*Last Play at Shea*, film, 2010)

Of all positive expressions, the vast majority refers to excellence, and there are a few dozen of synonyms for "excellent" found in our database:

*Dangelo promises to spend $14 million to repair the YMCA. Sounds **chido** [= excellent (Spanish)], right?* (*OC Weekly*, 2008)

*Frazier is **en fuego** [= excellent (Spanish)] indeed, so is the whole team. Go Gators!* (*Miami Herald*, 2014)

*Dude, you are sooo **ichiban** [= excellent (Japanese)]!* (Urban Dictionary, 2003)

*Your own response is **perfecto** [= excellent (Spanish)] for your particular case* (*Texas Monthly*, 2016)

The semantic field **human body** belongs to the so-called core themes because it is central to and characteristic of any slang in any language. This is linked with the human ability to experience the world via the senses and know the functions of our bodies. At the same time, as observed by Widawski ([2015] 2019: 84), social standards of propriety impose a different perception of this physical aspect: while common attitudes toward the body and its functions have become more tolerant in recent decades, this theme still constitutes a powerful sociocultural taboo. And taboo is a birthing ground for slang, which flourishes around themes considered socially unacceptable. It is thus no surprise that the body is also one of the largest semantic fields in informal borrowings, constituting over one-tenth of all expressions and representing borrowings from diverse donor languages. While this could be divided into various subfields, for the sake of this compact presentation let us distinguish here two main categories, the first one being body parts in general. See the following selection:

*We love to pump some maricon in his **culo** [= anus (Spanish)]* (Soda Head, 2009)

*He quickly undressed and showed her his **dingbat** [= penis (Dutch)]* (UCB student, 2013)

*He's been sitting on his **keister** [= buttocks (German)] all day* (Twitter, 2015)

*The shiners and injury to his **schnoz** [= nose (Yiddish)] were a result of a brutal hockey game with friends* (Washington Scene, 2012)

The other subfield consists of expressions associated with the peculiarities of the human body and its parts. Here is a handful of representative examples:

> *Ofelia the **Chichona** [= big-breasted woman (Spanish)] shows her juicy and tasty tits* (Amateur Album, 2014)
>
> *I might have ever so gently knocked my knee against his **kosher pickle** [= circumcised penis (Yiddish)]* (Huffington Post, 2011)
>
> *Ms. Johansson seemed slightly more **zaftig** [= curvaceous (Yiddish)] than I recalled from her many distinguished movie roles* (*Wall Street Journal*, 2015)
>
> *Who's the **zorro belly** [= someone who has an abdomen with post-operation scars (Spanish)]?* (Blogs, 2010)

A related category, **human physiology** (or **physiological functions**) is another core semantic field of informal borrowings. As remarked by Widawski ([2015] 2019: 85), this is understandable since the theme is almost entirely made up of references to what constitutes a cultural and social taboo in American culture. Informal language – especially its slang component – helps overcome this taboo by accepting these socially unsanctioned references. This field includes expressions for types of physiological processes, products, and related themes. Here are a few expressions linked with physiological processes:

> *The girl **ca-ca'ed** [= defecated (Spanish)] on his floor* (Tarheel Sack, 2006)
>
> *Nothing happened last night. She said she couldn't do it. **Rojo flow** [= menstruation (Spanish)], you know* (UNM student, 2014)
>
> *Do you **schvitz** [= sweat (Yiddish)] much during the summer?* (*Style at Home*, 2013)
>
> *My nephew **tossed his tacos** [= vomited (Spanish)] in a tennis ball can. Now that's talent!* (Date Hookup, 2010)

And here are some examples of other representative expressions within this semantic field, relating to products of physiological functions or otherwise connected to them:

> *You'll know them by their trail of **dreck** [= excrement (Yiddish)]* (Huffington Post, 2013)
>
> *She can't get impregnated by me if she rubs all my **mecos** [= semen (Spanish)] all over her panocha* (Soy Chicano, 2005)
>
> *He lifted his ass cheek and let a smelly **pedo** [= gas expelled from anus (Spanish)]* (UCB student, 2013)
>
> *He's been sitting on the **shittoir** [= toilet (French)] all morning* (UCLA student, 2014)

Another core lexical field includes **sex** and **sexuality**. This is another extensive theme in informal lexicon, possibly because sex is the most primal human activity and also because sex continues to be a powerful sociocultural taboo. Additionally, as observed by Chapman (1986: xxvi), the visible overlexicalization in this semantic field suggests that the standard vocabulary referring to sex is often either inadequate or overly scientific, and informal language comes in handy by providing various types of alternative, expressive vocabulary. This is also true about borrowing in informal American English. This field comprises expressions for a variety of things, people, states, and activities; some notable themes include sexual attractiveness, sexual orientation, and sex for profit. Here are a few samples related directly to sexual activity:

> *Try to find Trevor and have a **chowdown** [= oral sex (Chinese)] with him* (*Brooklyn Newspaper*, 2015)
>
> *A Cuban diplomat **jazzed** [= had sex with (Mandinka)] his wife* (Robert Olen Butler, 2015)
>
> *And for heaven's sake, I thought I told you to get some **nooky** [= sex (Dutch)] this week* (*National Review*, 2018)
>
> *Listen, stop kvetching and start **yentzing** [= having sex (Yiddish)]!* (Steve Stern, 2011)

And here is a selection of representative informal borrowings related to sexuality, broadly understood:

> *George Clooney is **en fuego** [= sexually attractive (Spanish)]!* (*News*, MTV-TV program, 2014)
>
> *How did he become a **lobo** [= male who frequents bars alone in the hope of finding a sexual companion (Spanish)]?* (*Be Careful*, film, 2011)
>
> *They told me that I would have to work as a **puta** [= prostitute (Spanish)]* (*New Yorker*, 2017)
>
> *I think you are **shtuppable** [= ready and willing to have sex (Yiddish)]. Look at this fucking love connection!* (OK Cupid, 2010)

Interestingly, one of the most visible subfields is sexual orientation, especially referring to homosexuality, which may be linked to the fact that it is still considered taboo in American culture. See the following expressions:

> *I don't know that many guys that see that show cause it's for **culeros** [= homosexual men (Spanish)]* (Anime Source, 2007)
>
> *That dirty **fagola** [= homosexual man (Yiddish)] is pushing the homo agenda* (Free Republic, 2012)

*I call her either a soft butch or a hard **femme** [= (in a homosexual relationship) the person who plays the passive, "feminine" role (French)]* (*Real L Word*, Showtime-TV series, 2010)

*Did you know your godson's a fucking **joto** [= homosexual man (Spanish)]?* (*La Mission*, film, 2009)

Crime and **violence**, considered here as a single entity, are also productive fields in informal American English, including informal borrowings. These are often connected with socioeconomic disadvantages suffered by minorities which, with upward mobility impossible, often resorted to crime. This vast theme includes expressions for various kinds and stages of crimes, the paraphernalia used to commit them, and types of criminals and their victims; some other notable themes feature law enforcement officials and undercover agents, as well as inmates and prison guards. Moreover, there are numerous expressions relating to physical violence, destruction, and killing. Here is a selection of expressions involving the criminal underworld:

*One of them I had known for a long time, he had been in the **clica** [= gang (Spanish)] with me* (David Montejano, 2010)

*Maxie relies upon the seductive charms of his **gun moll** [= female criminal or a criminal's female companion (Yiddish)] Ronnie* (*New York Times*, 2012)

*This cross-border thriller is populated with club owners and drug cartel **jefes** [= bosses of a drug cartel (Spanish)]* (*Los Angeles Review of Books*, 2013)

*I was introduced to some **traficantes** [= drug traffickers (Spanish)] although not much conversation took place* (Word Press, 2009)

And here is a handful of representative citational examples related to violence found in our database:

*I had a **chingaso** [= fight, especially a fistfight (Spanish)]. It means a fistfight here* (Twisting Nether Gazette, 2007)

*If you touch anything before I get it out, I'll **go jihad on your ass** [= to attack someone forcibly and mercilessly (Arabic)]* (Harry Hunsicker, 2007)

*The **slugfest** [= fistfight (German)] at the state fair was really a blessing* (*Simpsons*, Fox-TV series, 2000)

*Watch out, because Tracy will give you a **zetz** [= blow or punch (Yiddish)]* (*Examiner*, 2011)

Drugs and intoxication by drugs make up one of the largest lexical fields in informal lexicon (see Dalzell and Victor 2008). While illegal drugs share numerous characteristics ascribed to alcohol, they are more extreme, more addictive, and more closely associated with the criminal underworld. For these reasons, this field too is fertile ground for informal expressions. This huge theme is even more prominent among borrowings in informal American English, with an exceptionally sizable number of borrowings from Spanish. It includes various expressions for drugs in general, drug users and dealers, the effects of drug use, types of drugs, and their quality, quantity, and packaging. Again, this field may be split into several sub-fields, the first one being hard drugs:

> **Bazuko** [= *cocaine paste (Spanish)*] *is sold on the streets in small strawlike packages* (Patricia C. Marquez, 2001)
>
> *I had some* **hombrecitos** [= *hallucinogenic mushrooms (Spanish)*] *last night, man, I was tripping out* (Urban Dictionary, 2011)
>
> *She was addicted to* **schmeck** [= *heroin (Yiddish)*] (UCLA student, 2014)
>
> *He had not given up the* **tecata** [= *heroin (Spanish)*] (David Montejano, 2012)

The second subfield contains informal borrowings referring to soft drugs, predominantly marijuana:

> *Rastafarians are legally allowed to smoke* **ganja** [= *marijuana (Hindi)*] *for sacramental purposes* (*News*, ABC-TV program, 2021)
>
> *You smoke bud? I brought some* **hierba** [= *marijuana (Spanish)*] (*Blaze You Out*, film, 2013)
>
> *Do you want someone high on* **loco weed** [= *marijuana (Spanish)*] *baby sitting your kids?* (Free Republic, 2013)
>
> *"***Yesca** [= *marijuana (Spanish)*]?" "Bingo! I need to feel some reefer madness!"* (*Harsh Times*, film, 2005)

The third sizable subfield includes informal borrowings connected with drug users, addicts, or dealers. See the following:

> *Mexican* **burros** [= *Mexican smugglers of narcotics (Spanish)*] *smuggle drugs across the border* (Social Contract, 2014)
>
> *A* **dopehead** [= *illegal drug user (Dutch)*] *who OD'd? Sounds like someone the kids should emulate* (Philly Voice, 2019)
>
> *Monica doubted that such advances would ever benefit the* **tecatos** [= *heroin addicts (Spanish)*] *in northern New Mexico* (*Los Angeles Times*, 2012)
>
> *It's one* **wastoid** [= *alcohol or drug addict (Greek)*] *wasting another* (*Blue Bloods*, CBS-TV series, 2014)

A related category, **alcohol** and intoxication by alcohol, is usually considered one of the largest semantic fields in general informal lexicon and is also important in borrowings in informal American English. This can be explained in a few ways. Being drunk is socially taboo and may be punishable by law, yet at the same time it is something inherently human and encountered in all cultures. Informal language comes to one's aid. As noted by Chapman (1986: xxiv), its use is often a verbal attempt to convey our understanding and awareness of the condition. Another reason is the connection between the world of alcohol and the criminal underworld, itself a birthing ground for informal expressions, which was perhaps more visible in the past and highlighted during American Prohibition in the 1920s and early 1930s. This vast semantic field includes various expressions for alcohol, types of it, its quality, quantity, and packaging, as well as getting intoxicated. It can be conveniently split into three subfields, the first one being hard liquor:

> *Back in the day I used to drink **Adios Motherfuckers** [= strong, multi-liquor cocktails (Spanish)]* (Cafe Mom, 2011)
>
> *Hope you have a great b'day! I wish I could be there to drink **AMFs** [= strong, multi-liquor cocktails (Spanish)] with you!* (iPhoneogram, 2014)
>
> *Sheldon, what would it take for you to go into that liquor store and buy a bottle of **hooch** [= alcohol (Hoochinoo)]?* (Big Bang Theory, CBS-TV series, 2011)
>
> *You are willing to risk imprisonment for another bottle of **juke** [= liquor (Wolof)]?* (Narkive, 2005)

The other subfield is associated with lighter or less potent types of alcoholic beverages such as beer and wine. Consider the following selection of examples:

> *There's a cold **brewski** [= beer (Yiddish)] on the table. We must have just missed him* (CSI: Crime Scene Investigation, CBS-TV series, 2007)
>
> *This 4th of July be sure to have a cold **chela** [= beer (Spanish)] and some delicious food* (Cosmopolitan, 2014)
>
> *Throw in an extra $10 for a bottle of **dago red** [= cheap red wine, especially of Italian or Spanish origin (Spanish)]* (Los Angeles Times, 2008)
>
> *You'd be hard pressed to tell the difference between grand cru and **plonk** [= cheap and inferior wine (French)]* (Los Angeles Times, 2013)

Yet another sizable subfield contains borrowings associated with the psychological and physiological effects of consuming alcohol. See the following:

> *It is amazing to hear about the number of people who get **blitzed** [= drunk (German)] at office holiday parties* (New York Post, 2022)
>
> *He's too **borracho** [= drunk (Spanish)] to pray* (Under the Volcano, film, 1984)
>
> *He got so **plotzed** [= drunk (Yiddish)] that he urinated on himself* (Chicago Tribune, 1992)

*I thought Passover was the Jewish holiday to get **shickered** [= drunk (Yiddish)]
on Manischevitz (Harvard Crimson, 2009)*

Communication, an important lexical field, can be added to this listing
of core themes. It contains numerous expressions used in everyday communication but is also linked with **phatic function** (see Chapter 6) which
is used purely for social interaction, especially in starting communication,
continuing it, or gracefully ending it. Accordingly, this lexical field
includes several dozen semi-ritualistic expressions for greetings, attention-
grabbers, topic shifters, and farewells. Interestingly, many of these are
modified and playful. Consider the following examples:

Hola *[= hello (Spanish)], chicas! Elyse, good to see you again (American Pie
Presents: Band Camp, film, 2005)*

Oye *[= listen (Spanish)] mijo, did you see that game yesterday? (Sports, NBC-
TV program, 2015)*

*"Suzie, that boy is no good for you." "**Pero like** [= however (Spanish)], he's
super-hot" (Miami Herald, 2014)*

*I've got something to say: **sayonara** [= goodbye (Japanese)]! (Punisher, film,
1989)*

Another subfield contains expressions referring to understanding as well
as language manipulation or deception. Consider the following selection of
examples:

*Don't talk about the divorce unless they ask, **comprendo** [= do you understand
(Spanish)]? (Dexter, Showtime-TV series, 2006)*

*She'll be streetwise to the lies and the **jive talk** [= deceptive or misleading talk
(Wolof)] (Sliding Doors, film, 1998)*

*She bought my entire **spiel** [= persuasive or eloquent talk (Yiddish)]! (Gypsies,
Tramps and Thieves, film, 2006)*

*I know what kind of person he is, do you **savvy** [= understand (Spanish)]?*
(*News*, KWQC-TV program, 2016)

7.2   Culture-Specific

Semantic fields of borrowings in informal American English can also refer
to less universal themes. To paraphrase the American linguist Eble (1996:
51), informal lexicon of a group proliferates around topics of importance to
that group. While – as demonstrated above – most of the lexical fields of
borrowings in informal American English are virtually identical to those
found in general informal American English, there are certain themes that

exclusively refer to minorities and immigrants, their lifestyles and experiences. Put differently, these are the themes that reflect reality as experienced and seen from their perspective. Our database shows that such **culture-specific themes** include expressions connected with minorities and their experiences, but also racism, white people, linguistic diversity, and geography.

Minorities constitute a vast semantic field among borrowings in informal American English. There are numerous expressions for minorities in general, stereotypes relating to them, their body types with reference to skin color, and other features which are inherently connected with them or set them apart from the dominant white society. Interestingly, most of these borrowings come from Spanish. Here is a selection of expressions from this vast field:

> Some **chicanas** [= Mexican or Mexican American women (Spanish)] can pull off being blonde and look good, and others look terrible with blonde hair (Soy Chicano, 2005)
>
> All **eses** [= fellow Mexican male (Spanish)] from L.A. feel the same (YouTube, 2012)
>
> That's one messed-up **Polack** [= Pole or a person of Polish descent (Polish)], my brother (Veronica Mars, UPN-TV series, 2004)
>
> You're a thief, like that **Yid** [= Jew (Yiddish)], what's-his-name? (King of the Hill, Fox-TV series, 1993)

There are also finer divisions: borrowings within this semantic field may be more specific and may refer to specific subgroups within a larger group. Consider the following examples:

> I schooled some **chunts** [= Mexican nationals, especially if poor (Spanish)] in soccer today (Twitter, 2012)
>
> She sat down to pen her family's story in "Confessions of a **Jewish Shiksa** [= Jewish woman who is not Orthodox, pious, or observant (Yiddish)]" (Miami New Times, 2011)
>
> These **Mexiricans** [= persons of Mexican and Puerto Rican descent (Spanish)] are sucking up all the free health care (Red Tape, 2009)

A related category, **minority experience** is another significant semantic field in borrowings in informal American English. Expressions belonging to this field often provide labels for concepts and experiences that are particular to a minority or immigrant culture and lifestyle. Here especially, one will find expressions which, to paraphrase Pearce (2007: 165), grouped together can provide an insight into what the minorities regard as socially and culturally important. Naturally, this is a large field, including expressions for various people, things, actions, and qualities. One ever-present theme within this semantic field is immigration. Consider the following:

> *Thousands of **pollos** [= immigrants smuggled from Mexico to the USA (Spanish)] are out there and headed north (Tucson Weekly, 2004)*
>
> *You should call **la migra** [= the US Immigration and Naturalization Service (Spanish)], man. That bitch ain't legal (Southland, NBC-TV series, 2010)*
>
> *There are more Norwegians in the US than Norway, and **Tijuaneros** [= immigrants from Tijuana (Spanish)] in S.D. So what! (Twitter, 2014)*
>
> *Some of the Mexican American merchants have called him a **vendido** [= Mexican American who emulates behavior or values of the non-Hispanic majority (Spanish)] (Los Angeles Times, 2010)*

Racism (or **racial discrimination**) is another visible subfield discerned in borrowings in informal American English (see Dalzell 2010). Unfortunately, part of the experience of minorities, especially Latin Americans, continues to be connected with instances of racism, still present in American life. This fact is strongly reflected in informal lexicon – especially its slang subset – which tends to provide a verbal mirror of prevailing social conditions. Consider the following citational corroboration:

> *People could arrive on "**Chicano time** [= lack of punctuality (Spanish)]" (Tamis Hoover Renteria, 2013)*
>
> *She's a **gringa** [= white female from an English-speaking country (Spanish)] from California (Beverly Hills Chihuahua, film, 2008)*
>
> *The **mojados** [= illegal immigrants to the USA from Mexico (Spanish)] risked exposure by consenting to be filmed (New York Times, 2005)*
>
> *This show needs some girl dancing like a **shvartser** [= black-skinned person (Yiddish)] (Boardwalk Empire, HBO-TV series, 2011)*

Yet another notable lexical subfield involves expressions for **white people**. Much like with negative categorization, many of these are negative, with varying degrees of offensiveness. This is not surprising: the abundance of these terms suggests the strong emotional attitudes of minorities, reflecting their historically conditioned mistrust of white people and disappointment with the insufficient measures to combat discrimination (Kowalczyk 2010: 91). Here are a few representative expressions:

> *Working for **Anglos** [= white people who speak English (Spanish)] now posed no problems (Spanglish, film, 2004)*

*Hey **blanco** [= white man (Spanish)], I am a Florida native, born in Fort Meyers (Naples News, 2008)*

*Don't be getting mad at me because that **chica blanca** [= white woman, especially young one (Spanish)] turned you down (Bring It On: All or Nothing, film, 2006)*

*Things are pretty good for them in **Gringoland** [= English-speaking country, especially the USA (Spanish)] (New York Times, 2014)*

While **linguistic diversity** can be listed under the core theme of **communication** (see Section 7.1), it is presented here because it is closely connected with culture-specific themes. Informal borrowings provide numerous expressions for various languages, their variants, and language in general. Here is a selection of representative citational corroboration:

*Kids laughed the way I spoke **Americano** [= American English (Spanish)] (Samuelin Martínez, 2013)*

*I see, young man, that you speak **Kraut** [= the German language (German)] (Berkeleyside, 2014)*

*You had better get your translator ready if you don't speak the **lingo** [= foreign language (Portuguese)] (Yahoo Sports, 2018)*

*We don't speak the **parley-voo** [= the French language (French)] around here (Macleans, 2009)*

Interestingly, this field also includes several metalinguistic expressions for mixed or hybrid languages, slang, and related linguistic phenomena. The expressions from this field attest to the awareness of sociolinguistic variation of their users who often come from immigrant and ethnic minority backgrounds where such variation is the norm. See the following examples:

*The songs are written about Pachucos in **calo** [= Chicano street slang, especially with a heavy use of rhyming (Spanish)] (Arizona Daily Star, 2015)*

*You hear Stallworth straining to speak "**jive**" [= slang, especially African American slang of jazz musicians (Wolof)] while talking to his love interest (New Yorker, 2018)*

*No wonder kids rebel and take pot. In case you don't understand the **lingo** [= strange or unintelligible language of a particular group of people, esp. slang, jargon, or dialect vocabulary (Portuguese)], that's marijuana (USA Today, 2018)*

***Yinglish** [= variety of English that contains many Yiddish expressions, often modified (Yiddish)] is the marriage of Yiddish and English (Atlantic Monthly, 2014)*

Last but not least, there is **geography** (or **topography**), yet another culture-specific semantic field. As evidenced by Widawski and Kowalczyk (2011), geographical expressions – called **placenames** (and often loosely labeled **toponyms**) – constitute a significant yet undervalued part of informal lexicon. They are semantically rich and culturally meaningful, telegraphically describing the characteristics of places to which they refer, explaining the motivations of their coiners, and revealing the attitudes of their users. These expressions are also very popular in informal borrowings in American English where they function in a unique way, reflecting life from minority perspectives. This field includes expressions for various cities and parts of them, or geographical regions and districts. Here is a handful of examples referring to cities:

> *I live near El Paso, TX, which some people used to call* **Burrito City** *[= El Paso, Texas (Spanish)]* (Gaia Online, 2008)

> *Chula Vista is jokingly dubbed "***Chulajuana** *[= border town Chula Vista, California (Spanish)]," because it is becoming a de facto suburb of Tijuana* (Los Angeles Times, 1997)

> *I catch the bus every morning in* **Taco Town** *[= San Jose, California (Spanish)]* (First Nations, 2007)

> *How long is the travel from* **Tia Juana** *[= Tijuana, Mexico (Spanish)] to Palmdale?* (Road Route Map, 2014)

And here is a selection of representative borrowings referring to places and areas:

> *We had long since moved uptown to Riverside Drive,* **Allrightniks Row** *[= Manhattan's Riverside Drive, where many rich and successful Jewish immigrants live (Yiddish)]* (Erica Jong, 1997)

> *The tourist business there has suffered with the demise of the* **Borscht Belt** *[= the region in and near the Catskill Mountains north of New York City where many predominantly Jewish resort hotels once were found (Yiddish)]* (Ladykillers, film, 2004)

> *I went to school in* **Kosher Canyon** *[= neighborhood dominated by Jewish people (Yiddish)], and I love the stuff!* (Yelp, 2006)

> *Some major changes are coming to* **Loisaida** *[= the Lower East Side of New York's Manhattan (Spanish)]* (East Village, 2009)

7.3   Miscellaneous

Although most informal borrowings – especially the slang component – could be comprised within a few lexical fields such as those presented above, this is by no means an exhaustive list. In fact, informal expressions can serve as alternative synonyms for thousands of standard expressions (or stand for concepts for which there are no standard expressions yet) on various topics from nearly all spheres of life and can be categorized into diverse lexical fields which are collectively labeled here as **miscellaneous**. For instance, *The Oxford Dictionary of Slang* (Ayto 1998) lists over 170 lexical fields, while the even more extensive *NTC's Thematic Dictionary of American Slang* (Spears 1998) lists as many as 1,100 of them. The same can be said about borrowings in informal American English which can also function in the same way. Below is a catalog of such themes. It is partly based on Ayto's categorization (1998: iii– iv), with a sample of expressions representative of each field followed by citational evidence. Naturally, as the name "miscellaneous" suggests, this is more of a grab-all lexical field. However, its diversity and size are quite telling in themselves and amply illustrate the thematic scope of informal borrowings.

The body and its functions includes expressions for the body and its parts (*shnozz*), nakedness (*au naturel*), physique (*zaftig*), vision (*look-see*), smell (*el stinko*), bodily functions (*shvitz*), tiredness (*ausgespielt*), and illness (*touristas*). See the following:

> *We have to go and have a **look-see** [= look or inspection (Chinese)] (Rambo,* film, 2008)
>
> *The makeup didn't slide off my face when I **schvitzed** [= sweated (Yiddish)]* (*Elle Magazine*, 2018)
>
> *Now that I am getting sick, any magic remedies for a bit of **touristas** [= diarrhea, especially as contracted in a foreign country (Spanish)]?* (Trip Advisor, 2009)
>
> *Sometimes I would ask her if I looked big, and she would tell me I was looking a little **zaftig** [= curvaceous (Yiddish)]* (*Time*, 2014)

People and society is a vast semantic field that encompasses such themes as ethnic groups (*negrito*), national groups (*chuntaro*), people in general (*tipo*), children (*boychik*), relations (*vieja*), groups (*compania*), status (*chingaso*), social categories (*bourgie*), conventionality (*housefrau*), friends (*amiga*), sex (*shtup*), sexual orientation (*maricon*), prostitution (*kurveh*), crime (*norteños*), killing (*liquidate*), punishing (*potch*), police (*jura*), prison (*caboose*), politics (*politico*), the military (*semper fi*), and religion (*padre*). Consider these examples:

> *Those white **bourgies** [= upper-middle-class person (French)] cannot appreciate it* (*New York Press*, 2010)
>
> *He had brought his **compaña** [= group of friends (Spanish)] down to help* (Diane Whiteside, 2008)
>
> *Your grandmother Salome, if the truth be known, was something of a wild one, a **kurveh** [= prostitute (Yiddish)]* (Erica Jong, 1997)
>
> *Police said the suspects are members of the **Norteños** [= Mexican mafia from Northern California (Spanish)]* (*Los Angeles Times*, 2014)

Sustenance and intoxication contains such informal borrowings as those involving foodstuffs (*gringa taco*), eating (*ess and fress*), drinking (*drinkfest*), alcohol (*hooch*), tobacco (*frajo*), drugs (*yesca*). Here is a relevant sample:

> ***Ess and fress*** *[=eat, especially heartily, quickly or noisily (Yiddish)]! The all-you-can-eat buffet could very well be kosher* (*Village Voice*, 2008)
>
> *We played handball in the yard and bet **frajos** [= cigarettes (Spanish)], soap, and I would always win* (*Los Angeles Times*, 2011)
>
> *The Sheriff's here. Hide the **hooch** [= low-quality alcohol, especially if illegally produced (Hoochinoo)]!* (*Boardwalk Empire*, HBO-TV series, 2010)
>
> *On this day, the world's counterculture gather and pay a hazy homage to **yesca** [= marijuana (Spanish)]* (*OC Weekly*, 2011)

Articles and substances lists expressions for things (*dingus*), clothing (*schmatte*), accessories (*tchotchke*), tools (*filero*), containers (*keister stash*), weapons (*shiv*), dirt (*schmutz*), and cleanliness (*neatnik*). See the following:

> *So this little **dingus** [= anything one cannot name specifically (Dutch)] here is manufactured by Madrigal Electromotive?* (*Breaking Bad*, AMC-TV series, 2011)
>
> *It's just the **schmatte** [= shabby or unstylish garment (Yiddish)] I wear around the house* (*Californication*, Showtime-TV series, 2007)
>
> *You got some **schmutz** [= dirt (Yiddish)] on your cheek. My mistake, it's a mole* (*Frasier*, NBC-TV series, 1993)
>
> *Ricky also showed off his collection of **tchotchkes** [= playthings or trinkets (Yiddish)]* (Huffington Post, 2012)

Money, commerce, and employment includes expressions for money (*mucho dinero*), bribery (*schmear*), work (*fink*), business (*head honcho*), and dismissal (*get lost*). Let us present the following citational evidence:

> *Strikes had a tendency to degenerate into violence, with threats and assaults used against the "scabs" and "**finks**" [= strikebreakers (German)] who would replace striking workers* (*National Review*, 2012)
>
> *The new **head honcho** [= important person, especially a chief (Japanese)] will be tasked with rejuvenating the program* (*Des Moines Register*, 2015)
>
> *First of all, I'm Jim Carrey. You know what that means. **Mucho dinero** [= a lot of money (Spanish)], big bucks* (*Larry King Live*, CNN-TV program, 2018)
>
> *It's impossible to tell if that torrent of cash was an attempt to **schmear** [= bribe (Yiddish)] wavering Democrats* (Free Republic, 2008)

Behavior, attitudes, and emotions, one of the largest semantic fields, encompasses expressions for wanting (*porfa*), getting (*corral*), indifference (*not give a carajo*), excellence (*hondo*), beauty (*chula*), ugliness (*lobo*), unpleasantness (*nudgy*), bad quality (*schlock*), contemptibleness (*farkakte*), ineffectualness (*nebbish*), sentimentality (*schmaltz*), fairness (*mensch*), pleasure (*naches*), amusement (*tummel*), gratitude (*domo arigato*), hopelessness (*tough shitski*), confusion (*schnook*), trouble (*pedo*), excitement (*wow*), enthusiasm (*gung-ho*), effort (*blitz*), surprise (*chinga*), boredom (*blah*), composure (*shtarker*), anger (*mierda*), quarrel (*mano a mano*), violence (*bato loco*), nervousness (*shpilkes*), fear (*gevalt*), courage (*cojones*), cowardice (*culero*), boastfulness (*macher*), rudeness (*schlub*), contempt (*go to el carajo*), meanness (*chulo*), honesty (*mensch*), dishonesty (*ganef*), sincerity (*for real*), insincerity (*tokus licker*), lying (*fonfer*), deception (*jive*), cheating (*shtup*), betrayal (*dedo*), slyness (*juke*), secrecy (*omerta*), energy (*tummel*), and laziness (*huevon*). See the following:

> *"You're looking fine as fuck, **chula** [= attractive woman (Spanish)]!" "Don't touch me, please!"* (*Harsh Times*, film, 2005)
>
> *"You're gracious and kind. **Domo arigato** [= thank you very much (Japanese)]!" "You're welcome"* (*Mentalist*, CBS-TV series, 2013)
>
> *Why be a **huevón** [= lazy person, especially if also stupid (Spanish)] and not get to work?* (*OC Weekly*, 2012)
>
> *Would you save me the **schpilkes** [= nervousness or anxiety (Yiddish)] and stay retired for crying out loud?* (*You Don't Know Jack*, film, 2010)

Thought and communication is yet another field including such themes as belief (*kineahora*), disbelief (*no way Jose*), understanding (*capeesh*), knowledge (*savvy*), ignorance (*klutz*), skill (*dealmeister*), insanity (*meshugas*), foolishness (*dumb*), gullibility (*yold*), education (*phudnik*), communication (*shmooze*), greetings (*hola*), farewells (*sayonara*), complaining (*kvetch*), criticism (*flak*), assent (*si*), refusal (*nyet*), nonsense (*bushwa*), cursing (*puta madre*), and names (*Juanita*). Consider these citations:

> *The script has been whittled almost clean of expository dialogue and touchy-feely **bushwa** [= nonsense (French)]* (*New York Times*, 2015)
>
> *"Take him down, Teddy!" "**Nyet** [= no (Russian)]! No more!"* (*Rounders*, film, 1998)
>
> *You have some nerve to show here to **schmooze** [= converse idly or gossip (Yiddish)] with the tenure committee* (*Big Bang Theory*, CBS-TV series, 2013)
>
> *"Do you know the plan?" "**Si** [= yes (Spanish)], got it"* (*Employee of the Month*, film, 2006)

Arts, entertainment, and media comprises such themes as entertainment (*spaghetti western*), journalism (*spinmeister*), music (*krautrock*), dance (*juke*), sport (*bagel*), and gambling (*desperado*). Here is a representative selection of citations:

> *She beat Sharapova in the Olympics with a **bagel** [= tennis set won 6–0 (Yiddish)]* (Huffington Post, 2012)
>
> *You look more like a **desperado** [= degenerate gambler (Spanish)] than a fancy gambler* (Catherine Coulter, 2002)
>
> *As is his habit, he **juked** [= danced in a boisterous fashion (Wolof)] to the music, gesturing extravagantly* (South Florida Sun-Sentinel, 2012)
>
> *I was in that **spaghetti western** [= cowboy film made in Europe by Italian directors (Italian)], too* (Loss of Sexual Innocence, film, 2000)

Time and tide includes expressions for time (*bagel shift*), beginning (*from the get-go*), ending (*finito*), stopping (*enough already*), experience (*kishkes*), inexperience (*pisher*), stylishness (*plush*), and old (*alter kaker*). Consider this corroboration:

> *What makes you think a group of **alter kakers** [= old men, especially despicable ones] is gonna support a man who hasn't clipped his first nose hair yet?* (Distinguished Gentleman, film, 1992)
>
> *There's the ten-cylinder one, the twelve-cylinder one, and **finito** [= it is the end (Italian)]* (Jalopnik, 2014)
>
> *When I was considered for the board, I was affectionately referred to as "the **pisher** [= young inexperienced person (Yiddish)]," which means somebody who pees in his pants!* (Billboard Magazine, 1999)
>
> *How would you like to go back to my **plush** [= luxurious, stylish, and thus expensive (French)] suite at the Palace Hotel?* (Will & Grace, NBC-TV series, 2003)

Location and movement, yet another lexical field, encompasses expressions for places (*Tia Juana*), habitation (*borsht belt*), territory (*barrio*), remoteness (*boondocks*), movement (*shlep*), falling (*pull an el foldo*), speed (*chop chop*), arrival (*tsunami*), departure (*vam*), transportation (*shlep*), and vehicles (*ranfla*). Here is a representative sample:

> *The businesses in the **barrio** [= neighborhood (Spanish)] are trying to gentrify the neighborhood* (Arizona Republic, 2015)
>
> *I want them now. **Chop chop** [= quickly or instantly (Chinese)]!* (National Public Radio, 2014)
>
> *It was stunning when he **pulled an el foldo** [= collapsed (Spanish)]* (New York Daily News, 2015)
>
> *We're all standing in the middle of this digital **tsunami** [= arrival or occurrence of something in overwhelming amount (Japanese)] that's washing across the journalism landscape* (Ad Week, 2010)

Finally, **abstract qualities and states**, another vast lexical field, includes such themes as size (*jumbo*), quantity (*skosh*), fate (*mazel tov*), probability (*you should be so lucky*), certainty (*cinch*), risk (*bravo*), easiness (*no problemo*), difficulty (*megilah*), precision (*exacto*), approximation (*bissel*), correctness (*correctamundo*), mistakes (*fox paw*), success (*allrightnik*), ruination (*futz up*), failure (*desmadre*), defeat (*blitz*), victory (*schneider*), power (*shtarker*), influence (*mojo*), organization (*mafia*), subservience (*Tio Tomas*), genuineness (*kosher*), triviality (*bupkes*), insignificance (*pisher*), suitability (*arriba*), strangeness (*bizarro*), severity (*flak*), involvement (*macher*), abandonment (*vamoose*), and avoidance (*kineahora*). See the following:

> The Jackets **blitzed** [= defeated soundly (German)] them 7–1 (*St. Louis Today*, 2015)
>
> "So you're saying you're gonna get them occupied a couple of times a week?" "**Correctamundo** [= that is correct (Spanish)]!" (*Orange Is the New Black*, Netflix-TV series, 2016)
>
> As World Cup qualifying progressed, things deteriorated to the point that they became a total **desmadre** [= failure or disaster (Spanish)] (*News*, Fox-TV program, 2014)
>
> My dad will be 96 next month, **kineahora** [= let nothing bad happen, God forbid (Yiddish)], and the other day I asked him if he had any memories of FDR (*New Jersey Jewish News*, 2015)

Chapter Summary

In terms of themes, borrowings in informal American English can be divided into three main thematic types: core, culture-specific, and miscellaneous. The **core themes**, shared with those in general informal language, make up the majority of borrowings and include evaluative categorization, the human body, human physiology, sex and sexuality, crime and violence, and intoxication by drugs and alcohol. Most of these are social taboos in mainstream American culture and are virtually identical to those found in general informal American English, especially its slang component. The **culture-specific themes**, inherent to immigrants and minorities, include borrowings connected with minority experiences but also racial discrimination, white people, and geography viewed from their perspective. Especially frequent are borrowings involving minority lifestyles and experiences, but geographic expressions are also prominent. The **miscellaneous themes**, constituting an all-inclusive collection, include as many as 150 themes grouped under the following superordinate divisions: the body and its functions; people and society; sustenance and intoxication; articles and substances; money, commerce, and employment; behavior, attitudes, and emotions; thought and communication; arts, entertainment, and media; time and tide; location and movement; abstract qualities and states. This diversity and size are very telling in themselves, illustrating the thematic scope of informal borrowings and demonstrating that they are not a marginal part of lexicon, limited to only a few themes, but can be used to refer to virtually any aspect of human experience and the external world.

Conclusions

The **aim** of this book has been to provide a linguistic description of borrowings in informal American English and to serve as a practical resource documenting this type of language. These foreign-origin expressions, comprising both slang and colloquialism, constitute a vibrant sociolinguistic phenomenon resulting from language contact, and function as an important yet rarely discussed lexical contribution to American English. Their significance stems from the sociolinguistic significance of informal language in the United States, the strong presence of borrowings in American speech reflecting the immigrant nature of the country and the growing role of ethnic minorities, as well as the increasingly common use of this type of lexicon among larger segments of American society.

Drawing from the **methodological framework** of documentary linguistics and sociolinguistics, the description is based on lexical material from a large database of contextual citations extracted from diverse contemporary American sources to ensure the authenticity and representativeness of the material. The description is also multifaceted and aimed at showing informal borrowings from various perspectives, involving terms, donors, types, changes, functions, and themes of informal borrowings. It is amply supported throughout the text and in the Glossary with usage examples that illustrate particular linguistic patterns, show the sociocultural context in which they are used, and attest to the very existence of these expressions. The concluding assertions made in this book can be summed up as follows.

In terms of **terminology**, informal borrowings are defined as expressions taken from a foreign language and used in informal American English. They conform to the traditional typology of borrowings and include such main types as loanwords, loan translations, and semantic loans, but there are other finer distinctions, such as loanblends or foreignisms, much as there are certain terms often confused with borrowings, such as code switches or nonce borrowings. Informal language, in turn, refers to a type of vocabulary that is stylistically "lower" than the standard language and "below" the formal and neutral registers on the formality scale. It includes two subsets: colloquialism, which is composed of moderately informal and casual expressions, and slang, which is composed of highly informal and unconventional expressions, perceived as very expressive, deliberately undignified, and strongly linked with a sociocultural context. Again, there are several similar terms to account for this type of lexicon, such as nonstandard, jargon, or neologism, but their semantic scopes are different.

In terms of **donors**, borrowings in informal American English come from various languages. Unsurprisingly, Spanish has contributed the most expressions, accounting for almost half of the entire database; nearly all come from Mexican Spanish, with a handful of expressions borrowed from Puerto Rican and Cuban varieties. Borrowings from Yiddish are the second most frequent group, constituting one-third of the entire database; within these, Germanic Yiddishisms are most frequent, followed by Hebraic and Slavic ones. Other key language donors to informal American English are German, Italian, and French, followed by Japanese, Chinese, and Dutch. Lesser donors – languages that have contributed considerably fewer borrowings – include Slavic languages, Russian and Polish, followed by Arabic and two African languages, Wolof and Mandinka. Surprisingly, contributions from other languages – such as Hindi, Korean, Portuguese, Tagalog, or Vietnamese – feature in numbers that seem marginal given the sizable number of speakers of these languages in the United States; also surprising is the lack of any borrowings from such languages as Norwegian or Armenian, once spoken by large diasporas in the country. Interestingly, some expressions are a result of borrowing from not just one but two donor languages, typically involving Yiddish plus another language; other borrowings have a shared origin, as in the case of several expressions from German and Yiddish; still others are the result of pseudo-borrowing, a playful imitation of a foreign language specifically for a humorous effect. In general, findings corroborate the common perception that the top contributor of borrowings in informal American is Spanish, but they also reveal that the second position unquestionably goes to Yiddish, whose impact on informal American English is pronounced.

In terms of **types**, borrowings in informal American English can be classified according to a few main criteria. As for typology by borrowed material, one can distinguish loanwords (or borrowings proper), which are the most frequent in the database, followed by loanblends and loan translations, with semantic loans having a marginal occurrence; while, understandably, most loanwords come from Spanish, loanblends come largely from German, Dutch, and Yiddish, while loan translations come from Chinese and Yiddish. As for typology by part of speech, the majority of expressions are nouns, followed by adjectives and verbs, which is consistent with the part-of-speech distribution patterns found in noninformal borrowings; however, exclamations are surprisingly frequent while phrases, adverbs, affixes, pronouns, and prepositions feature in scant numbers. As for typology by assimilation, one can distinguish partially assimilated borrowings, which are most frequent, followed *ex aequo* by fully assimilated and unassimilated expressions; all of these types come from a variety of languages without any particular one constituting a majority. As for typology by modification, unmodified borrowings are the most frequent in the database, followed by partly modified and highly modified ones; again, all of these types come from various languages without any particular one standing out. As for typology by frequency, one can distinguish frequently used borrowings and restricted borrowings, followed by passive borrowings; expressions from Dutch and German feature prominently in the first group, those from Yiddish and Spanish in the second, without any particular language dominating the third. As for typology by register, most borrowings in informal American English are slang, the rest being colloquialisms; aside from Spanish and Yiddish, there are no other distinctive donor languages among those two types. Finally, as for typology by impact, non-vulgar borrowings constitute the majority of all expressions, with vulgar and potentially vulgar ones featuring in marginal numbers; a similar correlation is to be found among non-offensive, offensive, and potentially offensive expressions.

In terms of **changes**, borrowings in informal American English are often subject to various modifications. Phonological changes involve the modification of their pronunciation to conform to the phonological rules of American English; various changes can be observed in the original vowels, diphthongs, consonants, or accentuation, but particularly recurring is the change of /ñ/ into /n/ in borrowings from Spanish as well as that of /o/ into /ou/. Orthographical changes involve modification of the spelling of borrowed expressions; again, two notable instances are the Spanish acute accent over vowels resulting in /á, é, í, ó, ú/ and the tilde in /ñ/ which are often left out in spelling; the most startling changes concern borrowings from nonalphabetic languages like Chinese, Japanese, Korean, and Hindi, but also Dutch, Portuguese, and Irish Gaelic; finally, variation in the spelling of informal borrowings sometimes reflects regional differences in their donor languages, which is especially visible in the case of Yiddish. Morphological changes involve modification in the form of informal borrowings by means of adding or removing lexical material via standard wordbuilding processes: lengthening, which includes compounding, affixation, and phraseology; shortening, which includes clipping and initialisms (with acronyms notably absent); and other wordbuilding processes such as blending or corruption. Semantic changes involve modification in the meaning of informal borrowings by means of the processes of figuration and accompanying semantic shifting. Figuration, which accounts for one-third of all expressions, involves metaphor, metonymy, and several other processes; notable is the use of allusion, specific to immigrant culture and experience. Semantic shifting is extensive as well and involves generalization, specialization, melioration, and pejoration. Grammatical changes involve modification or conversion in the part of speech of informal borrowings; adjectivization and verbification are most common, with nominalization and a few other processes being rare; such grammatical conversion usually attests to a high degree of assimilation of borrowed expressions. Finally, register or stylistic changes involve modification (or lack thereof) in the original register of informal borrowings which may shift their stylistic status in American English; while most informal borrowings exhibit no such change and retain their informal status in American English, some reveal two notable patterns: from neutral to informal and, in rare cases, from formal to informal.

In terms of **functions**, borrowings in informal American English are used for several reasons. In the referential function, they are used to name things, essentially providing alternative synonyms for things already named in English (synonymous diversification) but also providing names for things yet to be named (neological enrichment). More often, however, informal borrowings are used instead of standard English to communicate additional information that is social, psychological, rhetorical, or cultural in nature. The social function involves group solidarity, social distancing, and rebellion; such use of informal borrowings serves especially the purpose of identifying members of immigrant and minority groups. Equally important is the psychological function, which includes the expression of emotions, humor, and toughness; surely, the most prominent usage concerns emotions: informal borrowings provide an extensive repertoire of expressions for a variety of emotional states and actions as well as emotive labels for people or things. The rhetorical function includes informality, conciseness, forcefulness, wordplay, and small talk; informality is obviously the most salient characteristic in that the use of informal borrowings always lowers the formality of communication. Finally, the cultural function involves expressing cultural identity, cultural crossing, and cultural stylization; while expressing cultural identity is the quintessential reason for using such expressions, cultural crossing and stylization are other notable phenomena accounting for the increasingly common use of this type of lexicon among larger segments of American society, regardless of their ethnic origin or mother tongue. Particularly interesting in the use of informal borrowings is the lack of the prestige function, considered to be one of the prime reasons for using noninformal borrowings.

In terms of **themes**, borrowings in informal American English can be divided into three main thematic types: core, culture-specific, and miscellaneous. The core themes, shared with those in general informal language, make up the majority of borrowings and include evaluative categorization, the human body, human physiology, sex and sexuality, crime and violence, and intoxication by drugs and alcohol. Most of these are social taboos in mainstream American culture and are virtually identical to those found in general informal American English, especially its slang component. The culture-specific themes, inherent to immigrants and minorities, include borrowings connected with minority experiences but also racial discrimination, white people, and geography viewed from their perspective. Especially frequent are borrowings involving minority lifestyles and experiences, but geographic expressions are also prominent. The miscellaneous themes, constituting an all-inclusive collection, include as many as 150 themes grouped under the following superordinate divisions: the body and its functions; people and society; sustenance and intoxication; articles and substances; money, commerce, and employment; behavior, attitudes, and emotions; thought and communication; arts, entertainment, and media; time and tide; location and movement; abstract qualities and states. This diversity and size are very telling in themselves, illustrating the thematic scope of informal borrowings and demonstrating that they are not a marginal part of lexicon, limited to only a few themes, but can be used to refer to virtually any aspect of human experience and the external world.

An important part of the book is the **Glossary**, forming over half of the entire text. Aside from serving as a quick and practical reference, its main purpose is to document and define the whole collection of borrowings in informal American English – many of which have been featured as illustrations in the main text of this book – with additional meanings and examples. Much like the entire book, it is based on a large database of citations reflecting the language used in natural contexts and collected from diverse contemporary US sources, notably those associated with immigrant groups and ethnic minorities, the prime users of informal borrowings. However, a much greater bulk of citations comes from more general or universal American sources, unrelated to immigrants and ethnic minorities. This demonstrates that informal borrowings are no longer limited in their use to the speech of these groups but have grown increasingly common among larger social segments, thus exerting a marked impact on American English in general. The Glossary lists almost 1,500 entries, each containing grammatical identification, usage labels, a definition in standard English, a quick bibliographical reference, three contextual examples with clearly identified sources and dates, as well as dating and etymological information. Usage examples are a particularly important part of the Glossary as they support the definitions, show the social, cultural, and ethnic context in which informal borrowings are used, attest to the very existence of these expressions, and contribute to a better understanding of both informal lexicon and borrowing. Because of its large size and in-depth description, the Glossary can easily stand as a dictionary in its own right.

A few final words. The aim of the book has been to document and describe borrowings in informal American English, but the scholarly and educational implications arising from this work go beyond the subject matter. For one thing, these expressions are an important lexical contribution to borrowing and informal language, and this multifaceted presentation reflects linguistic patterns applicable to both, thus increasing our understanding of these two phenomena in and of themselves. Moreover, the sociolinguistic observations made in this book are likely to enhance awareness and appreciation of linguistic diversity, something that one might call "sociolinguistic competence" and consider important, especially in the context of teaching English as a foreign language. Finally, this book has been meant to raise to the level of academic discussion a subject which so far has remained largely unresearched but continues to be linguistically and culturally significant, deserving attention and appreciation. I hope that this research-based, informative work will inspire discussion on the subject and contribute to the broader scholarship on borrowing and informal language.

Glossary

A

Abdul *n.* ARABIC *potentially offensive* an Arab or a person of Arab descent (JG, TD): **1999** *Three Kings*, film: *Don't make me smoke your ass, Abdul! We'll have no nonsense this time*; **2007** Free Republic: *Who knows if these Abduls know each other and have been to the same training places* || since 1991, from *Abdul*

Acapulco gold *n.* SPANISH a potent variety of marijuana, especially if grown in or imported from Acapulco de Juárez (JG, KC, TD): **2015** *Willamette Week*: *It's difficult to find any Acapulco Gold these days*; **2016** *Slate Magazine*: *Earlier that day Sabol had scored some Acapulco Gold on the beach* || since 1965, from *Acapulco* and *gold,* a reference to its leaves with a golden hue

adios amoebas *excl.* SPANISH goodbye (JG): **2007** Daily Strength: *I gotta go get some sleep, so adios amoebas!* **2014** Geo Cities: *Adios amoebas, we're outta here!* || since 1987, from *adiós* "goodbye" and *amoebas* and its resemblance to *amigos*

adios motherfucker *excl.* SPANISH *very offensive* goodbye (TD): **1997** *Lost Highway*, film: *I hope you have insurance, Jack. Adios motherfucker!* **2008** *Deal*, film: *"I need to say something." "How about 'Adios motherfucker'?"* || since 1963, from *adiós* "goodbye" and *motherfucker* "despicable person"

Adios Motherfucker *n.* SPANISH *very offensive* a strong, multi-liquor cocktail including vodka, rum, tequila, gin, blue Curaçao, sour mix, and 7-Up or ginger ale (TD): **2011** Cafe Mom: *Back in the day I used to drink Adios Motherfuckers*; **2012** Twitter: *I'm bout to listen to 80's Rock and drink Adios Motherfuckers all night* || dating unknown, from *adiós* "goodbye" and *motherfucker* "despicable person"

adios muchachos *excl.* SPANISH goodbye: **2007** *Borderland*, film: *Another inch, and I'd be "adios muchachos!"*; **2014** Huffington Post: *The Democrats said "Adios muchachos" to organized labor?* || dating unknown, from *adiós muchachos* "goodbye boys"

ad lib[1] *n.* LATIN a spontaneous speech or performance (AS, KC, JG): **2011** *Glee Project*, Oxygen-TV program: *Are you ready for some rap ad libs?* **2015** *Slate Magazine*: *Amy Schumer has a few great ad libs of her own* || since 1925, from *ad libitum* "as much as one desires"

ad-lib[2] *v.* LATIN to speak or perform spontaneously (AS, KC): **2005** *Madagascar,* film: *Who knows what you'll do. Make it up as you go along. Ad lib! Improvise!* **2009** *Family Guy,* Fox-TV series: *I ad-libbed that line* || since 1925, from *ad libitum* "as much as one desires"

ad-lib[3] *adj.* LATIN spoken or performed spontaneously: **2012** *Dallas Observer: There's no disputing his ad-lib acumen;* **2015** Denver Hypnosis: *He won an award for the best ad-lib speech at a Toastmasters group* || since 1925, from *ad libitum* "as much as one desires"

ad-lib[4] *adv.* LATIN spontaneously (AS, KC): **2015** UCLA student: *The prof talked ad-lib for an hour;* **2015** *Connecticut Magazine: I talked ad-lib about driving into Manhattan* || since 1925, from *ad libitum* "as much as one desires"

admeister *n.* GERMAN a specialist in advertising (KC): **1997** *New York Times: His former aide Peter Knight and his friend the admeister Carter Eskew are reaping big fees selling the tobacco deal;* **2016** *Washington Post: Trump's admeister smartly associated Clinton with it* || since 1960s, from ad and Meister "master"

again with something *excl.* YIDDISH something is brought up again or repeated: **2013** *People Magazine: Really? Again with the talk?* **2015** UCLA student: *Again with the complaints? I'm sick and tired of it* || dating unknown, from *shoyn vider mit epes* "again with something"

agita *n.* ITALIAN a feeling of agitation or anxiety (JG): **2006** *Sopranos,* HBO-TV series: *That fucking agita, T! I mean, do I blame myself for this life?* **2017** *Slate Magazine: Public transit can ferry people to airports reliably and with little agita* || since 1979, from *agitare* "agitate" or Southern dialectal pronunciation of *acido* "acid" or "heartburn"

A.K. *n.* YIDDISH an old man, especially a despicable one (KC, JG): **2007** Battle On: *I've known him since before he was an AK, and I've always liked him a lot;* **2010** Asheville Clicks: *The AK (short for Alter Kaker), my father in law, has been visiting with us in town for the past few weeks* || since 1920, from *alter ḵaker* "despicable old man," literally "old shitter"

a la *prep.* FRENCH in the style or manner of (AS): **2017** *New York Times: The way to stop it is not to go all wobbly-kneed a la Tillerson this week; nor is it to brandish wild military threats a la Trump;* **2018** *Autocar: This is a hybrid a la Toyota* || since 1700, from *à la mode de* "in the style of"

alambrista *n.* SPANISH a Mexican illegally present in the USA (TD): **2001** *San Diego Reader: I showed his picture to the alambristas there, but no one had seen him;* **2008** Armando Navarro: *An alambrista was a migrant who crossed the border illegally by presumably climbing over or cutting through a fence* || since 1974, from *alambrista* "wire-user" and reference to crossing the wire fences on the Mexico–US border

all right already *excl.* YIDDISH that is enough (KC): **2011** *Breaking Bad*, AMC-TV series: *"Tucker, will you shut the door?" "All right already! Jesus!"*; **2016** *Wall Street Journal*: *All-day Battery Life? All right, already! How much power will you get from this thing?* || dating unknown, from *genuk shoyn* "enough already"

allrightnik, alrightnik *n.* YIDDISH [1] someone who has succeeded financially, especially an affluent Jewish immigrant (JG): **2010** Yahoo Voices: *An alrightnik is a nouveau riche person who has no culture, a showoff*; **2012** *New York Times*: *He is sixty-five, a New York allrightnik who has made it big in real estate* [2] a conformist or someone who is easily assimilated: **2002** Ilana Abramovitch and Seán Galvin: *The neighborhood was known for its middle-class alrightniks – Jews who were culturally assimilated*; **2008** Esther Romeyn: *The allrightnik adopts all the customs of the new country* || since 1920, from *all right* and suffix *-nik,* and *olraytnik* "upstart" or "parvenu"

Allrightniks Row, Alrightniks Row *n.* YIDDISH Manhattan's Riverside Drive, where many rich and successful Jewish immigrants live: **1995** Irving L. Allen: *The slangy street name Allrightniks Row was given to Riverside Drive where certain affluent Jews came to live*; **1997** Erica Jong: *We had long since moved uptown to Riverside Drive, Allrightniks Row* || since 1920, from *all right* and suffix *-nik(s)* and *row*

aloha *excl.* HAWAIIAN [1] hello (AS, TD): **2004** *50 First Dates*, film: *Aloha, honey. What can I get for you?* **2007** *American Pastime*, film: *You know, aloha means "hello"* [2] goodbye (AS): **1990** *Twin Peaks*, ABC-TV series: *"Come on, one for the road. For old times' sake!" "Aloha!"*; **2013** *Mad Men*, AMC-TV series: *Aloha means hello and goodbye* || since 1800, from *aroha* "love"

already *adv.* YIDDISH immediately and with exasperation (JG): **2002** Jimmy Lerner: *After five minutes I accepted his apology and begged him to shut up already*; **2018** *Baltimore Sun*: *While speaking with him, he had several outbursts asking for me to just kill him already* || since 1941, from *shoyn* "already"

alrightnik *see* allrightnik

Alrightniks Row *see* Allrightniks Row

alter cocker, alter kaker *n.* YIDDISH an old man, especially a despicable one (JG, KC): **2008** *Spirit*, film: *Honey, I'm just an alter cocker, old fart*; **2016** Hollywood Reporter: *Guys, listen to an alter cocker here: The Oscars are a dinosaur* || since 1966, from *alter kaker* "despicable old man," literally "old shitter"

Americano *n.* SPANISH [1] an American, especially if white: **2004** *Arrested Development*, Fox-TV series: *"He's American." "Americano, eh? Just like me"*; **2010** *Wall Street Journal*: *The musical captures the island's essential appeal for Americanos* [2] American English: **2013** Samuelin Martínez: *Kids laughed the way I spoke Americano*; **2010** YouTube: *Maybe if you spoke Americano you would have a real job as legal citizens instead of this bullshit* || dating unknown, from *americano* "American"

AMF[1] *excl.* SPANISH goodbye (JG, TD): **2013** UCB student: *That's all what I got to say. Let me just say, "AMF!"*; **2014** Facebook: *I only heard an "AMF" and that was it* || since 1963, from *adiós* "goodbye" and *motherfucker* "despicable person"

AMF[2] *n.* SPANISH a strong, multi-liquor cocktail including vodka, rum, tequila, gin, blue Curaçao, sour mix, and 7-Up or ginger ale (TD): **2013** Drinks Mixer: *I've had AMFs in all sizes and variations*; **2014** Webstagram: *Patrick is drinking his AMF and Heineken* || dating unknown, from *adiós* "goodbye" and *motherfucker* "despicable person"

amiga *n.* SPANISH [1] a female friend: **2014** *Los Angeles Times*: *I'd rather hang out with my amigas on the bus*; **2016** *Maxim*: *He responded by calling her "amiga" and telling her she had a big heart* [2] a female: **2009** *Bring It On: Fight to the Finish*, film: *I'm guessing your little amiga hasn't seen the rest yet*; **2011** *Off the Map*, film: *Okay, okay, I'm trying to fix your amiga's boo-boo* || dating unknown, from *amiga* "female friend"

amigo *n.* SPANISH [1] a male friend (AS, JG, TD): **1990** *Miller's Crossing*, film: *We're just friends, you know, amigos*; **2015** *Las Vegas Review Journal*: *He also said that I was his amigo* [2] a male (JG, TD): **1997** *Men in Black*, film: *It looks like you fell off the bus in the wrong part of town, amigo*; **2015** Facebook: *For that, she needs a real amigo* || since 1897, from *amigo* "male friend"

andale (or **ándale**) *excl.* SPANISH get moving or hurry up: **2009** *Crank: High Voltage*, film: *You know the drill, bitch. Do it. Andale!* **2018** *Narcos: Mexico*, Netflix-TV series: *Andale, boys, let's deliver some freedom!* || dating unknown, from *ándale* "get moving" or "hurry up"

and how *excl.* GERMAN very much so (JG): **2005** Urban Dictionary: *"Man, that girl is a major bitch." "And how!"*; **2019** Wiktionary: *Did it create a disruption? And how!* || since 1865, from *und wie* "and how"

Anglo *n.* SPANISH *offensive* a white person who speaks English (AS, JG, TD): **2004** *Tucson Weekly*: *Urrea is a fronterizo, a man of the border, half Mexican and half Anglo*; **2015** *Houston Chronicle*: *Hispanics were in Texas before the Anglos* || since 1943, probably from *anglo* "Englishman" and *anglosajón* "Anglo-Saxon"

apparatchik *n.* RUSSIAN an official or staff member in a large organization, especially political (AS, KC): **2006** *Running Scared*, film: *I pick-pocketed a key off this apparatchik*; **2013** *Los Angeles Times*: *The right-wing apparatchik has decided workers are the enemy* || since 1940, from *apparatchik* "member of the Communist apparat"

apres fuck (or **après fuck**) *adj.* FRENCH *offensive* after sex: **2000** Christine Andreae: *I mean, I'm talking a whole lot more than an après-fuck buzz*; **2017** Dead Mule: *They lay in bed and shared an après-fuck cigarette* || dating unknown, from *après* "after" and *après ski* "after skiing"

arriba *excl.* SPANISH [1] I think it is excellent or agreeable: **1999** *Muppets from Space*, film: *"We're gonna blow you up!" "Arriba!"*; **2019** UCLA student: *"Let's grab something to eat!" "Arriba!"* [2] get moving or hurry up: **1981** *Prince of the City*, film: *We're going back! Come on, arriba!* **2001** *Double Take*, film: *Put on a little music. Goddamn, arriba, arriba!* || dating unknown, from *arriba* "up with it" or "hooray"

ATM *n.* SPANISH excellent: **2010** Twitter: *This club is totally ATM!* **2013** UCB student: *That busty amiga is ATM, a toda madre* || since 1974, from *a toda madre* "about every mother" or "all about mother"

a toda madre *phr.* SPANISH *potentially offensive* excellent (TD): **2000** *Los Angeles Times*: *The band is a toda madre*; **2014** Twitter: *Yes, Geneva is a toda madre, totally awesome* || since 1974, from *a toda madre* "about every mother" or "all about mother"

au naturel *adj.* FRENCH [1] natural: **2001** *Hannibal*, film: *It's perfectly au naturel to want to taste the enemy*; **2013** *Last Vegas*, film: *Next up is Christina, and she's a redhead. And let me tell you, it's au naturel* [2] naked (AS, TD): **1996** *ER*, NBC-TV series: *Lady Godiva was au naturel*; **2015** *House of Lies*, Showtime-TV series: *She was arrested in the yard of an ex-boyfriend. Au naturel. Twice* || since 1967, from *au naturel* "in one's natural state"

au reservoir *excl.* FRENCH goodbye: **1987** *Moonlighting*, ABC-TV series: *I can't really talk right now. Au reservoir!* **2007** Time Zone: *It's time to say "au reservoir," my friends. I'm off to France* || since 1980, from *au revoir* "goodbye" and *reservoir* and its resemblance to *au revoir*

ausgespielt *adj.* GERMAN exhausted or worn-out (KC): **2012** *New Yorker*: *Modernism and postmodernism are ausgespielt*; **2014** UCLA student: *When the season was over, he was totally ausgespielt* || dating unknown, from *ausgespielt* "played out"

ay excl. SPANISH oh: **1995** *Blue in the Face*, film: *Ay! What's this? Is this for me?* **2012** Fan Fiction: *Ay, chica, what are you doing here?* || dating unknown, from *ay* "oh"

ay carajo *see* carajo²

ay caramba *see* caramba

ay chihuahua *see* chihuahua

ay coño *see* coño²

ay-vay *excl.* YIDDISH oh: **2013** UCLA student: *Ay-vay! What a terrible thing to do!* **2015** Facebook: *Erica got her permit and, ay vay, she is driving!* || dating unknown, from oy vey "oh"

azul *n.* SPANISH a police officer or the police (KC): **2006** Tropical Fish: *The azuls were beating on them. The reason for such aggressiveness is not entirely clear*; **2016** Facebook: *Fuck the azuls!* || dating unknown, from *azul* "blue"

B

baby-femme *adj.* FRENCH suggesting youthful innocence combined with sexual abandon (TD): **2014** UCB student: *Guys loved her new baby-femme look*; **2015** Popculture Reviewed: *The baby femme style also includes color-rimmed baby T-shirts, baby-doll dresses, and Mary Jane shoes* || since 1995, from *baby* and *femme* "woman"

baby-san *n.* JAPANESE an East Asian child or young woman (TD): **1988** *Tour of Duty*, CBS-TV series: *I'm hanging out with this baby-san because I love her*; **2007** Charles Henderson: *They were sending the B-52s out dropping their tonnage on the Ho Chi Minh Trail, taking out a village full of mama-sans and baby-sans there* || since 1954, from *baby* and honorific title *san*

bagel¹ *n.* YIDDISH [1] a Jew (JG): **2002** *Chicago*, film: *They'll never know you're a bagel*; **2011** Amoeba: *It used to be commonly referred to as The Bagel District, but nowadays there sadly aren't as many bagels around* [2] a tennis set won 6–0 (KC): **2011** Bleacher Report: *Did you know that winning a set without losing a single game, 6–0, is referred to as a "bagel?"*; **2011** Tennis Planet: *Here's Nadal's interview after losing to Federer at WTF with a bagel* || in the first sense since 1957, in the second since 1980, from *beygl* "bagel"

bagel² *v.* YIDDISH to win a tennis set 6–0: **2004** Tennis Forum: *Who has the best record of bageling her opponents?* **2009** *Examiner: US Open Tennis 2009: Fernando Gonzalez disappoints, bageled in the third set by Rafael Nadal* || since 1980, from *beygl* "bagel"

bagel baby *n.* YIDDISH *offensive* [1] a young middle-class Jewish woman (JG): **2011** Hipster Jew: *Hey bagel baby, you lookin' sexy tonight*; **2014** Shesaurus: *Bagel baby is a young, wealthy Jewish gal* [2] a liberal and politically active young middle-class Jew (JG): **1983** *Maledicta: Middle-class young Jewish women who flocked to liberal causes were called bagel babies*; **2015** Blogger: *Don't call them bagel babies!* || in the first sense since 1970, in the second since 1983, from *beygl* "bagel" and *baby*

bagel bender *n.* YIDDISH *offensive* a Jew (JG): **2009** Yahoo Answers: *Why are Jewish people referred to as bagel benders?* **2011** Reckoning: *This guy ripped me off, what a bagel bender!* || since 1977, from *beygl* "bagel" and *bender*

bagel district *n.* YIDDISH a neighborhood dominated by Jewish people: **2011** Facebook: *The section of Fairfax Avenue filled with traditionally Jewish businesses is sometimes referred to by Angelenos as Kosher Canyon or The Bagel District*; **2012** Toronto Real Estate: *Highlights include the bagel district* || dating unknown, from *beygl* "bagel" and *district*

bagel meister *n.* YIDDISH AND GERMAN *offensive* a Jew: **2012** *Washington Post: Unangst also admitted to making remarks about "Jew money," and had called him a "bagel meister"*; **2013** Patch: *Cowher was also called "bagel" meister by some of the men* || since 1977, from *beygl* "bagel" and *mayster* "master"

bagel shift *n.* YIDDISH an early morning shift: **2009** Blip: *I couldn't go, no one would take my bagel shift. Sad!* **2011** Yahoo Answers: *I worked the bagel shift (2 am – 11:30 am)* || dating unknown, from *beygl* "bagel" and *shift*

Baghdad Boys *n.* ARABIC reporters from the CNN television channel (JG, TD): **2002** *Los Angeles Weekly*: *Ultimately, the film is a pean to CNN's "Baghdad Boys"*; **2002** Free Republic: *It's been eleven years since CNN's "Baghdad Boys" huddled in the hotel by candlelight, holding a microphone out a window to pick up the sounds of U.S. bombs* || since 1990, from *Baghdad* and *Boys*

Baja Bug *n.* SPANISH a Volkswagen Beetle, especially if modified for surfer use (TD): **2013** *Auto Week*: *He had bought the Baja Bug in Philadelphia*; **2014** *Los Angeles Times*: *He also designed the Baja Bug, a modified Volkswagen Beetle that was cheap and sturdy enough to open up off-roading to the masses* || since 1991, from *Baja* "bay," ultimately from the Mexican state *Baja California,* and *Bug* "VW Beetle"

bala *n.* SPANISH a capsule of the barbiturate Seconal: **2009** *San Diego Magazine*: *They earned the credit for taking balas across the border*; **2010** Twitter: *If you keep popping balas, you're going to die* || dating unknown, from *bala* "bullet" or "ball"

bam *n.* SPANISH amphetamine (JG): **1994** *Washington Post*: *Lucky was regularly injecting something called "bam," an amphetamine-like stimulant*; **2014** Wikipedia: *The street name for the drug in Washington D.C. was bam* || since 1969, from *bambita* "little bomb"

bamba *n.* SPANISH marijuana (JG): **2014** Penny Arcade: *I wish I had some bamba, the decision would be a lot easier*; **2014** Alcoholism: *Remember when he was referring to "bamba" he was talking about marijuana* || since 1938, from *bamba* "Mexican dance" and the title of Ritchie Valens' song *La Bamba*

bambino *n.* ITALIAN [1] a baby or young child (AS, KC): **1990** *Twin Peaks*, ABC-TV series: *To be honest, I wanted to talk to you about our bambino*; **1991** *Oscar*, film: *We're married real good. I got ten bambinos* [2] darling: **1988** *Married to the Mob*, film: *Just make with the beat, bambino!* **2022** Wattpad: *Hey bambino, what's your name?* || since 1920, from *bambino* "baby"

banzai¹ *adj.* JAPANESE berserk, behaving wildly (AS): **2009** *NCSI*, CBS-TV series: *Whoever trashed his apartment went banzai on his dinner plates with a hammer*; **2009** *National Enquirer*: *Tigers fans went banzai when they won the pennant in 1985* || since 1950, from a Japanese battle cry *banzai* "(let the Emperor live) ten thousand years"

banzai² *excl.* JAPANESE I am exhilarated and unafraid, especially to do something reckless (AS, JG): **1984** *Bachelor Party*, film: *Okay, gentlemen. The gods have answered your prayers! Banzai!* **2001** *Cats & Dogs*, film: *On my mark. Three, two one! Banzai!* || since 1905, from a Japanese battle cry *banzai* "(let the Emperor live) ten thousand years"

barrio (or **El Barrio**) *n.* SPANISH [1] a neighborhood: **1993** *Bound by Honor*, film: *You woke up all the babies in the barrio, ese!* **2013** El Paso Online: *It's a dangerous barrio* [2] Spanish Harlem (AS): **2005** *Carlito's Way: Rise to Power*, film: *So what brings you girls to el barrio?* **2012** *New York Times*: *In El Barrio, a New Bookstore Is Counting on Its Community* || dating unknown, from *el*, the definite article in Spanish, and *barrio* "town quarter or district in Spanish-speaking countries" or "neighborhood"

basuco *n.* SPANISH cocaine paste (AS, JG, KC, TD): **1989** *South Florida Sun-Sentinel*: *Many of them spend their meager earnings on basuco*; **2013** *News*, ABC-TV program: *They treat people who are addicted to basuco* || since 1983, from *bazuco* "cheap coca paste"

bato *n.* SPANISH [1] a person (JG, TD): **2000** *Porno*, film: *Come on, bato! Come on, hurry up!* **2010** David Montejano: *Juan recalled one bato who got hooked on heroin every time we kicked him out* [2] a person of Latin American descent (JG): **1996** *Los Angeles Times*: *You ever heard of a bato living in a fine place around here?* **2013** Alberto Arcia: *Don't call me "chief." You know I hate it when you mock my heritage. You don't hear me addressing you, "Hey bato!"* || since 1950 in the first sense, since 1971 in the second, from *bato* "simpleton" or "dude," ultimately from *chivato* "small goat"

bato loco *n.* SPANISH [1] a crazy person, especially of Latin American descent (JG, TD): **1995** *My Family*, film: *Carlitos grew up to be more of a problem than a bato loco*; **2014** *Los Angeles Times*: *But to the bato loco in the barrio this frustration is a luxury which he cannot afford* [2] a mentally unbalanced and violent member of a Mexican gang (JG): **2004** Ricardo L. Garcia: *They were bato locos and needed extra guarding*; **2014** Yahoo Groups: *Say hello to my bato locos, ese!* || since 1965, from *bato loco* "crazy person"

bazoo *n.* DUTCH the mouth (AS, JG, KC): **1997** *Frasier*, NBC-TV series: *I should mind my own business, keep my big bazoo shut*; **2017** UCLA student: *Why don't you shut your bazoo and leave me alone!* || since 1882, from *bazuin* "trumpet"

bazuko *n.* SPANISH cocaine paste (JG, KC, TD): **1988** *Orlando Sentinel*: *He began smoking marijuana when he was ten, a few years later he graduated to cocaine and bazuko*; **2001** Cannabis News: *He swore off booze and bazuko years ago* || since 1983, from *bazuco* "cheap coca paste"

beatnik *n.* YIDDISH a person who is alienated from society, especially a member of the Beat Generation subculture of the 1950s and 1960s (AS, JG, KC): **1995** *Nixon*, film: *Hoover says this Oswald checks out as a beatnik, a real bum*; **2016** *News*, CNN-TV program: *The doctor was a beatnik in the '60s* || since 1958, from *beat* and suffix -*nik*

beaucoup *adv.* FRENCH [1] extremely (JG): **2008** Susan Johnson: *He looked beaucoup sexy, smiling at her like that*; **2012** Philip Caputo: *You're telling us that we're beaucoup crazy?* [2] very much or a lot of (JG): **2017** *New Orleans Tribune*:

Those operators made beaucoup money off the backs of some of the most underserved public school children in Louisiana; **2018** *News*, CNN-TV program: *We don't want to shell out beaucoup bucks on all-new cookware that we'll only use once* ‖ since 1918, from *beaucoup* "very much"

be for real *phr.* YIDDISH be serious or truthful: **2016** *Washington Post*: *Is Donald Trump for real? We'll start getting an answer in Iowa*; **2016** *New York Newsday*: *Columnist Ted Bromund Writes, "The atom bomb was no more devastating than conventional U.S. air attacks." Is he for real?* ‖ since 1940, from *zaynen far emes* "to be for truth"

beso *n.* SPANISH a kiss: **2011** *Sitter*, film: *"We'll see you later, all right?" "Besos!"*; **2011** *Chuck*, NBC-TV series: *Sweet dreams, and besos, my flower!* ‖ dating unknown, from *beso* "kiss"

bicho *n.* SPANISH *offensive* [1] the penis (JG, KC): **1985** Elmore Leonard: *He was rough with her in the bed, and punished her with his bicho*; **2007** Yahoo Answers: *They request that a man should have a big bicho* [2] a despicable man, especially an insignificant one: **2004** Urban Dictionary: *That bicho sold us some poisoned mangos*; **2013** Cole Riley: *These bichos would kill you for a pack of cigarettes* ‖ since 1967, from *bicho* "small animal" or "insect"

big deal *excl.* YIDDISH this is not impressive (KC): **2000** *Requiem for a Dream*, film: *"Twenty-five pounds I've lost!" "Big deal!"*; **2015** *San Francisco Business Times*: *Large number of patients enrolled in your clinical trial? Big deal. Show me the results* ‖ since 1940, from *groyser kunst* "great mastery"

big enchilada *n.* SPANISH [1] an important person, especially a chief (AS, JG, KC): **1991** *JFK*, film: *I'll give you the name of the big enchilada*; **2015** *Baltimore Sun*: *We're going to go for the big enchilada, which is Hillary* [2] something important (AS): **1988** *Los Angeles Times*: *Dukakis was smart to pick Bentsen because Texas is the big enchilada*; **2010** *Examiner*: *The K-12 market is the big enchilada* ‖ since 1973, from *big* and *enchilada* "tortilla with meat and chili sauce"

big honcho *n.* JAPANESE an important person, especially a chief: **1995** *Los Angeles Times*: *I didn't want people to think I'm the big honcho*; **2000** *Cut Runs Deep*, film: *He was the big honcho, he was everybody's boss* ‖ since 1945, from *hanchō* "group leader"

Big J *n.* SPANISH Ciudad Juárez, Mexico (TD): **2010** Game Forge: *Did Juarez scare you? I was in Tijuana back in the 90s, never had a desire to go to the Big J*; **2014** Twitter: *He was born and raised in the Big J* ‖ since 1968, from *big* and *(Ciudad) Juárez*, a city in Mexico, ultimately from Benito Juárez, former president of Mexico

big kahuna *n.* HAWAIIAN [1] an important person, especially a chief (AS, KC, TD): **2002** *Skulls II*, film: *It means I'm the big kahuna around here*; **2013** *Hawaii Five-O*, CBS-TV series: *To start, let's meet the big kahuna, Lieutenant Commander Steve McGarrett* [2] an important thing: **2015** OpEd News: *This is the big kahuna* *that the press generally feels uncomfortable reporting*; **2015** Deadline: *China is the big kahuna* [3] a very large wave (AS): **1995** *Batman Forever*, film: *Surf's up, Big Kahuna!* **2015** Subway Surf: *Brody's riding on a big kahuna* || since 1950, from *big* and *kahuna* "medicine man" or "shaman"

big macher *n.* YIDDISH [1] a very important, influential, and well-connected person, especially involved in shady dealings: **2010** *Wall Street Journal*: *Madoff was a big macher outside prison*; **2011** *New York Magazine*: *Lyman was a big macher in the California GOP* [2] a boastful person: **2011** Facebook: *Another big macher who can't keep it in his pants!* **2012** *Chicago Tribune*: *What a big macher you are!* || since 1930, from *big* and *makher* literally "doer"

big megillah *n.* YIDDISH [1] great outrage, fuss, or complaining, especially over a trivial matter: **2009** *Jewish Journal*: *Don't make a big megillah about her age*; **2009** Reuters: *If the phone is available at Apple and AT&T, what's the big megillah?* [2] something big or important: **2000** *Los Angeles Times*: *For someone who loves to cover politics, this is the big Megillah*; **2014** *New York Post*: *This deal is a big megillah for the area* [3] a powerful, important, and especially arrogant person: **1995** National Board of Review of Motion Pictures: *They're making a big megillah out of a very ordinary person*; **2002** Payson Stevens: *They define a "big megillah" as a big shot who is full of air* || dating unknown, from *big* and *megile* "scroll" or "volume," especially the Book of Esther read aloud in its entirety at Purim celebrations

bimbette *n.* ITALIAN *potentially offensive* an attractive and hedonistic young woman, especially if also stupid (AS, KC, JG, TD): **2004** *Shall We Dance*, film: *No more underage bimbettes for me. Only real women from now on!* **2014** *Taxi Brooklyn*, NBC-TV series: *That may appeal to naive college girls and Brooklyn bimbettes* || since 1982, from *bimbo* "baby" and feminine suffix *-ette*

bimbo *n.* ITALIAN an attractive and hedonistic young woman, especially if also stupid (AS, JG, KC, TD): **2000** *American Psycho*, film: *You were hanging out with that bimbo Allison Poole; hot number!* **2014** Huffington Post: *He referred to Rep. Gloria Negrete McLeod as some bimbo* || since 1920, from *bambino* "baby"

bindle *n.* GERMAN a small packet of narcotics, especially when folded as an envelope (JG, KC): **2012** *Boardwalk Empire*, HBO-TV series: *I sell two bindles of powder on Elizabeth Street, Joe Masseria gets cut in?* **2018** *San Francisco Chronicle*: *Drug dealers sell hundreds of $10 bindles of cocaine* || since 1918, from *Büntel* "package"

bissel¹ *n.* YIDDISH a little bit (KC): **2012** *Examiner*: *This is only a bissel (a little bit) of the mountain of evidence that exists*; **2015** Huffington Post: *But wait a bissel. Don't think it's all gloom and doom* || since 1920, from *bisl* "piece"

bissel² *adv.* YIDDISH a little: **2000** Sylvia Barack Fishman: *African-American General Colin Powell famously declared that he speaks a bissel Yiddish*; **2012** *New York Magazine*: *It could make even him a bissel cool* || since 1920, from *bisl* "a little"

bizarro¹ *adj.* SPANISH strange or bizarre (AS, JG, KC): **2000** *Miss Congeniality*, film: *The only reason she won was because the winner got food poisoning. How bizarro is that?* **2018** *Billions*, Showtime-TV series: *Texas is a bizarro world* ‖ since 1971, probably from *bizarro* "bizarre," reinforced by a character called Bizarro in the *Superman* comic strips

bizarro² *n.* SPANISH a strange or bizarre person (JG, TD): **1995** Howard Stern: *The reclusive bizarro I've been goofing on for the past year wants to come on my radio show*; **2014** Yelp: *I've encountered some bizarros, but that makes it fun* ‖ since 1980, probably from *bizarro* "bizarre," reinforced by a character called Bizarro in the *Superman* comic strips

blah *adj.* FRENCH bland, dull, or featureless (JG, KC, TD): **2014** Trip Advisor: *The location is great but the place is blah*; **2015** Paleo Owl: *My hair is medium brown and very blah looking* ‖ since 1918, probably from *balsé* "bored" or "indifferent"

blanca *n.* SPANISH [1] *potentially offensive* a white woman: **2004** *Soul Plane*, film: *Hey there, blanca! Show me where it is*; **2010** Twitter: *Hey, blanca! You speak Spanish?* [2] an amphetamine tablet (JG, TD): **2012** Luis J. Rodriguez: *Blancas are white amphetamine pills*; **2014** Twitter: *Jessica Fuentes is on blancas!* ‖ since 1967 in the first sense, since 1967 in the second, from *blanca* and *blanco* "white"

blanco *n.* SPANISH [1] *potentially offensive* a white man (JG): **2008** *Prison Break*, Fox-TV series: *Time to fight, blanco!* **2014** Twitter: *Sometimes I like to speak Spanish at work just to mess with all the blancos in the office* [2] heroin (JG, TD): **2013** Twitter: *In case you don't know, blanco means heroin*; **2015** UNF student: *He got hooked on blanco* ‖ since 1967 in the first sense, since 1973 in the second, from *blanco* "white"

blitz¹ *v.* GERMAN [1] to defeat soundly (AS, JG, KC, TD): **2007** *1408*, film: *I'm gonna blitz the son of a bitch!* **2013** *Butler*, film: *The Marines moved out from the Army compound blitzed by the attack* [2] to win and leave an opponent scoreless (JG, KC, TD): **2014** *New York Times*: *She blitzed me, she just wiped me off the court*; **2015** *Los Angeles Times*: *The Clippers blitzed them for an 18–0 run in the third quarter* ‖ since 1940 in the first sense, since 1971 in the second, from *Blitzkrieg* "lightning war"

blitz² *n.* GERMAN [1] a sudden and heavy attack (AS, JG, KC, TD): **2002** *Rose Red*, film: *The Huskies were surprised by the blitz*; **2011** *Ides of March*, film: *They're gonna see a fucking blitz* [2] a concentrated effort (AS, JG, TD): **2011** *Parks and Recreation*, NBC-TV series: *We're doing a huge media blitz to publicize the Harvest Festival*; **2012** *Thousand Words*, film: *We want a full-scale media blitz* ‖ since 1940, from *Blitzkrieg* "lightning war"

blitzed *adj.* GERMAN [1] drunk (AS, JG, KC, TD): **1999** *EDtv*, film: *I got a little blitzed at the Christmas party*; **2017** *New York Post*: *Defense lawyer Laura Miranda argues that he was so blitzed that he was barely conscious and couldn't form murderous intent* [2] drug-intoxicated (AS, JG, TD): **1992** *Raising Cain*, film: *What's the matter* *with you? Are you blitzed again?* **2007** Grass City: *We ended up getting blitzed on weed* [3] exhausted (JG, TD): **2013** UCB student: *Two more laps and he was totally blitzed*; **2015** UNF student: *It was a very demanding task, and he came back home blitzed* || since 1966 in the first and second senses, since 1978 in the third, from *Blitzkrieg* "lightning war"

blow one's burritos *phr.* SPANISH to vomit: **2014** YouTube: *My dad looked kind of ashen and ready to blow his burritos*; **2015** UNF student: *He ate everything, and some twenty minutes later blew his burritos* || dating unknown, from *blow* and *burrito* "cornflour tortilla with savory filling," and analogy to *blow one's cookies* or *blow one's lunch*

blow one's tacos *phr.* SPANISH to vomit: **2012** NYU student: *He had too much beer and blew his tacos*; **2015** UNF student: *Blowing your tacos is vomiting* || dating unknown, from *blow* and *taco* "type of tortilla stuffed with various ingredients," and analogy to *blow one's cookies* or *blow one's lunch*

bobkes *see* bupkes

bodega *n.* SPANISH [1] a grocery store, especially Puerto Rican in New York City (AS, KC): **1994** *Above the Rim*, film: *Be up in that damn bodega with your mama food stamps*; **2006** New York Times: *The cost of a gallon of milk was 79 cents more in a bodega than in a supermarket* [2] a liquor store (AS, KC): **2003** *New York Times: He had been giving summons to workers in a bodega for selling liquor to minors*; **2015** Gothamist: *He's in the beer aisle of a bodega* || since 1850, from *bodega* "shop" or "cellar"

bolsa *n.* SPANISH a bag of narcotics, especially a ten-dollar bag of marijuana: **2009** International Cannagraphic: *I had a small bolsa for fifty pesos, that's less than $4*; **2013** Blogger: *They came back from Mexico with a bolsa of weed* || dating unknown, from *bolsa* "bag" or "pouch"

bombita *n.* SPANISH [1] an amphetamine pill or capsule (JG, KC, TD): **1985** *Life Magazine: Both cocaine and bombitas are stimulants, and either one combined with heroin, which is a depressant, produces a more pleasurable high than heroin alone*; **1998** Hilda González-Angiulo: *She recalls how drugs like cocaine, marijuana, LDS, and bombitas, were readily available at all hours* [2] a mixture of heroin and cocaine (JG): **2002** Thomas Nordegren: *Bombita is a colloquial term for a mixture of cocaine and heroin*; **2015** Greenwich Time: *Bombita is a very dangerous drug* || since 1966 in the first sense, since 1969 in the second, from *bombita* "little bomb"

bonanza *n.* SPANISH [1] prosperity or something profitable (JG): **2018** *USA Today: Here's how to make sense of the sales bonanza that starts July 16*; **2018** *Fortune: Oil majors like Exxon Mobil are betting that this bonanza has staying power* [2] a very large amount, especially of something desirable (JG): **2018** Bloomberg: *Where's President Trump's jobs bonanza?* **2018** *Chicago Reader: Chávez used a bonanza of cash from rising oil prices to fund extensive community services* || since 1876, from *bonanza* "good weather"

bonita *n.* SPANISH milk sugar (lactose) used to dilute heroin (JG, TD): 2007 Opiophile: *They used to slap it with bonita. Bonita being a Spanish trade name for lactose that was sold in bodegas*; 2013 David T. Courtwright: *When I first started shooting heroin they were cutting it with bonita, and coke with epsom salts* || since 1967, from *bonita* "pretty"

boo *n.* FRENCH a person's boyfriend or girlfriend (AS): 2019 Elite Daily: *Krieger posted this cute photo with her boo*; 2019 Cosmopolitan: *Planning the perfect date with your boo can be super romantic* || since 1980, from *beau* "boyfriend"

boobitas *n.* PSEUDO-SPANISH *potentially offensive* small female breasts (TD): 2006 Blogspot: *I sweat everywhere: in my head, under my boobitas, behind the knees*; 2015 Mr. Skin: *Catch a quick flick of Mariel's enhanced boobitas when she fans herself with a lifted shirt hem* || since 1963, from *boobs,* diminutive suffix *-ita,* and plural suffix *-s*

boo-coo (or **boo-koo**) *adv.* FRENCH [1] extremely (JG, TD): 1987 *Hamburger Hill,* film: *Water's boo-koo hot!* 2015 Instagram: *I was boo-coo crazy about you and you loved that* [2] very much or a lot of (JG, TD): 2010 *New York Times*: *There's bookoo traffic out there*; 2013 *Red Hook Summer,* film: *I got boo-coo square feet up in here* || since 1924, from *beaucoup* "very much"

boodle *n.* DUTCH money, especially money that has been acquired illegally (BK, JG): 1997 *New York Times*: *A bagman, in underworld parlance, is one who carries the boodle, or money, from the beneficiary of a corrupt deal to the grafter*; 2010 *Chicago Magazine*: *As Chicago grew in the 19th century and the boodle began to flow, opportunities for politicians to line their pockets multiplied* || since 1850, from *boedel* "property"

boojie *n.* FRENCH *potentially offensive* an upper-middle-class person (JG, TD): 2008 Black Agenda Report: *Those same boojies were madly in love with the Clintons before the arrival of Obama*; 2009 Education of Charlie Banks, film: *Danny, you're rich. You're pretty much boojie* || since 1970, from *bourgeois* "wealthy stratum of middle class"

boondocks *n.* TAGALOG a remote or isolated region (AS, JG, KC, TD): 1996 *3rd Rock from the Sun,* NBC-TV series: *I can't believe I'm gonna die on a flea-infested little planet in the boondocks of the galaxy*; 2015 Your Houston News: *Thomas would play gigs out in the boondocks* || since 1909, from *bundok* "mountain"

boozefest *n.* GERMAN a drinking party: 2012 *Besties,* film: *I'm drunk from your little boozefest*; 2013 *New York Daily News*: *It was a boozefest and it damaged the park* || dating unknown, from *booze* "alcohol" and *Fest* "festival"

bopkes *see* bupkes

border lingo *n.* PORTUGUESE [1] a hybrid mixture of Spanish and English used in the areas near the US–Mexican border: 2010 Gary Lee Berry: *I'd picked up a smattering of border lingo, comprende amigo?* 2016 American Thinker: *You think*

I'm going to let anyone off the hook for disastrous decisions? No way, Jose (a little border lingo) [2] the slang or jargon of the US Border Patrol agents: 2004 *Tucson Weekly*: *Pollos are smuggled immigrants in border lingo*; 2013 Jeffrey Prather: *We are experiencing a tremendous increase in OTMs, border lingo for "other than Mexicans"* || dating unknown, from *border* and *lingo*

borracho[1] *n.* SPANISH a drunkard (JG): 1987 *Miami Vice*, NBC-TV series: *I'm on the lookout for a few more investors. No drunks, no borrachos*; 2014 *Gang Related*, Fox-TV series: *Me and Manny robbed this borracho* || since 1623, from *borracho* "drunkard"

borracho[2] *adj.* SPANISH drunk: 1989 *Licence to Kill*, film: *You're borracho. Go to bed!* 2015 *Jackson Hole News & Guide*: *A full-fledged fiesta will be in swing, with the mariachi band and borracho locals* || since 1623, from *borracho* "drunkard"

borscht belt, borsht belt *n.* YIDDISH (sometimes capitalized) [1] the region in and near the Catskill Mountains north of New York City where many predominantly Jewish resort hotels once were found (AS, KC): 2004 *Ladykillers*, film: *The tourist business there has suffered with the demise of the Borscht Belt*; 2016 SF Gate: *The Catskill Mountain were known as the Jewish Alps or the Borscht Belt* [2] any neighborhood peopled with Russians, especially Russian Jews (KC): 2007 Daily XY: *The cultural epicentre for Toronto's nearly half million Russian immigrants is the Bathurst Borscht Belt*; 2011 *News*, ABC-TV program: *It's like the concentration of Japanese restaurants in Arlington Heights or the Russian Borscht Belt in Buffalo Grove* || from *borsht* "beet soup" and *belt*; in the first sense, since 1940, from the idea that borscht was a favorite dish of Jewish people, many of whom came from Eastern Europe where borscht is popular; in the second sense, since 1980s, from the popularity of borscht in Russia

borscht circuit, borsht circuit *n.* YIDDISH (sometimes capitalized) the resort hotels in the Catskill Mountains north of New York City, regarded as a circuit for entertaining (KC): 2010 *Chicago Tribune*: *He appeared in summer stock theater and on the Borscht Circuit in the Catskills*; 2012 *New York Times*: *He works reasonably steadily in nightclubs and the Borscht circuit* || since 1936, from *borsht* "beet soup" and *belt*, and the idea that borscht was a favorite dish of Jewish people, many of whom came from Eastern Europe where borscht is popular

borsht belt *see* borscht belt

borsht circuit *see* borscht circuit

boss[1] *n.* DUTCH a chief, manager, or the person in charge (AS, BK, JG): 2011 *Homeland*, Showtime-TV series: *I'm the boss around here*; 2012 *Django Unchained*, film: *You got to listen to your boss, white boy* || since 1806, from *baas* "master"

boss[2] *adj.* DUTCH excellent (AS, BK, JG): 2015 Mashable: *Riding zebras looked boss but was not chill at all*; 2016 *Los Angeles Times*: *If you lived in Southern California, you might have ridden in a VW dune buggy, maybe in Baja or at Pismo Beach. And it was boss* || since 1835, from *baas* "master"

boss around *v.* DUTCH to domineer, to direct or control someone in an authoritarian way (BK, JG): **2007** *Epic Movie*, film: *Every king needs subjects to boss around*; **2019** *San Francisco Chronicle*: *He quickly learned that he did not like being bossed around* || since 1856, from *baas* "master" and *around*

bossy *adj.* DUTCH domineering, controlling in an authoritarian way (AS, BK, JG): **2018** *Boston Magazine*: *He is also very bossy and gets super upset if things don't go exactly the way he wants them to*; **2019** *Washington Post*: *The 5-year-old can be bossy and independent all day* || since 1882, from *baas* "master" and suffix -*y*

bottom line *n.* YIDDISH the essence (JG, KC): **2015** *Orange County Register*: *The bottom line is we have no choice but to reduce our water usage*; **2015** *Florida Today*: *So what's the bottom line?* || since 1967, from *untershte shure* "bottom line"

bougie, bourgie *n.* FRENCH *potentially offensive* an upper-middle-class person (JG): **2010** *New York Press*: *Those white bourgies cannot appreciate it*; **2015** Yelp: *Bourgies probably haven't experienced a day of real hardship in their entire lives* || since 1970, from *bourgeois* "wealthy stratum of middle class"

boychik, boychick *n.* YIDDISH [1] a boy, especially young (KC): **2006** *Surf School*, film: *Boychik, I've been looking for you*; **2013** *Tablet Magazine*: *They are doing shitwork jobs that no self-respecting boychick wants to do* [2] (of a man) darling: **2006** *Shark Bait*, film: *What's the matter, boychik? You lost?* **2006** *Billable Hours*, Showcase-TV series: *Hold the door, I'm right behind you. Thank you, boychik!* || since 1951, from *boy* and suffix -*chik*

bozo *n.* SPANISH a stupid or foolish person, especially if also clumsy (AS, JG, KC): **1996** *Twelve Monkeys*, film: *I have nothing to do with those bozos*; **2018** *News*, Fox-TV program: *DeNiro called Trump a "national disgrace" as a candidate and referred to him as a "bozo"* || since 1916, from *bozal* "stupid"

bozo filter *n.* SPANISH a device that automatically excludes stupid or foolish people from computer networks (KC): **2018** *Globe and Mail*: *Instagram's new comment controls also feature something commonly called a "bozo filter"*; **2018** *Motherboard*: *It was possible to establish a bozo filter to screen out messages* || since 1990, from *bozal* "stupid"

bracero *n.* SPANISH [1] a Mexican laborer working in the USA (AS): **2005** *Houston Chronicle*: *Activists claim that some 150,000 former braceros have a right to the government money*; **2010** *Los Angeles Times*: *Nuño was a bracero, the name given to temporary workers contracted from Mexico* [2] *potentially offensive* any Mexican: **1996** *Lone Star*, film: *Over there, he's just another Mex bracero*; **2013** American History: *Braceros would compete for jobs* || since 1940, from *bracero* "day laborer"

brainwash ¹ *n.* CHINESE a forcible indoctrination (KC): **2014** *Winnipeg Free Press*: *The judge reprimanded them for what he called the "brainwash" of children*; **2015** *Napa Valley Register*: *I won't stand for segregation, degradation, the brainwash of an entire nation. Wake up, America!* || since 1950, from *xǐnǎo* literally "wash brain"

brainwash[2] *v.* CHINESE to submit to a forcible indoctrination (AS, KC): **2001** *Bandits*, film: *You took her away for two weeks and you brainwashed her*; **2005** *Constantine*, film: *I think they brainwashed her into stepping off that roof* || since 1950, from *xǐnǎo* literally "wash brain"

bravo *n.* SPANISH a Mexican or a Mexican American, especially if brave, bold, or reckless: **2007** Legends of America: *The conversation of these bravos drew my attention to a female character of the Texas frontier life*; **2011** Mary Hoffman: *These bravos were more like rival gangs of young aristocrats* || dating unknown, from *bravo* "fierce" or "wild"

brewski, brewskie, brewsky *n.* YIDDISH beer (AS, KC): **2007** *CSI: Crime Scene Investigation*, CBS-TV series: *There's a cold brewski on the table. We must have just missed him*; **2015** *Miami New Times*: *The most expensive place on the list to grab a brewski? Geneva, Switzerland, where the average bar beer will set you back over ten bucks* || since 1977, from *brew* and jocular suffix *-ski*

brewskie *see* brewski

brewsky *see* brewski

bronco *n.* SPANISH a young male recently initiated into homosexual sex, and thus somewhat rough (JG, KC, TD): **2006** Puerto Rico Online: *Get yourself a handsome bronco!* **2015** Homo Sex Info: *Bronco is a young homosexual male who is difficult to restrain during intercourse* || since 1933, from *bronco* "unbroken horse"

bruja *n.* SPANISH a despicable woman thought to have evil influence: **2012** *Modern Family*, ABC-TV series: *"The baby started kicking like crazy, like it's trying to claw its way out of me." "Bruja!"*; **2014** *Paranormal Activity*, film: *She's some bruja or witch or whatever* || dating unknown, from *bruja* "witch"

bubbe *see* bubby

bubbeh *see* bubby

bubbeleh *see* bubeleh

bubbie *see* bubby

bubby, bubbie, bubbeh, bubbe, bubeh, bube *n.* YIDDISH [1] a grandmother (AS, KC): **2012** *South Florida Sun-Sentinel*: *Don't rush your life! That's what my Bubby would always say to me*; **2013** Huffington Post: *When I visit, I pull up a chair from the kitchen so I can be close to my bubbie* [2] darling (KC): **1992** *Glengarry Glen Ross*, film: *This is how we keep score, bubby*; **2006** *South Park*, Comedy Central-TV series: *Hello bubbe, how was school today?* || in the first sense, from *bobe* "grandmother"; in the second sense, from *bobele* "darling"

bube *see* bubby

bubeh *see* bubby

bubeleh, bubbeleh *n.* YIDDISH darling (JG, KC): **2004** *Meet the Fockers*, film: *I haven't seen my bubeleh in months*; **2012** *Los Angeles Times*: *Did I ease your concerns, bubbeleh?* || since 1978, from *bobe* "grandmother" and diminutive suffix *-le*, literally "little grandma" and originally an endearment for baby girls

bubkes *n.* YIDDISH [1] nothing or an absurdly meager amount (JG, KC): **2001** *Race to Space*, film: *They got bubkes, zero, zilch*; **2012** *New York Magazine*: *All the other messages disintegrate to bubkes* [2] something absurdly trivial (JG): **2012** *Chicago Tribune*: *Romney offered bubkes in the way of specific policy proposals*; **2012** Twitter: *The stock market went so badly that he was left with just bubkes* || in the first sense since 1938, in the second since 1968, from *bobkes* "dung" or "manure"

buenas *excl.* SPANISH hello: **2010** Facebook: *Buenas, Emilio! How's it going?* **2013** Facebook: *Buenas! How have you been, guys?* || dating unknown, from *buenas días* "good day" or *buenas noches* "good evening"

bukkake¹ *n.* JAPANESE *potentially offensive* a sex act in which several men ejaculate on a woman or another man (JG): **2016** Cinema Blend: *Good thing both of your parents like bukkake*; **2016** Complex: *The streaming site gets more than twenty million unique visitors a day checking out everything from BBW to bukkake* || since 1995, from *bukkake* "sprinkling" or "splashing"

bukkake² *v.* JAPANESE [1] *potentially offensive* (of several men) to ejaculate on a woman or another man (JG): **2013** *Vancouver Sun*: *Matt is getting bukkake'd by a gang of HA's in prison*; **2013** IGN Boards: *It looks like two samurais bukkake'ing a chick in the middle* [2] to be swamped or inundated with something: **2011** Deadspin: *It's like I'm being bukkake'd with information*; **2016** Twitter: *My car got bukkake'd with pollen this morning* || since 1995, from *bukkake* "sprinkling" or "splashing"

bum *n.* GERMAN [1] a tramp or vagrant (AS, JG, KC): **1994** *Pulp Fiction*, film: *You decided to be a bum?* **2018** *Men's Health*: *Teasle thinks Rambo's a bum and runs him out of town* [2] a lazy person who avoids work (AS, JG, KC): **2014** Consumerist: *You Are Now Watching 93 Minutes Of Netflix A Day, You Lazy Bum*; **2018** *Newsweek*: *If Cohen is such a bum, why did you hire him?* || since 1864, from *bummer* and ultimately *from Bummler* "loafer"

bum around *v.* GERMAN to waste time doing nothing (AS, JG, KC, TD): **2012** *Ted*, film: *I've been bumming around with Ted too much*; **2018** *Santa Fe New Mexican*: *Martinez told his father he didn't know what he wanted to do other than bum around for a while* || since 1926, from *Bummler* "loafer"

bunco *n.* SPANISH [1] a swindle (AS, JG, KC): **2011** Blogger: *They were running a bunco and victimizing people*; **2013** Twitter: *That bunco was no joke* [2] a swindler (JG): **2010** Blogs: *The guy's a bunco!* **2014** John MacDonald: *The general method of these buncos is to attack housewives at their homes, although these men will canvass office buildings* || since 1883 in the first sense, since 1872 in the second, from *banca* "card game similar to monte"

bunco artist *n.* SPANISH a swindler (AS, JG, KC): **1993** *Short Cuts*, film: *Claire Kane is a bunco artist wanted in three states*; **2004** *New York Times*: *He plays a small-time bunco artist* ‖ since 1887, from *banca* "card game similar to monte" and *artist*

bunco game *n.* SPANISH a swindle (JG, KC): **2014** *Mobile Spokesman-Review*: *He was arrested for running a bunco game*; **2015** *San Diego Union-Tribune*: *What do we expect? A promise that you won't try this kind of bunco game again?* ‖ since 1875, from *banca* "card game similar to monte" and *game*

bupkes, bupkis, bobkes, bopkes *n.* YIDDISH [1] nothing or an absurdly meager amount (AS, JG, KC): **2013** *InformationWeek*: *Why does the U.S. Navy get all that money and we get bupkis?* **2013** *Seattle Times*: *For the fourth week in a row, we get bupkis* [2] something absurdly trivial (JG): **2006** *Walkout*, film: *"How much money do you make?" "As much as you do, which is bupkis"*; **2015** Market Watch: *Most of it adds up to bupkes* ‖ in the first sense since 1938, in the second since 1968, from *bobkes* "dung" or "manure"

burg *n.* GERMAN a town (JG, KC): **2018** *Reno News & Review*: *It winds its way through the hills and the valleys, and through the center of our burg*; **2019** *Capitol Weekly*: *Where, they ask, does one go to eat, drink and be merry in this burg?* ‖ since 1843, from *Burg* "town"

burrito *n.* SPANISH *offensive* [1] anyone of Latin American descent (JG): **1987** *Miami Vice*, NBC-TV series: *Do you believe the stones on this burrito?* **2010** Urban Dictionary: *"Yo, look at those Spanish people over there!" "That's one big burrito!"* [2] the penis, especially if big (JG): **2007** *Curious Girlfriend*: *Sandra thrusts his big burrito in the middle of her really lovely tatas*; **2012** Smut Post: *The guy stuffs his burrito in her pussy* ‖ since 1980 in the first sense, since 1989 in the second, from *burrito* "cornflour tortilla with savory filling"

Burrito City *n.* SPANISH El Paso, Texas (JG): **2008** Gaia Online: *I live near El Paso, TX, which some people used to call Burrito City*; **2012** PB Nation: *I live in Burrito City* ‖ since 1975, from *burrito* "cornflour tortilla with savory filling" and *city*

burro *n.* SPANISH a Mexican smuggler of contraband, especially narcotics, which is strapped to their back: **2004** Curtis Marez: *The contemporary practice of calling smugglers "mules" and "burros" goes back to the Mexican revolutionary times*; **2011** My San Antonio: *Burros smuggled booze during Prohibition and dope in recent times* ‖ dating unknown, from *burro* "donkey"

bushwa *n.* FRENCH nonsense (JG, TD): **2014** *Mother Jones*: *Was this little more than routine campaign trail bushwa?* **2022** *Salt Lake Tribune*: *Despite the bushwa spread by Fox News, anti-vaxxers aren't doing a single thing to preserve their own lives* ‖ since 1906, from *bois de vache* "dried cow dung"

buttinski, buttinsky *n.* YIDDISH someone who habitually interferes with someone else's affairs (AS, JG, KC): **2012** *New York Times*: *Ivy St. Helier is delicious as a painfully persistent buttinsky*; **2015** *New York Magazine*: *Not to be* *a buttinski, but I'd like to chime in and suggest something* || since 1902, from *butt in* and jocular suffix *-ski*

buttinsky *see* buttinski

by *prep.* YIDDISH [1] as far as concerns (JG, KC): **2011** *News*, ABC-TV program: *If the Bush tax cuts on the wealthy were left to expire, that's fine by you?* **2011** *Nashville Scene*: *Whatever the dude has to do to keep making records is cool by me* [2] at, at the place of (KC): **2012** Facebook: *I have arranged to meet by his place for dinner tonight*; **2013** Meet Up: *We could meet by my place* || since 1920s, from *bay* "as far as concerns" or "at the place of"

C

caballo *n.* SPANISH heroin (JG, KC, TD): **2009** Robert A. Wilson: *This compound was known as heroin to white people and caballo to Ed and Sam's Puerto Rican neighbors*; **2014** Home Spring: *You have to bring five grams of coke with you – but no caballo – these people don't go for caballo* || since 1969, from *caballo* "horse"

caboose *n.* SPANISH a prison, jail, or guardhouse (KC): **1996** Leon Pettiway: *They put me inside a caboose, and the caboose was full of rats*; **2013** Trip Advisor: *You get a certificate saying you "survived a night" in the caboose* || since 1865, from *calabozo* "jail or prison," ultimately from "dungeon"

cabron (or **cabrón**) *n.* SPANISH *offensive* a despicable man, especially if also stupid and brutish (TD): **2000** *Los Angeles Times*: *How Democrats would cheer to hear him call George W. Bush a cabron!* **2015** *Stanford Daily*: *Quit acting like a cabron* || since 1974, from *cabrón* "despicable man," literally "castrated goat"

ca-ca[1] (or **caca**) *n.* SPANISH [1] defecation or excrement (JG, TD): **1987** *Good Morning Vietnam*, film: *"I'm pretty sure you can step in crap." "Okay, we can stop with the debate on the ca-ca right now"*; **2005** *People Magazine*: *Our teacher commented it smelled of ca-ca* [2] nonsense (JG): **2006** Harmony Central: *Unless there are pics to prove otherwise, this story is ca-ca*; **2013** *Tulsa World*: *Ron, your long dissertation about what liberals believe is total ca-ca* || since 1952 in the first sense, since 1967 in the second, from *caca* "excrement" and *cagar* "to defecate"

ca-ca[2] (or **caca**) *v.* SPANISH to defecate (JG): **2012** Ayisha Monroe: *Skip was still ca-ca'ing all over the place*; **2013** Baby Gaga: *I tried putting her on the potty yesterday when she said she ca-caed, but after she sat there for a minute, I put her diaper back on* || since 1952, from *caca* "excrement" and *cagar* "to defecate"

calaboose *n.* SPANISH [1] a prison, jail, or guardhouse (AS, JG, KC, TD): **1990** *Los Angeles Times*: *The crime landed her in the calaboose*; **2015** *Avery Journal Times*: *He arrested Williams and placed him in the local calaboose* [2] a prison cell (KC): **1988** *Los Angeles Times*: *The idea of spending the night in the calaboose isn't appealing*; **2007** Roots Web: *The calaboose was 20 feet long by 10 feet wide by 12 feet high* || since 1792, from *calabozo* "jail or prison," ultimately from "dungeon"

Califas *n.* SPANISH California (TD): **2005** Indy Bay: *I grew up in the barrios in Califas*; **2010** *Los Angeles Times*: *I'm looking to move to Califas* ‖ since 1974, from *California* and *Las Californias*

calo (or **caló**) *n.* SPANISH Chicano street slang, especially with a heavy use of rhyming (JG): **1992** Luis Valdez: *They are speaking calo and calling themselves Chicanos*; **1995** *Los Angeles Times*: *The magazine takes its name from the calo, or slang, spoken and written by the Chicano graffiti artists since the 1930s* ‖ since 1970, from *calo* "slang of Spanish gypsies"

canamo (or **cáñamo**) *n.* SPANISH marijuana (JG): **2012** Drug War Chronicle: *Back then, it was known as canamo, the Spanish word for cannabis*; **2014** uKnowLingo: *Some canamo would be nice* ‖ since 1971, from *cáñamo* "hemp" or "reed"

canary *n.* YIDDISH someone or something perceived to bring bad luck (TD): **2007** Discovery Gaming: *Yeah, he's a canary, but don't let that put you off. Not like it's his fault*; **2012** Fan Fiction: *He hasn't had much luck with men. Maybe he's a canary* ‖ since 1968, from phonetic resemblance to *keyn eyn-(h)ore*, literally "(may) no evil eye (befall)"

canton (or **cantón**) *n.* SPANISH an apartment or a house: **2007** Urban Dictionary: *Let's meet up at my cantón later*; **2012** *Grimm*, NBC-TV series: *There is only my list, in my canton, on my conditions* ‖ dating unknown, from *cantón* "canton"

capeesh[1] *excl.* ITALIAN do you understand (AS, JG, TD): **1998** *Millennium*, Fox-TV series: *I'm trying to help you out here, capeesh?* **2003** *Los Angeles Times*: *Any of you makes any noise during this movie, you're dealing with me, capeesh?* ‖ since 1946, from *capisce* "do you understand" and *capire* "understand"

capeesh[2] *v.* ITALIAN to understand (JG, KC): **1995** *Simpsons*, Fox-TV series: *"Well, do you understand?" "Everything except 'capeesh'"*; **2013** Roominate: *Even though this was written by a lawyer, it's impossible not to capeesh* ‖ since 1946, from *capisce* "do you understand" and *capire* "understand"

capo *n.* ITALIAN the head of a local unit of the Mafia (AS, JG, KC, TD): **2006** Chicago Syndicate: *He is depicted as the capo in charge of the family's South Florida operations*; **2015** Topix: *The capo in the Gambino family was laundering money through mortgage fraud* ‖ since 1952, from *capo* "head"

capo di tutti capi *n.* ITALIAN the senior figure in the Mafia, the chief of all chiefs (JG, KC): **1992** *Chicago Tribune*: *The reputed capo di tutti capi remains at large*; **2011** *Shameless*, Showtime-TV series: *I'm married to the head of a family now, capo di tutti capi* ‖ since 1952, from *capo di tutti capi* "head of all heads"

carajo[1] *n.* SPANISH *offensive* [1] the penis: **2013** YouTube: *He can suck my carajo*; **2014** Guestbook: *Man, he was so proud of his carajo!* [2] a despicable person: **2013** Urban Dictionary: *Some carajo just nicked my bike*; **2017** *Snowfall*, FX-TV series: *Look at me, carajo. I'm not gonna run* [3] nonsense or a lie: **2007** *We Own the Night*, film: *What carajo did you tell him?* **2013** UCB student: *Do you believe this carajo?* [4] something annoying, worthless, or of bad quality: **2007** *Rise of the Footsoldier*, film: *What carajo have you made?* **2014** Word Press: *Just don't invite me over to dinner with that carajo on your pizza* || dating unknown, from *carajo* "penis"

carajo² (or **ay carajo**) *excl.* SPANISH *offensive* [1] I am irritated: **1997** *Dance with the Devil*, film: *Carajo! What the fuck is this?* **2006** *Scanner Darkly*, film: *We almost died, carajo!* [2] I am surprised: **1990** *Fresh Prince of Bel-Air*, NBC-TV series: *Maybe she's fine, like — ay carajo — like your sister!* **2005** *Conversations with Other Women*, film: *Carajo! What time is it?* || dating unknown, from *carajo* "I am irritated" or "I am surprised," ultimately from "penis"

caramba (or **ay caramba**) *excl.* SPANISH [1] I am irritated (AS): **1991** *Adventures of Tintin*, film: *Caramba! I missed again!* **2007** *Los Angeles Times*: *Country charm? Ay caramba!* [2] I am surprised (AS): **2008** Reuters: *They expect me to take my sword and . . . caramba! I left my sword at home!* **2012** Rómulo Gallegos: *Oh! Caramba! What an honor to have you come to see me!* || dating unknown, from *carajo* "I am irritated" or "I am surprised," ultimately from "penis"

cardenales *n.* SPANISH barbiturates (TD): **2010** *News*, NBC-TV program: *He became addicted to cardenales, barbiturates*; **2014** UNM student: *Cardenales are barbiturates* || since 1997, from *cardenales* "cardinals (birds)"

carga *n.* SPANISH heroin (JG, TD): **1998** Reyes Ramos: *I can buy an ounce of carga [heroin] easier*; **2005** Urban Dictionary: *Hey, holmes, who's got the carga?* || since 1968, from *carga* "charge" or "load"

carnal *n.* SPANISH a close male friend, especially from the neighborhood (JG, TD): **1992** *American Me*, film: *I'm telling you this because you're my carnal*; **1993** *Bound by Honor*, film: *I'll always love you for it, carnal* || since 1950, from *carnal* "fleshy"

carnalito *n.* SPANISH a close male friend: **2009** *Los Angeles Times*: *I miss you a lot carnalito, wish you were here right now*; **2014** *Dallas Morning News*: *He read a poem to their carnalito* || since 1950, from *carnalito* "little close male friend," ultimately from *carnal* "fleshy"

carne *n.* SPANISH [1] heroin (JG): **2010** Blogger: *The police seized ten kilo of carne*; **2010** Twitter: *He OD'd on carne* [2] *offensive* the penis: **2008** Forums: *Some strange Mexicano dude is grabbing your wife's hips and grinding his carne into her rear*; **2014** Twitter: *Liam has a big carne* || since 1982, from *carne* "meat"

carucha *n.* SPANISH a car, especially old and battered one: **2009** Mustang World: *You roll around blasting them oldies in your carucha*; **2010** LA Eastside: *My dad stopped his carucha abruptly in the middle of an intersection* || dating unknown, from *carucha* "carriage"

casa *n.* SPANISH a brothel (JG): **2002** City X Guide: *It's 250 pesos ($6) to take out the girls from the casa*; **2004** International Sex Guide: *It's regardless of whether you do* *the girl in the casa or your hotel, and then the girl negotiates her price with you* ‖ dating unknown, from *casa* "house"

casabas *n.* TURKISH *potentially offensive* a woman's breasts, especially if large (AS, JG, KC, TD): **2001** *Los Angeles Times*: *Did you check out her casabas?* **2003** *American Wedding*, film: *Titties, tatas, casabas, bazoongas, all up in our faces! Buck up, fellas! Show some enthusiasm!* ‖ since 1939, from *casaba* "kind of melon"

Catholic bagel *n.* YIDDISH a nontraditional bagel, especially flavored (KC): **2005** Daily Kos: *Poppyseed is one flavor of a new line of Catholic bagels that seek to take over the bagel market from the Jews*; **2011** Chowhound: *While I'd come to accept Catholic bagels (raisins and cinnamon), I'd never seen a cheddar cheese bagel before* ‖ dating unknown, from *Catholic* and *beygl* "bagel," and the idea of departing from traditional Jewish ways

cazzo *n.* ITALIAN *offensive* [1] the penis (JG): **2018** Michael Anderson: *His confusion grew to breaking point when he realized that his cazzo had become stiff*; **2018** Pornhub: *Handsome Italian Guy Wanks His Cazzo* [2] a despicable person: **1996** *Gotti*, film: *Nobody gives a fuck about this greedy cazzo*; **1997** *Kiss Me, Guido*, film: *"Me? Hey, I was only with her once ... well, twice!" "Cazzo!"* ‖ dating unknown, from *cazzo* "penis"

cement kimono *n.* JAPANESE a casing of cement containing a corpse for disposal in deep water (JG, KC): **1991** *Oscar*, film: *You're lucky you didn't upset me today. You'd be wearing a cement kimono!* **2014** Ed Falco: *Dutch killed Bo, put him in a cement kimono, and dropped him in the East River because he thought he was conspiring with Luciano* ‖ since 1940, from *cement* and *kimono* "loose traditional Japanese robe"

chacha *n.* SPANISH [1] a woman: **2006** *Black Snake Woman*, film: *"This here's my woman." "That chacha will do you no good"*; **2013** Twitter: *Call your mom, call your chacha. Tell 'em to hook me up with them* [2] *potentially offensive* the vagina: **2013** Porno4Portable: *As soon as the guy sticks his schlong in her chacha, she starts screaming*; **2015** Freeones: *She let him touch her chacha* ‖ dating unknown, from *muchacha* "young girl" or "young maid"

chale *excl.* SPANISH I say no (JG, TD): **2010** Laura E. Garcia et al.: *But the city of San Diego said "chale" (no way) we're going to make a highway patrol substation there*; **2012** David Montejano: *Alberto kept telling Primo that we had to kill for la raza, to which Primo said, "Chale [no]!"* ‖ since 1950, from old Spanish *chale* "crazy"

Charlie Cong *n.* VIETNAMESE Viet Cong or its member (TD): **1989** *Tour of Duty*, CBS-TV series: *We kicked Charlie Cong's butt at Tet*; **2015** *Wall Street Journal*: *Ain't nobody here but Charlie Cong, as in Viet Cong* ‖ since 1970, from *Charlie* and *(Viet) Cong* "Vietnamese Communist Army"

cheapo[1] *adj.* PSEUDO-SPANISH cheap (JG, KC): **1999** *Bone Collector*, film: *I need you to buy me one of those cheapo cardboard cameras*; **2015** Cleveland Online: *He's a pilot for a cheapo airline* ‖ since 1967, from *cheap* and mock Spanish suffix *-o*

cheapo[2] *n.* PSEUDO-SPANISH [1] something cheap (JG, KC): **2004** Twin Turbo: *I bought some cheapos from good old Ebay.com*; **2005** Democratic Underground: *There are some cheapos available at any music store* [2] a stingy or parsimonious person (JG, KC): **2004** *White Chicks*, film: *You promised to give us $5 each. Cheapo!* **2008** *One, Two, Many*, film: *"Yeah, I'll have a beer. Are you buying?" "Oh, you're such a cheapo!"* || since 1976, from *cheap* and mock Spanish suffix *-o*

cheeba *n.* SPANISH marijuana, especially if potent (JG, KC, TD): **1999** *Big Daddy*, film: *I'm puffing the cheeba*; **2006** *Big Momma's House 2*, film: *Child smoking the cheeba?* || since 1970, from *chiba* "marijuana"

cheechako *n.* CHINOOK a newcomer or novice (AS, JG, KC): **2009** *Wyvern*, film: *"I couldn't sleep!" "Most cheechakos can't"*; **2012** Fodor's: *Newcomers are referred to as cheechakos, which is Chinook for "newcomer"* || since 1897, from *chee chako* "newcomer"

chela *n.* SPANISH beer: **2014** *Cosmopolitan*: *This 4th of July be sure to have a cold chela and some delicious food*; **2014** *Latin Life*: *While you're enjoying a cold chela or a margarita, the music plays live in the background* || dating unknown, from *chela* "beer," literally "blonde"

chiba *n.* SPANISH marijuana (JG, KC, TD): **2001** *Super Troopers*, film: *These local mothers have got a hundred keys of chiba and I don't know it?* **2019** Maurice Broaddus: *That's an excuse to smoke chiba, not a real religion* || since 1981, from *chiba* "marijuana"

chica *n.* SPANISH a woman, especially young one: **2003** *Bad Boys II*, film: *This black chica working for the Russians was a maniac lunatic*; **2008** *Beverly Hills Chihuahua*, film: *Don't you speak any Spanish, chica?* || since 1940, from *chica* "girl" or "young woman"

chica blanca *n.* SPANISH a white woman, especially young one: **2006** *Bring It On: All or Nothing*, film: *Don't be getting mad at me because that chica blanca turned you down*; **2009** *Unforgiven*, film: *Hey, chica blanca! How are you?* || since 1940 from *chica* "girl" and *blanca* "white"

Chicana *n.* SPANISH a Mexican or Mexican American woman (AS): **2003** *Los Angeles Times*: *It is dedicated to social empowerment of Chicanas through higher education*; **2012** *Dallas Observer*: *I'm not a Mexican, I'm a Chicana, and that's different* || since 1947, from *Chicana* "a female American of Mexican descent, usually first generation and born in the North of the USA," ultimately from *Mexicana* "female Mexican"

Chicano *n.* SPANISH a Mexican or Mexican American (AS, TD): **2005** *Silicon Valley's Metro*: *It's something that resonates with a lot of Chicanos*; **2020** *Los Angeles Times*: *Perera was among the young Chicanos who had come looking for trouble that day* || since 1947, from *Chicano* "a male American of Mexican descent, usually first generation and born in the North of the USA," ultimately from *Mexicano* "male Mexican"

Chicano time *n.* SPANISH *offensive* a lack of punctuality (TD): **2005** Urban Dictionary: *"He still isn't here, I thought we said two o'clock." "I'm sure he's OK, Chicano time"*; **2006** José Casas: *Alex, come on! The school doesn't run on chicano time!* || since 1972, from *Chicano* "an American of Mexican descent, usually first generation and born in the North of the USA," ultimately from *Mexicano* "male Mexican," and *time*

chicharra *n.* SPANISH marijuana or marijuana cigarette, especially its leftovers (JG): **2002** Thomas Nordegren: *Chicharra is a colloquial term for leftovers of a joint of marijuana*; **2014** Word Meaning: *We will smoke us a chicharra* || since 1960, from *chicharra* "cicada"

chichi *n.* JAPANESE *offensive* female breasts (AS, KC): **1990** *Taking Care of Business*, film: *Nice tits! Nice chichi!* **2015** Daviant Art: *This gal is thick! Big chichi* || since 1879, from Japanese *chichi* "female breasts" or "milk"

chichis *n.* SPANISH *potentially offensive* female breasts (JG): **2014** Deborah Rodriguez: *I loved Analisa and her chichis*; **2022** *Marvelous Mrs. Maisel*, Amazon-TV series: *It's a strip club, girls are shaking their chichis* || since 1966, from Spanish *chiches* "female breasts"

chichona *n.* SPANISH *potentially offensive* a big-breasted woman: **2008** *Harper's Magazine*: *She was a chichona and it was hard not to know that, especially when she was wearing a bathing suit*; **2008** Soy Chicano: *She truly is a chichona* || dating unknown, from *chichona* "big-breasted woman," ultimately from *chichis* "female breasts"

chicle *n.* SPANISH heroin (TD): **2007** *88 Minutes*, film: *"Chicle?" "No, thank you"*; **2015** International Living: *It was once a center for shipment of chicle* || since 1994, from *chicle* "gum"

chico *n.* SPANISH a young person of Latin American descent, especially a Mexican (JG): **2010** Topix: *Hey chico, I'm just curious, do you know anything about English grammar?* **2014** Tweet Tunnel: *Hola chico, how ya doing?* || since 1966, from *chico* "boy" or "young man" and *Chico,* popular Mexican name

chido *adj.* SPANISH excellent: **2008** *OC Weekly*: *Dangelo promises to spend $14 million to repair the YMCA. Sounds chido, right?* **2014** Twitter: *Your hair looks chido* || dating unknown, from *chido* "excellent"

chihuahua (or **ay chihuahua**) *excl.* SPANISH [1] I am annoyed or disgusted: **2013** *News*, CNN-TV program: *Ay, chihuahua! Not this again!* **2022** Tumblr: *Ay chihuahua! Get those fucking beans out of my face!* [2] I am surprised: **2004** *Laws of Attraction*, film: *"I want you." "Ooh, chihuahua! Nice opening line, I like it"*; **2012** Huffington Post: *Chihuahua! My body has never experienced this kind of intensity* || dating unknown, from *ay chihuahua* "I am disgusted or surprised," perhaps from *chingar* "to copulate," ultimately from *Chihuahua,* a city in Mexico

chinch *n.* SPANISH [1] a bedbug (AS, JG): 2010 *New York Magazine*: *It issued a warning about a bug called cimex lextularius, known as a "chinch"*; 2014 Bedbug King: *Bedbugs are sometimes called chinches* [2] an annoying or despicable person: 2010 Urban Dictionary: *Frank didn't want to reimburse me for the fees. He's such a chinch*; 2014 Blogs: *I was scared I'd never get to meet you and call you a chinch* || since 1861, from *chinche* "bug" or "bedbug"

chinch pad *n.* SPANISH a cheap hotel or a room in such a hotel: 1995 Irving L. Allen: *Vermin-infested flops were also called flea houses, bug houses, and chinch pads*; 2013 Keith Huff: *He still lives in this one-room chinch pad looking over an alley* || since 1944, from *chinche* "bug" or "bedbug" and *pad* "lodging"

chinfest *n.* GERMAN an idle or gossipy conversation session (JG, KC): 2015 E-Reading Club: *I've had a chinfest with Pedro*; 2015 Facebook: *We have decided to postpone our chinfest till the fall* || since 1940, from *chin* "talk" and *Fest* "festival"

chinga *excl.* SPANISH *very offensive* [1] I am irritated: 2008 Blogspot: *Chinga! That's inconvenient!* 2014 Facebook: *Chinga! Where are my shoes?* [2] I am surprised: 2005 *Havoc*, film: *It's the jura! Chinga!* 2013 UCB student: *Chinga! What are you doing here?* || dating unknown, from *chingar* "to copulate"

chingado *excl.* SPANISH *offensive* I am irritated: 2008 Deviant Art: *Chingado! What did she just call me?* 2013 Fiction Press: *Chingado, what's the matter with you?* || since 1995, from *chingar* "to copulate"

chingao *excl.* SPANISH *offensive* I am irritated (JG): 2007 MSF High: *I was pissed. I shouted, "Chingao, it's me, pendejo!"*; 2011 Open Writing: *He was able to regain his balance just long enough to shout "chingao" before again flipping backward* || since 1995, from *chingar* "to copulate"

chingaso *n.* SPANISH [1] an important and influential person, especially one's chief (JG): 2006 Urban Dictionary: *Hector will kick your ass; he is the chingaso around here*; 2015 UNF student: *He pretended to be some big chingaso* [2] a fight, especially a fistfight (TD): 2007 Twisting Nether Gazette: *I had a chingaso. It means a fistfight here*; 2008 *Surfer Magazine*: *She looks like she'll throw a chingaso* || since 1990 in the first sense, since 1965 in the second, from *chingazo* "tough man"

chingo *adv.* SPANISH a great deal (JG): 2010 Forum Mazda Miata: *I didn't have to pay a chingo of money to have someone else do it for me*; 2014 Facebook: *You'll make chingo of people happy* || since 2003, from *chingo* "a lot of"

chingon[1] (or **chingón**) *n.* SPANISH an important and influential person, especially one's chief (JG, TD): 2003 Urban Dictionary: *That Eddie Cruz guy is one tough chingon*; 2012 *OC Weekly*: *He had packed a four-course meal with more than a few highlights showing what a chingón he really is and will be in this spot* || since 1974, from *chingazo* "tough man"

chingon[2] (or **chingón**) *adj.* SPANISH excellent: **2003** Urban Dictionary: *That was the most chingon game I've ever played*; **2013** *Houston Press*: *Houston music is chingon!* || since 1974, from *chingazo* "tough man"

chintzy *n.* HINDI cheap or inferior but showy (AS, KC): **1996** *Seinfeld*, NBC-TV series: *The doormat? Pretty chintzy, huh? Considering the money she makes*; **2007** *Grizzly Man*, film: *He had a chintzy felt hat and a cheap plastic apron* || since 1850, from *chintz* "stained or printed cotton fabric regarded as cheap and unstylish," ultimately from *chīṃṭ* "stain"

chiquita *n.* SPANISH a young woman, especially if attractive (JG): **2002** *Tribe Magazine*: *I just want to laze by the pool with a beer and some chiquitas*; **2022** Blogspot: *This place is filled with sexy chiquitas* || since 1942, from *chiquita* "little girl," a diminutive version of *chica* "girl" or "young woman"

chiquita banana *n.* SPANISH an attractive young woman (JG): **2014** Groove Shark: *I'm a chiquita banana*; **2014** *Glamour*: *William, we think she looks smashing! Do you think she looks like a chiquita banana?* || since 1969, from *chiquita* "little girl" and *banana*

chisme *n.* SPANISH gossip or rumors (TD): **2002** *Los Angeles Times*: *Tattlin's book is balanced between carefully observed reportage and chisme, or gossip*; **2002** Denise Chavez: *It was a family-type neighborhood where too many people knew enough chisme about me to make things uncomfortable* || since 1974, from *chisme* "gossip" and *cisma* "schism or separation"

chiva *n.* SPANISH heroin (JG, TD): **1998** *He Got Game*, film: *You got the uppers, the downers, the chiva, crystal meth*; **2014** *Albuquerque Journal*: *Young women were doing chiva (heroin) with friends* || since 1967, from *chiva* "heroin"

chocha *n.* SPANISH *offensive* the vagina (JG, KC): **2003** Raquel Z. Rivera: *Mention is made of a Latin chick smuggling drugs in her chocha*; **2012** *San Francisco Weekly*: *She is unafraid to talk about shaving her chocha* || since 1967, from *chocha* "vulva," literally "woodcock"

chochke, chotchke *n.* YIDDISH [1] a plaything or trinket (JG, KC): **2010** *Sons of Tucson*, Fox-TV series: *I got chotchkes and doodads*; **2016** *News*, NJTV-TV program: *We don't like spending money on chotchkes* [2] a cute and adorable person, especially a child (JG, KC): **2014** UCLA student: *She's a cute little chochke. What's her name?* **2019** Blogger: *I love to take pictures of my little chotchkes* || since 1964, from *tshatshke* "bauble" or "trinket," variant of *tsatske*

cholo *n.* SPANISH *offensive* [1] a young and tough Mexican American (AS, JG, TD): **2008** *In Plain Sight*, film: *A couple of years from now, you're just gonna be another hairnet-wearin' cholo*; **2010** *Los Angeles Times Magazine*: *My husband is a cholo (Hispanic Tough Guy) with his shaved head and tattoos* [2] a Mexican American teenage gang member (AS, JG, KC): **1992** *Gas, Food, Lodging*, film: *He's a cholo. Pure gangster*; **2004** *Criminal*, film: *I look like a businessman, and you look like a fucking* *cholo* || since 1971 in the first sense, since 1974 in the second, from *cholo* "halfbreed" and *Cholollán*, a district of Mexico

chonga *n.* SPANISH *potentially offensive* (especially in South Florida) a working-class, sexualized, and aggressive young woman: **2014** *Jersey Shore Massacre*, film: *If that chonga gives me one more look, I swear, I'm gonna fuck her up*; **2015** *Latina*: *Being a chonga means I do not have to apologize for my feminism* || since 1990, from *chonga* "working-class, sexualized young woman"

chooch[1] *n.* SPANISH *offensive* the vagina (KC): **2010** *National Spectator*: *Lady Gaga shows her her chooch*; **2011** *You Be Mom*: *Is your chooch bleeding?* || since 1920, from *chocha* "vulva," literally "woodcock"

chooch[2] *n.* ITALIAN *offensive* a stupid person (JG): **2004** *New York Times*: *The film does succeed in demonstrating why someone might call him a chooch*; **2014** *Intelligence*, CBS-TV series: *You think we don't know what you're doing, chooch?* | since 1935, from *ciuccio* "fool," literally "donkey"

chop chop *adv.* CHINESE quickly or instantly (JG, KC): **2007** *Avatar*, film: *Come on, Louise, chop chop!* **2016** TMZ: *Let's go. Chop chop!* || since 1830, from Anglo-Chinese Pidgin *chap chap* "quickly"

chopped liver *n.* YIDDISH [1] an insignificant or trivial amount: **1990** *Los Angeles Times*: *Twenty years ain't chopped liver*; **2006** *Washington Post*: *$400 million isn't chopped liver* [2] something insignificant or trivial: **2009** *New York, I Love You*, film: *She'll go to the prom with you tonight, and that's not chopped liver*; **2016** *New York Times*: *This is one of the great centers of learning in the country. I'm not in a position to think that that's chopped liver* [3] someone insignificant or trivial: **1991** *Last Boy Scout*, film: *"Let's wait inside." "What am I, chopped liver?"*; **2016** TVLine: *Time to realize you have a daughter, and that she's not chopped liver* || dating unknown, from *gehakte leber* "chopped liver"

chorizo *n.* SPANISH *offensive* the penis (TD): **2011** Topix: *I heard he has a big chorizo*; **2014** Homosexual Tube: *He strokes off his big chorizo and shoots his load all over himself* || since 1995, from *chorizo* "spicy pork sausage"

chota *n.* SPANISH [1] a police informer (JG): **1989** Earthlink: *He's a chota, a known informant*; **2007** Soy Chicano: *Maybe he's a chota* [2] police (JG, TD): **2007** *Day Break*, ABC-TV series: *See, this chota, he tried to sell me out to Booth*; **2010** Twitter: *They shouted, "Chota's coming!"* || since 1967 in the first sense, since 1971 in the second, from *choto* "informer"

chotchke *see* chochke

chow[1] *n.* CHINESE food (JG, KC): **1993** *Fugitive*, film: *I'm starving. Had enough prison chow*; **2000** *Men of Honor*, film: *What's for chow, Cookie?* || since 1856, from Anglo-Chinese Pidgin *chow* "mixture of food"

chow[2] *v.* CHINESE to eat (JG, KC): **1991** *Barton Fink*, film: *All right, let's chow!* **2009** Reddit: *We chowed and drank a few beers* || since 1907, from Anglo-Chinese Pidgin *chow* "mixture of food"

chow down *v.* CHINESE to eat voraciously or set to eating (JG, KC): **2010** *Due Date*, film: *It's time to roll to Chili's and chow down with my guys*; **2013** *Los Angeles Times*: *He chowed down on tacos gringas* [2] to perform oral sex; **2012** YouTube: *I would love to chow down on her pussy*; **2015** Red Tube: *Two Japanese hotties chow down on a hard dong* || since 1907 in the first sense, since 1951 in the second, from Anglo-Chinese Pidgin *chow* "mixture of food" and *down*

chow-down *n.* CHINESE [1] an act of eating (JG): **2008** *Five Dollars a Day*, film: *What do you say to a chow-down?* **2007** Chowhound: *We had a chow-down at Henry's* [2] oral sex (JG): **2013** Tribesone: *He is known as a chowdown champion and sex machine*; **2015** *Brooklyn Newspaper*: *Try to find Trevor and have a chowdown with him* || since 1939 in the first sense, since 1951 in the second, from Anglo-Chinese Pidgin *chow* "mixture of food" and *down*

chowhound *n.* CHINESE an enthusiastic eater (JG, KC): **2010** *Family Guy*, Fox-TV series: *You're a chowhound, aren't ya, Pete?* **2010** Trip Advisor: *It's a must stop for chowhounds!* || since 1917, from Anglo-Chinese Pidgin *chow* "mixture of food" and *hound* "enthusiast," and analogy to *boozehound* "alcoholic"

chow time *n.* CHINESE a mealtime, especially in an institution (JG): **2004** *Meet the Fockers*, film: *I invented something to ease his anxiety during chow time*; **2001** *Los Angeles Times*: *At 3 p.m., it's chow time for the center's twelve young but hungry sharks* || since 1907, from Anglo-Chinese Pidgin *chow* "mixture of food," *time,* and analogy to *sack time* "bed time"

chuc *n.* SPANISH [1] a young and tough Mexican American (TD): **2003** My Diary: *She's really nice but all the chucs take advantage of her*; **2014** UNM student: *He hangs out with some chucs* [2] a Mexican American gang member (JG, TD): **2009** Reality Mod: *The only thing that can defeat a chuc is a chuc*; **2010** Blogs: *Don't fuck around with the chucks!* || since 1963 in the first sense, since 1966 in the second, from *pachuco* "flashily dressed or vulgar"

chuco *n.* SPANISH [1] a young and tough Mexican American (TD): **2007** Yahoo Groups: *Not all cholos and chucos are criminals*; **2009** Laura Lee Cummings: *Bob met some chucos from New Mexico* [2] a Mexican American gang member (JG, TD): **2013** Radical Riders: *These chucos fused and blended together with the rural bandit types*; **2014** Wattpad: *All the chucos were cruisin with their Impalas* || since 1966, from *pachuco* "flashily dressed or vulgar"

Chuco Town *n.* SPANISH El Paso, Texas: **2006** Soy Chicano: *I'm from Chuco Town and I nearly fell off my chair from laughing*; **2013** *San Jose Mercury News*: *The city of El Paso was typically referred to as Chuco Town* || since 2005, *(pa)chuco* "flashily dressed or vulgar" and *town*

chula *n.* SPANISH an attractive woman: **2005** *Harsh Times*, film: *"You're looking fine as fuck, chula!" "Don't touch me, please!";* **2014** Twitter: *Maybe one day you'll meet a chula who can do it* ‖ dating unknown, from *chula* "attractive woman"

Chulajuana *n.* SPANISH *potentially offensive* border town Chula Vista, California: **2013** *San Diego Reader*: *I am headed to Chulajuana;* **2014** *Voice of San Diego*: *Chula Vistans are tired of their city being called "Chulajuana"* ‖ dating unknown, from *Chula (Vista)* literally "beautiful view," and *Tijuana,* a city in Mexico

chulo *n.* SPANISH [1] an attractive man: **2013** Urban Dictionary: *Look at that little chulo over there with the chubby cheeks! He's so cute!* **2015** Facebook: *Who's the chulo in the middle?* [2] an annoying or despicable man: **2003** *South Park*, Comedy Central-TV series: *How am I supposed to make an album with those chulos?* **2007** *Dexter*, Showtime-TV series: *That chulo's gonna walk again!* ‖ dating unknown, from *chulo* "attractive man" or "pimp"

chunt *n.* SPANISH *offensive* a Mexican national, especially if poor (TD): **1988** James Diego Vigil: *Mexican nationals are referred to as chuntaros or chunts;* **2010** Topix: *Stupid chunts are like the plague. When is Fontana going to clean up their act and make the city livable again?* ‖ since 1988, from *chúntaro* "someone from the Mexican state of Michoacán" or "Mexican with a bad taste"

chuntaro *n.* SPANISH *offensive* a Mexican national, especially if poor (TD): **2007** *San Diego Union-Tribune*: *The chuntaros from el barrio are back;* **2014** *Phoenix New Times*: *The firm handshake is the hallmark of the older generation and chúntaros* ‖ since 1988, from *chúntaro* "someone from the Mexican state of Michoacán" or "Mexican with a bad taste"

churro *n.* SPANISH [1] *potentially offensive* the penis: **2005** Urban Dictionary: *His churro is nice and thick;* **2007** Brown Pride: *She's talking about a guy who said that he had a big churro aka big dick* [2] a marijuana cigarette: **2013** *We're the Millers*, film: *It's a cute little drug-dealing community. They probably sell churros;* **2014** Instagram: *Let's smoke a churro!* ‖ dating unknown, from *churro* "penis" or "marijuana cigarette," literally "strip of fried dough dusted with sugar or cinnamon"

chutspa *see* chutzpah

chutzpah, chutzpa *n.* YIDDISH [1] arrogance or insolence (AS, JG, KC): **2012** *New York Times*: *Chutzpah, according to the old definition, is when you murder your parents and, then plead for mercy because you're an orphan;* **2016** *South Florida Sun-Sentinel*: *Malachi Love-Robinson, the teen who posed as a doctor, is now holding press conferences. What chutzpah!* [2] bravery and courage (AS, JG): **2007** *I Want Candy*, film: *You've got chutzpah, I like that. I give you two minutes;* **2013** *Contra Costa Times*: *I don't believe our state legislators have the chutzpah to pass a legalization bill* ‖ since 1883, from *khutspe* "impudence" or "audacity"

chutz-spa *n.* YIDDISH an expensive, pretentious spa, catering to rich and pampered Jewish females: **2003** *Los Angeles Magazine*: *A Visit to the Chutz-Spa;*

2003 *Jewish Journal*: *Two Jewish New Yorkers are relaxing at a California health club called The Chutz Spa* ‖ since 1990s, from *chutz(pah)* and *spa* and the phonetic resemblance

ciao *excl.* ITALIAN [1] goodbye (AS, JG, KC): **2009** *New York Times*: *He nodded slightly and said, "Ciao!"*; **2021** *News*, CBC-TV program: *Nobody agrees with my loss of basic freedom rights, so ciao!* [2] hello (AS, KC): **2018** *Los Angeles Times*: *Welcome to Los Angeles. Ciao. I just landed*; **2021** *Good Housekeeping*: *Ciao guys, welcome to my new restaurant in London* ‖ since 1919, from *ciao* "goodbye," ultimately from *schiavo* "I am your slave"

cinch *n.* SPANISH [1] something certain (AS, JG, KC): **2008** NOLA: *That seems to be a cinch, as Mendoza has not mounted much of a campaign*; **2014** *Chicago Tribune*: *It's a cinch that many of her critics haven't read the book themselves* [2] something easily done (AS, JG, KC): **1993** *Seinfeld*, NBC-TV series: *"Did you get it?" "It was a cinch"*; **2000** *New York Times*: *Getting to Williamsburg is a cinch* ‖ since 1887, from *cincha* "saddle girth," which, when tight, fosters certainty

clica *n.* SPANISH a gang (JG): **2013** *Los Angeles Times*: *They prove their loyalty to the clica*; **2013** Stranger: *They purchase weapons for the clica, pay lawyers for those in prison* ‖ since 1991, from *clica* "clique"

cliterati *n.* ITALIAN *potentially offensive* [1] influential women, especially lesbian or feminist writers: **2015** Word Press: *"You're nothing but a wet hole" may be my new standby insult for the cliterati*; **2016** Facebook: *Brush your teeth, and always remember to read some cliterati* [2] men who know how to satisfy women orally: **2004** *New York Times*: *Urging men to become members of the cliterati, he deconstructs the female anatomy and arousal cycle*; **2015** Wired: *The result is an innovative vibrator for the cliterati* ‖ since 2000, from *clit* "clitoris" and plural suffix *-ati*, analogous to *literati*

coca *n.* SPANISH cocaine: **2001** *Blow*, film: *I do not trust $600,00 worth of coca to someone I don't know*; **2011** *Los Angeles Times*: *In my last severe depression, I took coca again* ‖ dating unknown, from *cocaína* "cocaine"

cock *n.* FRENCH *potentially offensive* the vagina (JG): **1997** Gini Sikes: *To them, Coco said, cock meant pussy*; **2013** Twitter: *She got a vacuum cleaner that fits her cock* ‖ since 1833, from *coquille* "cockleshell" or "cowrie"

cojones *n.* SPANISH [1] *potentially offensive* testicles (AS, JG, TD): **1994** *Speed*, film: *You got some big, round, hairy cojones*; **2006** *Los Angeles Times*: *What's a male without his cojones?* [2] courage or audacity (AS, JG, KC, TD): **2005** *Fun with Dick and Jane*, film: *I think it takes a lot of cojones to do what you two have done today*; **2015** *Wall Street Journal*: *It boils down to technique, concentration, and cojones* ‖ since 1932, from *cojones* "testicles"

colorado *n.* SPANISH a red barbiturate capsule (TD): **2006** Academia: *There's these other pills that we'd call colorados (reds)*; **2013** Blogs: *Can you OD on colorados?* ‖ since 1971, from *colorado* "the color red"

compa *n.* SPANISH a close friend (JG, TD): **2007** *Los Angeles Times*: *Like many of his compas, Castro was moved to support the guerilla cause*; **2014** iPhoneogram: *I got it for Christmas from your compa and I love it too!* ‖ since 2003, from *compadre* "godfather"

compadre *n.* SPANISH a close friend (AS, JG, TD): **2006** *Dexter*, Showtime-TV series: *You know, compadre, she's got a hot body, but her face?* **2010** *El Paso Times*: *My regards to El Teo and his compadre, Muletas* ‖ since 1833, from *compadre* "godfather"

companera (or **compañera**) *n.* SPANISH a female companion, especially in illegal activity: **2006** *Los Angeles Times*: *Her companera considers fiction a form of "high gossip"*; **2010** *South Florida Sun-Sentinel*: *When I opened my eyes, I saw my companeras dead* ‖ since 1845, from *compañera* "female companion" or "female partner"

companero (or **compañero**) *n.* SPANISH a companion, especially in illegal activity: **2002** *Los Angeles Times*: *His compañeros muttered that while he sat pretty in the States, they were risking all in the Caribbean*; **2015** *New Statesman*: *I mentioned this to my compañero* ‖ since 1845, from *compañero* "companion" or "partner"

compania (or **compaña**) *n.* SPANISH a group of friends: **2008** Diane Whiteside: *He had brought his compaña down to help*; **2014** Mexican Cupid: *I want to be with my compania* ‖ dating unknown, from *compañía* "company" or "circle of friends"

comparo *n.* PSEUDO-SPANISH a comparison: **2017** Auto Evolution: *Chevy's latest weapon easily outguns the Challenger Hellcat (we just couldn't help the comparo)*; **2018** Drive: *They published a comparo between the Model 3, the Chevy Bolt and the Nissan Leaf* ‖ dating unknown, from *comparison* and pseudo-Spanish suffix *-o*, ultimately meant to resemble Spanish *comparación* "comparison"

complicado *adj.* SPANISH complicated: **2011** *Love Ranch*, film: *"How come?" "Because it's, like, complicado"*; **2011** *Californication*, Showtime-TV series: *Life is mucho complicado right now, Stu. I'm kind of in the final death throes of a marriage* ‖ dating unknown, from *complicado* "complicated"

comprende[1] *excl.* SPANISH do you understand (TD): **2007** *Rockaway*, film: *We gotta get paid upfront, comprende?* **2021** Dodgers Nation: *I just couldn't envision him wanting to end his career by leaving in the second inning. Comprende?* ‖ since 1994, from *comprende* "do you understand" and *comprender* "to understand"

comprende[2] *v.* SPANISH to understand: **1997** Spinning Globe: *Can't you comprende that? That's your side of the line*; **2009** *Miss March*, film: *Juanita, I'm trying to do something. Do you comprende?* ‖ since 1994, from *comprende* "do you understand" and *comprender* "to understand"

comprendo[1] *excl.* SPANISH do you understand: **2008** *Pathology*, film: *You wanna play, you gotta bring something to the table. Comprendo?* **2010** *Undocumented*, film: *That's one thousand dollars, comprendo?* ‖ since 1994, from *comprende* "do you understand" and *comprender* "to understand"

comprendo² *v.* SPANISH to understand: **2009** *Escapist Magazine*: *"That's all." "I don't comprendo"*; **2014** Newsmax: *He has sufficient brain power to comprendo* || since 1994, from *comprende* "do you understand" and *comprender* "to understand"

computerati *n.* ITALIAN computer-proficient people, especially programmers: **2008** *Los Angeles Times*: *Hourlong episodes were broken into six eight-minute installments for the attention span impaired computerati*; **2016** *Chicago Tribune*: *Judges will be hearing plenty of evidence from computerati about why Apple's technical argument is right* || since 1990, from *computer* and plural suffix *-ati*, analogous to *literati*

coño¹ *n.* SPANISH *very offensive* [1] the vagina (JG): **2011** Fiction Press: *I put it in her coño and had sex!* **2014** World Sex Guide: *She wouldn't let me touch her coño* [2] women as sexual objects (JG): **2005** Blogspot: *She can be excused for believing that youth are ignorant and mainly interested in material possessions and getting some coño*; **2013** ASU student: *These guys came here looking for coño* || since 2007, from *coño* "vagina"

coño² (or **ay coño**) *excl.* SPANISH *very offensive* [1] I am irritated (JG): **2007** *Grindhouse*, film: *"Coño! You said ten!" "I'm sorry"*; **2012** *Miami New Times*: *Coño! If people knew what was going on!* [2] I am surprised: **2000** *Before Night Falls*, film: *Coño, he even has a private chauffeur!* **2014** Tumblr: *Coño! Why are you so cute?* || since 1936, from *coño* "I am surprised," ultimately from "vagina"

corral *v.* SPANISH to acquire, secure, or find (AS, JG, KC): **1990** *Baltimore Sun*: *He spent the day corraling votes*; **2013** Golf News Now: *I say let Mark Steinberg corral the money and employ a better publicist for Tiger* || since 1859, from *corral* "enclosed place"

correctamundo *adv.* PSEUDO-SPANISH correctly (TD): **2011** *Nurse Jackie*, Showtime-TV series: *"Zoey, right?" "Correctamundo"*; **2015** *Chicago Now*: *You can opt out any time, but then who would entertain you? Uh, no one. Correctamundo* || since 1992, from *correct* and *-mundo* "world"

Cosa Nostra *n.* ITALIAN an organized crime syndicate (AS): **1998** *Witness to the Mob*, film: *You are now part of the Cosa Nostra as a member of the Gambino family*; **2018** *Washington Times*: *Carmine Persico has been identified by the FBI as the longtime head of the New York Cosa Nostra* || since 1960, from *cosa nostra* "our thing"

coyote *n.* SPANISH a smuggler of illegal immigrants from Mexico into the USA (JG, KC): **2017** *New York Post*: *Alfredo paid a coyote $3,500 per person to get us across in a series of vans*; **2022** Florida Politics: *Where do border crossers find the coyotes transporting them into the country? Sometimes they just look on Facebook* || since 1923, from *coyote* "someone who acts as an intermediary, taking advantage of it"

crapfest *n.* GERMAN a nonsensical talk or presentation: **2009** *Los Angeles Times*: *I hope this doesn't turn into another crapfest*; **2013** *Lost Girl*, Showcase-TV series: *All I know is that this latest crapfest caused a whole mess of paperwork* || dating unknown, from *crap* "something worthless or nonsensical" and *Fest* "festival"

cruda (or **la cruda**) *n.* SPANISH hangover: **1987** *Los Angeles Times*: *It is a legendary early-morning cure for a hangover, or "la cruda"*; **2014** Facebook: *I'm drinking some more to recover from la cruda* || dating unknown, from *la cruda* "hangover," literally "raw"

Crutches *n.* SPANISH Las Cruces, New Mexico (TD): **2010** Blogs: *He was born in Crutches*; **2014** Facebook: *He was originally from Crutches* || since 1970, from phonetic resemblance, ultimately from Spanish *las cruces* "the crosses"

cruz *n.* SPANISH opium, especially of Mexican origin (JG): **2009** That's Poppycock: *Cruz is opium from Veracruz, Mexico*; **2014** UNM student: *The junkie was hooked on cruz* || since 1955, from *Veracruz*, a city in Mexico, ultimately from Spanish *vera cruz* "true cross"

cucaracha *n.* SPANISH [1] *offensive* the vagina: **2012** Urban Dictionary: *My cucaracha is itchy and sore from last night. I wonder if he gave me something*; **2014** Facebook: *OMG! Her cucaracha is out!* [2] an old and battered car: **2010** Car Lounge: *So are you really driving a cucaracha? And will you be driving it to the show?* **2011** Motorcycle USA: *I see you drive a cucaracha* || dating unknown, from *cucaracha* "vagina," literally "cockroach"

culero *n.* SPANISH *offensive* [1] a homosexual man: **2009** Yahoo Answers: *I asked my girl if she'd ever take it up the booty, and she said that's for culeros (gays)*; **2012** YouTube: *He will fuck you in your ass like a real culero* [2] a despicable person: **2006** Trance Addict: *Get the fuck out of this thread you fucking culero!* **2007** *New York Times*: *They talk to a culero like Chavez on his level and expect him to understand* [3] a coward: **2003** Teen Spot: *Manny, don't be a culero and let me use the freakin' word!* **2011** YouTube: *Don't be a culero and say what race are you. Don't try to hide in that ghetto talk!* || dating unknown, from *culero* "homosexual man," ultimately from *culo* "anus" and nominal ending *-ero*

culo *n.* SPANISH *offensive* [1] anus: **2002** *25th Hour*, film: *You're upstairs, taking it in the culo*; **2013** *Tucson Weekly*: *He can stick that up his culo* [2] buttocks (JG): **1995** *Blue in the Face*, film: *It's the little waitress with the fat culo, isn't it?* **2002** *Shark Attack 3*, film: *Are you afraid that something is going to swim up and bite your culo?* || since 1967 in the second sense, from *culo* "buttocks" or "anus"

cumare *n.* ITALIAN a mistress: **1999** *Sopranos*, HBO-TV series: *She's not his wife anyway. She's his cumare*; **2019** *Esquire*: *He's the only one without a cumare (a mistress)* || dating unknown, from dialectal *cumare* "mistress"

cushy *adj.* HINDI [1] easy (AS, JG, KC, TD): **2005** *Land of the Dead*, film: *Who'd you blow to get this cushy job?* **2015** *Voice*, film: *Friday I had a pretty cushy gig* [2] comfortable, providing comfort (AS, JG, KC, TD): **2010** *Life As We Know It*, film: *All right, here you go. Big cushy chair, new monitors. Drinks are in the fridge*; **2018** Eater SF: *I don't mind sinking into a cushy armchair* || since 1915, from *khush* "pleasure" and ultimately from Persian *khosi*

D

dago *n.* SPANISH *offensive* [1] a Hispanic person (AS, JG, KC, TD): 2009 Democratic Underground: *No dagos, wops or Irish need to apply*; 2012 Hispanic Post: *President Theodore Roosevelt called Colombians "dagos" when he stole Panama* [2] an Italian (AS, JG, KC, TD): 1998 Los Angeles Times: *Battistoni had overheard Daley refer to her as a dago*; 2012 Kill the Irishman, film: *"You know who the Gambinos are?" "Sure. Big dagos in New York"* || since 1832 in the first sense, since 1857 in the second, from *Diego* "James," used in the seventeenth century to mean "Spaniard"

Dago *n.* SPANISH San Diego, California (JG, TD): 2012 Aging Rebel: *I wonder if there are any locals from San Diego. I live in Dago, I have not seen them around at all*; 2014 Moe Lane: *Pete Wilson was mayor when I lived in Dago* || since 1931, from *Diego* "James" and the modified second part of the city's name

dago red *n.* SPANISH *offensive* cheap red wine, especially of Italian or Spanish origin: 2014 Zagat: *Bottles of Dago red are still $15*; 2015 Pine Island Eagle: *I don't want to be considered a "wine snob" so let me also say that I have enjoyed a bottle of dago red* || since 1906, from *Diego* "James," used in the seventeenth century to mean "Spaniard," and *red*

dago town *n.* SPANISH *offensive* a Latin American part area of a US town or city (JG): 1988 Don DeLillo: *He met his sisters at the streetcar stop in Dago Town*; 2014 Fulton History: *It's just about like dago town in Rochester, about half a dozen nice buildings, nearly all Spanish* || since 1927, from *Diego* "James," used in the seventeenth century to mean "Spaniard," and *town*

da kine *adj.* HAWAIIAN excellent (JG, TD): 1995 Los Angeles Times: *Surf shops offered boards and wheels that were "da kine"*; 2013 News, CBS-TV program: *Bruno has a very "da kine" Hawaiian style* || since 1851, from Hawaiian respelling of *that kind* "anything of which one forgets the precise name"

dama blanca (or **la dama blanca**) *n.* SPANISH cocaine (JG, TD): 1985 New York Times: *Even some of the street names for cocaine – lady, girl, mistress, dama blanca – link the drug to women*; 2010 Blogspot: *I would be tossed out into the street if our employer caught us snorting some dama blanca* || since 1976, from *dama blanca* "white lady"

das *definite article* GERMAN (someone or something) involved in or characterized by what is indicated, sometimes associated with Germany: 2009 Word Press: *I tried hard to do das German thing*; 2015 Halifax Chronicle Herald: *Das Scandal: Canadian VW Owners Furious with Volkswagen Deception* || dating unknown, from German definite article *das*

dealmeister *n.* GERMAN a skillful negotiator or a specialist in making deals (KC): 2007 Billboard Magazine: *The division is headed by veteran Rolling Stones dealmeister Michael Cohl*; 2007 New York Times: *With the hiring of new-media* *dealmeister Quincy Smith, everybody has been wondering what the company has in store* || since 1960s, from *deal* and *Meister* "master"

dedo *n.* SPANISH a police informant (TD): **2006** *El Paso Times*: *"He's a dedo, a finger, an informant," says Raul Loya, a Dallas lawyer*; **2010** *Vanity Fair*: *A traitor to a narco-cartel is known as a dedo* || since 1995, from *dedo* "finger"

deja nu *n.* YIDDISH AND FRENCH a feeling of repetition or recurrence of the present situation, especially when an instant action is required: **1981** *New Statesman*: *It left me with feelings of both deja vu and deja nu*; **2004** *New York Times*: *Theater Review. Déjà Nu? Stars Return!* || since 1990, from *déjà vu* "already seen" and *nu* "well" or "so"

deja vu all over again *phr.* FRENCH a feeling of repetition or recurrence of the present situation (JG, KC, TD): **2015** *News*, CNBC-TV program: *In biotech, it's deja vu all over again*; **2022** *Huntington Herald-Dispatch*: *Yogi Berra once said, "It's like deja vu all over again." That's how it felt on Friday night at Logan* || since 1970, from *déjà vu* "already seen" and *all over again*

Delhi belly *n.* HINDI diarrhea, especially as contracted in a foreign country (JG, KC, TD): **2015** *New York Times*: *They serve delicious khati rolls that won't give you "Delhi belly"*; **2017** *Travel*, CNN-TV program: *For those who fear the dreaded Delhi belly we've included some recommendations* || since 1944, from *Delhi*, capital of India, and *belly*

der *definite article* GERMAN (someone or something) involved in or characterized by what is indicated, sometimes associated with Germany: **2011** *Seibertron*: *Crazy people making der crazy toys!* **2018** *Core77*: *Every part of this thing looks so dangerous that it should be called Der Widowmaker* || dating unknown, from German definite article *der*

desmadre *n.* SPANISH a failure or disaster (TD): **2008** *LA Eastside*: *That event soon deteriorated in a real desmadre*; **2012** *Topix*: *His actions were the cause of a desmadre* || since 1974, from *desmadrar* "to destroy" or "mess up"

desperado *n.* SPANISH a degenerate gambler (JG, KC): **2002** Catherine Coulter: *You look more like a desperado than a fancy gambler*; **2009** *Triggerman*, film: *Let's go and take care of that desperado you locked up, all right?* || since 1956, from *desperado* "desperate man"

diablito (or **el diablito**) *n.* SPANISH a mixture of marijuana, cocaine, heroin, and phencyclidine (JG): **2010** *Lolly Dream*: *I need some el diablito. I can pay*; **2014** *Parenting Teens*: *El diablito is marijuana, cocaine, heroin and PCP* || since 2001, from *el diablito* "little devil"

diablo (or **el diablo**) *n.* SPANISH a mixture of marijuana, cocaine, heroin, and phencyclidine (JG): **2008** *Urban Dictionary*: *Wanna go smoke some el diablo?* **2015** *Las Vegas Sun*: *The drug, sold under name diablo, is part of larger category of synthetic drugs* || since 2001, literally *el diablo* "devil"

dildo *n.* ITALIAN [1] an artificial penis used as a sex toy (KC): **2001** *American Pie 2*, film: *Holy shit! There's a dildo in my drawer*; **2005** *Who's Your Daddy?*, film: *You gave my mom a dildo?* [2] a stupid and despicable person (JG, KC, TD): **1997** *South Park*, Comedy Central-TV series: *Dude, don't call my brother a dildo*; **2016** *Outside*: *Out of the way, you stupid dildo!* || since 1600 in the first sense, since 1960 in the second, from *diletto* "women's delight"

dinero *n.* SPANISH money (AS, JG, KC): **1990** *Air America*, film: *Sorry, I have no local dinero*; **2012** *Wired*: *I found an ATM for some dinero* || since 1856, from *dinero* "money," itself from a medieval Spanish currency

dingbat *n.* DUTCH [1] anything one cannot name specifically (JG, KC): **2011** Bright Hub: *You can do a search on Google for this dingbat*; **2015** UNF student: *How much did you pay for this dingbat?* [2] the penis (JG): **2010** Blogs: *He had a small dingbat*; **2015** UNF student: *With a dingbat like this, he should be in the movies* [3] a stupid person: **1998** *Fear and Loathing in Las Vegas*, film: *He's not just some dingbat! He's a foreigner*; **2000** *Scary Movie*, film: *They'd probably cast some dingbat like Jennifer Love Huge Tits to play me* || since 1905 in the first sense, since 1916 in the second, from *ding* "thing" and *bat*

dingus *n.* DUTCH [1] anything one cannot name specifically (AS, JG, KC, TD): **1997** *Mr. Magoo*, film: *I will not pass my cash until I get a close look at the dingus*; **2011** *Breaking Bad*, AMC-TV series: *So this little dingus here is manufactured by Madrigal Electromotive?* [2] the penis (JG, KC, TD): **2008** *Hottie and Nottie*, film: *I can't do this, my dingus will fall off*; **2015** Dennis Doph: *He buried his big dingus in my ass* [3] a stupid person: **1994** *Airheads*, film: *Get in the truck, dingus!*; **1996** *Friends*, NBC-TV series: *I'm such a dingus!* || since 1876 in the first sense, since 1888 in the second, since 2014 in the third, from *ding* "thing"

disgusto *adj.* SPANISH disgusting: **1990** *Los Angeles Times*: *So what's like not insulting to someone who thinks bein' a movie queen is disgusto?* **2007** Type Pad: *He kept farting, which was disgusto and amusing by turns* || since 1981, from *disgusto* "disgust"

ditto[1] *n.* ITALIAN a duplicate or copy, especially of a document: **2009** Blogspot: *This enables each person to send out several dittos every day*; **2019** Tumblr: *Do they multiply and just create more dittos?* || since 1670, from Tuscan *ditto* "said"

ditto[2] *adv.* ITALIAN as said before, similarly (AS): **2019** *New York Times*: *You might say the same about Vermont. Ditto for small blue states like Rhode Island, Delaware, Hawaii*; **2019** *Deseret News*: *When the race he conceived hit the 20-year mark he got a call. Same at 30. Ditto at 40* || since 1670, from Tuscan *ditto* "said"

dittohead *n.* ITALIAN an unquestioning supporter of an idea or opinion, especially as expressed by a journalist or politician (KC): **2007** *Mother Jones*: *I wouldn't say that dittoheads lack the ability to reason*; **2018** *New York Times*: *That's probably an accurate assessment of the rage that will consume loyal dittoheads if their hero goes down* || since 1992, from *ditto* "as said before" and *head*

dodo *n.* PORTUGUESE an old-fashioned and ineffective person (AS, KC): **2016** *Cosmopolitan*: *He's a dodo. There's no polite way to put this*; **2018** *Washington Post*: *She expressed her worry that contemporary feminists had made her feel like a dodo* || since 1600, from *doudo* "simpleton"

do-goodnik *n.* YIDDISH a well-intentioned, selfless, or altruistic person, especially if naive or self-righteous: **1999** *New York Times*: *Stephen Antiuk is a self-described do-goodnik*; **2011** Chronicle of Higher Education: *They're hanging around the campus being busy-beavers and do-goodniks without pay* || dating unknown, from *do-good(er)* and suffix *-nik*

domo arigato *excl.* JAPANESE thank you very much: **2005** *How I Met Your Mother*, CBS-TV series: *"I liked your performance." "What, the karaoke? Domo arigato!"*; **2013** *Mentalist*, CBS-TV series: *"You're gracious and kind. Domo arigato!" "You're welcome"* || since 1980, from *dōmo arigatō* "thank you very much"

don't give me a canary *excl.* YIDDISH I am hereby warding off the envy of others: **2000** James A. Matisoff: *Rosten reports a further corruption of the expression to "canary," as in "Don't give me a canary!"*; **2010** Word Mavens: *We're supposed to leave next week for vacation, so don't give me a canary* || since 1968, from *canary* "evil eye" and phonetic resemblance to *keyn eyn-(h)ore*, literally "(may) no evil eye (befall)"

dope *n.* DUTCH [1] an illegal drug or drugs (AS, JG, KC, TD): **1994** *Léon*, film: *We pick up the dope, and it tests 90 percent pure*; **1999** *American Beauty*, film: *My dad caught me smoking dope* [2] a stupid person (AS, JG, KC): **1994** *Hudsucker Proxy*, film: *Your friends call you "dope"?*; **2006** *Click*, film: *Dope is for dopes, buddy!* [3] information, especially confidential (AS, JG, KC, TD): **2015** Twitter: *Anyone has any dope on the girl?* **2015** *Baltimore City Paper*: *Bartender Joey Smith gave us the dope about dealing with a hangover* || since 1888 in the first sense, since 1851 in the second, since 1901 in the third, from *doop* "sauce for dipping"

doped *adj.* DUTCH under the influence of drugs (JG): **2010** Blogger: *She was doped on vicodin*; **2015** UCB student: *He got doped pretty quickly* || dating unknown, from *doop* "sauce for dipping"

dope fiend *n.* DUTCH a drug addict or user (JG, TD): **1998** *Fear and Loathing in Las Vegas*, film: *The dope fiend fears nothing*; **2016** *New York Times*: *It's pretty hard having a dope fiend for a mother* || since 1886, from *doop* "sauce for dipping" and -head

dopehead *n.* DUTCH a drug addict or user (JG, TD): **1994** *Last Seduction*, film: *You know, kid, you don't look like a dopehead*; **2007** *New York Times*: *At least he didn't end up a dopehead* || since 1903, from *doop* "sauce for dipping" and *-head*

dopenik *n.* DUTCH AND YIDDISH a drug addict: **2000** *Village Voice*: *As a trio of Brighton Beach dopeniks, they are all subsumed by the formal hootenanny*; **2011**

American Spectator: You want to call him a "dopenik?" || dating unknown, from *dope* "drugs" and suffix *-nik*

doper *n.* DUTCH an illegal drug user (AS, JG, KC, TD): **1997** *Jackie Brown*, film: *The only people he ever sold to were dopers;* **2004** *Sopranos*, HBO-TV series: *We don't do drugs, we're not some stupid dopers* || since 1916, from *doop* "sauce for dipping" and *-er*

doradilla *n.* SPANISH marijuana (JG): **2014** Tripod: *Doradilla is slang for cannabis;* **2014** UCLA student: *We took a trip to Tijuana to buy some doradilla* || since 1973, from *doradilla* "fern"

double sawski, double sawsky *n.* YIDDISH a twenty-dollar bill (JG): **2006** Railroad Forum: *Double sawbucks, a.k.a double sawskies, are $20. Fins are $5;* **2008** Democratic Underground: *I'll bet a double sawski that he was a bully when he was a kid* || since 1953, from *double saw* "twenty dollars" and suffix *-ski*

dreck, drek *n.* YIDDISH [1] excrement (JG): **2011** Yahoo Finance: *Having HPD4 respond to you is like having dreck on your shoe;* **2011** Blogger: *The place smelled of dreck* [2] something worthless or of inferior quality (AS, JG, KC): **2012** Huffington Post: *I just wish Spielberg hadn't made that last dull piece of dreck;* **2013** Democratic Underground: *99% of the films today are pure dreck* [3] nonsense (AS): **1999** *Family Guy*, Fox-TV series: *It's dreck and you know it. Don't have the guts to respond, huh?* **2015** *Florida Sun Sentinel: People have started to realize that a lot of what he says is dreck* || since 1920s, from *drek* "filth" or "excrement"

drecky *adj.* YIDDISH [1] worthless or of inferior quality (AS, JG): **2009** Chowhound: *I live in NY and the food here is generally too expensive and drecky;* **2015** *Arkansas Times: The "Star Wars" franchise has been rescued from the drecky prequels* [2] nonsensical (AS): **2010** Daily Kos: *That intoxicating feeling is gone from this site, mired in the drecky argument between people who love and people who hate Obama;* **2014** *Atlanta Journal Constitution: It is one possible reason for getting yourself involved in Spark's drecky idea of romance* || since 1920s, from *drek* "filth" or "excrement" and adjectival suffix *-y*

drek *see* dreck

drinkfest *n.* GERMAN a drinking party: **2004** *New York Times: New Year's Eve in Moscow is a rowdy, convivial drinkfest;* **2010** *Los Angeles Times: The guest list for this particular drinkfest is as follows* || dating unknown, from *drink* and *Fest* "festival"

drive someone loco *phr.* SPANISH to make someone crazy: **2003** Tom Coffey: *He talked about it so much he was driving her loco;* **2012** *Sports*, NBC-TV program: *It still drives me loco that the Bengals got rid of him* || dating unknown, from *drive someone crazy* and loco "crazy"

du jour *adj.* FRENCH currently popular (AS, KC): **2010** *Newsweek: It is the vehicle du jour;* **2013** *Boston Herald: A scandal du jour hits the capital* || since 1990, from *du jour* "of the day"

dumb *adj.* GERMAN stupid (KC): **1997** *L.A. Confidential*, film: *Maybe White's not so dumb after all*; **2014** Twitter: *Michael gave a dumb explanation* || since 1823, from *dumm* "stupid"

dumb-ass[1] *adj.* GERMAN *potentially offensive* stupid (KC): **2009** *Hangover*, film: *We stole it from this dumb-ass cop*; **2015** *Los Angeles Times*: *I found your dumbass clients* || since 1934, from *dumm* "stupid" and suffix *-ass*

dumb-ass[2] *n.* GERMAN *potentially offensive* a stupid person (KC): **1998** *Armageddon*, film: *Stop interrupting her, dumb-ass!* **2015** Twitter: *These dumbasses did not know they misspelled the name* || since 1958, from *dumm* "stupid" and suffix *-ass*

dumb-bell *n.* GERMAN a stupid person (KC): **2013** Celebitchy: *"Yes" for the looks alone, "no" because he's a dumb-bell*; **2009** Fan Fiction: *I would have it if I hadn't been such a dumb-bell and flunked eighth grade* || since 1918, from *dumm* "stupid" and *bell*

dumb down *v.* GERMAN [1] to make simpler or easier (JG, KC): **2016** *Forbes*: *As a result, entrepreneurs face the temptation to constantly dumb down product features and design*; **2016** *San Diego Union-Tribune*: *Why did you think it necessary to dumb down your article on the loss of USS Indianapolis?* [2] to make stupid: **2015** *News*, CBS-TV program: *How to dumb down your Smart TV so it can't track you?* **2016** *Washington Blade*: *Both parties dumb down discourse* || since 1933, from *dumm* "stupid" and *down*

dumbfuck *n.* GERMAN *very offensive* a stupid person (JG, TD): **2002** *8 Mile*, film: *Look at y'all standin' here freezin' like dumb-fucks!* **2011** YouTube: *You're such a dumbfuck. You need to shut up!* || since 1952, from *dumm* "stupid" and *fuck*

dumbhead *n.* GERMAN a stupid person (KC): **1998** *Advocate*: *Kennedy was in some cases a real dumbhead on our issues*; **2012** *Los Angeles Times*: *I realized what a dumbhead I was* || since 1887, from *Dummkopf* "stupid head"

dumbo *n.* GERMAN a stupid person (JG): **2003** *Los Angeles Times*: *He treated us like we're a bunch of bums and dumbos*; **2014** Twitter: *I was a real dumbo, I didn't know anything* || since 1932, from *dumm* "stupid" and suffix *-o*, reinforced by the Walt Disney cartoon character *Dumbo*

dumbshit *n.* GERMAN *offensive* a stupid person (JG, KC, TD): **2005** *Longest Yard*, film: *You scared him away, dumbshit!* **2018** *Kominsky Method*, Netflix-TV series: *"Who do I have?" "Me, you dumbshit!"* || since 1960, from *dumm* "stupid" and *shit*

dummy *n.* GERMAN [1] a stupid person (JG): **1994** *Forrest Gump*, film: *Hey, dummy! Are you dumb or just plain stupid?* **1996** *Fargo*, film: *How the fuck do you split a fuckin' car, you dummy?* [2] a mute (JG): **1990** *Home Alone*, film: *I'm upstairs, dummy!* **1999** *Green Mile*, film: *You hear what he was yelling when we brought the dummy in?* || since 1812 in the first sense, since 1874 in the second, from *dumm* "stupid" and suffix *-y*

dummy up *v.* GERMAN to stop talking and be quiet (JG): **2001** *Sopranos*, HBO-TV series: *Promise me that you'll dummy up about this*; **2004** *CSI: Miami*, CBS-TV series: *Our victim's dad here dummied up* ‖ since 1928, from *dummy* "mute" and *up*

dupa *n.* POLISH *potentially offensive* [1] buttocks (JG): **2000** *Allentown Morning Call*: *I volunteered because I probably needed a kick in the dupa to get going*; **2013** *Weather*, Fox8-TV program: *The snow is up to my dupa!* [2] self: **2019** Facebook: *You'll get your dupa sued*; **2022** Pinterest: *Move your dupa. Make sure you're stretching!* ‖ dating unknown, from *dupa* "buttocks" or "anus"

E

easy-schmeezy, easy-shmeezy[1] *adj.* YIDDISH very easy: **2008** Word Press: *The recipe is easy-schmeezy. I'll post a couple of photos at the bottom*; **2018** Sport Bikes: *The wiring is easy-shmeezy, just splice in new connectors* ‖ dating unknown, from reduplication of *easy* and infix *-schm-*, and based on *easy-peasy* "very easy"

easy-schmeezy, easy-shmeezy[2] *adv.* YIDDISH very easily: **2007** *Bionic Woman*, NBC-TV series: *We can override that easy-schmeezy*; **2014** Kickstarter: *Many Jews enjoy kvelling about their kids and that book has made building a rapport with them very easy shmeezy* ‖ dating unknown, from reduplication of *easy* and infix *-schm-*, and based on *easy-peasy* "very easy"

el *prefix.* SPANISH (someone or something) involved in or characterized by what is indicated, sometimes associated with a Spanish-speaking country or people (JG, KC, TD): **2011** Gizmodo: *El fake-o reviews also used more verbs, while honest reviews used more nouns*; **2016** *San Diego Free Press*: *So El Stupido in the White House reacted to this news with his own "alternative facts"* ‖ since 1929, from Spanish prefix *el*

El Barrio *see* barrio

el cheapo[1] *adj.* PSEUDO-SPANISH cheap (JG, KC): **2009** Roadbike Review: *I guess I'll have to buy some somewhat el cheapo parts to use for learning*; **2012** *Miami Herald*: *That el cheapo owner will sell the team before he has to pay* ‖ since 1967, from *cheap* and mock Spanish prefix word *el* and suffix *-o*

el cheapo[2] *n.* PSEUDO-SPANISH [1] something cheap (JG, KC): **2009** *PC World*: *The el cheapos don't have an oil lube system for the pump valves*; **2014** Cheeky Chicago: *You can mix and match el cheapos with something slightly more expensive, if you wish* [2] someone cheap or parsimonious: **2009** Yelp: *If you really like her, then keep in mind that she's an el cheapo and hard to get*; **2014** Geek Hack: *The el cheapos usually have issue with the new model* ‖ since 1967, from *cheap* and mock Spanish prefix word *el* and suffix *-o*

El Chuco *n.* SPANISH El Paso, Texas: **2012** *El Paso Times*: *It's been a curious week in El Chuco*; **2013** Borderzine: *A mere five years later after first hitchhiking to El Paso* *in 1989, Welsh would be back to "El Chuco" for good* || since 1965, from *el* and *(pa) chuco* "flashily dressed or vulgar"

el diablito   *see* diablito

el diablo   *see* diablo

El Dog *n.* PSEUDO-SPANISH a Cadillac Eldorado automobile (TD): 2013 Jalopnik: *My dream car has been Cadillac Eldorado, or as I like to call it, the El Dog*; 2011 *Motor Trend*: *In my teens, I wanted an El Dog, a red Eldorado Caddy* || since 1975, from resemblance to *El Dorado*

el dorko[1]   *n.* PSEUDO-SPANISH a stupid or incompetent person (JG): 2011 NYU student: *You two look like complete el dorkos! Get rid of these shirts!* 2015 Salon: *The kid was called "el dorko"* || since 1990, from *dork* "stupid or incompetent person" and mock Spanish prefix word *el* and suffix *-o*

el dorko[2]   *adj.* PSEUDO-SPANISH stupid or incompetent: 2010 E-Cigarettes: *I had to tell the el dorko story about why I have to get a new one*; 2008 Sox Talk: *I have to go out with the el dorko frames* || since 1990, from *dork* "stupid or incompetent person" and mock Spanish prefix word *el* and suffix *-o*

el floppo *n.* PSEUDO-SPANISH a failure (JG): 1999 Silicon Investor: *I was intrigued by the hype surrounding this film, and I would have hated to have it be an el floppo*; 2011 *New York Post*: *He had an el floppo with this season's "Women on the Verge of a Nervous Breakdown"* || since 1936, from *flop* "failure" and mock Spanish prefix word *el* and suffix *-o*

el foldo *n.* PSEUDO-SPANISH a failure (JG, KC): 2006 *New York Times*: *If the Jets were hoping for an el foldo from Oakland, it's not happening, not yet*; 2006 *Honolulu Advertiser*: *It's precisely the kind of el foldos that have Smith in hot water now* || since 1943, from *fold* "failure" and mock Spanish prefix word *el* and suffix *-o*

el guapo   *see* guapo[1]

El Lay *n.* SPANISH Los Angeles, California (TD): 2008 Democratic Underground: *Barstow is only one hour away from El Lay so it ain't that bad*; 2015 *Las Vegas Weekly*: *Goss is talking of moving to Las Vegas, cutting off the commute he has been making from El Lay* || since 1951, from *L.A.* initials in *Los Angeles*, and their pronunciation resembling Spanish

el magnifico   *see* magnifico

el primo   *see* primo

el ropo *n.* PSEUDO-SPANISH a cigar, especially inferior (JG, KC, TD): 2011 Cigar Chronicles: *If it's harsh and strong, you have yourself an el ropo*; 2011 Missouri Whitetails: *It takes a real man to smoke an el ropo* || since 1940, from *ropo* "cheap cigar" and mock Spanish prefix word *el* and suffix *-o*

el sleazo *adj.* PSEUDO-SPANISH despicable, corrupt, and immoral (JG): 2003 Free Republic: *I have no doubt that Governor Doofus is el sleazo, but the CA electorate re-elected him and they deserve to get what they voted for*; 2010 Blogger: *Her boyfriend is el sleazo* || since 1937, from *sleazy* and mock Spanish prefix word *el* and suffix *-o*

el stinko[1] *n.* PSEUDO-SPANISH a cheap and strong cigar (JG): 1998 *Cigar Aficionado*: *In the early '80s I started to make money, so I went from smoking El Stinkos to Cubans*; 2015 *North Shore News*: *He would have reeked of ten-cent el stinkos* || since 1940, from *stink* and mock Spanish prefix word *el* and suffix *-o*

el stinko[2] *adj.* PSEUDO-SPANISH [1] stinking: 2010 Garage Journal: *Why ruin a power wagon with an el stinko diesel?* 2013 ASU student: *This food is totally el stinko!* [2] contemptible or miserable: 2000 *Philadelphia Inquirer*: *What lies beneath is an el stinko ending*; 2009 Leland Report: *I agree with your assertion that this was an el stinko day* || since 1940, from *stink* and mock Spanish prefix word *el* and suffix *-o*

el supremo *see* supremo

el zilcho *n.* PSEUDO-SPANISH nothing (JG, KC): 2006 Democratic Underground: *We get what we want, and they get el zilcho*; 2014 YouTube: *The rich get richer and you get el zilcho* || since 1979, from *zilch* "nothing" and mock Spanish prefix word *el* and suffix *-o*

Eme (or **EME, La Eme**) *n.* SPANISH [1] the Mexican mafia (TD): 2008 *Los Angeles Times*: *The Mexican Mafia, known as the Eme, imposed new rules on Southern California Latino street gangs*; 2012 Hood Up: *Joe Morgan was a figurehead for the EME for over twenty years* [2] a Mexican American prison gang (TD): 2008 Free Republic: *The first murder attributed to the Eme beyond prison walls occurred in 1971*; 2014 LA Weekly: *They face the wrath of the Eme when they end up behind bars* || since 1978, from the Spanish pronunciation of the letter "M"

empanada *n.* SPANISH *offensive* the vagina: 2009 Urban Dictionary: *Check out that ass! Did you see the empanada, too?* 2010 Huddle: *I'd like to put my chorizo in her empanada* || dating unknown, from *empanada* "stuffed pastry baked or fried"

enchilada *n.* SPANISH [1] everything or totality (KC): 2014 *Dallas Morning News*: *Here in San Antonio we want our Spurs to win the entire enchilada*; 2021 Politico: *They don't want the package without the non-partisan assessment on how much the enchilada will cost* [2] a chief (KC): 2011 *Texas Magazine*: *I told him I didn't know, which is not what the Chief Enchilada wanted to hear*; 2015 UNF student: *Who's the enchilada around here?* || since 1973, from *enchilada* "tortilla with meat and chili sauce"

enchilada eater *n.* SPANISH *offensive* a Mexican: 2010 Topix: *See what happens to you when you marry one of them enchilada eaters*; 2013 ASU student: *He referred to Mexicans as "enchilada eaters"* || dating unknown, from *enchilada* "tortilla with meat and chili sauce" and *eater*

Ene (or **ENE, La Ene**) *n.* SPANISH the Nuestra Familia prison gang (TD): 2008 Brown Pride: *The Ene claimed victory and became a major player in prison life*; 2014 Idaho Gangs: *The Nuestra Familia (La ENE) originated in the mid 1960s at Soledad Prison in California* || since 1995, from the Spanish pronunciation of the letter "N"

en fuego *adj.* SPANISH [1] excellent (TD): 2014 *Instyle*: *Jared Leto's Oscars Hair is En Fuego!* 2014 *Miami Herald*: *Frazier is en fuego indeed, so is the whole team. Go Gators!* [2] sexually attractive: 2010 Facebook: *Wow, that Rachel chick is en fuego!* 2014 *News*, MTV-TV program: *George Clooney is en fuego!* || since 1997, from *en fuego* "on fire"

enjoy *excl.* YIDDISH enjoy yourself (KC): 1998 *Big Lebowski*, film: *"The old man told me to take any rug in the house." "Well, enjoy!"*; 2008 *Kung Fu Panda*, film: *You are free to eat. Enjoy!* || since 1980, from *genis* "enjoy"

enough already *excl.* YIDDISH that is enough (AS): 2009 *Zombieland*, film: *Hey, for fuck's sake! Enough already!* 2016 Huffington Post: *Similar sentiments are common in these times. Enough already! Slavery ended more than 150 years ago* || dating unknown, from *genuk shoyn* "enough already"

enough with something *excl.* YIDDISH I do not want to hear any more of something: 2010 *Toronto Star*: *Enough with the talk. It's time for action*; 2016 *Chicago Tribune*: *If you don't want to change your country, don't try to change ours. Enough with this political correctness!* || dating unknown, from *genuk mit epes* "enough with something"

esa (or **ésa**) *n.* SPANISH [1] (used especially as a term of address) a fellow Mexican woman: 2000 *Next Friday*, film: *We're gonna party now, esa*; 2007 Brown Pride: *Damn, these esas know how to shop and where to shop!* [2] (used especially as a term of address) a streetwise young woman: 1992 *American Me*, film: *You're gonna like it, esa*; 2007 Urban Dictionary: *Don't worry about those putas. I got your back, esa* || since 1961, feminine version of *ese bato* "that simpleton" and *ese* "that"

ese (or **ése**) *n.* SPANISH [1] (used especially as a term of address) a fellow Mexican male (JG): 1995 *Desperado*, film: *It's cool, ese, cool!* 2012 YouTube: *All eses from L.A. feel the same* [2] (used especially as a term of address) a streetwise young man (JG, TD): 2007 Street Gangs: *The brothas don't speak on ese's like that, I don't know where the fuck you got that shit*; 2016 *Ray Donovan*, Showtime-TV series: *What the fuck are you so mad about, ese?* || since 1961, from *ese bato* "that simpleton" and *ese* "that"

-ese *suffix* LATIN a language denoting character or style: 2015 *New York Times*: *My colleague Patrick LaForge unearths more examples of journalese*; 2015 *Popular Science*: *That's a lot of Pentagonese* || dating unknown, based on Latin *-ensis*

-esque *suffix* FRENCH typical of or resembling what is indicated: 2016 Yahoo Movies: *NASA Discovers a New "Star Wars"-esque Planet*; 2016 *News*, ABC-TV program: *Dionne says Clinton has optimistic Reagan-esque view of America* || dating unknown, from suffix *-esque*

ess and fress *phr.* YIDDISH to eat, especially heartily, quickly, or noisily: **2006** *Los Angeles Magazine*: *The neighborhood deli is a land of ess and fress*; **2008** *Village Voice*: *Ess and fress! The all-you-can-eat buffet could very well be kosher* || dating unknown, from *esn un fresn* "to eat heartily"

essay *n.* SPANISH **[1]** (used especially as a term of address) a fellow Mexican (JG): **2011** *Highline Times*: *Hey, essay, you know what they do to homeboys like you?* **2013** Blogs: *He showed up with a bunch of essays from Tijuana* **[2]** (used especially as a term of address) a streetwise young man (JG): **2009** Blogspot: *Today I went to school with my fellow essays*; **2014** Yahoo Groups: *Hi essay, how are you?* || since 1961, from *ese bato* "that simpleton" and *ese* "that"

estuffa *n.* SPANISH **[1]** stuff: **2013** YouTube: *I'm just letting y'all in on what's up and estuffa*; **2013** Twitter: *Get rid of this estuffa!* **[2]** a drug, especially heroin (JG): **2008** Urban Dictionary: *Man, you gotta hook me up with some of that estuffa*; **2010** Addiction Blog: *Estuffa? In my experience, heroin can be called anything* || since 1984, from English *stuff* and Spanish prefix *e-* and suffix *-a*

exactamundo *adv.* PSEUDO-SPANISH exactly: **1993** *Teenage Mutant Ninja Turtles*, CBS-TV series: *"I'll bet my shell it's Shredder!" "Yeah! My thoughts exactamundo!"*; **2019** *Stranger Things*, Netflix-TV series: *"It creates electromagnetic field." "Exactamundo!"* || since 1982, from *exacto* "exact" and *mundo* "world"

exacto *excl.* SPANISH exactly (TD): **2006** *Behind the Mask*, film: *"Don't you forget something?" "The alibi!" "Exacto!"*; **2009** *Wall Street Journal*: *"The best is yet to come." "Exacto!"* || since 1991, from *exacto* "exact"

Eyetie (or **Eytie**) *n.* PSEUDO-ITALIAN *offensive* an Italian or a person of Italian descent (AS, JG, KC, TD): **1992** *Far and Away*, film: *The club is crawling with Eyeties*; **2005** Urban Dictionary: *Don't call him eyetie, he'll punch you out* || since 1919, from a humorous imitation of an Italian speaker pronouncing *Italian*

F

Facebooknik *n.* YIDDISH someone addicted to Facebook, a social networking service and website: **2008** *Forbes*: *Obama is a textbook Facebooknik*; **2012** Campaign Outsider: *It's a wake-up call for every one of the 800 million Facebookniks* || since 2004, from *Facebook* and suffix *-nik*

factoid *n.* GREEK a presumed fact of dubious validity (KC): **2001** Free Republic: *The left-wing LA Times never lets a little thing like a factoid interfere with its agenda*; **2012** *Atlantic Monthly*: *I had thought a factoid was a diminutive form of fact more than a derogatory one* || since 1970, from *fact* and suffix *-oid*

fagola *n.* YIDDISH a gay man (KC): **2012** Free Republic: *That dirty fagola is pushing the homo agenda*; **2015** Hollywood Reporter: *He was acting like a fagola* || since 1961, from *feygl* or *feygele* "little bird"

fancy-schmancy, fancy-shmancy *adj.* YIDDISH [1] overly elegant, ornate, or sophisticated: **2013** *Chicago Tribune*: *You are greeted by marble columns, a fancy-shmancy lamp and some opera posters*; **2021** *Duluth News Tribune*: *The dressing tastes like a very fancy-schmancy restaurant dressing full of complex flavors* [2] pretentious or affected: **1991** *Only the Lonely*, film: *I hope your fancy-schmancy ballet was worth it*; **2005** *Third Wish*, film: *You can't just waltz in off the street and throw out some fancy-schmancy words with that phony accent of yours* ‖ since 1929, from reduplication of *fancy* and infix *-schm-*

fandango *n.* SPANISH nonsense: **1997** *Baltimore Sun*: *I don't like all this fandango, or whatever you want to call it*; **2012** YouTube: *Please, stop all this fandango and let me create a document* ‖ dating unknown, from *fandango* "kind of fast-moving Spanish dance"

fanook *n.* ITALIAN *potentially offensive* a homosexual man: **1999** *Sopranos*, HBO-TV series: *It's a sign of weakness and possibly a sign that you're a fanook*; **2021** *Many Saints of Newark*, film: *You're gonna have to work for those two fanooks* ‖ dating unknown, from *finocchio* "fennel"

farkakte, farkakter *adj.* YIDDISH despicable or accursed (JG, KC): **2006** *Queer Duck: The Movie*, film: *Martin, will you put down the farkakte trumpet?* **2012** *USA Today*: *The studio is 43 degrees and I'm in those farkakte little shorts* ‖ dating unknown, from *farkakt*, literally "shitty"

farklemt, farklempt *adj.* YIDDISH overcome with emotion: **2009** Dining Chicago: *It makes me a little farklemt every time I see that clip*; **2012** *Metro Weekly*: *Maybe you're not Jewish, but you get farklempt when you see Barbra Streisand* ‖ dating unknown, from *farklemt* "emotionally disturbed"

farmisht *adj.* YIDDISH confused (JG): **2005** *New York Times*: *When it was published, Person was farmisht and did not take any action*; **2015** *Curve Magazine*: *As her sexual orientation evolves, Horvitz feels farmisht and tries to resist her attraction to women* ‖ since 1960, from *farmisht* "confused" or "disoriented"

farshikkert, farshikert *adj.* YIDDISH drunk: **2007** Daily Kos: *Perhaps he's a tad farshikkert in this video clip, nu?* **2011** Gear Page: *I proceeded to get completely farshikkert on cheap beer* ‖ dating unknown, from *farshikert* "drunk"

farshtinkener, farshtinkene *adj.* YIDDISH [1] stinking (JG): **1999** *Freaks and Geeks*, NBC-TV series: *I'm farshtinkener and I'm showering!* **2019** UCLA student: *He has farshtinkene feet* [2] despicable or accursed: **2005** *New York Observer*: *I'm an old person, and it was a real eye-opener for me to go over there and see what had happened to farshtinkener Brooklyn*; **2011** *Newark Star-Ledger*: *We spit on that farshtinkener Hitler* ‖ since 1968, from *farshtinkert*, literally "stinking"

fartootst, fartoost, fartutst, fartust *adj.* YIDDISH confused or disoriented: **1987** *Miami Herald*: *The guy got you all fartootst when he ordered his plate*; **1993** *New York*

Times: *Fartootst means "mixed up"* || dating unknown, from *fartutst* "confused" or "disoriented"

fartumelt, fartummelt *adj.* YIDDISH dizzy or confused, especially when surprised: **1993** *New York Times Magazine*: *Chung gave her reaction to the ordeal to the USA Today: "I'm fartumelt! Fartootst! Farmisht!"*; **2013** Twitter: *I'm fartumelt, you mean to tell me Santa isn't Jewish?* || dating unknown, from *fartumelt* "disoriented"

fartutst *see* fartootst

fatmouth[1] *n.* MANDINKA someone who talks too much (JG, KC): **2010** Free Republic: *Here comes the fatmouth!* **2014** American Conservative: *He's a total grandstander and a fatmouth* || since 1926, from *da ba* "fat mouth"

fatmouth[2] *v.* MANDINKA to talk too much (JG, KC, TD): **2010** *Washington Post*: *Since we're all fatmouthing here late at night, imagine this*; **2022** *American Conservative*: *When I hear him fatmouthing about how the US ought to risk nuclear war with Russia over Ukraine, it chills me to the bone* || since 1962, from *da ba* "fat mouth"

fatmouthed *adj.* MANDINKA talking too much (JG, TD): **2010** Daily Beast: *The fatmouthed Republicans have sold to the Tea Baggers*; **2015** Air Talk: *Australia is a nation of fatmouthed gutless rats* || since 1952, from *da ba* "fat mouth" and *-ed*

faux *adj.* FRENCH artificial or false (AS, KC): **2012** *Goats*, film: *"This is faux turkey." "It smells wonderful"*; **2008** *Sex and the City*, film: *They spare me a week of faux soul-searching* || since 1980, from *faux* "false"

faygeleh, faygelah, feygeleh, feygelah *n.* YIDDISH [1] a little girl: **2005** Live Journal: *I can't bear the thought of that happening to my little feygeleh*; **2010** *News*, ABC-TV program: *This is my little faygeleh and she will sing a song for you and your heart will just melt* [2] a gay man (JG, KC): **2006** *Queer Duck: The Movie*, film: *They told me he was faygeleh, but, frankly, I don't see it*; **2012** *New York Post*: *How does it feel to be married to a faygeleh?* || since 1968, from *feygl* or *feygele* "little bird"

feh *excl.* YIDDISH [1] what a terrible smell (KC): **2004** Gothamist: *Feh! It stinks!* **2005** Linda Glasser: *It smelled like rotten food, stinking bodies, and stale air. Feh!* [2] I am disgusted (AS, KC): **2009** *New York Times*: *Feh! What would you expect from a culture that doesn't allow women to drive?* **2013** *Washington Post*: *First Amendment? Robust Democracy? Feh!* || since 1950s, from *fe* "ugh"

femme[1] *n.* FRENCH (in a homosexual relationship) the person who plays the passive, "feminine" role (AS, JG, KC, TD): **2003** Urban Dictionary: *Eva's girl is a high maintenance femme*; **2010** *Real L Word*, Showtime-TV series: *I call her either a soft butch or a hard femme* || since 1934, from *femme* "woman"

femme[2] *adj.* FRENCH (in a homosexual relationship) involving the passive, "feminine" role (JG, KC, TD): **2005** *Just Friends*, film: *I know it might sound* *a little femme*; **2015** BuzzFeed: *I like dating as a femme lesbian* || since 1963, from *femme* "woman"

feria *n.* SPANISH money (JG): **1993** *Bound by Honor*, film: *Remember, I'm paying you a lot of feria, ese*; **2012** *Sons of Anarchy*, FX-TV series: *That still brings the feria in your pocket* || dating unknown, from *feria* "fair"

-fest *suffix* GERMAN a prolonged or intense activity characterized by what is indicated (AS, KC): **2013** Death and Taxes: *The Conversation quickly turned into a mutual complainfest*; **2016** *Washington Post*: *Trump bantered with the host of the popular radio raunchfest about whether he could have nailed her* || since 1865, from *Fest* "festival"

feygelah *see* faygeleh

feygeleh *see* faygeleh

filero *n.* SPANISH a knife or knife-like weapon: **1992** *American Me*, film: *"You're bleeding, carnal!" "Hey, the dude had a filero. He cut me, man"*; **2005** Urban Dictionary: *He got stabbed with a filero* || dating unknown, from *filero* "sharp object" and *filo* "sharp"

fin *n.* YIDDISH [1] a five-dollar bill (JG, KC): **1995** *Clueless*, film: *Pass me a fin, I'll pay you back*; **2009** *Surfer Magazine*: *You owe me a fin!* [2] a hand (KC): **2008** Barbara Kipfer and Robert Chapman: *Reach out your fin and grab it*; **2013** Fan Fiction: *Get your dirty fins off of Alan!* || in JG the first sense since 1909, in the second since 1920s, from *finf* "five"

finif *n.* YIDDISH a five-dollar bill (JG, KC): **1982** *New York Magazine*: *Mom would send me a finif now and then, sometimes a ten or a twenty*; **2009** Bike Forums: *I rarely carry ID with me, just a finif for coffee and bagel* || in the first sense since 1859, in the second since 1859, from *finf* "five"

finito[1] *adj.* ITALIAN ended or finished (AS, JG, KC): **2000** *Bring It On*, film: *Our free cheer service is over as of this moment. Finito*; **2012** *News*, CBS-TV program: *McCabe told Richards that he's finito* || since 1963, from *finito* "finished"

finito[2] *excl.* ITALIAN it is the end (JG): **2001** *Blow*, film: *I'm out! Finito! Last fuckin' party!* **2010** *Boardwalk Empire*, HBO-TV series: *No more monkey business!. Finito!* || since 1977, from *finito* "finished"

fink[1] *n.* GERMAN [1] a strikebreaker (AS, JG, KC): **1995** *Get Shorty*, film: *I never met a fink and I hope I never do*; **2012** *National Review*: *Strikes had a tendency to degenerate into violence, with threats and assaults used against the "scabs" and "finks" who would replace striking workers* [2] an informer (AS, JG, KC, TD): **2001** *New York Times*: *The film seems to be setting her up as a fink and a traitor*; **2021** *Toronto Sun*: *Caifano found out his partner was a fink* || since 1892 in the first sense, since 1902 in the second, from *Fink* "student not belonging to the students association"

fink² *v.* GERMAN to inform on (AS, JG, KC, TD): 2002 *Gilmore Girls*, WB-TV series: *Who finked?* 2010 *New York Daily News*: *Fitzgerald finked on his old jailhouse pal because he had killed his pet cat* || since 1925, from *Fink* "student not belonging to the students association"

finski, finsky *n.* YIDDISH a five-dollar bill: 2010 Black Planet: *Looks like you owe me a finsky*; 2016 *Los Angeles Times*: *See what a finski can do to a guy's attitude?* || since 1952, from *fin(f)* "five" and jocular suffix *-ski*

fin-spot *n.* YIDDISH a five-dollar bill (JG, KC): 2010 Urban Spoon: *I had the special Detroit coneys for five dollars. They were super good. And worth a fin spot for sure*; 2011 Blogspot: *I picked it up for a fin spot (that means $5, right?)* || since 1909, from *finf* "five" and *spot*

flak *n.* GERMAN [1] anti-aircraft fire (AS, JG, KC): 1991 *Flight of the Intruder*, film: *It's too quiet. Where's the goddamn flak?* 2001 *Pearl Harbor*, film: *We got flak everywhere* [2] severe criticism (AS, JG, KC, TD): 1991 *InfoWorld*: *The team took some flak because of that*; 2000 *How the Grinch Stole Christmas*, film: *He never catches any flak for it* [3] problems (KC, TD): 1991 *JFK*, film: *Either we pull out now or we go through heavy flak together*; 2002 *People I Know*, film: *I caught a lot of flak about that* || since 1937 in the first sense, since 1968 in the second, since 1956 in the third, from *Fliegerabwehrkanone* "pilot-defense gun"

flopski *n.* YIDDISH a failure: 2010 *Arizona Daily Sun*: *"Toy Story 3" is a flopski in Russia*; 2012 Bear Insider: *The legacy adds to a big flopski on the national stage* || dating unknown, from *flop* "failure" and suffix *-ski*

folksmensch, folksmensh *n.* YIDDISH [1] a common person: 2010 *Wall Street Journal*: *Schneer repeatedly calls him a folks-mensch, a Yiddish term meaning a man of the people*; 2011 Coney Island Online: *Hopefully, we can get someone a little more folksmensch next time around* [2] an accomplished person who is not a snob: 2010 *Bookmarks Magazine*: *Weizmann was a Zionist hero, the folksmensch who charmed British high society*; 2011 NYU student: *We're looking for a folksmensh, someone cool* || dating unknown, from *folksmentsh*, literally "man of the people" or "common man"

fonfer *n.* YIDDISH [1] a boastful or lying person who does not deliver: 2007 *South Florida Sun-Sentinel*: *Don't vote for a fonfer. Vote for a mensh*; 2009 Democratic Underground: *They called the sonorous fonfers on both sides as essentially empty suits playing pre-recorded talking points* [2] someone who wastes times doing nothing: 1996 Leo Rosten: *Did you ever hear of such a fonfer?* 2011 NYU student: *Tell that fonfer to quit goofing around* || dating unknown, from *fonfer*, literally "someone who talks through the nose"

fooey *excl.* YIDDISH [1] what a terrible smell: 2012 Blogspot: *They began to smell bad. Fooey!* 2013 UCB student: *This place stinks! Fooey!* [2] I am disgusted (KC): 2012 Investors Hub: *Ah, fooey! What an inauspicious conclusion!* 2010 *Los Angeles Times*: *I'm still hoping the affair lasts long enough for a spinoff, but with the dalliance* *now made public, Diane seems likely to keep her passion in check in the future. Fooey* || since 1902, from *fui* "ugh"

for free *phr.* YIDDISH without charge (KC): **1994** *Forrest Gump*, film: *I cut that grass for free*; **2008** *Dark Knight*, film: *If you're good at something, never do it for free* || since 1940, from *far gornisht* "for nothing"

for instance *phr.* YIDDISH an example (KC): **2005** *Sin City*, film: *By way of a for instance, I killed three men tonight*; **2015** *Minneapolis Star-Tribune*: *That's just a for instance* || since 1940, from *tsum bayshpil* "for example"

for real *excl.* YIDDISH seriously or truthfully (KC): **2011** NYU student: *You're from Poland? For real?* **2016** *News*, CBS-TV program: *I mean, for real, there ain't nothin' but poor black and Latino people in jail* || since 1940, from *far emes* "for truth"

fox paw *n.* PSEUDO-FRENCH an embarrassing mistake (KC): **1992** *Married with Children*, Fox-TV series: *We're gonna raise the money to get you out of this fox paw*; **2005** Urban Dictionary: *It was a fox paw to think they came to repair the leak* || since 1785, from phonetic respelling of *faux pas* "false step"

frajo *n.* SPANISH [1] a marijuana cigarette (JG): **2013** Twitpic: *I'm smoking a frajo and working out*; **2014** Twitter: *I'm smoking a frajo in my room, cuz I'm too lazy to get up*; [2] a cigarette (JG): **2011** *Los Angeles Times*: *We played handball in the yard and bet frajos, soap, and I would always win*; **2013** *Blaze You Out*, film: *Care for a frajo?* || since 1952 in the first sense, since 1992 in the second, from *frajo* "cigarette butt"

free gratis *phr.* LATIN without charge (KC): **2004** *Deadwood*, HBO-TV series: *The vaccine will be distributed free gratis*; **2015** Twicsy: *It's free gratis, no need to pay* || since 1883, from *free* and *gratis* "free"

freier *n.* YIDDISH a gullible or naive person: **2007** *America Magazine*: *Shtinker was prison slang for a rat, freier or patsy*; **2015** *Vox*: *This combines with his legendary fear of being seen as a "freier" (sucker) in front of his people* || dating unknown, from *fraier* "patsy"

fress *v.* YIDDISH [1] to eat, especially heartily, quickly, or noisily: **1998** *New York Times*: *Go ahead, fress a bissel! Try it, you'll like it*; **2013** Urban Spoon: *I happily fressed on the chicken salad* [2] to perform cunnilingus or fellatio (JG): **2011** NYU student: *Look at her lips, she sure likes to fress*; **2015** UNF student: *That chick likes to fress* || since 1885 in the first sense, since 1967 in the second, from *fresn* "to devour" or "to gorge oneself"

fresser *n.* YIDDISH [1] someone who eats heartily, quickly, or noisily (JG): **1999** *Los Angeles Magazine*: *Herewith is a roundup of the best places in LA for a vegetarian to feast like a fresser*; **2013** *South Florida Sun-Sentinel*: *There was enough food for everyone from noshers to fressers* [2] someone who performs cunnilingus or fellatio (JG): **2007** Urban Dictionary: *A fresser is someone who goes down on another*; **2011**

NYU student: *She's a great fresser* ‖ since 1885 in the first sense, since 1967 in the second, from *freser* "glutton"

frijole eater *n.* SPANISH *offensive* a Mexican (JG): **2002** Planet Ice: *An unknown man from the army opened fire on fifteen unsuspecting frijole eaters*; **2010** Topix: *Look, white people aren't near as scared as the frijole eaters* ‖ since 1983, from *frijoles* "beans" and *eater*

frijole guzzler *n.* SPANISH *offensive* a Mexican (JG): **2013** Patricia M. Montilla: *They were referred to as "chilis," "taco chokers," "frijole guzzlers"*; **2014** Atlas Tales: *Various characters refer to a group of Mexican bandits as "chili eaters," "frijole guzzlers," and "greasers"* ‖ since 1983, from *frijoles* "beans" and *guzzler*

frito *n.* SPANISH *offensive* a Mexican (JG): **2014** Deviant Art: *Hello, my fellow fritos, it's me again!* **2014** Twitter: *There was a frito who used to copy my stuff* ‖ since 1978, from *frito* "fried" or "fried food," reinforced by advertisements for Frito Bandito which feature a stereotypical Mexican bandit

Fritz *n.* GERMAN *potentially offensive* a German or a person of German descent (AS, JG, KC): **2006** *New York Times*: *The Fritzes are running away from us*; **2007** *Leningrad*, film: *The Fritzes, they're digging in* ‖ since 1883, from *Fritz*, diminutive of proper name *Friedrich*

fritz *v.* GERMAN [1] to break down or malfunction (AS, JG, TD): **2011** *Time*: *The electrical system fritzed, the communications died*; **2014** *American Conservative*: *Whenever a light bulb burned out, or an appliance fritzed, she attributed it to a visit from her mom* [2] to make something break down or malfunction (JG, KC): **2012** *New York Times*: *Some malignancy has fritzed the instruments!* **2015** Facebook: *I could end up fritzing the entire national grid* ‖ since 1918 in the first sense, since 1949 in the second, from *Fritz*, diminutive of proper name *Friedrich*, and propagandist dislike of all things German

fritz out *v.* GERMAN [1] to break down or malfunction (JG, TD): **2012** *Wired*: *The Russians are pretty sure they know why their Mars moon probe fritzed out*; **2014** *Missoulian*: *Microphones needed new batteries. Cords fritzed out and had to be replaced* [2] to make something break down or malfunction: **1993** *Forbes*: *Several times geckos slithering inside TSC3s would electrocute themselves, fritzing out the sensors*; **2014** Apple Discussions: *I spilled a drink on my Macbook pro, probably fritzing out the motherboard* ‖ since 1960, from *Fritz*, diminutive of proper name *Friedrich*, and propagandist dislike of all things German

from one's kishkas, from one's kishkes *phr.* YIDDISH from one's deepest emotional experience: **2008** Got Poetry: *Here is a poem that came from my kishkas*; **2010** Heeb Magazine: *His music changed me forever and he taught me to stop writing for "radio" and start writing from my kishkas* ‖ since 1959, from *fun kishkes*, literally "from one's guts"

fronterizo *n.* SPANISH someone who lives near the US–Mexico border: **1997** *Los Angeles Times*: *If the fronterizos belonged to one country, the bustling Tijuana-San*

Diego metropolitan sprawl would be their capital; **2011** *Examiner*: *Contemporary fronterizos in Southern Arizona refuse to accept the separation between North and South* || dating unknown, from *fronterizo* "borderlander"

fuckfest *n.* GERMAN *very offensive* a prolonged sex session, especially an orgy: **1998** *Sex and the City*, HBO-TV series: *A Wall Street honcho seeks two horny gals for an East Hampton fuckfest*; **2014** *Village Voice*: *That didn't stop him from turning it into a fuckfest* || since 1897, from *fuck* "sex" and *Fest* "festival"

fuete *n.* SPANISH a hypodermic needle (JG): **2004** Emmanuel Frost: *Fuete is a hypodermic needle*; **2012** Blogspot: *Paula tells him he doesn't need his fuete* || since 1973, from *fuete* "whip"

futz¹ *n.* YIDDISH [1] a stupid and despicable person, especially older (JG, KC): **1995** *Judge Dredd*, film: *Olmeyer, you stupid futz! I don't believe it. You just wasted three hours*; **2006** Democratic Underground: *Aw geez, he's such a futz!* [2] the vagina (JG, KC): **2011** Blogs: *What if Palin sent pics of her futz?* **2013** UCB student: *That perv wanted to touch her futz* || since 1935 in the first sense, since 1941 in the second, from *fartsn* "to flatulate"

futz² *v.* YIDDISH [1] to waste time doing nothing (AS, JG): **2003** *O.C.*, Fox-TV series: *"I think you could stop futzing." "No, I can't"*; **2012** Motley Fool: *He's waiting for me to quit futzing and get some work done* [2] to temper, meddle, or manipulate (JG, KC): **2009** *Broken Hill*, film: *I futzed it, so we could get done sooner*; **2012** *PC World*: *It took days of futzing to identify what was wrong* || since 1932 in the first sense, since 1965 in the second, from *fartsn* "to flatulate"

futz around *v.* YIDDISH to waste time doing nothing (AS, KC): **2007** Investor Village: *He had a good run but has futzed around since then*; **2012** *Globe and Mail*: *India is forging ahead with fundamental health reform, while Canada continues to futz around* || since 1932, from *fartsn* "to flatulate" and verbal particle *around*

futz around with *v.* YIDDISH [1] to provoke or play with someone: **2012** *Tucson Weekly*: *It's OK to futz around with her*; **2013** *Wall Street Journal*: *You don't futz around with Uncle Sam* [2] to temper, meddle, or manipulate with (KC): **2013** *Rolling Stone*: *We perform everything together, with very little futzing around with it after it's done*; **2013** *Atlantic Monthly*: *The two women futzed around with their synthpads and sampling gear* || since 1930s, from *fartsn* "to flatulate" and verbal particles *around with*

futzed up *adj.* YIDDISH [1] confused (KC): **2010** Free Republic: *Any boy who has a dream about who wins "American Idol" has got their life priorities so totally futzed up as to be beyond my comprehension*; **2012** Express Milwaukee: *What a futzed up mess we've allowed ourselves to be in!* [2] ruined or botched (KC): **2006** *Chicago Tribune*: *Finally he gave up and announced that any futzed-up dialogue would be rerecorded in the studio*; **2007** *Dallas Morning News*: *No matter which way the city goes on this thing, it will be a futzed-up deal* || since 1947, from *fartsn* "to flatulate"

futzer *n.* YIDDISH [1] someone who wastes time doing nothing: **1997** Michio Kaku: *He's a futzer. He arrives in the morning with four or five wild ideas, most of* *them wrong*; **2007** Urban Dictionary: *Man, you gotta be such a futzer all the time?* **[2]** someone who ruins or botches something: **2010** *Chicago Tribune*: *Finally, says Cohen, who calls herself "an inveterate futzer," be sure to make the loaf compact. Pat solidly, so when you cut it into slices, the cookies won't crumble*; **2013** UCB student: *The guy's a futzer, never does anything right* || since 1939 in the first sense, since 1965 in the second, from *fartser* literally "someone who flatulates"

futz up *v.* YIDDISH **[1]** to confuse: **2012** Rational Wiki: *I was totally going to vote for you but you futzed me up*; **2013** Facebook: *This is the way medicine used to be practiced before the do-gooder fools futzed everything up* **[2]** to ruin or botch (JG): **2000** *Milwaukee Journal Sentinel*: *He got the sequence mixed up, which futzed up the scanning equipment*; **2009** Gate World: *Look how many complained when they futzed up the "Threads" episode when Season Eight was released* || since 1947, from *fartsn* "to flatulate" and verbal particle *up*

futzup *n.* YIDDISH **[1]** confusion: **2012** NYU student: *The first month of college was an epic futzup*; **2015** Facebook: *The futzup lasted too long* **[2]** something ruined or botched: **2014** Steam Community: *I'm at a loss how this futzup happened in the first place*; **2018** Fark: *I watched a futzup happen beyond my control* || since 1947, from *fartsn* "to flatulate" and verbal particle *up*

futz with *v.* YIDDISH **[1]** to provoke or play with someone: **2002** *Minority Report*, film: *You think I might, you know, futz with him?* **2006** Free Republic: *Send the message to all who would futz with us* **[2]** to temper, meddle, or manipulate with (KC): **1997** *Chasing Amy*, film: *Would you stop futzing with your fuckin' bag? We're late already*; **2010** *Fashion Magazine*: *Angel Chen wants to dress well but has no time or inclination to futz with her clothes* || dating unknown, from *fartsn* "to flatulate" and verbal particle *with*

futzy *adj.* YIDDISH **[1]** stupid and despicable: **2007** Freak Angels: *It's a good place to start finding out how these futzy little buggers are doing*; **2013** Wordnik: *Hey, you don't have to do that futzy old boring research anymore* **[2]** older or old-fashioned: **2005** *Washington Post*: *Your hobbies consist of futzy little mechanical things (clock repair)*; **2013** *New York Observer*: *It doesn't give a damn for the musings of a futzy professor* || dating unknown, from *fartsn* "to flatulate" and adjectival suffix *-y*

G

gabacho *n.* SPANISH *offensive* a white person (TD): **1993** *Bound by Honor*, film: *You wanna bust me? Well, come on, gabacho. You're the law!* **2015** *Washington Post*: *You a vato or a gabacho?* || since 1950, from *gavacho* "white person," originally "French person"

gabfest *n.* GERMAN an idle or gossipy conversation session (AS, JG, KC, TD): **1994** *Northern Exposure*, CBS-TV series: *Are we having a poker game or a gabfest here?* **2000** *Los Angeles Times*: *At the gabfest, one hairdresser responded this way* || since 1897, from *gab* "talk" and *Fest* "festival"

gaga *adj.* FRENCH crazy or irrational, especially as a result of old age or excitement (AS, JG, KC): **2009** *I Love You, Man*, film: *He's gaga over you. It's adorable*; **2011** *Eye of the Storm*, film: *Can't you see our mother's completely gaga?* || since 1905, from *gaga* "senile person"

galoot *n.* SPANISH a boorish and awkward man (KC): **2010** Laurie Fox: *If I'm such a galoot, then let me prove to ya how gentle I can be*; **2015** Huffington Post: *I have never carried myself like a ballerina but I'm no lumbering galoot either* || since 1864, from *galeoto* "galley slave"

gam *n.* FRENCH a leg, especially a woman's leg (AS, JG, KC): **1999** *Life*, film: *That girls had gams*; **2014** *Neighbors*, film: *Hold that gam steady!* || since 1785, from *jambe* "leg" and Northern French *gambe* "leg"

ganef, ganif *n.* YIDDISH [1] a thief (JG, KC): **1993** *Me and the Kid*, film: *"Why don't you just give me all your money?" "You ganef!"*; **2009** *Vanity Fair*: *Many of the victims I visited were widows, including a lady with the mouth of a truck driver who cursed "that ganef, that thief, that nasty son of a bitch"* [2] a crooked, dishonest or unethical person (AS, JG, KC): **2009** *Desert Sun*: *Have you noticed the mind-blowing fact that the pharmaceutical and medical insurance ganefs have increased their commercials on TV?* **2013** *New York Daily News*: *She had to know what a ganef the guy was when he got the boot from the charity* || since 1839 in the first sense, since 1860 in the second, from *ganev* "thief"

ganif *see* gonif

ganja *n.* HINDI marijuana (AS, JG, KC, TD): **2002** *8 Mile*, film: *Want to smoke some ganja?* **2006** *Children of Men*, film: *Ganja is still illegal* || since 1858, from *gāṁjā* adopted via Caribbean usage

gantseh macher, gantse macher *n.* YIDDISH [1] a very important, influential, and well-connected person, especially involved in shady dealings: **2012** Fan Fiction: *You might be a gantseh macher in the shmata business but that means bupkis around here*; **2017** *East Bay Express*: *Matthew, his father's favorite, is a busy financial gantse macher* [2] a boastful person: **2011** Tom Collins: *You are the gantse macher with the Ph.D. in economics*; **2013** Facebook: *He behaves like a gantseh macher* || since 1930, from *gantse* "whole" and *makher* "doer"

gantseh megillah, gantse megillah *n.* YIDDISH [1] anything very long or complicated (JG): **2009** NJOP: *Whether it's a long-winded tale or a story overloaded with details – it's called a gantseh megillah!* **2011** Blogger: *It's great that the gantse megillah is over* [2] everything or totality: **1995** *New York Times*: *I want the whole gantse megillah*; **2015** UNF student: *I'm talking about the gantse megillah, all of it* [3] great outrage, fuss, or complaining, especially over a trivial matter: **2011** Talker Bill: *Enough with the gantseh megillah over our environment and gas drilling!* **2013** *New Orleans Review*: *It was such a gantseh megillah, such a big deal* || since 1909 in the first sense, since 1954 in the other two, from *megile* "scroll" or "volume," especially the Book of Esther read aloud in its entirety at Purim celebrations

gato *n.* SPANISH heroin (JG): **2003** *Rundown*, film: *How much is your gato worth?* **2012** Topix: *Got some gato. Let me know if you're interested* || since 1980, from *gato* "cat"

gaucho *n.* SPANISH *offensive* a Mexican: **1999** *Held Up*, film: *What are these gauchos? Now you can hang with the homeboys?* **2001** *Tremors 3: Back to Perfection*, film: *"Cool watch!" "Gift from the gauchos"* || dating unknown, from *gaucho* "cowboy of South American Pampas"

gavacho *n.* SPANISH *offensive* a white person (JG, TD): **2004** Michael Kearney: *I was surprised when I found out last year that some of these gavachos speak Spanish*; **2013** Twitter: *None of these gavachos have done shit for la raza* || since 1950, from *gavacho* "white person," originally "French person"

gazabo *n.* SPANISH a man (JG, KC): **1999** *Slight Case of Murder*, film: *Give me the toughest gazabo you've got*; **2013** Facebook: *You can't get away with it. I'm a pretty prominent gazabo* || since 1889, from *gazapo* "smart fellow," ultimately from *gazapo* "young rabbit"

gelt *n.* YIDDISH money (JG, KC): **2008** *Detroit Times*: *That could cost him a lot of gelt before he breaks it all together*; **2008** *Village Voice*: *The Dolan family has enough gelt to spend $650 million to buy the behemoth Long Island newspaper* || since 1698, from *gelt* "money," literally "gold"

geronimo *excl.* APACHE I am exhilarated and unafraid, especially when leaping from a great height (AS, JG): **1997** *Conspiracy Theory*, film: *You'll be screaming "geronimo" the whole way down*; **1999** *Toy Story*, film: *Okay, fellas, let's roll! Geronimo!* || since 1941, from *geronimo* "one who yawns," nickname of Apache leader Goyathlay

geronimo *n.* APACHE an alcoholic drink mixed with a barbiturate (JG, TD): **2003** Urban Dictionary: *Geronimo is an alcoholic beverage (especially wine) mixed with a barbiturate sleeping pill*; **2018** Ocean Breeze Recovery: *It is known as Geronimo when mixed with alcohol* || since 1950, from *geronimo* "exclamation of exhilaration," ultimately from "one who yawns," nickname of Apache leader Goyathlay

get lost *phr.* YIDDISH to leave someone alone (JG): **1994** *Léon*, film: *You guys get lost. I don't want to see you*; **2015** *Los Angeles Times*: *She could have told them to get lost and retreated into her grief* || since 1950, from *ver farblondzhet* "get lost"

get schlonged, get shlonged *phr.* YIDDISH to be defeated or victimized: **2015** *Forbes*: *If at first you get schlonged, try again!* **2016** Huffington Post: *Trump will most definitely get schlonged if he continues to repel female voters with it* || since 2015, from *shlang* "penis," literally "snake," and analogy to *get dicked* "to be cheated or victimized"

gevalt *excl.* YIDDISH [1] I am surprised (KC): **2002** *Shanghai Ghetto*, film: *Gevalt! Who did this to me?* **2015** UNF student: *Gevalt! What is this little thing?* [2] I am alarmed, terrified, or worried (KC): **1993** *New York Times*: *Oy Gevalt! New Yawkese An Endangered Dialect?* **2012** *Chicago Tribune*: *Gevalt! Keeping up with the Steins has made me all ferklempt* || since 1960s, from *gevald* or *gvald* "for heaven's sake," literally "violence" or "force"

give someone shpilkes, give someone schpilkes *n.* YIDDISH to make someone nervous or anxious (JG): **2005** Len Cohen: *Artie, please stop that, you're giving me shpilkes*; **2015** *Sports*, CBS-TV program: *The commercial gives me chills, even shlipkes* || since 1982, from *shpilkes* "nervousness" or "impatience," literally "pins," and *zitsn oyf shpilkes* "to be nervous or impatient," literally "to sit on pin and needles"

give someone some skin *phr.* MANDINKA to slap hands in greeting or congratulation (JG, KC): **2000** *Romeo Must Die*, film: *Come on, give me some skin!* **2006** *After School Special*, film: *What's up, buddy? Give me some skin!* || since 1939, from *i golo don n bolo* "place your skin in my hand"

glitch[1] *n.* YIDDISH [1] a malfunction, especially sudden (JG, KC): **2000** *Space Cowboys*, film: *I assure that we we'll fix this problem. It's just a glitch*; **2013** *PC Magazine*: *Apple today rolled out iOS 6.1.3, which fixes a glitch that allowed scammers to circumvent the lock screen on iOS gadgets* [2] an interruption, especially sudden (KC): **1997** *Dead Silence*, film: *Make sure there are no more communication glitches like that one*; **1997** *Contact*, film: *It must have been the glitch in the timing!* || since 1962, from *glitshn zikh* "to slip," "to slide," or "to skid"

glitch[2] *v.* YIDDISH [1] to malfunction or cause to malfunction, especially suddenly: **2010** *Sharktopus*, film: *The software is glitching*; **2011** *Houston Chronicle*: *The site's viewership counter seems to be glitching* [2] to interrupt or be interrupted, especially suddenly: **2010** Digital Digest: *This somehow glitched the quest and it was not possible to proceed*; **2015** UNF student: *The production glitched unexpectedly* || since 1962, from *glitshn zikh* "to slip," "to slide," or "to skid"

glitchy *n.* YIDDISH [1] malfunctioning: **2011** *New York Times*: *Buyers have criticized its glitchy touch screen, clunky controls, and slow web browser*; **2012** *Globe and Mail*: *These range from condensation inside the headlights to glitchy heater blower motors* [2] interrupted or erratic: **2011** *Examiner*: *It's a hip-hop tempo banger, with glitchy rhythms and buildups that crash down into melodic bleeps and bloops*; **2012** *Chicago Tribune*: *He inserts clever spoken commands into the glitchy collages* || since 1962, from *glitshn zikh* "to slip," "to slide," or "to skid"

glitterati *n.* ITALIAN famous and glamorous people (AS, JG, KC, TD): **2000** *Body and Soul*, film: *Why don't you go grab a seat and pretend you're part of the glitterati?* **2010** *Glee*, Fox-TV series: *Everybody looks at us differently. We're glitterati* || since 1946, from *glitter* and plural suffix *-ati*, analogous to *literati*

glitz[1] *n.* YIDDISH flashiness or showiness (JG, KC): **2005** *Muppets' Wizard of Oz*, film: *I know you think show business is all glitz and glamour, but it's not*; **2010** *Naples News*: *If you filtered all the glitz out of Miami, you'd get Naples, Florida* || since 1978, since 1970s, from *glitsern* "to glitter"

glitz² *v.* YIDDISH to make flashy or showy (KC): **1998** *Wired*: *Here in Los Altos, new money has driven up the cost of living, yet it hasn't glitzed the environment as it would almost anywhere else in America*; **2010** Community Baby Center: *How do I get started glitzing a dress?* || since 1970s, from *glitsern* "to glitter"

glitz up *v.* YIDDISH to make flashy or showy (KC): **2005** *Chicago Tribune*: *They're running park programs and they've glitzed the place up*; **2013** Wicked Local: *The house needs interior updates such as glitzing up the bathrooms* || since 1970s, from *glits(ern)* "to glitter" and verbal particle *up*

glitzy *adj.* YIDDISH flashy or showy (JG, KC): **1991** *Delirious*, film: *People like the Hedisons just the way they are: rich, ruthless, glitzy*; **2013** *News*, CNN-TV program: *For some, it's the glitzy stores of New York and Paris. For others, it's the designer ateliers of Rome and Amsterdam* || since 1966, from *glits(ern)* "to glitter" and adjectival suffix *-y*

go figure *phr.* YIDDISH imagine this (KC): **2003** *American Splendor*, film: *We even won a couple of National Book Awards. Go figure!* **2022** *St. Louis Post-Dispatch*: *Medicines for erectile dysfunction are far cheaper, go figure* || dating unknown, from *gey visn* "go learn"

go jihad on someone's ass *phr.* ARABIC *offensive* to attack someone forcibly and mercilessly: **2007** Harry Hunsicker: *If you touch anything before I get it out, I'll go jihad on your ass*; **2014** Reddit: *I'm about to go jihad on his ass* || since 2007, from *jihād* "struggle on behalf of Islam" and analogy to *go medieval on someone's ass* "attack someone forcibly and mercilessly"

go loco *phr.* SPANISH [1] to become crazy: **2013** *Atlantic Monthly*: *Short skirts and high heels make men go loco*; **2014** *New York Times*: *He's going loco from thirst and heat in the desert* [2] to get intoxicated with marijuana: **2007** Cannabis Culture: *Many commented he went loco on the weed*; **2013** Naira Land: *After smoking the second wrap, the guy started going loco* || dating unknown, from *go crazy* and *loco* "crazy" and *loco weed* "marijuana"

goma *n.* SPANISH [1] inferior heroin: **2014** *Washington Post*: *Whatever goma the farmers harvest is sold to middlemen or cartel lab operators*; **2014** Borderland Beat: *The guys here are saying that Mexican cartels improved on the refining of goma* [2] opium (JG): **1997** Google Groups: *They owe their good fortune not only to the profits of goat raising but to mota (marijuana) and goma (opium)*; **2004** Urban Dictionary: *Goma is Mexican slang for opium* || since 1967, from *goma* "gum"

gonif, gonef *n.* YIDDISH [1] a thief (JG, KC): **2003** *Boston Globe*: *He called Lehman a gonif, Yiddish for thief*; **2009** *Robin Williams: Weapons of Self Destruction*, film: *He took our 401 k. The gonif's coming back for the house* [2] a crooked, dishonest, or unethical person (AS, JG, KC): **2010** *Mad Men*, AMC-TV series: *Damn it! Those gonifs at CBS are screwing me again!* **2021** *News*, NBC-TV program: *My mother would have called Madoff a "gonif." It means a thief or at* *a minimum a dishonest person* ‖ since 1839 in the first sense, since 1860 in the second, from *ganev* "thief"

goober *n.* KONGO [1] an uneducated or unsophisticated person (AS, KC, TD): 2007 *Sydney White*, film: *Sydney and her band of goobers are screwing with our plans*; 2021 *Boston Herald*: *It is about time that the goobers in the flyover country should pay more* [2] a stupid person (JG, KC): 2004 *7th Heaven*, WB-TV series: *He's being a big goober about it*; 2022 *Florida Today*: *That had more to do with me acting like a goober* ‖ since 1862 in the first sense, since 1919 in the second, from *nguba* "peanut"

goodnik *n.* YIDDISH a well-intentioned, selfless, or altruistic person, especially if naive or self-righteous: 2005 *New York Times*: *These days you're what Roth might call a goodnik*; 2012 *New York Post*: *Beards somehow connote villains, not heroes. Henry VIII was a bad boy. Ho Chi Minh? A pig. Lenin? Shove it. Persia's ruler Xerxes also not such a goodnik* ‖ dating unknown, from *good* and suffix *-nik*, and possibly from *do-goodnik*

goomah *n.* ITALIAN a mistress: 2007 *Sopranos*, HBO-TV series: *Phil's at his goomah's every Friday night*; 2019 *GQ Magazine*: *Each mobster has a "goomah" like the rest of us have a winter coat* ‖ dating unknown, from dialectal *comare* "godmother"

goombah *n.* ITALIAN [1] a close male friend (JG, KC, TD): 1997 *Donnie Brasco*, film: *You have to find yourself a new goombah*; 2001 *See Spot Run*, film: *Your sister is married to my goombah* [2] an Italian American (JG): 1992 *Hoffa*, film: *This goombah, this guinea, reached under his coat, takes out his piece*; 1996 *NYPD Blue*, ABC-TV series: *The goombahs are loudmouths* [3] a member of the Italian American Mafia (AS, JG): 1993 *Another Stakeout*, film: *I can't take this goombah into court with a bunch of circumstantial crap!* 1999 *Sopranos*, HBO-TV series: *They're two goombahs from the old neighborhood* ‖ since 1954 in the first sense, since 1960 in the second, since 1969 in the third, from dialect pronunciation of *compare* "companion" or "godfather"

gordita *n.* SPANISH a short and obese woman: 1988 *Stand and Deliver*, film: *Don't call me "gordita," pendejo!* 2007 International Sex Guide: *I might want to hook up with a busty gordita for some sweet dinner* ‖ dating unknown, from *gordita* "thick pancake filled with meat, cheese, and vegetables"

go to ca-ca (or **go to caca**) *phr.* SPANISH to be ruined: 2007 *Seattle Post Intelligencer*: *The service at the Clinton branch went to ca-ca*; 2010 *Los Angeles Times*: *It's so depressing that individuals have let this area go to caca* ‖ dating unknown, from *caca* "excrement" and analogy to *go to shit*

go to el carajo *phr.* SPANISH *potentially offensive* [1] to leave someone alone: 2007 Pablo Medina: *He shrugged his shoulders and told the older man to go to el carajo*; 2012 Facebook: *Oscar, just go to el carajo!* [2] to hold someone in contempt: 2008 Topix:

Go to el carajo! El Salvador rocks! Go finger yourself! 2010 Blogs: *If you don't like it, go to el carajo!* || dating unknown, from *go to hell* and *carajo* "penis"

goy *n.* YIDDISH a non-Jew (AS, JG): **1991** *New York Times*: *Malamud and Roth demanded the right to juggle ideas in full view of the public, but this right is never conceded to us goys*; **2009** *Chicago Tribune*: *My best friend, being a goy, can't understand why anyone would eat gefilte fish* || since 1841, from *goy* "gentile man"

goyesque *adj.* YIDDISH not Jewish: **2008** *New York Times*: *With its cloistered patios and latticed grills, the look is very goyesque*; **2013** UCB student: *It's a very goyesque place* || since 1990s, from *goy* "gentile" and adjectival suffix *-esque*

goyfriend *n.* YIDDISH a non-Jewish boyfriend of a Jewish person: **2016** *New York Newsday*: *Sarah Goldman considers herself a nice Jewish girl who's courting heresy in the form of an itching-to-marry goyfriend*; **2021** Your Tango: *One woman explains why she dates Catholic men so she can find a "goyfriend," or a man who is non-Jewish, to celebrate Christmas with* || dating unknown, from *goy* "gentile man" and *friend*

goyish *adj.* YIDDISH not Jewish (AS, JG): **2011** *Chicago Tribune*: *This Irish Catholic writer is as goyish as they come, so, why matzo?* **2013** *New York Post*: *He's the East Coast intellectual, she's the handsome, California horseback-riding goyish goddess* || since 1890, from *goyish* "gentile"

goyishe kop, goyisher kop *n.* YIDDISH [1] non-Jewish way of thinking, especially being stupid: **1999** *New York Observer*: *Maybe she's no shiksa, but it looks like she has a goyishe kop*; **2012** *Tablet Magazine*: *To say that someone had a goyishe kop meant that they were willfully idiotic* [2] someone who thinks in a non-Jewish way, especially if stupid: **2006** *Washington Post*: *We're too damn smart for you, goyishe kops*; **2009** Blogspot: *A person who wouldn't listen was a goyishe kop* || dating unknown, from *goyisher kop*, literally "gentile head"

goy toy *n.* YIDDISH an attractive young non-Jewish male used like the plaything of a Jewish woman: **2005** *Out Magazine*: *Fran Drescher brings her nasal charms back to the tube with Living with Fran, the WB sitcom in which she's a sexy divorcee with a goy toy*; **2013** *New York Times*: *She plays a fiery leftist and Robert is her coolly apolitical goy-toy* || since 2000, from *goy* "gentile man" and *toy*, and analogy to *boytoy* "an attractive young man used like the plaything of a woman or a man" or "an attractive young woman used like the plaything of a man"

greefa *n.* SPANISH marijuana or marijuana cigarette (JG, KC, TD): **1999** Cannabis News: *The only health risk in smoking greefa is the smoking itself. Smoking anything, whether hash or tobacco, causes lung cancer and other respiratory diseases*; **2013** Facebook: *We're smoking greefa and having fun* || since 1931, from *grifo* "bushy or unruly hair" or "untidy person" and *grifa* "female drug addict"

griffa *n.* SPANISH marijuana or marijuana cigarette (JG, TD): **2011** Twitter: *"In the need of some griffa!" "Quit smoking weed!"*; **2013** UCSD student: *Where can I score some griffa?* || since 1931, from *grifo* "bushy or unruly hair" or "untidy person" and *grifa* "female drug addict"

gringa *n.* SPANISH [1] *offensive* a white female from an English-speaking country (KC, TD): 1992 *Los Angeles Times*: *Marjorie was surprised to discover so much female complicity in machismo, from Latin women to gringas alike*; 2011 *Dallas Observer*: *Why is a knocked-up Mexican girl a tramp, while a gringa is a "victim?"* [2] a taco in a white flour tortilla with gyros-like pork filling: 2014 *Columbus Dispatch*: *Los Guachos Taqueria (5221 Godown Rd.) has really good tacos, pork tacos and gringas*; 2015 *Village Voice*: *Everyone is ordering gringas ($8.50), flour tortillas folded over melted cheese and grilled meats* ‖ since 1849 in the first sense, since 2000 in the second, from *gringa* "white woman from an English-speaking country"

gringa taco *n.* SPANISH a taco in a white flour tortilla with gyros-like pork filling: 1996 *Santa Fe New Mexican*: *One gringa taco came served with lettuce, tomato and a choice of Charro beans or Fideo*; 2014 *Dallas Entree Journal*: *You can get a gringa taco with a flour tortilla. That's why it's called a gringa, because it's the American way* ‖ since 1995, from *gringa* "white woman from an English-speaking country" and *taco*

gringo *n.* SPANISH *offensive* a white person from an English-speaking country (AS, KC, TD): 2000 *Space Cowboys*, film: *These instructions were probably translated by some gringo, an expatriate American*; 2018 *Narcos: Mexico*, Netflix-TV series: *Don't cross the border, the gringos are waiting* ‖ since 1849, from *gringo* "white man from an English-speaking country"

Gringo Gallop *n.* SPANISH *offensive* diarrhea suffered by tourists in Mexico or Latin America (JG, TD): 2007 *Trip Advisor*: *Montezuma's Revenge is also known as the Gringo Gallop and the Aztec Two-step*; 2012 *Health 24*: *It's something I'd had opportunity to perfect some years ago when stricken with a spectacular case of Gringo Gallop* ‖ since 1960, from *gringo* "white person from an English-speaking country" and *gallop* with reference to diarrhea

Gringoland *n.* SPANISH *offensive* an English-speaking country, especially the USA: 2006 *Free Republic*: *Gee, actions have consequences in Gringoland!* 2012 *News*, Fox-TV program: *We need more people coming from Gringoland* ‖ dating unknown, from *gringo* "white person from an English-speaking country"

guapa[1] *n.* SPANISH a good-looking woman: 1985 *Miami Vice*, NBC-TV series: *"I'm a man, guapa!" "I doubt it!"*; 2014 UNM student: *Who's that busty guapa?* ‖ dating unknown, from *guapa* "handsome"

guapa[2] *adj.* SPANISH (of a woman) good-looking: 2014 Tumblr: *I miss my guapa girlfriend so much!* 2013 UCB student: *Yo, chica, you're looking guapa!* ‖ dating unknown, from *guapa* "handsome"

guapo[1] (or **el guapo**) *n.* SPANISH a handsome man: 2007 *Cold Case*, CBS-TV series: *Stay a little longer, guapo!* 2015 Yelp: *There were so many good looking people there. Even the staff were guapos!* ‖ dating unknown, from *guapo* "handsome"

guapo[2] *adj.* SPANISH handsome: 2010 *Eastbound & Down*, HBO-TV series: *Do I look guapo in this outfit?* 2011 *American Dad!*, Fox-TV series: *Hello, Ricky Martin! You're looking guapo, as usual* ‖ dating unknown, from *guapo* "handsome"

guero (or **güero**) *n.* SPANISH *potentially offensive* [1] a blond-haired and light-skinned person: **1995** *Streets of Laredo*, film: *"You say he's a guero? He's what?"* *"Guero. That means a blond-haired Mexican"*; **2008** *Gamefaqs*: *My cousin would beat down Mexicans whenever they called him a guero* [2] a white person: **1993** *Bound by Honor*, film: *You speak Spanish, guero?* **1997** *Perdita Durango*, film: *"If we're gonna do a kidnapping, we should get a gringo." "A guero? It'll be impressive!"* || dating unknown, from *guero* "blondie," ultimately from *huero* "empty" and *huevo huero* "empty egg lost during incubation" associated with sickness

gun *n.* YIDDISH a thief, especially a pickpocket (JG, KC): **2007** Lawrence Jeffrey Epstein: *A gun, a pickpocket or general thief, is probably derived from gonif, Yiddish for "thief"*; **2009** Tom Dalzell: *A gun is a pickpocket* || since 1857, from *gonif* and *ganev* "thief"

gung-ho *adj.* CHINESE zealous, committed, enthusiastic (AS, KC): **2013** *Chicago Fire*, NBC-TV series: *"Where's gung-ho Joe?" "I don't think he's coming back"*; **2021** *Politico*: *There are more Americans skeptical of going to war with Russia than those who are gung-ho* || since 1945, from *gōng hé* "work together"

gun moll *n.* YIDDISH a female criminal or a criminal's female companion (JG, KC): **2004** *News*, CBS-TV program: *Zellweger landed her first leading role as the trailer-trash gun moll Starlene in "Love and .45"*; **2011** *New York Post*: *Its acquiescence in gun violence would have rung a tad more true if he hadn't himself arranged a sweet deal for the youthful gun moll at the center of the case* || since 1908, from *gonif* and *ganev* "thief" and *moll*

gunsel *n.* YIDDISH [1] a gay man's partner, especially sexually vulnerable (JG, KC): **1990** Peter Lehman: *Spade refers to him as a "gunsel," a term meaning gunman, but also meaning a boy used in pederasty*; **2008** Elise Chenier: *At the beginning of the twentieth century, prisoners and hoboes called young, inexperienced boys, especially homosexuals, gunsels* [2] a thug or petty criminal (AS, KC): **2007** *Jesse Stone: Sea Change*, film: *He just got out of prison. Freelance gunsel. Works for Gino on occasion*; **2012** *Globe and Mail*: *Burt Lancaster waxed a bit of nostalgia for the 1940s while playing Lou, the aged small-time gunsel in the 1980 Oscar-nominated feature "Atlantic City"* || in the first sense since 1914, from *gandzl* "gosling"; in the second since 1940s, from *gonif* and *ganev* "thief"

guru *n.* HINDI an influential or popular expert (AS, JG, KC): **2011** *Source Code*, film: *Do you know any good gurus?* **2015** *New York Times*: *Republican political guru Karol Rove used the issue against Democrats* || since 1960, from *guru* "spiritual teacher"

H

habibi *n.* ARABIC darling (JG): **2005** Urban Dictionary: *"Holy shit, I look fat!" "Aw, habibi, you look great"*; **2008** *You Don't Mess with the Zohan*, film: *You're a good guy, habibi. I just don't know what to do* || since 2000, from *habibi* "beloved"

hache *n.* SPANISH heroin (JG, TD): **2004** Wiki Spaces: *Hache is slang for heroin*; **2005** Blogspot: *Can I have some money for some smack? Please. how about some cash for some hache?* || since 1955, from the Spanish pronunciation of the letter "H"

haimish, haymish *adj.* YIDDISH **[1]** homelike and cozy (KC): **2004** *Cutting Edge: The Magic of Movie Editing*, film: *She cut her films at her house in the San Fernando Valley, and it was a very haimish kind of a workplace*; **2009** *Los Angeles Times*: *It's very haimish here, it's homey* **[2]** unpretentious, natural, or informal (KC): **2011** *New York Times*: *She was looking glamorous and haimish at the same time*; **2012** Tripod: *A haimish person judges you by your character, not your money* || since 1960s, from *heymish* "homelike" or "cozy"

haji *n.* ARABIC an Arab: **2010** *Esquire*: *He thought he was coming here to get into fights with some hajis to get some, but instead he got stuck with teaching the hajis how to wield a baton*; **2014** *Lone Survivor*, film: *The second they run down there, we got 200 hajis on our backs* || since 1990, from *haji* "Muslim who has been to Mecca as a pilgrim"

halal *adj.* ARABIC approved or acceptable (JG): **2015** Reddit: *Taking a road trip to Florida is probably a halal thing to do*; **2017** *Jewish News*: *Is it halal to love one's nation?* || since 2000, from *ḥalāl* "permissible, especially with regard to food and drink"

Hanoi Hilton *n.* VIETNAMESE a prisoner-of-war camp in Hanoi during the Vietnam War (JG, TD): **2016** *Washington Times*: *He had been tortured for five years in the Hanoi Hilton*; **2019** *Billions*, Showtime-TV series: *The guy is as loyal as John McCain in the Hanoi Hilton* || since 1970, from *Hanoi* and *Hilton* "chain of luxurious hotels"

hasta *excl.* SPANISH goodbye (JG): **2003** Boxing Scene: *Hasta, guys. Talk to you Monday*; **2013** Twitter: *Hasta! See you next week, hermano!* || since 1989, from *hasta mañana* "till tomorrow"

hasta la bye-bye *excl.* SPANISH goodbye (JG, TD): **2008** *Beverly Hills Chihuahua*, film: *This is highly inappropriate. Hasta la bye-bye!* **2013** *New York Times*: *If you aren't nice to them, it's hasta la bye-bye, baby!* || since 1990, from *hasta la vista* "goodbye" and *bye-bye*

hasta la pasta *excl.* PSEUDO-SPANISH goodbye (JG): **2013** Yelp: *I'm on the go. Hasta la pasta, baby*; **2013** Fan Fiction: *You know I can be impatient, so hasta la pasta!* || since 1989, from *hasta la vista* "goodbye" and *la pasta*, mocking Spanish

hasta la vista *excl.* SPANISH goodbye (TD): **1997** *Jungle 2 Jungle*, film: *"Hasta la vista!" "Hey, stop! You can't leave me here!"*; **2015** *Entertainment Tonight*: *I'm going to have a little bit of lunch with my family, so hasta la vista!* || dating unknown, from *hasta la vista* "until the next time"

hasta lumbago *excl.* PSEUDO-SPANISH goodbye (TD): **1985** *Last Dragon*, film: *"Hasta lumbago!" "Sayonara!"*; **2008** Free Republic: *Seriously, dude, I can't take you seriously, so hasta lumbago!* || since 1977, from *hasta luego* "until later"

hasty banana *excl.* PSEUDO-SPANISH goodbye (JG, TD): **2007** *Washington Post*: *I should say "hasty banana." Good night, all!* **2013** ASU student: *I should be going. Hasty banana, dudes!* || since 1949, from *hasta mañana* "see you tomorrow" and *banana*

hausfrau *n.* GERMAN a woman whose primary interests are keeping house and raising children (AS, KC): **2014** *National Geographic*: *We are talking here about the idealized homemaker: the hausfrau who can whip up a roast leg of lamb with parsnip mash and madeira sauce without breaking a sweat*; **2015** *USA Today*: *Anna is a hausfrau with a blond banker husband and two little blond boys* || since 1918, from *Hausfrau* "housewife"

haymish *see* haimish

head honcho *n.* JAPANESE an important person, especially a chief (AS, JG): **2015** *Des Moines Register*: *The new head honcho will be tasked with rejuvenating the program*; **2022** *New York Magazine*: *Jeff Zucker was the president of CNN Worldwide, making him its head honcho* || since 1945, from *head* and *hanchō* "group leader"

healthnik *n.* YIDDISH someone obsessed with health, especially healthy diet: **2011** *South Florida Sun-Sentinel*: *Healthniks were working out at gyms, jogging or taking walks*; **2012** Twitter: *We're not healthniks by any means, but we do like good food that's made fresh* || dating unknown, from *health* and suffix -*nik*

hentai *n.* JAPANESE *potentially offensive* pornographic cartoon or animated cartoon film, especially Japanese in origin or style: **2013** *Internship*, film: *"What's hentai?" "Japanese comic books where women get penetrated by octopus tentacles"*; **2017** *Cosmopolitan*: *A common practice in hentai is to stretch the sex acts beyond the boundaries of normal human sex* || since 1990, from *hentai seiyoku* "perverse sexual desire"

hierba *n.* SPANISH marijuana: **2013** *Blaze You Out*, film: *You smoke bud? I brought some hierba*; **2014** UNM student: *Hierba is legal in Colorado* || since 1967, from *hierb* "herb"

hija *n.* SPANISH (especially as a term of address) a young woman you like: **2011** *Off the Map*, film: *"You're abandoning me, hija?" "I just need a little time for myself"*; **2014** *Seattle Post Intelligencer*: *He introduces them to his hija all the time* || dating unknown, from *hija* "daughter"

hijo *n.* SPANISH (especially as a term of address) a young man you like: **2005** SF Gate: *OK, hijo, help me out here. What should I say?* **2013** *Houston Chronicle*: *Her hijo is a good person* || dating unknown, from *hijo* "son"

hijo de puta *phr.* SPANISH *offensive* a despicable man: **1990** *Die Hard 2*, film: *Hijo de puta! It's McClane again!* **2012** Blaze: *That hijo de puta would have been court-martialed* || since 1890, from *hijo de puta* "despicable man," literally "son of a bitch"

himbo *n.* ITALIAN an attractive and hedonistic young man, especially if also stupid (JG, KC, TD): **2012** Flavorwire: *Originally presented as an empty-headed looker with womanizing streak, he's recently turned the himbo stereotype on its head*; **2016** Hollywood Reporter: *She chooses the himbo with the cut abs* || since 1988, from *he* and *bimbo* "attractive and hedonistic young woman, especially if also stupid" which comes from *bambino* "baby"

hip *adj.* WOLOF [1] fashionable or popular (KC): **1997** *Face/Off*, film: *He ain't too hip now, but I can dig that*; **2010** *Scott Pilgrim vs. the World*, film: *Me? I'm what's hip! I'm what's happening!* [2] aware, knowing, or understanding (KC): **2009** Jim Carlton: *At age 73, he's very hip to what's happening on the jazz scene today*; **2015** Verbotomy: *Maurice thinks he's very hip about all computer related information but he's actually clueless* || since 1932, from *hepi* "knowing"

hipster *n.* WOLOF [1] a person who wants to be fashionable or popular (KC): **2010** *Community*, NBC-TV series: *Do hipsters walk around wearing $300 jeans?*; **2010** *Lie To Me*, Fox-TV series: *They're hipsters, not hippies* [2] a devotee of jazz or swing music (KC): **1994** *Flintstones*, film: *I know a place where the hipsters go*; **2004** *Ray*, film: *You've come to the place where the sophisti-cats and hipsters hang their bebop hats* || since 1941, from *hepi* "knowing" and *-ster* ending

hock¹ (or **hok**) *v.* YIDDISH [1] to chatter all the time (KC): **2002** *Surfer Magazine*: *A relative gave one of those workout things Chuck Norris and Kristy Brinkley are hocking all the time*; **2004** *Elvis Has Left the Building*, film: *Do you think you could stop that? You've been hocking for the past hour* [2] to nag (KC): **2007** *Big Bang Theory*, CBS-TV series: *Bernadette's been hocking me to take her roller skating*; **2009** Flickr: *My friends are hocking me to start a business making ceramic urns for our past beloved pets* || since 1961, from *hakn* "to chop" or "to knock," and *hakn a tshaynik* "to chatter constantly," literally "to knock a teakettle"

hock² *v.* DUTCH to pawn (JG, KC): **2004** *Kill Bill: Vol. 2*, film: *You hocked a Hattori Hanzo sword?* **2018** *Kominsky Method*, Netflix-TV series: *You were going to hock it for drugs* || since 1878, from *hok* "hutch" or "debt"

hock shop *n.* DUTCH a pawn shop (JG, KC): **2015** SF Gate: *His father, a Russian immigrant, operated a hock shop*; **2017** *News*, ABC-TV program: *I took my sewing machine to a hock shop and hocked it to get the money* || since 1886, from *hok* "hutch" or "debt" and *shop*

hocus-pocus *n.* PSEUDO-LATIN [1] magic: **2015** *Cosmopolitan*: *You might even say there's some hocus-pocus happening*; **2021** *Forbes*: *Add some hocus pocus with your smart bulbs inside and outside your home* [2] trickery (KC): **2012** *Wall Street Journal*: *The tricks of their trade are flashlights, night-vision cameras and gadgets with blinking lights that are pure hocus-pocus*; **2013** Huffington Post: *Democrats are mocking Paul Ryan's budget plan as hocus pocus* || since 1694, from imitating the Church Latin phrase *hoc est corpus* "this is the body"

hola *excl.* SPANISH hello: **2005** *American Pie Presents: Band Camp*, film: *Hola, chicas! Elyse, good to see you again*; **2015** *Santa Cruz Sentinel*: *Hola, how are you tonight?* || dating unknown, from *hola* "hello"

holdupnik *n.* YIDDISH a robber: **2002** Henry L. Feingold: *Jews drawn to vice and crime were rarely burglars or holdupniks*; **2004** *Jewish Daily Forward*: *The holdupniks didn't ask many questions and demanded that everyone hand over their valuables* || dating unknown, from *holdup* and suffix *-nik*

Hollywoodnik *n.* YIDDISH a person from Hollywood: **2010** *Los Angeles Times*: *It would enable Hollywoodniks to write screenplays on their iPhones*; **2012** *New York Post*: *Most people we know have quit handing our money over to these Hollywoodniks* || dating unknown, from *Hollywood* and suffix *-nik*

holy guacamole *n.* SPANISH [1] I am surprised: **1993** *Teenage Mutant Ninja Turtles*, CBS-TV series: *I don't believe I'm seeing this. Holy guacamole!* **2002** *Little Secrets*, film: *"I'll be at your house next Wednesday at 2:00." "Holy guacamole!"* [2] I am annoyed or disgusted: **2002** *Felicity*, WB-TV series: *Holy guacamole! I need to talk to you, it's kind of an emergency*; **2003** *South Park*, Comedy-Central-TV series: *"Payback time!" "Holy guacamole!"*; **2017** UCLA student: *Holy guacamole! I forgot my driver's license* || dating unknown, from *holy* and *guacamole* "avocado-based dip," based on *holy shit*

holy shitski, holy shitsky *n.* YIDDISH [1] I am surprised: **2004** Grease Car: *Holy shitsky! $2.53 a gallon? Oh man!* **2009** Tumblr: *Holy shitsky! I turned sixty!* [2] I am annoyed or disgusted: **2016** Newser: *Holy shitsky! I could have lost some serious dough*; **2016** Tumblr: *Holy shitski! This is utterly ridiculous* || dating unknown, from *holy shit* and suffix *-ski*

hombre *n.* SPANISH a man (AS, JG, TD): **1996** *Bulletproof*, film: *Those fellas messed with the wrong hombre*; **1999** *American Beauty*, film: *You need a little more than that, my little hombre* | since 1854, from *hombre* "man"

hombrecitos *n.* SPANISH hallucinogenic mushrooms (JG): **2007** Shroomery: *These species are called hombrecitos*; **2011** Urban Dictionary: *I had some hombrecitos last night, man, I was tripping out* || since 1977, from *hombrecitos* "little men" and reference to creatures seen after taking the hallucinogen

hombrito *n.* SPANISH a man: **2013** *R.I.P.D.*, film: *You gotta learn the lingo, hombrito*; **2017** UCLA student: *Hey, hombrito, let me help you!* || since 1980, from *hombre* "man" and affectionate suffix *-ito*

honcho[1] *n.* JAPANESE an important person, especially a chief (AS, JG, KC, TD): **1997** *Hercules*, film: *Now he's a honcho, he's a hero*; **2001** *Kate and Leopold*, film: *You're going to be the top New York honcho* || since 1945, from *hanchō* "group leader"

honcho[2] *v.* JAPANESE to lead or direct (AS, JG, KC): **2003** *Chicago Tribune*: *Jenny Bricks is honchoing the project*; **2015** *Los Angeles Daily News*: *UCLA basketball* *coach Steve Alford gets $2.6 million a year to honcho the hoops squad* || since 1958, from *hanchō* "group leader"

hondle, hondel *v.* YIDDISH to negotiate, especially on the price of something: **2013** *New York Magazine*: *She shows up at Bee's Doll Shop to hondel over the merchandise*; **2014** *Esquire*: *Hondle! It's about shamelessness, about asking and asking and not caring when you get shot down* || since 1920, from *handlen* "to haggle or bargain"

hondo *adj.* SPANISH excellent (KC, TD): **1986** *Los Angeles Times*: *"If a guy is better than cool, you say, "He's really hondo," a female student said*; **2010** Deviant Art: *That is such a hondo song* || since 1980, from *hondo* "deep"

Hongcouver *n.* CHINESE Vancouver, British Columbia: **2015** Conversation: *Vancouver became such a popular destination that locals refer to it as Hongcouver*; **2015** *Los Angeles Times*: *Some locals have dubbed it "Hongcouver"* || since 1990, from *Hong (Kong)* and *(Van)couver*

hooch *n.* HOOCHINOO low quality alcohol, especially if illegally produced (AS, JG, KC): **2010** *Boardwalk Empire*, HBO-TV series: *The Sheriff's here. Hide the hooch!* **2014** *Miami New Times*: *What's the difference between the $12 bottle of hooch and all these expensive rums?* || since 1897, from *hoochinoo* "liquor made by the Hoochinoo Indians of Alaska"

hoopla *n.* FRENCH unnecessary fuss or commotion (JG): **2019** *Wall Street Journal*: *The art of negotiating is to concede things you don't care for, while making a big hoopla about it*; **2019** *Dallas Morning News*: *I don't want to make a big hoopla, I don't think there's any reason for that* || since 1877, from *houp-là* "expression accompanying a sudden movement, especially of some trick on stage"

hoosegow *n.* SPANISH a jail or prison (AS, JG, KC, RS, TD): **2012** *CSI: Crime Scene Investigation*, CBS-TV series: *It looks like you're going to the hoosegow*; **2014** *Los Angeles Times*: *He was hauled to the hoosegow* || since 1908, from *juzgado* "tribunal" or "court"

hot chihuahua¹ *excl.* SPANISH [1] I am surprised: **2012** Tumblr: *Hot chihuahua! This is a beautiful piece of art!* **2013** UCLA student: *Hot chihuahua! This tastes good!* [2] I am annoyed or disgusted: **2010** Twitter: *Hot chihuahua! What a mess!* **2015** UNF student: *Hot chihuahua! What is it this time?* || dating unknown, from *hot (damn)* and *(ay) chihuahua* "I am surprised" or "I am annoyed," perhaps from *chingar* "to copulate," ultimately from *Chihuahua*, a city in Mexico

hot chihuahua² *n.* SPANISH a sexually attractive person: **2004** *News*, MTV-TV program: *Before joining the Road Rules cast, he was dating a hot chihuahua*; **2008** Flickr: *I hope that hot chihuahua heading my way notices me* || dating unknown, from exclamation *hot chihuahua* "I am surprised," perhaps from *chingar* "to copulate"

hot taco *n.* SPANISH a sexually attractive woman, especially of Hispanic origin (TD): **2011** *InSecurity*, CBC-TV series: *You all come out for some piping hot tacos*;

2014 UNM student: *She's a hot taco, and she's not your league* || since 1974, from *hot* "sexually attractive" and *taco* "type of tortilla stuffed with various ingredients"

housefrau *n.* GERMAN a woman whose primary interests are keeping house and raising children: **2018** *Forbes: She is seeking something beyond the future as a bourgeoise housefrau that her parents have planned for her*; **2018** *Albuquerque Journal: I tell my husband, "You didn't marry a housefrau"* || since 1918, from *house* and *(Haus)frau* "housewife"

how come *phr.* YIDDISH why: **1998** *Truman Show*, film: *How come he wants to go to Chicago?* **1999** *Sixth Sense*, film: *You asked a lot of questions about Dad today. How come?* || dating unknown, from *vi kumt es* "how does it come"

huevon (or **huevón**) *n.* SPANISH *potentially offensive* a lazy person, especially if also stupid (TD): **2004** Urban Dictionary: *That huevón wouldn't know his ass from a hole in the ground!* **2007** Yahoo Answers: *You are a huevon, as we say in South Dallas* || since 1960, from *huevos* "eggs" or "testicles" and the image of the man who is so lazy that his testicles grow large

huevos *n.* SPANISH [1] *potentially offensive* testicles (JG, TD): **2008** *Stiletto*, film: *I will cut his huevos off*; **2012** *Washington Post: There are many stories, but the most popular one, it has to do with his huevos (testicles)* [2] courage (TD): **2007** *Man in the Car*, film: *Now, go get him. Show some huevos*; **2022** *Tucson Sentinel: We admire his huevos* || since 2000, from *huevos* "eggs" or "testicles"

hustle¹ *v.* DUTCH [1] to swindle or victimize (AS, BK, JG): **2005** *Match Point*, film: *You'd better watch out for this one: he's made a living out of hustling*; **2014** *Horrible Bosses 2*, film: *Listen, I hustle, I don't steal* [2] to pressure someone into doing something, especially buying something (AS, BK, JG): **2018** *San Antonio Current: In the lawsuits, Duncan claimed Banks had encouraged, promoted, and hustled him into investing in a series of bad ventures*; **2019** Cinema Blend: *He hustled him into paying for a free paper* [3] to work as a prostitute (AS, BK, JG): **2018** *Albuquerque Journal: The girl had made comments about Sanchez making her hustle*; **2019** *South Florida Gay News: He often struggled with waiting tables in the summer and felt he had no choice but to hustle and often made more money doing so* || since 1890 in the first two senses, since 1926 in the third, from *hutselen* "shake" or "toss"

hustle² *n.* DUTCH [1] a swindle (AS, BK, JG): **2019** *New York Post: None of them been charged in the sprawling scam and the schools were not involved in the hustle*; **2019** *Augusta Chronicle: Many people see that as a chance to break the law, run a hustle* [2] pressuring someone into doing something, especially buying something (BK, JG): **1997** *Lost World: Jurassic Park*, film: *When you try to sound like Hammond, it comes off as a hustle*; **2018** *LA Sentinel: She was trying to convince them to rent their property to her and they replied they were not interested in her hustle* [3] working as a prostitute (BK, JG): **2012** *New York Times: Some were escaping the hustle and danger of illegal sex work*; **2017** *Esquire: There are a lot of hassles that come with the hustle, and both the cops and prostitutes have to play a part in this grand performance* || since 1940, from *hutselen* "shake" or "toss"

hustler *n.* DUTCH [1] a swindler (AS, BK, JG): **1992** *Diggstown*, film: *Never try to hustle a hustler*; **1995** *Casino*, film: *All I know is that Green was an Arizona real estate hustler* [2] a person who pressures someone into doing something, especially buying something (AS, BK, JG): **2002** *Road to Perdition*, film: *Call the cops! I know hustlers when I see them*; **2019** Hilton Head Island Pocket: *I'm a hustler. I was trying to sell the man some property* [3] a prostitute (AS, BK, JG): **2005** *New York Times Magazine*: *JT was a teenage hustler who'd been pimped out as a cross-dressed prostitute by his mother*; **2018** *South Florida Gay News*: *Historically, Miami Beach, Fort Lauderdale, and West Palm Beach all had known areas where hustlers would loiter and look for work* || since 1886 in the first two senses, since 1924 in the third, from *hutselen* "shake" or "toss" and *-er*

hypemeister *n.* GERMAN a specialist in publicity or public relations, especially insincere (KC): **1995** *San Francisco Weekly*: *Before you dismiss me as a hypemeister, you should ask yourself if laziness and passivity are sabotaging your opportunities*; **2011** *Time Out New York*: *It was an uncharacteristically quiet way for this media-savvy hypemeister to unveil new work* || since 1960s, from *hype* and *Meister* "master"

I

ichiban *adj.* JAPANESE excellent (JG, TD): **1992** *Quantum Leap*, NBC-TV series: *You're an ichiban liar, man!* **2015** Wordnik: *It is voiced by Phil LaMarr, who is pretty ichiban* || since 1900, from *ichiban* "number one"

in big kimchi *phr.* KOREAN in serious trouble (TD): **2007** Ecoustics: *If you can't figure out how to use a remote, then you're in big kimchi!* **2014** Georgia Outside News: *You get in that water when it is 20 degrees outside, you are in big kimchi* || since 1979, from *kimchi* "Korean dish made from fermented cabbage"

in deep kimchi *phr.* KOREAN in serious trouble (JG): **2018** Reuters: *The world economy will be in deep kimchi if the current trade war between the United States and China drags on*; **2021** *Sports Illustrated*: *At 5–7, the Vikings are toast, and coach Mike Zimmer is in deep kimchi* || since 1979, from *kimchi* "Korean dish made from fermented cabbage"

indocumentado *n.* SPANISH an immigrant without legalized stay and without the necessary documents: **1994** *Chicago Tribune*: *Lost your job? Blame it on the indocumentados*; **1995** *Los Angeles Times*: *"The industry can't survive without the indocumentados," said the contractor, himself a onetime illegal immigrant from Mexico* || since 1970, from *indocumentado* "undocumented"

influyente *n.* SPANISH an important person, especially in a drug ring: **2004** Fred C. Collom: *I gained the respect and friendship of many Mexican influyentes*; **2012** Blogspot: *If our local DA chooses not to prosecute or pursue charges against the influyentes, are we screwed?* || dating unknown, from *influyente* "influential"

infobahn *n.* GERMAN a high-speed computer network (KC): **2013** *Seattle Times*: *The speedier infobahn doesn't entirely remake life*; **2014** *Kansas City Star*: *Complaints* *about the sometimes inconvenient construction of Google's infobahn grow* || since 1990, from *information* and *Autobahn* "highway"

in hock *phr.* DUTCH in debt, especially to a pawnbroker (AS, JG, TD): **2014** *New Republic*: *The coalition is in hock to big business*; **2015** Global News: *Ottawa is in hock to the tune of $600 billion* || since 1883, from *in* and *hok* "hutch" or "debt"

in one's kishkes, in one's kishkas *phr.* YIDDISH in one's deepest emotional experience: **2014** *Charlotte Observer*: *He knew in his kishkes Benjamin would be there*; **2016** *Wall Street Journal*: *I know every second of it. It's in my DNA. It's in my kishkes* || since 1959, from *fun kishkes,* literally "from one's guts"

-itis *suffix* GREEK a condition or tendency involved in or characterized by what is indicated, which is compared to a disease (JG, KC): **2013** *New Yorker*: *I had a terrible attack of lazyitis*; **2018** *News*, WGME-TV program: *CBS spoke with psychologists about a new term called the "worry-itis"* || since 1912, from Greek feminine adjectival ending *-itēs*

Ivan *n.* RUSSIAN *offensive* a Russian or a person of Russian descent (AS, JG, TD): **2004** *National Review*: *What about the Ivans on the street?* **2015** Quizlet: *How did the Ivans relate to the West?* || since 1944, from popular name *Ivan*

J

jaina *n.* SPANISH a woman, especially sexually attractive one (JG): **2017** *Snowfall*, FX-TV series: *How come you talk to me like you know me, jaina?* **2018** Urban Dictionary: *OMG, I am cute? Does that mean I'm a jaina?* || since 1992, from *jaina* "one's girlfriend" and female name *Jaina*

jalopy *n.* SPANISH a battered old car or airplane (JG, KC): **1999** *At First Sight*, film: *I still haven't got that old jalopy fixed*; **1999** Inspector Gadget, film: *Can't you make this jalopy go any faster?* || since 1924, possibly from the mispronunciation of Jalapa, a Mexican city to which many US used cars were sent

Jane *n.* SPANISH marijuana (JG, KC): **2006** *Marijuana Magazine*: *I don't notice any change in my motor skills while high on jane*; **2012** Date Hookup: *My cousins are stuck in LA, having nothing to do but smoke jane and get drunk* || since 1972, from *Mary Jane* "marijuana," literally translated from María Juanita

jazz *v.* MANDINKA to have sex with: **2011** Blogspot: *Some rich politician jazzed her vagina*; **2015** Robert Olen Butler: *A Cuban diplomat jazzed his wife* || since 1924, from *jasi* "pleasurable activity"

jazz up *v.* MANDINKA to make lively, stimulating, or exciting: **2015** *U.S. News & World Report*: *Here's four ways to jazz up your résumé*; **2015** *Time*: *Always incorporate high-flavor add-ons to jazz up veggies, like sautéing with olive oil garlic* || since 1917, from *jasi* "pleasurable activity," *up*, and analogy to *spice up*

jazzy *adj.* MANDINKA lively, stimulating, or exciting: **2015** *Cherry Hill Courier Post*: *He pronounced the new interior "pretty jazzy"*; **2015** *Columbus Dispatch*: *The songs are jazzy and fun* || since 1917, from *jasi* "pleasurable activity" and suffix *-y*

J-City *n.* SPANISH Ciudad Juárez, Mexico: **2009** *New York Post*: *My friends and I thought of going to our favorite bar in J-City to eat avocado sandwiches*; **2011** Topix: *Supposedly the two factions duking it out in J-City are the Juarez Cartel and the Sinaloa Cartel* || since 1968, from *(Ciudad) Juárez*, a city in Mexico, ultimately from *Benito Juárez*, former president of Mexico, and City

jefe *n.* SPANISH [1] a chief (AS): **1996** *Lone Star*, film: *Any man with a badge is his jefe*; **2002** Blade II, film: *You thought you had me on a short leash, didn't you, jefe?* [2] a boss of a drug cartel: **1997** *New York Times*: *Pablo Escobar Gaviria was the jefe of the Medellin cartel*; **2013** *Los Angeles Review of Books*: *This cross-border thriller is populated with club owners and drug cartel jefes* [3] one's father: **2013** iPhoneogram: *I asked my jefe where he wanted to go for his birthday dinner*; **2011** *Lowrider Magazine*: *The younger Hernandez did his jefe proud* || since 1900, from *jefe* "male chief"

Jewish shiksa, Jewish shikse *n.* YIDDISH (used especially by Orthodox Jews) a Jewish woman who is not Orthodox, pious, or observant: **1991** Mordechai Schreiber: *Joe was counseling a Jewish shiksa with straight blond hair down to her rump and a peace emblem sewn on the seat of her pants*; **2011** *Miami New Times*: *She sat down to pen her family's story in "Confessions of a Jewish Shiksa"* || since 1892, from *Jewish* and *shikse* "gentile woman"

Jihad Jane *n.* ARABIC *offensive* a militant, antiwestern Muslim woman: **2014** *News*, CNN-TV program: *Jihad Jane was indicted on four counts, including conspiring to support terrorists*; **2014** National: *Jihad Janes are the most despicable type of women* || since 2007, from *jihād* "struggle on behalf of Islam" and *Jane*

jiu-jitsu *n.* JAPANESE something involving dexterity and flexibility, especially a particular technique: **2013** *Entertainment Weekly*: *More recent historians have credited him with being a master of political jiu jitsu*; **2018** *Vice*: *If you are a huckster or a shyster, this is a great place to pull off the jiujitsu of conning people* || since 1995, from *jūjutsu* "Japanese martial art and method of unarmed combat"

jive¹ *n.* WOLOF [1] deceptive or misleading talk (KC): **2015** *New York Post*: *I don't have a relationship with de Blasio. It's all jive*; **2015** Blogs: *Quit talking jive, man!* [2] slang, especially African American slang of jazz musicians: **2001** *Royal Tenenbaums*, film: *I'll talk some jive like you've never heard*; **2018** Conversation: *Some of us speak King's English, some of us speak jive* || since 1929 in the first sense, since 1938 in the second, from *jev* "false talk"

jive² *v.* WOLOF [1] to deceive or mislead (KC): **2004** *Ray*, film: *"I'd like to discuss your future." "Don't jive me now. I ain't for sale"*; **2008** Democratic Underground: *Willy kept jiving him until Jimmy finally left* [2] to use slang, especially African American slang of jazz musicians: **2010** Xbox 360: *I wish I knew how to jive like in*

"*Airplane*"; **2015** Twitter: *Can you jive better than this guy?* ‖ since 1928 in the first sense, since 1938 in the second, from *jev* "false talk"

jive artist *n.* WOLOF a deceptive or misleading person: **2014** *Sports*, NBC-TV program: *Were you going to send the money back today or are you just a jive artist?* **2021** *Texas Monthly*: *Testimony in that trial portrayed Davis as a jive artist who convinced 70 customers that bullfrog farming was the wave of the future* ‖ since 1939, from *jev* "false talk," *artist*, and analogy to *bullshit artist* "deceitful person"

jive-ass[1] *n.* WOLOF a deceptive or misleading person (KC): **1990** *Q & A*, film: *And then some jive-ass gives me that stick and gun shit*; **2006** Topix: *Now you sound like a jive-ass* ‖ since 1940, from *jev* "false talk" and suffix *-ass*

jive-ass[2] *adj.* WOLOF deceptive or misleading (KC): **1993** *Bound by Honor*, film: *That man was no jive-ass punk*; **2018** *New York Magazine*: *Weinstein's a jive-ass motherfucker, wouldn't return my calls* ‖ since 1940, from *jev* "false talk" and suffix *-ass*

jive talk *n.* WOLOF [1] deceptive or misleading talk (KC): **1998** *Sliding Doors*, film: *She'll be streetwise to the lies and the jive talk*; **2015** Cowboy Job: *Also, no more job talk, please* [2] slang, especially African American slang of jazz musicians (KC): **2002** *Piñero*, film: *He's busy perfecting his jive talk*; **2006** *Everybody Hates Chris*, UPN-TV series: *Sorry, I couldn't understand your jive talk* ‖ since 1930 in the first sense, since 1944 in the second, from *jev* "false talk" and *talk*

jive-talk *v.* WOLOF [1] to deceive or mislead: **2008** Urban Dictionary: *Bush speeches are nearly jive talkin!* **2012** Twitter: *Are you jive-talking me?* [2] to use slang, especially African American slang of jazz musicians: **1980** *Ebony Magazine*: *She jive-talked with the boys*; **1992** *Simpsons*, Fox-TV series: *Are there any jive-talking robots in this play?* ‖ since 1930 in the first sense, since 1944 in the second, from *jev* "false talk" and *talk*

jodido[1] *n.* SPANISH *potentially offensive* a contemptible person: **2004** Ralph M. Flores: *Bring me some rope and I'll tie it around that jodido*; **2011** Rudy Apodaca: *Don't call me that, jodido!* ‖ dating unknown, from *jodido* "despicable"

jodido[2] *adj.* SPANISH *potentially offensive* contemptible: **1999** Marco McPeek Villatoro: *Wipe that jodido grin off your face!* **2010** *Phoenix News Times*: *No need to play the superiority game among ourselves, we're equally jodido* ‖ dating unknown, from *jodido* "despicable"

Joe Schmo, Joe Schmoe, Joe Shmo, Joe Shmoe *n.* YIDDISH an undistinguished and average person, especially unfortunate (AS, KC): **2004** *Hustle*, film: *Your client would still be a Joe Shmoe from Poughkeepsie if I had not dug this story*; **2012** *Chicago Tribune*: *At least I'm still ahead of Joe Schmo in the net income category* ‖ since 1948, from *Joe* and *schmo* "naive and gullible person" or "average person," the latter being an alteration of *schmuck* which itself comes from *shmok* "penis" or "despicable person," literally "jewel"

Johnny Jihad *n.* ARABIC *offensive* a militant, antiwestern Muslim (TD): 2006 *New York Times*: *His cousins learned to ignore words like "camel jockey" and "Johnny Jihad"*; 2011 Officer: *Johnny Jihad walks in and starts indiscriminately shooting up the place* ‖ since 2006, from *Johnny* and *jihād* "struggle on behalf of Islam"

jokenik *n.* YIDDISH a jocular person, especially someone who tells jokes: 1994 *Los Angeles Times*: *A jokenik, she deflects most questions with her highly idiosyncratic brand of humor*; 2011 NYU student: *Her dad was a real jokenik, made us laugh all the time* ‖ dating unknown, from *joke* and suffix *-nik*

Jose (or **José**) *n.* SPANISH *offensive* a Spanish-speaking person, especially a Puerto Rican: 2006 Yahoo Answers: *They got thrown deeper into poverty hole just because some Jose wants to come here illegally*; 2010 *Examiner*: *This isn't Mexico, and if some Jose wants to fly his Mexican flag, he can do it in his own country* ‖ since 1976, from name *José*

joto *n.* SPANISH *potentially offensive* a homosexual man (JG): 2009 *La Mission*, film: *Did you know your godson's a fucking joto?* 2015 Huffington Post: *Being called a joto, or fag, was a common occurrence for me* ‖ dating unknown, from *joto* "Jack from a deck of cards"

J-Town *n.* SPANISH Ciudad Juárez, Mexico: 2013 *El Paso Times*: *I convinced a group of friends to tag along on a day trip to J-Town. Juárez is definitely not what it used to be*; 2014 Trip Advisor: *It's always a good place to eat burritos, one of the most recommended in J-Town* ‖ since 1968, from *(Ciudad) Juárez*, a city in Mexico, ultimately from *Benito Juárez*, former president of Mexico, and Town

Juan *n.* SPANISH *offensive* a person from Puerto Rico (JG): 2010 Baby Center: *I feel compelled to add that I am from Long Island and yes, there are quite a few of Juans here*; 2011 *Vicksburg Daily News*: *Some Juan wanted us to tell you that you're sexy* ‖ since 1992, from *Juan*, a popular name

Juana *n.* SPANISH marijuana (JG): 2010 Urban Dictionary: *Wanna go smoke some Juana?* 2013 Cool Tweets: *We smoked juana all day and listened to Bieber all night* ‖ since 1938, from *María Juanita* "marijuana," reinforced by the clipping of *marijuana*

Juan Doe *n.* SPANISH *offensive* an unidentified Hispanic male (TD): 2004 *New York Times*: *Here Lies Juan Doe*; 2016 *Orange County Register*: *Most likely the registered owned was a Juan Doe that no one could find* ‖ since 1993, from the popular name *Juan*, based on *John Doe*

Juanita *n.* SPANISH [1] marijuana (JG): 2013 Facebook: *Have you been smoking juanita?* 2014 My Space: *Me smoking some juanita!* [2] prostitute: 2001 *Crazy Beautiful*, film: *Hey, look at the Juanita!* 2013 XXX Bunker: *A big-assed Juanita has a fine doggystyle fuck in a minivan* ‖ since 1938 in the first sense, from *María Juanita* "marijuana," in the second from *Juanita*, a popular name

Juanita Doe *n.* SPANISH *potentially offensive* an unidentified Hispanic female: 2013 Mugshots: *It's not the Juanita Doe you were looking for?* 2015 *New York Times*: *We have a style of liturgy that speaks to Juanita Doe* || since 1993, from the popular name *Juanita*, based on *Jane Doe*

Juanita weed *n.* SPANISH marijuana: 2010 Blogs: *I got some killer Juanita weed. Interested?* 2013 ASU student: *They have been smoking Juanita weed all day* || since 1938, from name *Juanita* and *weed*

jubilesta *n.* SPANISH a festive jubilee: 2011 Soap Opera Network: *A man I had worked with at the Center Theater happened to be directing the jubilesta*; 2013 Blogs: *They're throwing a jubilesta on Friday Cool!* || since 1930, from *jubilee* and *fiesta* "party"

juke[1] *n.* WOLOF [1] liquor (KC): 2006 Ercille Christmas: *It would be hard not to drink the bottle of juke*; 2011 Blogger: *We were drinking juke and having fun* [2] a coin-operated record player in a bar (JG, KC): 1997 *U-Turn*, film: *Got a quarter for the juke?* 2008 *Honeydipper*, film: *It must be a short circuit in the juke here* || since 1941, from *dzug* "disorderly action"

juke[2] *v.* WOLOF [1] to dance in a boisterous fashion (JG, KC, TD): 2012 *South Florida Sun-Sentinel*: *As is his habit, he juked to the music, gesturing extravagantly*; 2015 Sound Cloud: *I know you love to juke!* [2] to deceive, mislead, or manipulate (KC, TD): 2008 *Office*, NBC-TV series: *You juked the stats*; 2004 *Wire*, HBO-TV series: *We were under pressure to keep the crime down, to juke the stats district by district* || since 1939, from *dzug* "disorderly action"

juke and jive *phr.* WOLOF [1] to dance in a boisterous fashion: 2005 *People Magazine*: *We were juking and jiving*; 2013 Lipstick Alley: *I can't tell you how many black people were juking and jiving to his latest album* [2] to deceive or mislead: 2015 *Winnipeg Sun*: *As a couple of Ticats zeroed in on him, Anderson started to juke and jive*; 2015 *Lincoln Journal Star*: *He didn't juke and jive, he just ran* || since 1970, from *dzug* "disorderly action" and *jev* "false talk"

jukebox *n.* WOLOF a coin-operated record player in a bar (KC): 1999 *Los Angeles Times*: *Hanna had never seen a jukebox before immigrating to the United States*; 2001 *Jimmy Show*, film: *He's buying a song on a juke box* || since 1930, from *dzug* "disorderly action" and *box*

jukehouse *n.* WOLOF [1] a brothel (KC): 2000 Robert Hendrickson: *A juke house is a house of ill repute*; 2015 Tumblr: *Do you know what goes on in a juke house? There's drinking and a whole lotta hot women* [2] a bar with a coin-operated record player (JG): 2015 *News*, MTV-TV series: *Kimbrough turned it into a juke house in 1991*; 2015 Houston Culture: *Lonnie found it near the porch of a juke house* || since 1940, from *dzug* "disorderly action" and *house*

juke joint *n.* WOLOF a bar with a coin-operated record player (JG, KC): 1996 *Last Man Standing*, film: *"Where are we headed?" "A juke joint outside of town"*; 2011 *Los Angeles Times*: *This is the last of the real Mississippi Delta juke joints* || since 1935, from *dzug* "disorderly action" and *joint* "bar"

jumbo *adj.* KONGO very big in size (KC): **2006** Sharleen Cohen: *I've got onion rings and jumbo cheeseburgers*; **2015** Facebook: *A jumbo pack costs $19.99* || since 1897, from *nzamba* "elephant"

junque *n.* PSEUDO-FRENCH old and discarded things, junk (KC): **2006** Urban Dictionary: *I always find some neat junque when I go to the flea market*; **2014** Blogspot: *In addition to produce, she sells a lot of junque* || dating unknown, from *junk* "things" and the pseudo-French spelling *-que* which lends some chic to the material

jura *n.* SPANISH a police officer or the police: **2005** *Havoc*, film: *Oh shit, homes! It's the jura!* **2009** Brown Pride: *Then the pinche jura came, and one of the vatos had a knife* || dating unknown, from *jura* "police," literally "oath"

K

kabayo *n.* SPANISH heroin (JG): **2003** Urban Dictionary: *Nigga, I be dope sick. Go down to Ave. And get me some kabayo*; **2014** Alcoholism: *When he was referring to kabayo, he was talking about heroin* || since 1969, from *caballo* "horse"

kahuna *n.* HAWAIIAN [1] an important person, especially a chief (AS, JG, TD): **2003** *Law & Order*, NBC-TV series: *So you're after the cosmetics kahuna?* **2008** *Christmas Cottage*, film: *His wife is the big kahuna here* [2] an important thing (JG, TD): **1998** *Safe Men*, film: *That was only a test of your abilities, this one is the kahuna*; **2008** *Universe*, History-TV series: *The Big Kahuna in our solar system is Jupiter* [3] a very large wave (AS): **2013** Twitter: *It's a beautiful morning to catch a kahuna*; **2015** Twitter: *Watch surfers ride a big kahuna* || since 1964, from *kahuna* "medicine man" or "shaman"

ka-ka¹ *n.* SPANISH [1] defecation or excrement (JG, TD): **2012** Break: *The staff went crazy asking which child did ka-ka on the toilet*; **2013** UCB student: *You've got some ka-ka on your shoe* [2] nonsense (JG): **2013** Facebook: *This is complete and utter ka-ka!* **2013** YouTube: *I can't listen to this ka-ka* || since 1952 in the first sense, since 1967 in the second, from *caca* "excrement" and *cagar* "to defecate"

ka-ka² *v.* SPANISH to defecate (JG): **2011** Baby Center: *He later told me that he ka-ka'ed on the floor*; **2012** Blogspot: *He finally ka-ka'ed in this potty today* || since 1952, from *caca* "excrement" and *cagar* "to defecate"

kamikaze *adj.* JAPANESE reckless and self-destructive (AS, KC): **2011** *Rolling Stone*: *It's kind of a kamikaze move, and it's a pretty difficult thing*; **2012** *Washington Post*: *In the race's final days, Romney has adopted what you might call a kamikaze strategy* || since 1960, from *kamikaze* "pilot of a suicide mission" and "divine wind"

kaput *adj.* GERMAN [1] out of order, inoperative, or useless (AS, JG, KC, TD): **2012** *Madagascar 3*, film: *The plane's totaled. Kaput*; **2015** Jalopnik: *The A/C compressor is kaput, there's a dent in the hood, and the dash is cracked* [2] finished or done (JG): **2011** *Californication*, Showtime-TV series: *We're done. Kaput.*

Splitsville; **2015** Riverfront Times: *But while the friendship remains, the partnership is kaput* || since 1914 in the first sense, since 1925 in the second, from *kaputt* "out of order"

keed *n.* PSEUDO-SPANISH a young person (KC, TD): **2003** *Anger Management*, film: *You gotta get load of this, keed*; **2017** *Riverfront Times*: *Who's gonna support dem keeds?* || since 1920, from a humorous imitation of a Spanish speaker pronouncing *kid*

keister[1] *n.* GERMAN the buttocks (JG, KC, TD): **2015** *News*, WFTV-TV program: *They gave me a royal shaft in the keister*; **2015** *Sports*, NBC-TV program: *My father would have kicked me in the keister if I cried to him* || since 1882, from *Keist* "chest" or "box"

keister[2] *v.* GERMAN to hide (contraband) in the rectum (JG, TD): **2011** Smoking Gun: *Vogt keistered the contraband to get it into the lockup*; **2011** *Up All Night*, NBC-TV series: *It's not in her purse, but she's keistering it for sure* || since 1992, from *Keist* "chest" or "box"

keister bandit *n.* GERMAN an aggressive male homosexual who takes the active role in anal sex (JG, TD): **2010** Facebook: *The guy's a keister bandit*; **2015** Gold Eagle: *It has been dominated during that time by keister bandits* || since 1950, from *Keist* "chest" or "box" and *bandit*, analogous to *ass bandit* "aggressive male homosexual"

keister stash *n.* GERMAN a tube-like container of contraband hidden in the rectum (JG, TD): **2012** Blogspot: *Both men and women often use a keister stash to conceal contraband up their asses*; **2013** Mr. Conservative: *They call it a keister stash, a jailhouse purse* || since 1967, from *Keist* "chest" or "box" and *stash*

kibitz *v.* YIDDISH [1] to offer unwanted commentaries, especially while watching a game or performance (JG, KC): **2011** *Time Out Chicago*: *I'm a noted local sportscaster who likes to kibitz here*; **2015** *Toronto Star*: *You can almost hear Woody Allen kibitzing in the background* [2] to chat, especially in a joking or teasing manner (JG, KC): **2003** *Down with Love*, film: *I'll spend all day up front kibitzing with the customers*; **2008** *Chicago Tribune*: *In the town square, the old men sit together kibitzing and elbowing each other as the women walk by* || since 1927, from *kibetsn* "to make unwanted comments"

kibitz around *v.* YIDDISH to chat, especially in a joking or teasing manner: **2011** Mac Forums: *It's a great place to kibitz around with others*; **2011** *Montreal Gazette*: *Reality shows are really just an excuse for me to kibitz around* || since 1927, from *kibetsn* "to make unwanted comments" and verbal particle *around*

kibitzer *n.* YIDDISH [1] someone who offers unwanted commentaries, especially while watching a game or performance (JG, KC): **2009** Word Press: *After a great tsimmes over some disobedient technology and a dozen of kibitzers offering solutions, we got rolling*; **2011** *Inquirer*: *When he reached the fire scene, he saw lots of kibitzers* [2] someone who likes to chat, especially in a joking or teasing manner (KC): **1990**

Philly: *Ritchie was described by colleagues as a kibitzer and practical joker*; 2007 *Torontoist: Maybe it's because his father is a kibitzer, a prankster, I mean* || since 1922, from *kibetsn* "to make unwanted comments"

kibitz with *v.* YIDDISH to chat with someone, especially in a joking or teasing manner: 2010 *Los Angeles Times: Gerber always took extra time to roam the halls, stopping to kibitz with everyone from pages to secretaries to junior executives*; 2012 *Globe and Mail: She kibitzed excitedly with her supporters* || since 1927, from *kibetsn* "to make unwanted comments"

kibitzy *adj.* YIDDISH [1] offering unwanted commentaries, especially while watching a game or performance: 2004 *Washington Post: What struck Shaffer was the way this colorful, kibitzy character would suddenly flatline*; 2011 Diplomacy World: *Chris even had to shush me from a kibitzy comment* [2] talkative, especially in a joking or teasing manner: 2007 *Washington Post: At 11 o'clock you can find a highly excitable, endlessly kibitzy 67-year-old dentist from Freeport, Long Island, in the middle of a circle of TV news cameras*; 2011 Yelp: *All waitresses are pretty nice and kibitzy* || dating unknown, from *kibets(n)* "to make unwanted comments" and adjectival suffix *-y*

kielbasa *n.* POLISH *potentially offensive* the penis, especially if big (JG): 2007 Michelle Kane: *Don't forget to put a rubber on his kielbasa!* 2016 Tube Porn Classic: *This she does by slipping out of her panties and wolfing down his kielbasa* || since 1978, from *kiełbasa* "sausage"

kinderwhore[1] *n.* GERMAN *potentially offensive* a young woman whose dress suggests both youthful innocence and sexual abandon (TD): 2010 In Character: *Durham exposes the phenomenon of kinderwhores*; 2012 Grace Carol: *That's what happens when one dates kinderwhores instead of charming employed women* || since 1994, from *Kinder* "children" and *whore*

kinderwhore[2] *adj.* GERMAN *potentially offensive* (of a young woman's dress) suggesting both youthful innocence and sexual abandon: 2010 Style Rookie: *Courtney Love popularized the kinderwhore look in the early 90's*; 2015 Nashville Scene: *There were so many kinderwhore outfits* || since 1994, from *Kinder* "children" and *whore*

kineahora *excl.* YIDDISH let nothing bad happen, God forbid (TD): 1994 *Los Angeles Times: "She's so beautiful, kineahora," Pearlie tells me, invoking one of her oft-chanted expressions to ward away the evil eye*; 2015 *New Jersey Jewish News: My dad will be 96 next month, kineahora, and the other day I asked him if he had any memories of FDR* || since 1994, from *keyn eyn-ore* "no evil eye"

kishkes, kishkas *n.* YIDDISH [1] intestines (AS, JG, KC): 1997 *New York Times: When everything else fails, give 'em a clout in the kishkes*; 2011 *Boardwalk Empire*, HBO-TV series: *What do you call a horse when they cut off his kishkes?* [2] one's deepest emotional experience or consciousness: 1995 Nicholas A. Cummings: *This time I want you to really reach down into your kishkas and come up with the reason*;

2007 *Los Angeles Times*: *The idea hit him right in the kishkes* [3] inner workings or the inside: 2011 Computer: *Defrag and clean out its kishkes*; 2012 *Tablet Magazine*: *Shove the disc into the kishkes of the DVD, and make us all watch it* || since 1902 in the first two senses, since 1959 in the third, from *kishkes* "inner feelings," literally "guts"

kit and caboodle *phr.* DUTCH everything entirely (AS, JG, KC): 2015 *San Jose Mercury News*: *Get rid of the whole kit and caboodle!* 2016 *Omaha World-Herald*: *It can be all yours for fees ranging from $30 to $300 per months, which includes the whole kit and caboodle* || since 1961, from *kit* "collection" and *boedel* "property"

klutz *n.* YIDDISH [1] a clumsy or inept person (AS, JG, KC): 2003 *Cooler*, film: *"I'm so sorry. I'm such a fucking klutz!" "No, this stuff happens"*; 2009 *Powder Blue*, film: *I'm a klutz and I spill everything* [2] a stupid person (AS, JG, KC): 1994 *Dumb and Dumber*, film: *You know what the klutz did? He came home one night dead drunk*; 2013 *Canadian Living*: *You wouldn't insult your best friend by calling her a loser or a klutz every time she makes a mistake* || since 1968, from *klots* "clumsy idiot," literally "block"

klutz around *v.* YIDDISH [1] to behave in a clumsy or inept way (KC): 2004 Velocity Reviews: *I need to buy a new set instead of klutzing around with these ones*; 2011 *Time Out*: *You start to realize these people are klutzing around in a very average way* [2] to behave in a stupid way (KC): 2011 My Space: *I can't wait to klutz around with you*; 2012 Huffington Post: *Sandler will dress as a woman and klutz around* || since 1968, from *klots* "clumsy idiot," literally "block" and verbal particle *around*

klutzy *adj.* YIDDISH [1] clumsy or inept (AS, JG, KC): 2002 *Chicago Tribune*: *She is bright but extremely klutzy*; 2012 *Chicago Sun-Times*: *I'm klutzy and uncoordinated* [2] stupid (AS, KC): 2009 Carrie Cobb: *Becky was embarrassed that she had done something so klutzy in front of her*; 2011 *San Francisco Chronicle*: *It's Santa's klutzy son* || since 1968, from *klots* "clumsy idiot," literally "block" and adjectival suffix *-y*

knacker *see* knocker

knish *n.* YIDDISH *potentially offensive* the vagina: 2006 Richard Sand: *Keep your eye on the road instead of her knish*; 2012 Word Press: *How do you say "lick my knish" in French?* || since 1968, from *knish* "dumpling with a savory filling"

knocker, knacker *n.* YIDDISH a powerful, important, and especially arrogant person (JG, KC): 1998 Mordechai Richler: *She told my wife that I was such a knacker*; 2012 Bossip: *Save some of that material for a real knocker* || since 1960, from *knaker* literally "one who snaps a whip"

kompromat *n.* RUSSIAN compromising information collected for use in blackmailing or discrediting someone, especially for political purpose: 1997 *Chicago Tribune*: *He might soon release a flood of kompromat, real or fabricated materials about tawdry financial schemes*; 2018 *News*, CNN-TV program: *Does Russia have kompromat on Trump?* || since 1997, from *kompromat*, itself a blend from *kompro-metiruyushchiy material* "compromising material"

kosher *adj.* YIDDISH [1] authentic, genuine, or proper (AS, JG, KC): **1994** *Beverly Hills Cop III*, film: *I checked with Washington, Fulbright's kosher. He's working on something classified*; **2011** *Bay Area Reporter*: *The comedy is kosher, the food is not*; **2011** *New York Times*: *Thomas is a kosher character* [2] legitimate, legal, or lawful (AS, JG, KC): **1997** *Man Who Knew Too Little*, film: *"License?" "Relax, the van's kosher!"*; **2011** *New York Daily News*: *Judge David Schmidt ruled last week the spoof was kosher* [3] approved or acceptable (JG, KC): **1991** *Switch*, film: *Would it be kosher if I prayed for a little help?* **2009** *Los Angeles Times*: *Would it be kosher to make a joke about Sasha holding hands with a pedophile?* [4] (especially in gay usage) a circumcised penis (JG): **2014** YouTube: *I have a kosher penis*; *Does that mean that a gay Jew has to suck off a kosher dick?* **2015** Twitter: *It's a kosher cock* || since 1986 in the first three senses, since 1972 in the fourth, from *kosher* "ritually pure or fit to eat," and hence "acceptable"

Kosher Canyon *n.* YIDDISH a neighborhood dominated by Jewish people: **2005** Blogspot: *To his credit, he did drive me back to Kosher Canyon*; **2011** Facebook: *The section of Fairfax Avenue filled with traditionally Jewish businesses is sometimes referred to by Angelenos as Kosher Canyon or The Bagel District* || since 1975, from *kosher* "ritually pure or fit to eat," and hence Jewish, and *Canyon*

kosher pickle *n.* YIDDISH (especially in gay usage) a circumcised penis: **2009** Free Gay Pix: *I had seen his kosher pickle in the locker room many times*; **2011** Huffington Post: *I might have ever so gently knocked my knee against his kosher pickle* || since 1986, from *kosher* "ritually pure or fit to eat," and hence Jewish, and *pickle* "penis"

kraut *n.* GERMAN *offensive* [1] a German or a person of German descent (AS, JG, KC, TD): **1998** *Big Lebowski*, film: *I told that fucking kraut thousand times I don't roll on shabbes!* **2014** *Monument Men*, film: *Can I talk to the kraut?* [2] the German language (JG, TD): **2015** Facebook: *The movie is about a German drill sergeant, for those who understand kraut*; **2010** Jim Miller: *I can't speak kraut* || since 1837 in the first sense, since 1948 in the second, from *Sauerkraut* "chopped pickled cabbage"

kraut-eater *n.* GERMAN *offensive* a German or a person of German descent (JG): **2006** Timothy Morrisroe: *Minnesota is full of kraut-eaters*; **2011** Free Republic: *The kraut-eaters want reparations for that* || since 1839, from *Sauerkraut* "chopped pickled cabbage" and *eater*

krauthead *n.* GERMAN *offensive* a German or a person of German descent (JG, KC, TD): **2008** Word Press: *Nobody does Weissbier better than the krautheads*; **2015** Men Stuff: *He kept company with krautheads, polacks, etc.* || since 1928, from *Sauerkraut* "chopped pickled cabbage" and *head*

krautland *n.* GERMAN *offensive* Germany (JG, TD): **1993** *King of the Hill*, film: *Did he take a steamer back to krautland?* **2015** Pinterest: *Greetings from Krautland!* || since 1955, from *Sauerkraut* "chopped pickled cabbage" and *land*

krautrock *n.* GERMAN *potentially offensive* a genre of minimalistic electronic music that originated in Germany: **2009** *New York Times*: *It's a gritty hybrid of Krautrock, dance-rock and part-punk*; **2015** *Los Angeles Times*: *Their music was part of a movement that came to be called "krautrock," a term Froese hated* || since 1970, from *Sauerkraut* "chopped pickled cabbage" and *rock*

krauty *adj.* GERMAN *offensive* [1] German (JG, TD): **2015** Yelp: *I found the beer very krauty and heavy*; **2015** Blogs: *The car looks very krauty* [2] of minimalistic electronic music that originated in Germany: **2015** Brooklyn Vegan: *They are melting glitchy electronics and krauty indie rock together with skill*; **2015** Reddit: *They have a similar krauty sound* || since 1965 in the first sense, since 1970 in the second, from *Sauerkraut* "chopped pickled cabbage" and adjectival ending *-y*

kudos *n.* GREEK compliments or congratulations (AS, KC): **1997** *Game*, film: *"I took the test today!" "You did? Kudos!"*; **2018** *Gay Times Magazine*: *I give kudos to everyone who came out during the biggest part of their career* || since 1920, from *kydos* "praise"

kurveh, kurve *n.* YIDDISH a prostitute: **2004** *Modern Jewish Studies*: *The kurves came to have their corsets fitted*; **2004** *City Journal*: *That was once a famous house of prostitution, where the kurves, or prostitutes, lived* || dating unknown, from *kurve* "prostitute"

kvell *v.* YIDDISH [1] to be proudly happy, especially because of a child's achievement (AS, JG, KC): **2004** *House, M.D.*, Fox-TV series: *"I had a job interview lined up at New York Mercy yesterday." "Hospital for Manhattan's glitterati. Big coup. Your homies must be kvelling"*; **2011** *PC World*: *Readers weren't kvelling about their Windows phones* [2] to enjoy someone's defeat or humiliation: **2009** Facebook: *Don't kvell over his mistake*; **2011** *Seattle Weekly*: *Women of a certain age will kvell* || since 1964, from *kveln* "to beam" or "to be delighted"

kveller *n.* YIDDISH someone who is proudly happy, especially because of a child's achievement: **2011** Jewish Baltimore: *I'm a kveller. I take great pride in the good things happening around me*; **2011** Twitter: *Toby is a kveller maybe, but not a yeller* || dating unknown, from *kveln* "to beam" or "to be delighted"

kvetch, kvetsh¹ *v.* YIDDISH to complain or grumble (AS, JG, KC): **2005** *Munich*, film: *If I can't kvetch, I can't do my job*; **2007** *New York Times*: *Let the kvelling and kvetching commence!* || since 1950, from *kvetshn* "to complain," ultimately from "to press" or "to squeeze"

kvetch, kvetsh² *n.* YIDDISH a chronic complainer or grumbler (AS, JG, KC): **2005** *South Florida Sun-Sentinel*: *If you find it difficult to understand, don't be a kvetch*; **2007** *New York Times*: *She gets the last word, she's also something of a kvetch* || since 1964, from *kvetshn* "to complain," ultimately from "to press" or "to squeeze"

kvetcher, kvetsher *n.* YIDDISH a chronic complainer or grumbler: **2010** *Wall Street Journal*: *A Woody Allen-type nebbish, Lenny is a kvetcher; he frets about his age,* *his baldness, and his parents*; **2011** *PC World*: *Call me a kvetcher, but I'm tired of spam* || since 1964, from *kvetshn* "to complain," ultimately from "to press" or "to squeeze," and suffix *-er*

kvetchfest, kvetshfest *n.* YIDDISH AND GERMAN a session of complaining: **2008** *New York Times*: *Today's NYT includes an overview of the kvetchfest*; **2011** *Examiner*: *He could get distracted and go on a kvetchfest* || since 1990s, from *kvetshn* "to complain," ultimately from "to press" or "to squeeze," and *Fest* "festival"

kvetchy, kvetshy *adj.* YIDDISH complaining or grumbling (JG): **2005** *Chicago Tribune*: *He's a nervous, kvetchy Philadelphia office furniture salesman separated from his wife*; **2010** *Los Angeles Times*: *He supports his sister Beryl, a kvetchy "filmmaker" who hasn't worked in years* || since 1945, from *kvetsh(n)* "to complain," ultimately from "to press" or "to squeeze," and adjectival suffix *-y*

kvetsh *see* kvetch

kvetsher *see* kvetcher

kvetshy *see* kvetchy

L

la *prefix.* SPANISH (someone or something) involved in or characterized by what is indicated, sometimes associated with a Spanish-speaking country or people: **2015** Huffington Post: *You were the first woman I saw in person, who fought for la raza*; **2018** *Billboard*: *I got what you need. The white girl . . . la gringa!* || dating unknown, from Spanish prefix *la*

labonza *n.* ITALIAN the stomach (JG, KC): **2001** *Simpsons*, Fox-TV series: *Me and him are going to whack you in the labonza!* **2009** *Los Angeles Times*: *They take a blast right in the labonza!* || since 1934, from *la pancia* "paunch"

la cruda *see* cruda

la dama blanca *see* dama blanca

La Eme *see* Eme

La Ene *see* Ene

landsman *n.* YIDDISH someone who comes from the same hometown or country (KC): **2006** *Scoop*, film: *"What's your name? Tell them your name!" "Sondra Pransky!" "A landsman! United States! Fantastic!"*; **2010** *Examiner*: *If you think Bob Arun was rooting for his landsman, Foreman, you ain't seen nothing yet* || since 1940s, from *landsman* "compatriot"

la pinta *see* pinta

La Raza *see* Raza

la roca *see* roca

leño (or **leno**) *n.* SPANISH marijuana or marijuana cigarette (JG): **2010** David Montejano: *Some would smoke a leno (joint) and really get high*; **2014** Bebo: *I'm smoking a leno and kicking it with my friends* || since 1955, from leño "log" or "piece of firewood"

lingo *n.* PORTUGUESE [1] a strange, unusual, or unintelligible language of a particular group of people, especially slang, jargon, or dialect vocabulary (AS, KC): **2018** *USA Today*: *No wonder kids rebel and take pot. And, Mrs. Johnson, in case you don't understand the lingo, that's marijuana*; **2018** Extra: *In the movie, Butler plays a submarine captain, but how well does he know the lingo?* [2] a hybrid language, especially used in an area where different languages come into contact: **2013** Blogs: *Spanglish is the lingo some of them use*; **2018** *Time Out*: *Singlish is the local lingo. The beauty of it is the fact that its melting pot of words originating from various languages* [3] a foreign language (AS): **2018** Yahoo Sports: *You had better get your translator ready if you don't speak the lingo*; **2018** *New Yorker*: *On tours of duty in Yemen, he picked some of the lingo* || since 1660, from *lingoa* "tongue" and ultimately from Latin *lingua*

liquidate *v.* RUSSIAN to kill, especially by violent means (AS, KC): **1991** *JFK*, film: *He himself was then liquidated by a patriotic Muscovite*; **2015** *Newsweek*: *A powerful bomb liquidated him in the same way he had killed so many others* || since 1924, from *likvidirovat'* "to liquidate" or "to wind up"

lobo *n.* SPANISH [1] a male who frequents bars alone in the hope of finding a sexual companion: **2011** *Be Careful*, film: *How did he became a lobo?* **2013** Blogs: *Watch out, the guy's a real lobo* [2] an ugly person (JG): **2010** Blogs: *Her new boyfriend is an awful lobo*; **2014** UNM student: *I can't believe she's dating such a lobo* || since 1947, from *lobo* "grey wolf" reinforced by the American English *wolf* "man assertive and zealous in his pursuit of women"

loca *n.* SPANISH a crazy woman: **1997** *Los Angeles Times*: *These locas speak at the speed of rancheras music*; **2007** Junot Díaz: *Your mother was a loca when it came to love. It almost killed her* || since 1852, from *loca* "crazy (woman)"

loco[1] *n.* SPANISH [1] a crazy man (JG, KC): **2001** Fan Fiction: *You're a loco. And you're going to get yourself killed one of these days*; **2011** Street Advisor: *Put simply, you would have to be a loco to want to live in this neighborhood* [2] marijuana (JG, TD): **2010** Blogs: *The guy was high on loco*; **2013** ASU student: *They were smoking loco and drinking beer* || since 1852 in the first sense, since 1969 in the second, from *loco* "crazy"

loco[2] *adj.* SPANISH crazy (AS, JG, KC, TD): **2010** *Modern Family*, ABC-TV series: *Taking him to a horror movie, that's loco!* **2019** *New York Post*: *Mayor Bill de Blasio must be loco if he thinks this is a good idea* || since 1887, from *loco* "crazy"

loco weed (or **locoweed**) *n.* SPANISH marijuana (AS, JG, RS, TD): **2010** *Mountain Eagle*: *I have never used illegal drugs or smoked loco weed (marijuana)*; **2012** *News*, NBC-TV program: *Did you also try smoking loco weed as a kid?* || since 1924, from *loco* "crazy" and *weed* "marijuana"

Loisaida *n.* SPANISH the Lower East Side of New York's Manhattan (TD): **2008** *New York Daily News*: *Loisaida's Melonie Díaz is quietly becoming a Hollywood fixture*; **2009** East Village: *Some major changes are coming to Loisaida* || since 1981, from a Spanish adaptation of English, borrowed back into English

look-see *n.* CHINESE a look or inspection (JG): **1997** *Con Air*, film: *Muchacho, check out the tower! Have a look-see, yeah?* **2013** *New York Times*: *Take a look-see, missy* || since 1854, from *kànjiàn* literally "look-see"

loot *n.* HINDI money (JG): **2015** Bustle: *They outgrow their clothes on the quick, so spending a lot of loot seems wasteful*; **2018** *Los Angeles Review of Books*: *This is where they make a lot of loot* || since 1900, from *lūṭ* "plunder"

los niños *see* niños

luego *excl.* SPANISH goodbye (JG): **2013** Blogs: *He said "luego," and left*; **2014** UNM student: *"I gotta go, so luego, dude!" "Luego!"* || dating unknown, from *hasta luego* "until later"

luftmensch, luftmensh *n.* YIDDISH [1] an impractical, dreamy, sensitive, and poetic person: **1993** *New York Magazine*: *Lionel was something of a luftmensch, his obliviousness to reality was nothing compared with the misjudgment and self-absorption of so many intellectuals in the thirties*; **2012** *Chicago Tribune*: *Manny is the inventor, though to Boris he's a luftmensch (dreamer)* [2] someone without an occupation: **2012** *Chicago Now*: *Travel bloggers are the worst. A vast majority of them can be best described as a luftmensch*; **2015** *Toronto Star*: *Bob wrote a memoir about his old man, who was what you might call luftmensch, a man who was doing fine with no visible means of support* || dating unknown, from *luftmentsh* "impractical dreamer with no occupation," literally "air man"

M

macaroni *n.* ITALIAN *offensive* an Italian or a person of Italian descent (JG, KC, TD): **2014** Blogspot: *They called him a macaroni*; **2015** Tumblr: *I didn't kill the macaroni* || since 1845, from *maccaroni* or *maccheroni* "Italian pasta in the shape of narrow tubes"

macaroni bender *n.* ITALIAN *offensive* an Italian or a person of Italian descent (JG): **2011** NYU student: *Who are you calling a "macaroni bender"?* **2014** St. Louis Racing: *My grandmother, born in Italy, was called a "macaroni bender" in the second grade!* || since 1956, from *maccaroni* or *maccheroni* "Italian pasta in the shape of narrow tubes"

macha *n.* SPANISH a tough or assertive woman, especially a feminist: **2004** Urban Dictionary: *Only the modern macha manages to give the declining male what he really deserves*; **2007** Democratic Underground: *I was a real "macha"* *woman, tougher than most* || dating unknown, from *macha* "tough or assertive woman, especially a feminist"

macher *n.* YIDDISH [1] an important, influential, and well-connected person, especially one involved in shady dealings (AS, JG): **2011** *New York Daily News*: *Wonder arises anew with the discovery that Liu hired a Wall Street macher named Kevin Davis*; **2011** *Boardwalk Empire*, HBO-TV series: *"He's busy!" "Yes, he's a macher now"* [2] a boastful person (AS): **2010** Jerry Oppenheimer: *Bernie envisioned himself making it big. He was a macher*; **2011** Facebook: *He's a showboating macher* || since 1909, from *makher* "someone important and powerful," literally "doer"

machisma *n.* SPANISH blatant female assertiveness or aggression (KC): **1995** *Los Angeles Times*: *They continue the traditions of their forlorn ancestors but with the liberated machisma of '90s Americanized women*; **2012** *Psychology Today*: *Has the feminine mystique been replaced by media machisma?* || since 1970, from *machismo* and *-a*, based on *machismo*

machismo *n.* SPANISH blatant male aggression or virility (AS, KC): **2002** *Scrubs*, NBC-TV series: *This overbearing machismo is usually just compensation for a lap-pinkie*; **2005** *Viva Cuba*, film: *You're an abusive man, full of machismo* || since 1960, from *machismo* "aggressive masculinity"

macho¹ *n.* SPANISH an aggressively masculine male (AS, KC): **1999** *Models*, film: *You're the machos, you're the men! You carry one!* **2016** *Macleans*: *She was bullied by the machos and the feminists* || since 1960, from *macho* "male"

macho² *adj.* SPANISH aggressively masculine (AS, KC, TD): **2005** *Denver Post*: *Some see "macho mentality" as a link in three soldiers' suicides*; **2015** *Dallas Voice*: *Men are still expected to be very macho, very hypermasculine* || since 1960, from *macho* "male"

Macho Burger (or **macho burger**) *n.* SPANISH a hamburger with onions: **2012** Eater: *The signature item is Macho Burger, which comes with chorizo, Oaxaca cheese, caramelized onions, and sauce*; **2013** *Miami New Times*: *Motz was in Miami and ate a macho burger from Latin Burger and Taco food truck about two years ago, and fell in love with it* || since 1965, from *macho* "male" and *burger*, reinforced by A&W brand of hamburgers called *papa burger* containing two beef patties as opposed to *mama burger* containing just one

macho drama *n.* SPANISH something glorifying aggressive masculinity: **1998** *Village Voice*: *In 1991, the U.S. media not only acted as cheerleader for war, but also couched conflict as a macho drama*; **2015** *Men's Journal*: *You could argue that history has all been one long macho drama* || since 1970, from *macho* "male" and *drama*

macho it out *phr.* SPANISH to behave in an aggressively masculine way (KC): **2008** *New York Times*: *If Kerry had taken this approach, instead trying to macho it out with Bush, he might have won in 2004*; **2011** *Chicago Tribune*: *Don't keep going* *because you made the decision and now you need to macho it out* || since 1970, from *macho* "aggressively masculine" and *it out*

macho man *n.* SPANISH an aggressively masculine male: **2006** *Time*: *Mitch was acting like a macho man*; **2015** *Salinas Californian*: *Jesse doesn't claim to be a macho man* || since 1965, from *macho* "male" and *man*

mack¹ *n.* FRENCH a pimp (JG, KC): **2001** Virginia McConnell: *His attire made Phillips think he was a mack*; **2011** Cecil Brown: *I'm tired of these women always tryin' to get you to come to be their mack* || since 1887, from *maquereau* "pimp"

mack² *v.* FRENCH to work as a pimp with (JG, KC): **2011** Escapist Magazine: *I just macked bitches, I was a little pimp*; **2012** *San Diego Reader*: *Williams could have been macking sluts* || since 1900, from *maquereau* "pimp"

madam *n.* FRENCH a woman who runs a brothel (JG): **2018** *Knoxville News-Sentinel*: *She turned to running prostitution rings and became Knoxville's most famous madam*; **2018** *News*, Fox-TV program: *It's been 25 years since Hollywood madam Heidi Fleiss became one of the most notorious women in America* || since 1719, from *madame* "lady"

madon *excl.* ITALIAN [1] I am irritated (TD): **2010** *Hawthorne*, TNT-TV series: *"The wedding is Saturday, and against my good advice, they went there!" "Madon!"*; **2019** UCLA student: *Madon! What are you doing?* [2] I am surprised (TD): **2010** *Good Guys*, Fox-TV series: *Madon! I thought you was dead*; **2009** Queerty: *Oh madon! What a man!* || since 1964, from *Madonna* "Virgin Mary"

mafia *n.* ITALIAN a group of influential people, suspected of controlling an organization or institution (AS, KC): **2007** *Washingtonian*: *Goldberg calls his friends "the conservative mafia"*; **2015** *Ottawa Citizen*: *The Liberal mafia will continue to steal and rob us taxpayers. Why vote?* || since 1960, from *mafia* "organized group of criminals"

magnifico (or **el magnifico**) *adj.* SPANISH excellent (JG): **2009** Google Groups: *He's el magnifico. But people who race in F1 need to be young*; **2014** Catholic Philly: *Philadelphia is magnifico!* || since 1993, from *el magnifico* "something magnificent"

make a tsimmes, make a tzimmes *phr.* YIDDISH to create a great outrage, fuss, or complaining, especially over a trivial matter (AS): **1997** *Los Angeles Times*: *Why are you making such a tsimmes over everything?* **2012** Orange County Register: *She makes such a tzimmes about it* || since 1968, from *tsimes* "fuss and confusion," literally "stew of sweetened vegetables or fruit"

mamacita *n.* SPANISH a woman, especially a young and attractive one (JG): **2011** Pop Crush: *She's quite a mamacita*; **2013** *Los Angeles Times*: *The elderly woman longs for the days when she was considered a mamacita* || since 1973, from *mamacita* "little mother"

mama coca *n.* SPANISH cocaine (JG): **1989** Edmundo Morales: *It should not be enough reason to argue that "mama coca" has ever had a sacred meaning in the Andean culture*; **2014** Huffington Post: *American slang has a knack for giving stimulants the feminine names: White Lady, China Girl, Mama Coca* || since 1983, from *mama* "mother" and *coca* "cocaine"

mamada *n.* SPANISH *potentially offensive* fellatio: **2005** Urban Dictionary: *That ruca gives one hell of a mamada*; **2014** Boyz Tube: *Cute Aggie wanders in to give him a mamada* || dating unknown, from *mamada* "fellatio" and *mamar* "to suck"

mama-san *n.* JAPANESE [1] a brothel madam (AS, TD): **2005** Urban Dictionary: *Look for mama-san, she knows how to help you have a good time*; **2017** News, ABC-TV program: *The investigators raided the brothel, isolated and arrested the mama-san and rescued several girls* [2] an East Asian child or young woman: **2004** *Cold Case*, CBS-TV series: *Yo, mama-san! What's up?* **2010** *Freeway Killer*, film: *My unit rolled into this hamlet. This little baby-faced mama-san came running to the tent* || since 1946, from *mama* and honorific ending *san*

mami (or **mamí**) *n.* SPANISH a woman, especially, an attractive one (JG): **2014** *Miami New Times*: *They'll do whatever it takes to get the sexy mamis moving*; **2014** Perez Hilton: *Nobody can hold this sexy mami down!* || since 2000, from *mamí* "little mother"

mami chula (or **mamí chula**) *n.* SPANISH a sexually attractive woman: **2012** *CSI: Crime Scene Investigation*, CBS-TV series: *Mami chula, you want my money, you're gonna have to earn it the hard way*; **2011** Twitter: *Look at that mami chula!* || dating unknown, from *mamí chula* "attractive woman," literally "attractive mother"

mamma mia *excl.* ITALIAN [1] I am irritated: **1995** *Grumpier Old Men*, film: *Be gentle! Mamma mia!* **2010** Facebook: *We lost? Mamma mia!* [2] I am surprised: **1999** *Talented Mr. Ripley*, film: *"Dickie has a fianceé!" "Mamma mia!"*; **2007** *Mad Men*, AMC-TV series: *He made you all this and it was platonic? No petting, nothing? Mamma mia!* || dating unknown, from *mamma mia* "my mother"

mana *n.* SPANISH (especially as a term of address) a woman: **2010** *Perrier's County*, film: *Mana, will you pay attention?* **2012** Tumblr: *Hey mana! What time is it there?* || since 1967, from *mana* "female friend," ultimately from *hermana* "sister"

mandingo *n.* MANDINKA *potentially offensive* a strong and big-built African American man (GS, JG): **2015** TMZ: *I bet you secretly fantasize about bedding a Mandingo since Bob isn't getting it done*; **2016** Inquisitr: *I'm six feet tall, and I'm strong. Strong! I mean, look at me, I'm a Mandingo!* || dating unknown, from *mandingo* "member of the Mandinka people"

mano *n.* SPANISH (especially as a term of address) a man (JG, TD): **1994** *Fresh*, film: *It looks like you got the wrong apartment, mano*; **2007** *Half Past Dead 2*, film: *I told you to back off, mano* || since 1967, from *mano* "male friend," ultimately from *hermano* "brother"

mano a mano[1] *n.* SPANISH a one-on-one confrontation, especially a hand-to-hand fight or duel (AS, KC, TD): **2005** *Pit Fighter*, film: *I hear that El Julio is wanting to do a mano a mano*; **2014** *Billboard*: *Drake is on tour battling Lil Wayne, but that doesn't mean he can't break from the mano a mano* ‖ since 1968, from *mano a mano* "hand to hand"

mano a mano[2] *adv.* SPANISH involving a one-on-one confrontation, especially a hand-to-hand fight or duel (AS): **2003** *Mother Jones*: *Confronted by father, Bush suggests they settle it mano a mano*; **2014** Yelp: *Like gentlemen, both of you should take it outside and handle things mano a mano* ‖ since 1968, from *mano a mano* "hand to hand"

maracas *n.* SPANISH *potentially offensive* female breasts (JG, KC): **2011** *Washington Post*: *Nancy Grace's wardrobe malfunction happened when she went over to listen to the judges commentary, briefly exposing one of her maracas*; **2017** Bustle: *She joked the actor shouldn't look down at her big maracas when she dances* ‖ since 1939, from *maracas* "rounded gourd-rattles"

Maria *n.* SPANISH marijuana: **2009** International Sex Guide: *I want to make some trips to Netherlands to smoke some Maria*; **2014** OK Cupid: *I'm playing World of Warcraft while smoking some Maria* ‖ dating unknown, from *María* "Mary"

Maria Juanita *n.* SPANISH marijuana: **2009** *Spine Health*: *The ones I know wouldn't even give an aspirin if they knew someone was smoking Maria Juanita*; **2010** Twitter: *He was high on Maria Juanita* ‖ dating unknown, from *María Juanita* "Mary Jane"

maricon (or **maricón**) *n.* SPANISH *potentially offensive* a homosexual man (KC): **2005** *Michigan Daily*: *While in Miami on Spring Break, I was called a maricón more than once*; **2013** *Los Angeles Times*: *Paret called Griffith – who had been rumored to be gay – a maricon, a nasty Spanish slur for homosexual* ‖ since 1932, from *maricón* "homosexual or effeminate man"

mariposa *n.* SPANISH *potentially offensive* [1] a homosexual man: **2008** Johnny Miles: *They all said he was a mariposa. That he sucked dick and took it up the ass*; **2012** Literotica: *He was still angry at Tom for mocking him and calling him a mariposa, a homosexual* [2] a prostitute: **2010** Twitter: *She's a mariposa, a working girl*; **2013** *OC Weekly*: *Wow, this really does confirm your status as a mariposa* ‖ dating unknown, from *mariposa* "butterfly" and reinforced by *mariposa de la noche* "night butterfly"

marone *excl.* ITALIAN [1] I am irritated (JG): **2002** *Sopranos*, HBO-TV series: *Marone! What are you doing?* **2018** *New York Post*: *"Marone!" proclaimed one perturbed fan* [2] I am surprised (JG): **2019** *Esquire*: *Marone! The Sopranos is 20 and hasn't changed a day*; **2021** *Many Saints of Newark*, film: *"I bet she pays $100." "Marone!"* ‖ since 1964, from dialectal pronunciation of *Madonna* "Virgin Mary"

marrano *n.* SPANISH a disgusting and despicable person: **2017** *Snowfall*, FX-TV series: *I'd rather die than be fucked by these marranos*; **2017** Urban Dictionary: *Those* *marranos are fucking savages, they are always under the influence and fuck shit up everywhere they go* || dating unknown, from *marrano* "pig" and *Marrano* "a (Medieval) Jew who converted to Christianity"

Mary *n.* SPANISH marijuana (JG): **2010** Grass City: *I don't have a bong yet, I'm pretty new to smoking mary*; **2010** Indeed: *If you smoke Mary and you're a light smoker, it will be removed from your urine system in three weeks* || since 1936, from *Mary Jane* "marijuana," literally translated from *María Juanita*

Mary J. (or **Mary J**) *n.* SPANISH marijuana (JG): **2013** Gay Speak: *I'm tired of being asked if I smoke Mary J*; **2014** Village Voice: *There were also police officers who seemed to ignore the casual use of Mary J* || since 1928, from *María Juanita* "Mary Jane"

Mary Jane *n.* SPANISH marijuana (JG, TD): **2013** News, NBC-TV program: *He must have smoked some Mary Jane*; **2014** Vibe: *The video was filmed in Washington State where recreational use of Mary Jane has been legalized* || since 1928, from *María Juanita* "Mary Jane"

Mary Juana *n.* SPANISH marijuana (TD): **2001** Meta Filter: *I'm goin' to Mexico and smokin' some Mary Juana!*; **2008** Gamefaqs: *Let's smoke some mary juana!* || since 1928, from *María Juanita* "Mary Jane" and phonetic similarity to marijuana

maven, mavin *n.* YIDDISH an expert or a connoisseur (AS, JG, KC): **2003** *Anything Else*, film: *Then there's Tom, the money market maven, and Perry, the travel agent guy. But no, she wants more*; **2012** Chicago Magazine: *Gene Siskel, a maven of real estate, advised them on which house to buy* || since 1950, from *meyvin* "expert"

mayate *n.* SPANISH *offensive* a black person (JG): **1992** *American Me*, film: *What the hell are the mayates doing with the Italians?* **2015** *Orange Is the New Black*, Netflix-TV series: *Give it to the fat mayate so she don't get all sad* || since 1969, from *mayate* "figeater beetle"

mazel *n.* YIDDISH luck (TD): **2010** New York Times: *If you have the mazel to find a shade tree in either of these parks, consider yourself lucky*; **2015** Facebook: *We would like to wish you a lot of mazel and health* || since 1968, from *mazal* "star constellation" or "luck"

mazels *excl.* YIDDISH congratulations: **2005** *Munich*, film: *Mazels on the baby, and all that!* **2018** Cosmopolitan: *All the mazels, Khloe! So happy to hear you're doing well and can't wait to see your baby* || since 1862, from *mazal tov* "good star constellation" or "good luck"

mazel tov *excl.* YIDDISH congratulations (AS): **2009** *Defiance*, film: *You have a new profession! Mazel tov!* **2014** New York Times: *Years later, the people who had shouted "mazel tov" at our wedding asked "What happened?"* || since 1968, from *mazal tov* "good star constellation" or "good luck"

mazula, mazoola *n.* YIDDISH money, especially ready cash (JG, KC): **1990** *Havana*, film: *Twin sisters from St. Louis are loaded with mazoola*; **2007** World Wide Words: *Elvis Presley will make more mazoola this year than all of the presidents of* *our five top universities combined* || since 1951, from *mazuma* and *mezumen* "ready cash"

mazuma, mazooma *n.* YIDDISH money, especially ready cash (AS, JG, KC): **2002** *Los Angeles Times*: *This may not be a good time to lay out a lot of mazuma at a fancy resort*; **2011** Jewish Holiday: *During the Depression, a nickel was a lot of mazuma* || since 1901, from *mezumen* "ready cash"

mega[1] *adj.* GREEK very large (AS, JG, TD): **2006** *Zoom*, film: *His speed could create a mega vortex*; **2008** *Tropic Thunder*, film: *It is financed by hotheaded mega mogul Les Grossman* || since 1966, from *megas* "great"

mega[2] *adv.* GREEK extremely (JG): **2015** *Henderson Daily Dispatch*: *That is mega crazy*; **2015** *Spartanburg Herald Journal*: *Americans admire the mega rich and don't resent them* || since 1966, from *megas* "great"

megabucks *n.* GREEK a lot of money (AS, JG, KC, TD): **2006** *Las Vegas*, NBC-TV series: *They were gonna hit megabucks that evening*; **2009** *Being Erica*, CBS-TV series: *Her parents are rich. I mean, megabucks* || since 1946, from *megas* "great" and *bucks* "money"

megillah *n.* YIDDISH [1] anything very long and tedious (JG, KC): **2003** *In the Cut*, film: *"It's a megillah!" "We're all doing overtime"*; **2012** *Chicago Tribune*: *It took four months for the paint to come from Europe, such a megillah to get that color* [2] anything unnecessarily complicated or overly extended (JG, KC): **1997** *Buffy the Vampire Slayer*, WB-TV series: *A lot of parents are doing it. It's part of this cultural exchange megillah*; **1998** *New York Times*: *Don't make a megillah out of every little thing* || since 1909, from *megile* "scroll" or "volume," especially the Book of Esther read aloud in its entirety at Purim celebrations

-meister *suffix* GERMAN an expert at what is indicated (AS, JG, KC): **2014** *New York Times*: *For many years as a Republican campaign-meister, he knew that to get attention he needed a stunt*; **2015** *Arizona Daily Star*: *It reminds us what a talented songmeister he was* || since 1960, from German *Meister* "master," perhaps also from Yiddish *mayster* with the same meaning

mensch, mensh *n.* YIDDISH [1] a decent, noble, and honorable person (AS, JG, KC): **1999** *Family Guy,* Fox-TV series: *I have faith that Chris will grow up to be a real mensch*; **2004** *Desperate Housewives*, ABC-TV series: *I should probably send a thank you letter to my parole officer. He's being such a mensch about this* [2] a respected and admired person (KC): **2005** *Wedding Crashers*, film: *Lou Epstein, I want you to meet a real mensch, Chuck Schwartz*; **2011** *Tucson Weekly*: *He's actually a lovely and charming guy, a real mensch* || since 1909, from *mentsh* "decent person," literally "person"

mercy buckets *excl.* PSEUDO-FRENCH thank you (JG): **1993** *Northern Exposure*, CBS-TV series: *"I'll drive it around." "Mercy buckets!"*; **2006** Urban Dictionary: *"Here you go!" "Mercy buckets!"* || since 1960, from phonetic respelling of *merci beaucoup* "thank you very much"

mercy buttercups *excl.* PSEUDO-FRENCH thank you (JG): **1995** *InfoWorld: Bon voyage! Mercy buttercups!* **2011** Paul Collins: *It's not "mercy buttercups," you morons, it's merci beaucoup* || since 1981, from phonetic respelling of *merci beaucoup* "thank you very much"

meshuga¹, meshugga, meshuge, meshugge *adj.* YIDDISH crazy (AS, JG, KC): **1996** *New York Times: Some people would say that's a meshugge schedule*; **1999** *Man on the Moon*, film: *That kid is totally meshuga* || since 1888, from *meshuge* "crazy"

meshuga², meshugga, meshuge, meshugge *n.* YIDDISH a crazy person (JG): **1996** *Los Angeles Times: People regard her as a meshuga, or crazy person*; **2011** *New York Times: What a meshuga! Who knows if he's angry or just releasing his inner child?* || since 1900, from *meshuge* "crazy"

meshugas, meshuggas, meshugaas, meshuggaas *n.* YIDDISH craziness or insanity (AS, JG, KC): **2004** *Ocean's Twelve*, film: *Danny's had enough of this meshugaas*; **2012** *Los Angeles Times: What kind of director in his right mind would want to stage this? Such meshugas doesn't come cheap, so where might funding be found?* || since 1958, from *meshugas* "craziness"

meshugener¹, meshuggener *n.* YIDDISH a crazy man (AS, JG, KC): **2010** *Atlantic Monthly: He has a devoted corps of meshuggeners hanging on his every word*; **2011** *Love, Wedding, Marriage*, film: *Stop acting like some kind of meshuggener in front of your daughters!* || since 1910s, from *meshugener* "crazy person"

meshugener², meshuggener *adj.* YIDDISH crazy (JG): **1998** *Price Above Rubies*, film: *She's running around like a meshuggener thing*; **2004** *Meet the Fockers*, film: *"Jack's angry." "He's also a bit meshuggener"* || since 1910s, from *meshugener* "crazy person"

meshugenut, meshuggenut *n.* YIDDISH a crazy person: **2002** Payson Stevens: *A meshugenut is a nutty person who can drive you crazy*; **2004** Bladesmith's Forum: *Did you meet any other fascinating meshugenuts?* || since 2000, from *meshuge* "crazy" and *nut*

Mexicali revenge *n.* SPANISH diarrhea (JG, TD): **2009** Deep Politics Forum: *Nearly all of his guests developed classic cases of "Mexicali revenge" after being fed local produce*; **2013** Blogs: *He had a nasty case of Mexicali revenge* || since 1973, from *Mexicali*, a city in Mexico, itself a blend of *Mexico* and *California*, and revenge

Mexicana *n.* SPANISH *potentially offensive* a female Mexican: **2013** *Phoenix New Times: About 33 percent of Mexicanas who marry a gabacho are college-educated*; **2014** *San Diego Reader: Mommy is a Mexicana, Daddy is a gringo* || dating unknown, from *Mexicana* "female Mexican"

Mexicano *n.* SPANISH *potentially offensive* a male Mexican (AS): **2003** *Painted House*, film: *You like my sister, Mexicano?* **2007** Lubbock Online: *In a lot of Mexicanos' eyes, Texas is still Mexico* || dating unknown, from *Mexicano*, "male Mexican"

Mexirican *n.* SPANISH *offensive* a person of Mexican and Puerto Rican descent: 2009 Red Tape: *These Mexiricans are sucking up all the free health care*; 2012 St. Augustine Online: *As Mexirirans get wealthy, they want to vote Republican* || dating unknown, from *Mexicano* and *Puerto Rican*

mierda¹ *n.* SPANISH *offensive* [1] excrement (JG): 2005 Blogspot: *I leave pieces of mierda on your doorsteps*; 2014 Tumblr: *Bitch, I'll smear mierda on your bedroom walls!* [2] something annoying, worthless, or of bad quality: 2005 *Dirty*, film: *None of that pinche mierda would have happened if you'd told me you was protecting H. A. now*; 2008 *Weeds*, Showtime-TV series: *She comes back with nothing but the mierda she buys in line at the crossing* [3] nonsense or a lie: 2012 *Savages*, film: *"Men will say anything to stop the pain." "Mierda. You're stupider than you look"*; 2014 YouTube: *Why do people listen to this mierda?* || dating unknown, from *mierda* "excrement"

mierda² *excl.* SPANISH *offensive* [1] I am irritated: 2005 *Headspace*, film: *Mierda, now I have to go*; 2019 UCLA student: *Mierda! There's something wrong* [2] I am surprised: 2009 *Miss March*, film: *Mierda! I can't believe Cindi would do this*; 2004 *Day Without a Mexican*, film: *Oh mierda! Don't shoot!* || dating unknown, from *mierda* "excrement"

migra (or **la migra**) *n.* SPANISH the US Immigration and Naturalization Service; the Border Patrol: 2008 *Los Angeles Times*: *The car stopped. A moment of tension. The migra gave the Chevy the OK to leave*; 2014 *San Jose Mercury News*: *Many migrants illegally crossing the border fear La Migra* || since 1970, from *la migra* "border patrol," ultimately from *la inmigración* "immigration"

mija *n.* SPANISH (especially as a term of address) a young woman you like: 2009 *Bring It On: Fight to the Finish*, film: *Come on, mija, you know I love you*; 2015 *Houston Chronicle*: *My dad calls me "mija"* || dating unknown, from *mija* "my dear," ultimately from *mi hija* "my daughter"

mijo *n.* SPANISH (especially as a term of address) a young man you like: 2010 *Law & Order*, NBC-TV series: *"She looked like a cheap whore." "Don't use that word, mijo"*; 2015 *Twin Falls Times-News*: *My mother told me time and again, "mijo, you were born in the US and you aren't taking advantage of it"* || dating unknown, from *mijo* "my dear," ultimately from *mi hijo* "my son"

mishmash *n.* YIDDISH a confused mixture or hodge-podge (KC): 2000 *Gift*, film: *This is just mishmash. I told you this wouldn't lead to nothing*; 2012 *Chicago Tribune*: *What began with a quirky mish-mash of opening ceremony ended with a thumping celebration of London and British music* || dating unknown, from *mishmash* "confused mixture"

moi *pron.* FRENCH me (AS): 2006 *Love Wrecked*, film: *"You can't tell anyone, ok?" "Moi? Spill the beans? Not a chance"*; 2012 *Forger*, film: *"You did that on purpose." "Moi? Never!"* || dating unknown, from *moi* "me"

mojado *n.* SPANISH *potentially offensive* an illegal immigrant to the USA from Mexico: **2005** *New York Times*: *The mojados risked exposure by consenting to be filmed*; **2019** *Brooklyn Rail*: *He accuses her of opening a hotel for mojados in her backyard* || dating unknown, from *mojado* "wet," derived from the image of swimming across the Rio Grande from Mexico into Texas

mojo *n.* FULA [1] a charm or amulet worn against evil (KC): **1998** *He Got Game*, film: *This mojo works! It worked on your ass!* **2015** E-Poetry: *He's got some mojo around his neck* [2] influence, power, or charisma (JG, KC, TD): **2007** *Two and a Half Men*, CBS-TV series: *The girl digs my mojo*; **2009** *Ebony*: *Prince lost the mojo* [3] sex appeal or sex drive (KC, TD): **1995** *Pinky and the Brain*, WB-TV series: *That man gets my mojo workin'*; **2003** Urban Dictionary: *Man, that girl has mojo!* || since 1926, from *moco* "medicine man"

momzer *n.* YIDDISH [1] an illegitimate child: **2009** Jeanne Barrack: *My mother was unwed when she had me; that makes me a momzer*; **2019** Quora: *If a married Jewish woman has a child by another man, that child, though Jewish, is a momzer* [2] a despicable and untrustworthy person (JG, KC): **1990** *Chicago Tribune*: *I wouldn't trust that louse. Gussie, you married a real momzer*; **2011** Daily Kos: *That idiot Cantor is a momzer and a liar!* [3] a parasitic person (KC): **2002** Shirley Shapiro: *Pray that the momzers would stay away from us*; **2021** *Hill*: *This man was a momzer and would cheat his own grandmother for fifty cents* || since 1914, from *mamzer* "bastard"

mondo¹ *adv.* SPANISH [1] extremely (JG): **2009** Tumblr: *He was mondo sexy in that suit*; **2014** Pinterest: *Pretty boy Efron is mondo hot in this clip* [2] very much or a lot of (JG): **2001** *Los Angeles Magazine*: *Chandler would become eligible to be a free agent and sign for mondo dollars*; **2002** *Big Fat Liar*, film: *We're talking mondo bucks* || since 1966 in the first sense, since 1985 in the second, from *mundo* "world"

mondo² *adj.* SPANISH [1] extreme: **1995** *Basketball Diaries*, film: *The little kid's got a mondo fever*; **2014** Facebook: *Lindsay Lohan just oozes mondo sex appeal* [2] very large or substantial (JG): **2001** *Knockaround Guys*, film: *It's definitely super mondo wheels, man*; **2008** Urban Dictionary: *That's a mondo car* || since 1968 in the first sense, since 1985 in the second, from *mundo* "world"

mondo bizarro *adj.* SPANISH very strange or bizarre (JG): **1993** *Homeward Bound*, film: *Will you look at this guy? This is, like, mondo bizarro*; **2021** *Chicago Reader*: *Grayson has had some mondo-bizarro scene partners. The craziest was Kevin, who had magnets implanted into his fingers* || since 1966, from *mundo* "world" and *bizarro* "bizarre or strange"

mondo weirdo *adj.* SPANISH very strange or weird (JG): **2009** Blogspot: *I have developed an allergic reaction to most mondo weirdo 9/11 theories*; **2013** News, NBC-TV program: *His live show traces through his nearly-50-year career as a mondo weirdo moviemaker* || since 1966, from *mundo* "world" and *weirdo* "weird or strange"

monte *n.* SPANISH marijuana, especially of good quality (JG): **2007** Blogspot: *Ask him about getting some monte (weed)*; **2013** Blogger: *Where can I score some monte?* ‖ since 1980, from *monte* "thicket" or "bush"

moose *n.* JAPANESE a Japanese or Korean prostitute, especially in the Korean war (JG, KC, TD): **2015** Wikipedia: *In that episode a "moose" was defined as a Korean girlfriend*; **2015** Angelfire: *They explain to them that she is a moose* ‖ since 1952, from *musume* "girl"

moota *n.* SPANISH marijuana or marijuana cigarette (JG, KC, TD): **2013** Twitter: *I am about to smoke moota*; **2014** Drug Library: *Moota, as the drug was known in the city, was popular throughout the red-light district* ‖ since 1937, from *mota* "speck or tiny bit" or "clod of dirt"

mother of all *phr.* ARABIC the most epic, extreme, or sizable example of something (JG, KC, TD): **2012** *Chasing Ice*, film: *The Ilulissat glacier in Greenland is the mother of all glaciers*; **2016** Fortune: *After all, the U.S. Treasury is the mother of all piggy banks* ‖ since 1991, from *umm al-ma'ārik* "mother of all battles," popularized by Saddam Hussein in reference to the Gulf War

mox nix¹ *excl.* PSEUDO-GERMAN it is irrelevant or unimportant (TD): **2008** Urban Dictionary: *"Do you want ice cream or pie for dessert?" "Mox nix. Just surprise me"*; **2008** Blogspot: *Hillary is so experienced, right? Mox nix, though* ‖ since 1955, from *(es) macht nichts* "it does not matter"

mox nix² *adj.* PSEUDO-GERMAN irrelevant or unimportant: **2008** Weapon Evolution: *Ultimately it looks like a mox nix deal to me*; **2018** Twitter: *Why is the press so concerned about the communications of a mox nix reporter being gathered?* ‖ since 1955, from *(es) macht nichts* "it does not matter"

Mr. Cheapo *n.* SPANISH someone cheap or parsimonious (KC): **1996** *She's the One*, film: *I'll pay the $12, Mr. Cheapo*; **2005** Ripoff Report: *Fixing it will be much less expensive in the long run, but Mr. Cheapo doesn't care about the future* ‖ dating unknown, from prefix *Mr.-*, *cheap*, and mock Spanish suffix *-o*

mu *n.* SPANISH a marijuana cigarette (JG, KC): **2010** Blogger: *That dude wanted to score some mu*; **2014** Twitter: *They were smoking some mu and having a good time* ‖ since 1936, from *muta* "marijuana" or "herbs"

muchacha *n.* SPANISH [1] a female friend: **2012** *Lay the Favorite*, film: *"Call me sometime?" "I will. Adios muchacha!"*; **2016** *Orange Is the New Black*, Netflix-TV series: *Tell your muchachas how poor choices can ruin your life* [2] a woman (AS): **1992** *Encino Man*, film: *You see that muchacha over there?* **1995** *Crossing Guard*, film: *You wanna dance with the muchachas?* ‖ dating unknown, from *muchacha* "girl"

muchacho *n.* SPANISH [1] a male friend: **2003** *Miami Trail*, film: *You, Zeus, muchacho! How's it hanging?* **2004** *In Good Company*, film: *It's going to be okay, muchachos* [2] a man (AS): **2004** *Starsky and Hutch*, film: *You're gonna give me some* *answers, comprende, muchacho?* **2014** *Tucson Weekly*: *What is that crap? Screw you, muchacho!* ‖ dating unknown, from *muchacho* "boy"

mucho *adv.* SPANISH [1] much or many (AS, JG, KC, TD): **2014** Angelfire: *I need mucho chicks, I'm always horny*; **2021** *Forbes*: *You can save mucho dollars* [2] extremely (AS, JG, TD): **1996** *Striptease*, film: *"You're happy?" "Oh, mucho happy!"*; **2005** *Hard Candy*, film: *Your complete honesty will be mucho appreciated* ‖ since 1942 in the first sense, since 1957 in the second, from *mucho* "much"

mucho dinero *phr.* SPANISH a lot of money (KC, TD): **1990** *Nobody's Perfect*, film: *That will cost mucho dinero*; **2007** *CSI: Crime Scene Investigation*, CBS-TV series: *Izzy's music library was for sale. Mucho dinero to be gained* ‖ since 1942, from *mucho* "much" and *dinero* "money"

muchos *adv.* SPANISH much or many (JG): **2006** Greg Caldwell: *We repeat this operation many times, saving muchos people*; **2011** Blogspot: *Muchos things to do, I got a lot of things to do* ‖ since 1942, from *mucho* "much"

muj *n.* ARABIC a Mujahideen, Muslim guerilla fighter engaged in a holy war: **2007** *Charlie Wilson's War*, film: *The CIA estimates that seven out of every ten times the muj fires a Stinger, a Soviet chopper or a plane falls out of the sky*; **2012** *Memorial Day*, film: *All that muj had was an AK* ‖ since 2000, from *mujāhid* "one who fights a holy war"

mula *n.* SPANISH [1] a Mexican smuggler of contraband, especially narcotics: **2009** *Houston Chronicle*: *All were first-time offenders but part of a growing wave of mulas, female smugglers*; **2011** Facebook: *In the movie "Maria Full of Grace," the mulas swallow the cocaine in packages of condoms* [2] a gay person who assumes the passive role in sex: **2007** James Alex Garza: *Mulas were homosexual prisoners sporting nicknames like "La Camelia" and "La Princessa"*; **2010** Blogs: *He was a mula in jail* ‖ since 1972, from *mula* "female mule"

mundo[1] *adv.* SPANISH [1] extremely: **2004** Live Journal: *I'm mundo happy for you*; **2009** Muppet Central: *I might go there next week and I'm mundo excited* [2] very much or a lot of: **2005** Ars Technica: *I'm looking for all opinions here before I drop mundo dollars on a device*; **2014** UNM student: *Don't worry, you've got mundo options* ‖ since 1966 in the first sense, since 1985 in the second, from *mundo* "world"

mundo[2] *adj.* SPANISH very large: **2004** Urban Dictionary: *That's one mundo screen*; **2015** UF student: *He shows up in his mundo ride, Cadillac Escalade* ‖ since 1985, from *mundo* "world"

muta *n.* SPANISH a marijuana cigarette (JG, KC, RS, TD): **2013** Drug Test: *Mexicans who had just slipped over the border arrived with their muta*; **2014** Brush Beat: *They were listening to records and smoking "muta" (marijuana)* ‖ since 1937, from *mota* "drugs," literally "speck or tiny bit" or "clod of dirt"

N

naca *n.* SPANISH an uneducated or unsophisticated woman from a lower socioeconomic class, especially from the countryside: **2003** Urban Dictionary: *Loria looks like a naca wearing crusty long acrylic toe nails*; **2015** *Los Angeles Times*: *Laura Bozzo breaks her silence about Mark Tacher's diss and calls herself a "naca" in an interview* || dating unknown, from *naco* "country bumpkin"

naches, nachas *n.* YIDDISH joy and pride, especially because of one's children: **1995** *New York Magazine*: *Ferklempt but stable divorced Jewish nonsmoker seeks man of integrity and compassion to share life's nachas and tzuris*; **2016** *Washington Post*: *When Lieberman ran for vice president, Jews swelled with naches* || dating unknown, from *nahkes* "contentment at another's success"

naco *n.* SPANISH an uneducated or unsophisticated man from a lower socioeconomic class, especially from the countryside: **2006** *Houston Chronicle*: *I can't drive my BMW to downtown. We should go camping in Colorado instead, at least there the nacos won't be rebelling against us*; **2006** *Los Angeles Times*: *Only the nacos, the people who are dying of hunger, will vote for him* || dating unknown, from *naco* "country bumpkin"

nada *n.* SPANISH nothing (AS, JG, TD): **2013** *Dallas Buyers Club*, film: *"Anything to declare?" "No sir. Nada"*; **2016** *News*, CBC-TV program: *This has nada to do with Mexico* || since 1914, from *nada* "nothing"

nash *see* nosh

nash on *see* nosh

nasher *see* nosher

nasherei *see* nosherei

nashery *see* noshery

neatnik *n.* YIDDISH someone obsessed with cleanliness and neatness: **2005** *New York Times*: *"Are kitchen materials like copper and marble more trouble than they're worth?" "Either would require a household to have at least one neatnik"*; **2011** *Boston Globe*: *Being a neatnik myself, I feel for you living with a hoarder and all that useless junk* || since 1959, from *neat* and suffix *-nik*

nebbish[1] *n.* YIDDISH [1] a weak, timid, ineffectual, or pitiful person (AS, JG, KC): **2003** *Capturing the Friedmans*, film: *They make him sound like some kind of brutal sadist, whereas I had always thought of him as being kind of a nebbish*; **2012** *New York Times*: *He's a classic British comic type, the nebbish who endures constant humiliation* [2] an unimportant or mediocre person (JG, KC): **2006** *For Your*

Consideration, film: *I only invited the best ones, the ones whose daddies were professionals. There wasn't a nebbish in the group*; 2008 Ilene Schneider: *I don't understand what she sees in such a nebbish* ‖ since 1941, from *nebech* "pitiful person"

nebbish² *adj.* YIDDISH [1] weak, timid, ineffectual, or helpless: 2011 *Atlantic Monthly*: *Owen Wilson's persona often lapsed into little more than an impression of his director's famous nebbish persona*; 2011 *Deseret News*: *All the offhand criticisms would be comfortable coming from Allen in his familiar nebbish screen persona* [2] unimportant or mediocre: 2002 Payson Stevens: *The central character is so nebbish he has not even a name*; 2011 *Pittsburgh Post Gazette*: *Surly over circumstances that force them to live at home with nagging, nebbish parents, the drunken off-duty researchers repeatedly start fights* ‖ since 1941, from *nebech* "pitiful person"

nebbishy *adj.* YIDDISH [1] weak, timid, ineffectual, or helpless (AS, JG, KC): 2011 *New Yorker*: *He stars as the nebbishy Warren Nefron, whose bleak identity is defined by the opening scenes, in which he tries and fails to commit suicide*; 2012 *Tablet Magazine*: *Comedy guru Robert Weide examines the life and work of Woody Allen, film's iconic nebbishy New York Jew* [2] unimportant or mediocre (JG): 2011 New World News: *It suggests a very nebbishy university*; 2022 *Spokane Spokesman-Review*: *The movie tells the story of a nebbishy film professor who suspects his wife of having an affair* ‖ since 1979, from *nebech* "pitiful person" and adjectival suffix *-y*

need something like a hole in the head *phr.* YIDDISH not to need something at all (JG, KC): 2005 *Rescue Me*, FX-TV series: *I don't want him here. We need the guy like a hole in the head*; 2015 Hollywood Life: *You need Tyga and his latest drama like a hole in the head* ‖ since 1945, from *darfn epes vi a lokh in kop* "to need something like a hole in the head"

negrita *n.* SPANISH *potentially offensive* a black-skinned female, especially an African American: 1990 *Havana*, film: *There was a Chinese, a negrita, and I think the other one was Danish*; 2014 Black Planet: *I'm gonna be livin on campus, so any guy looking for a sexy negrita, give me a call!* ‖ dating unknown, from *negrito* "little black woman"

negrito *n.* SPANISH *potentially offensive* a black-skinned male, especially an African American: 2003 *Kill the Poor*, film: *Negrito, don't start with me!* 2014 *School Dance*, film: *And your little friend from school, is he a negrito?* ‖ dating unknown, from *negrito* "little black man"

netnik *n.* YIDDISH someone obsessed with the Internet: 1997 Daily Beast: *Let's start with Yahoo. The company is being touted as profitable by many netniks*; 2001 *Newsweek*: *With money virtually burning holes in their pockets, netniks ordered Cisco products as if there were no tomorrow* ‖ since 1990s, from *net* and suffix *-nik*

nieve *n.* SPANISH cocaine (JG, TD): 2009 International Sex Guide: *They would purchase pounds of marijuana and half-kilos of nieve*; 2013 David Dobson: *"I'm looking for some nieve." "Nieve? What does a white boy like you want with cocaine?"* ‖

since 1993, from *nieve* "snow," perhaps as a translation of or reinforced by American English *snow* "cocaine" or "heroin"

nig *n.* SPANISH *very offensive* a black or dark-skinned person: 2008 *Shield*, FX-TV series: *There's plenty of nigs out there*; 2014 *Top Five*, film: *It's strictly for me and my nigs* ‖ since 1932, from *nigger* and ultimately from Spanish *negro* and Latin *niger* "black"

nigga *n.* SPANISH *very offensive* a black or dark-skinned person: 2007 *American Gangster*, film: *What? Y'all niggas never seen hoochie before?* 2018 *Ray Donovan*, Showtime-TV series: *You fucked with the wrong nigga!* ‖ since 1925, from *nigger* and ultimately from Spanish *negro* and Latin *niger* "black"

nigger *n.* SPANISH *very offensive* a black or dark-skinned person: 2005 *Million Dollar Baby*, film: *You know, I've got nothing against niggers*; 2005 *40 Year Old Virgin*, film: *Listen to me, you are fucking with the wrong nigger* ‖ since 1600, from Spanish *negro* and Latin *niger* "black"

-nik *suffix* YIDDISH AND RUSSIAN (someone or something) involved in or characterized by what is indicated (AS, JG, KC, TD): 2012 *New York Post*: *That stretch of Amsterdam Avenue in the upper 70s was hailed a healthnik's haven*; 2016 *New York Post*: *Alain Vigneault is the coach with the reputation as a peacenik* ‖ since 1929, from *-nik*

ninja *n.* JAPANESE a tough person: 2005 Urban Dictionary: *Ninjas don't sweat*; 2014 *San Francisco Weekly*: *You can be a ninja, or a gangster* ‖ since 1990, from *ninja* "martial arts expert"

niños (or **los niños**) *n.* SPANISH hallucinogenic mushrooms: 1985 Mayan Heritage: *Before Wasson, nobody took los niños simply to find God*; 2014 Medi Lexicon: *Can you OD on niños?* ‖ since 1975, from *niños,* literally "little children"

nip *n.* JAPANESE *offensive* [1] a Japanese or a person of Japanese descent (AS, JG, TD): 2001 *Man Who Wasn't There*, film: *The man disappeared into thin air like the nips at Nagasaki*; 2002 *Windtalkers*, film: *You do look like a nip* [2] the Japanese language (JG): 2014 4Plebs: *Since I don't speak nip, I can't really tell*; 2015 Tumblr: *I can't understand nip, so what's the point of watching an anime in their language?* ‖ since 1942, from *Nippon* "Japan"

nitwit¹ *n.* DUTCH a stupid person (JG, KC): 2015 Mediaite: *Trump may be a nitwit, but he's running for president*; 2016 *Cycling Weekly*: *I have nothing to prove to a nitwit like you* ‖ since 1922, from *niet weet* "I don't know"

nitwit² *adj.* DUTCH stupid (JG, KC): 2007 *Philadelphia Weekly*: *He's also, with all due respect, a nitwit guy*; 2015 Down Trend: *It was a nitwit thing to say* ‖ since 1922, from *niet weet* "I don't know"

nix¹ *n.* GERMAN [1] nothing (JG, KC): 2004 *New York Daily News*: *Mike Feud Means Nix to Knicks*; 2010 *Skills*, film: *There is no reception. Nix, no reception* [2] a refusal, rejection, or veto KC): 1992 BioWorld: *ABC Applauds Bush's Nix of*

Treaty; **2013** *News*, Fox-TV program: *The President's fix gets a big nix* ‖ since 1789 in the first sense, since 1951 in the second, from *nix*, a colloquial variant of *nichts* "nothing"

nix² *v.* GERMAN to refuse, reject, or veto (JG, KC, TD): **2009** *It's Complicated*, film: *You're sure? You nixed the last twenty things*; **2015** *Selma*, film: *And please consider nixing the speech at the Capitol* ‖ since 1903, from *nix*, a colloquial variant of *nichts* "nothing"

nix sign *n.* GERMAN a sign that forbids something (KC): **1994** Sam Dworkis: *Next to selected photographs you'll see the nix sign. This means the photograph depicts a wrong way to do an exercise*; **2005** Blogs: *I saw a nix sign there* | since 1990, from *nix*, a colloquial variant of *nichts* "nothing" and *sign*

no big deal *excl.* YIDDISH [1] this is not impressive: **2010** *Kick-Ass*, film: *Rear-view cameras, no big deal!* **2013** Trip Advisor: *It was pretty noise but hey, no big deal* [2] do not worry, it is all right: **1997** *Men in Black*, film: *No big deal, you can come with me, Redge*; **2014** *Whiplash*, film: *"I'm sorry!" "No big deal!"* ‖ since 1940, from *groyser kunst* "great mastery" and *no*

no bueno *adj.* SPANISH no good: **2012** *Men in Black 3*, film: *If Boris gets to him before we do, that's no bueno*; **2018** *Daily Californian*: *I've come to realize that refined sugars are the second or third thing on the ingredients list – which is no bueno* ‖ dating unknown, from *no bueno* "not good"

no comprende *excl.* SPANISH I do not understand (TD): **2010** *Virginity Hit*, film: *"Open!" "No comprende, I am from Mexico"*; **2015** *Overdrive Magazine*: *I did it but the answer was "no comprende"* ‖ since 1971, from *no comprendo* "I do not understand"

no comprendo *excl.* SPANISH I do not understand (JG): **2010** *Main Street*, film: *"Who's in charge here?" "No comprendo!"*; **2016** *Orange Is the New Black*, Netflix-TV series: *"I need to pee." "Sorry, no comprendo"* ‖ since 1971, from *no comprendo* "I do not understand"

nooky (or **nookie**) *n.* DUTCH *potentially offensive* [1] sexual intercourse (JG, KC, TD): **1997** *Dante's Peak*, film: *Sometimes couples sneak up here for some hot nookie*; **2008** *Five Dollars a Day*, film: *First time I got nookie was in this car* [2] a woman or women considered as a sex object (JG, KC, TD): **2012** Word Press: *He's looking for a nookie*; **2015** Facebook: *She's a hot nookie* ‖ since 1928, from *neuken* "to have sex"

no problemo *excl.* SPANISH [1] do not worry, it is all right (JG): **1994** *Pulp Fiction*, film: *"I can't, I gotta be someplace." "No problemo"*; **1998** *Big Lebowski*, film: *"Forgive me!" "No problemo, man!"* [2] you are welcome (TD): **2002** *Six Feet Under*, HBO-TV series: *"Thank you, David." "No problemo"*; **2005** *How I Met Your Mother*, CBS-TV series: *"Thanks, Pete!" "No problemo, Marsh!"* ‖ since 1963 in the first sense, since 1989 in the second, from *no problemo* "no problem"

no way Jose (or **no way José**) *excl.* SPANISH [1] no, never (JG, KC): 2016 National Public Radio: *My first response to them was "No way Jose. We don't do that"*; 2016 *Los Angeles Daily News*: *No way, Jose!" Mexicans aren't about to pay for Trump's wall* [2] I do not believe it (JG): 2008 Prelude Power: *We got seat sensors? No way Jose! Really?* 2013 Twitter: *No way Jose! Wow! Tell me more!* || since 1960 in the first sense, since 1997 in the second, from *no way* and *Jose*

nochschlepper, nochshlepper *n.* YIDDISH a dependent or parasitic person: 2010 *Chicago Tribune*: *Lieberman threw in many Yiddish words, including fairly obscure ones like nochschlepper, which means a tag-along, and his audience laughed*; 2010 *OC Weekly*: *It was a slang term in my elementary school for a tagalong, a nochshlepper, you know* || dating unknown, from *nokhshleper* "someone who tags along"

no-goodnik *n.* YIDDISH [1] an irresponsible or unreliable person (JG, KC): 2008 *Washington Post*: *Who's the no-goodnik who busted us on the On Parenting blog?* 2011 *Toronto Sun*: *Ali's talking about him as an Uncle Tom and no-goodnik* [2] a worthless person, especially one who wastes time doing nothing (KC): 1990 *Simpsons*, Fox-TV series: *I was born a no-goodnik and I will die a no-goodnik*; 2012 *Wall Street Journal*: *It's more serious than a no-goodnik getting a free ride* [3] a shady character, especially a petty criminal (KC): 2009 Huffington Post: *The no-goodnik threatened to kill the young woman's mother*; 2012 *Time Out Chicago*: *Her new paramour is a no-goodnik who frames Eddie for murder* || since 1944, from *no-good* and suffix *-nik*

Norteños (or **Nortenos**) *n.* SPANISH the Mexican mafia from Northern California: 2011 *San Jose Mercury News*: *Sanchez found protection in a rival gang, the Norteños*; 2014 *Los Angeles Times*: *Police said the suspects are members of the Norteños* || dating unknown, from *norteños* "northerners"

nosh¹ *n.* YIDDISH [1] a snack, especially between meals (AS, JG, KC): 2000 *Requiem for a Dream*, film: *You want something to eat? A little nosh, piece of cake? I could go and get something*; 2004 *Laws of Attraction*, film: *You must both stay for some nosh* [2] oral sex, especially fellatio (JG): 2011 NYU student: *A good nosh is something I need*; 2012 Blogs: *No money, no nosh!* || since 1941 in the first sense, since 1998 in the second, from *nash* "snack"

nosh² *v.* YIDDISH [1] to have a little snack to eat, especially between meals (AS, JG, KC): 2012 *Kelowna Daily Courier*: *The guys were eating in style, too, noshing at some of Kelowna's most talked about restaurants*; 2012 *New York Times*: *In the grand ballroom of the Baccarat mansion, they noshed on foie gras* [2] to practice oral sex, especially fellatio (JG): 2011 NYU student: *She's not particularly into noshing*; 2015 Facebook: *She's great at noshing, if you know what I mean* || since 1931 in the first sense, since 1972 in the second, from *nashn* "to eat a snack"

nosher *n.* YIDDISH [1] someone who likes to eat, especially snacks (JG): 2003 *Chicago Tribune*: *The first location is Katz's Delicatessen. That's where Meg Ryan demonstrated to an embarrassed Billy Crystal and a diner filled with pastrami* *noshers* how women feign sexual pleasure; **2012** *USA Today*: *The place is always crowded with noshers ordering the famous all-beef franks and papaya drinks* [2] someone who practices oral sex, especially fellatio (JG): **2011** NYU student: *She's a great nosher*; **2015** UNF student: *They say she's a fantastic nosher* || since 1969 in the first sense, since 1978 in the second, from *nasher* "someone who likes to eat snacks"

noshery *n.* YIDDISH a bar or small restaurant, especially where one can eat snacks (AS, JG, KC): **2000** *New York Times*: *He has run the 75-seat Jerry and Harvey's noshery in Marlboro*; **2010** *New York Post*: *"I wanted the space to be nicer but I also wanted to have fresher ingredients," she says of her nouveau noshery* || since 1952, from *nasherei* "snack place"

not care a carajo *phr.* SPANISH *potentially offensive* to not care at all: **2007** *Gone Baby Gone*, film: *Don't you care a carajo?* **2008** *Felon*, film: *Nobody cares a carajo* || dating unknown, from *not care a damn* and *carajo* "penis"

not give a carajo *phr.* SPANISH *potentially offensive* to not care at all: **2007** Tim Bugansky: *They don't give a carajo about anything*; **2014** Soda Head: *I don't give a carajo about your sexuality* || dating unknown, from *not give a damn* and *carajo* "penis"

not know from nothing *phr.* YIDDISH to know nothing about something (KC): **1991** *Out for Justice*, film: *"Where's Richie?" "I don't know from nothing"*; **2006** *Everwood*, WB-TV series: *I may not know from nothing, but I think Roses's concerns are natural* || since 1936, from *nit tsu visn fun gornisht* "not know from nothing"

nu *excl.* YIDDISH well, so: **2007** Chowhound: *Nu, so what happened? We're sitting on shpilkes here*; **2011** *New York Times*: *"Nu? Is this 2nd Avenue?" "No, it's Lincoln Center"* || dating unknown, from *nu* "well" or "so"

nudge[1] *n.* YIDDISH a boring, nagging, or annoying person (JG, KC): **1994** *Don't Drink the Water*, film: *They're paranoid, and you're a nudge for the whole trip*; **2003** Direct Marketing News: *He apologizes for being such a nudge* || since 1968, from *nudne* "boring" and *nudien* "to bore"

nudge[2] *v.* YIDDISH to bore, nag, or annoy (JG, KC): **1997** *Deconstructing Harry*, film: *If I tell you why I did it, do you promise not to nudge me?* **2007** *Chicago Tribune*: *They have been nudging Jones to change her Internet and phone service* || since 1971, from *nudne* "boring" and *nudien* "to bore"

nudgy *adj.* YIDDISH boring, nagging, or annoying (JG): **2009** *Variety*: *All the picture lacks is a nudgy mother constantly asking, "So when are you going to get a best friend already?"*; **2009** *New York Times*: *Thaler has gotten all nudgy* || since 1969, from *nudne* "boring" and *nudien* "to bore," and adjectival suffix *-y*

nudnik *n.* YIDDISH a boring, nagging, or annoying person (AS, JG): **2008** *Boulder Weekly*: *It's too bad Allen falls into the old trap of painting characters like*

Vicky's nudnik fiancé as a nudnik simply because he's into golf and finance; **2010** *Los Angeles Times*: *Funny how those nudniks a few years back were going on about global warming* || since 1925, from *nudnik* "boring person"

numero uno *n.* ITALIAN AND SPANISH [1] the best person or thing (AS, JG, TD): **2009** *Road of No Return*, film: *I am American and America is numero uno*; **2010** *Chosen One*, film: *Tell him I was numero uno in sales last year* [2] the most important or influential person or thing (AS, JG, KC): **2014** *Management Today*: *Facebook is still numero uno*; **2016** *Bay Area Reporter*: *Oscar night on ABC is still numero uno* [3] oneself (JG, TD): **2005** Urban Dictionary: *In the end, the only person I really need to worry about is numero uno*; **2010** Mormon Discussions: *I'm talking about numero uno here* || since 1942 in the first two senses, since 1977 in the third, from *numero uno* "number one"

Nuyorican *n.* SPANISH *potentially offensive* a Puerto Rican, especially one living in New York City (AS): **2006** *El Cantante*, film: *It feels good to be a Nuyorican holding up a trombone instead of a tray*; **2016** *American Spectator*: *They can't do anything if Nuyoricans move in* || since 1970, from *New York* and *Puerto Rican*

nyet *part.* RUSSIAN no: **1998** *Rounders*, film: *"Take him down, Teddy!" "Nyet! No more!"*; **2013** *Assassins Run*, film: *"You promise?" "Nyet!"* || dating unknown, from *nyet* "no"

O

-o *suffix* PSEUDO-ITALIAN AND PSEUDO-SPANISH (something or someone) having the indicated characteristics (KC): **2016** *Dallas Morning News*: *The Mavericks did not want to go into that extended layoff on the heels of a stinko performance*; **2016** *Denver Post*: *I get your point about wacko right wingers* || since 1896, from *-o*

ocupado *adj.* SPANISH occupied: **2017** BuzzFeed: *The bathroom is ocupado*; **2021** *The Mitchells vs. The Machines*, film: *"Do you want to see my special effects?" "Sorry, Katie, I'm a little ocupado"* || dating unknown, from *ocupado* "occupied"

-oid *suffix* PSEUDO-GREEK (something or someone) resembling or imitating what is indicated (AS, KC): **2016** Quora: *Russia under Putin is democratoid*; **2016** *Fairfield Daily Republic*: *This factoid seems tailor-made for Vermont Sen. Bernie Sanders* || since 1800, from suffixes *-oeides* and *-eidos*

old cocker *n.* YIDDISH an old man, especially a despicable one (JG, KC): **1995** *South Florida Sun-Sentinel*: *Portrait also includes current-day interviews with a collection of old cockers who were part of Dean's formative years*; **2006** *Holiday*, film: *I'm wondering why a beautiful girl like you would spend Saturday night with an old cocker like me* || since 1968, from *alter kaker* "despicable old man," literally "old shitter"

old futz *n.* YIDDISH a stupid and despicable older person: **1994** *Mediaweek*: *These are things of the past and anyone even mentioning them will be exposed as a pathetic,* *obsolete old futz*, 2006 *Salem News*: *You sound like a cool young dude and I am an old futz compared to you* || since 1930s, from *alter fartser* "despicable old person," literally "someone who flatulates"

old futzer *n.* YIDDISH a stupid and despicable older person: 2008 *Rocky Mountain News*: *It referred to former President Dwight Eisenhower as the old futzer*; 2014 *Tri-City Herald*: *The old futzer recommends that you try wines that vary in style* || since 1930s, from *alter fartser* "despicable old person," literally "someone who flatulates"

old kaker *n.* YIDDISH an old man, especially a despicable one (JG, KC): 2008 Type Pad: *The old kaker doesn't even try*; 2016 Blogger: *He's a senile old kaker with nothing to lose* || since 1968, from *alter kaker* "despicable old man," literally "old shitter"

old kocker *see* old cocker

omerta *n.* ITALIAN a code of silence, especially the one used by members of the Italian mafia (AS): 1998 *Witness to the Mob*, film: *If you violate the law of omerta or betray the brotherhood, may your soul burn as this saint!* 2017 Hollywood Reporter: *Omerta has never taken deep root in the media-entertainment industrial complex* || since 1960, from *omertà* "humility"

on shpilkes, on schpilkes *phr.* YIDDISH [1] nervous or anxious: 2001 *New York Daily News*: *Even so, NBC's president, Robert C. Wright, seems unusually out of sorts, perturbed, troubled, or, as they say at the Harvard Business School, on shpilkes*; 2005 *Confessions of an American Bride*, film: *I'm on shpilkes. No son of mine is being married in a church* [2] impatient or overabundant with energy: 2010 *New York Times*: *I'm sitting on shpilkes waiting for an answer*; 2011 Crown Heights: *The other is more of a wanderer and is always on shpilkes* || since 1982, from *shpilkes* "nervousness or impatience," literally "pins," and *zitsn oyf shpilkes* "to be nervous or impatient," literally "to sit on pin and needles"

on the fritz *phr.* GERMAN broken or malfunctioning (AS, JG, KC, TD): 1995 *Casino*, film: *I had our pilot tell him the plane was on the fritz*; 2015 Arkansas Online: *The cable is on the fritz. It could be a while* || since 1903, from *Fritz*, diminutive of proper name *Friedrich*, and propagandist dislike of all things German

on the hustle *phr.* DUTCH living as a swindler (BK, JG): 2017 *Washington Post*: *The latest conservative scam got exposed. The entire GOP is on the hustle*; 2019 *Billboard*: *McFarland was on the hustle and his scams became more audacious and bold over time* || since 1950, from *hutselen* "shake" or "toss"

open the kimono *phr.* JAPANESE to make a full disclosure of data (TD): 2015 *Time*: *He hopes that users will open the kimono on their personal data*; 2015 *Computer World*: *Many manufacturers may not want to open the kimono to its customer base* || since 1974, from *open* and *kimono* "loose traditional Japanese robe"

opinionmeister *n.* GERMAN an opinion-maker or expert (KC): **1997** *New York Magazine*: *The difference between neutral news anchor and opinionmeister is blurry*; **2008** *Time*: *The* New York Times *opinionmeister gives the Delaware Senator a glowing recommendation for veep* || since 1960s, from *opinion* and *Meister* "master"

orale (or **órale**) *excl.* SPANISH [1] hello (TD): **1993** *Bound by Honor*, film: *Orale, carnalito! What's up, ese?* **2022** Facebook: *Orale, guys! Great looking ranflas* [2] all right: **1992** *American Me*, film: *"Make sure nothing happens to these guards." "Orale"*; **2013** *Line of Duty*, film: *"Let me get a picture of you guys real quick." "Orale"* || since 1950, from *órale* "now," ultimately from *ahora* "now"

out the ying-yang *n.* CHINESE to the extreme, to excess (JG, TD): **1997** *Los Angeles Times*: *If we sent these kids to war, you'd have sick calls out the ying yang*; **2015** *State*: *We already pay out the ying-yang for everything. We can't stand any more taxes* || since 1965, from *ying-yang* "rectum" (ultimately from *yīng-yáng* "Chinese philosophy yin-yang") and analogy to *out of one's ass* "to the extreme"

oy *excl.* YIDDISH [1] I am surprised (KC): **2006** Blogspot: *Oy! Is this for real?* **2015** Trip Advisor: *The perplexed: oy, where do I start?* [2] I am alarmed, terrified, or worried (AS, KC): **2009** *Los Angeles Times*: *Oy, what am I getting myself into?* **2010** Old Jews Telling Jokes: *Oy, he says, I think we're in trouble* || since 1892, from *oy* "ay"

oye *excl.* SPANISH listen: **1992** *Aces: Iron Eagle III*, film: *Oye, vato, put that shit back in the van!* **1993** *Bound by Honor*, film: *Oye, narco, you like busting dope dealers?* || dating unknown, from *oye* "listen"

oy gevalt *excl.* YIDDISH [1] I am surprised (KC): **2003** *Chicago Tribune*: *Oy gevalt, me and my lover just won a Grammy!* **2009** *Variety*: *Shirley shouts "oy gevalt" and "oh my gaad" every ten seconds* [2] I am alarmed, terrified, or worried (KC): **1993** *New York Times*: *Oy Gevalt! New Yawkese An Endangered Dialect?* **2006** *For Your Consideration*, film: *Oy Gevalt! What have I done!* || since 1921, from *oy* and *gevald* or *gvald* "for heaven's sake," literally "violence" or "force"

oy vey *excl.* YIDDISH oh: **2011** *Wall Street Journal*: *Oy vey! Yiddish is making a comeback at colleges*; **2011** *Albany Times Union*: *Oy vey! Here's a Hanukkah story guaranteed to flip your yarmulke*; **2016** *Washington Post*: *Donald Trump thinks Ben Carson is an education expert! Oy vey!* || since 1992, from *oy vey* "oh"

P

pachanga *n.* SPANISH a big and noisy party, especially with music and dancing: **2000** *Los Angeles Times*: *She arranged the pachanga, or bash, for the Latino students who could not make it home for Thanksgiving*; **2015** *Miami New Times*: *Perez is turning his pachanga into a two-day fiesta for them* || dating unknown, from *pachanga* "big and noisy party"

pachuca *n.* SPANISH [1] a female Mexican American gang member: 2012 *San Jose Mercury News*: *A lot of people thought of the pachucos as lowlife gangsters and pachucas as their cheap girlfriends*; 2014 Megalomaniac: *Female gang members, the pachucas, also engaged in street warfare* [2] a young and tough Mexican American female: 2009 Laura Lee Cummings: *The post-World War II pachucas continued to project the tough demeanor*; 2012 *San Jose Mercury News*: *A modern pachuca is a woman who has the courage to be herself* || since 1943, from *pachuco* "flashily dressed or vulgar"

pachuco *n.* SPANISH [1] a Mexican American gang member (AS, JG, TD): 1995 *My Family*, film: *Chucho was one of the baddest pachucos on the whole East Side*; 2015 *News*, KCET-TV program: *Those pachucos, they only wanna fight when it's five or more of them* [2] a young and tough Mexican American (JG, TD): 1995 *My Family*, film: *I told you I don't want you playing with no pachuco*; 1996 *Courage Under Fire*, film: *"Where'd you get those pictures?" "Some pachuco gave them to me"* || since 1943, from *pachuco* "flashily dressed or vulgar"

padre[1] *n.* SPANISH a priest, especially a military chaplain (AS, JG, KC): 2011 *Killing*, AMC-TV series: *What's with the security, padre?* 2011 *Combat Hospital*, ABC-TV series: *We're trying to save this kid's life, padre* || since 1792, from *padre* "father"

padre[2] *adj.* SPANISH excellent: 2013 Facebook: *Luv ya! This is really padre on your part*; 2014 Weebly: *This class is very padre because the teacher is amazing* || dating unknown, from *padre* "excellent," literally "father"

paesan *n.* ITALIAN someone who comes from the same hometown or country (KC): 1987 *Miami Vice*, NBC-TV series: *There's this lawyer, Sordoni. Paesan*; 2001 *Sopranos*, HBO-TV series: *"That's a good one!" "You like it, you can use it on your paesans"* || since 1930, from *paesan* "compatriot"

paisan (or **paisano**) *n.* ITALIAN a fellow Italian or Italian American (AS, JG, TD): 1996 *Friends*, NBC-TV series: *Yo, paisan! Can I talk to you for a sec?* 2008 *Californication*, Showtime-TV series: *Mario, this is Hank, paisan* || since 1947, from *paisan* "peasant"

pal *n.* ROMANY a friend, especially a close one (AS, JG, KC, TD): 1999 *American Beauty*, film: *Janie, what happened? We used to be pals*; 2018 *Indianapolis Star*: *His pal seemed to like the idea but unfortunately didn't remember their discussion the next day* || since 1760, from *pal* "brother"

pal around *v.* ROMANY to associate or socialize (AS, JG, KC, TD): 2000 *Angel*, WB-TV series: *If you just want to pal around, call us*; 2002 *Abandon*, film: *I'd love to just pal around and talk about the past* || since 1879, from *pal* "brother"

pal around with *v.* ROMANY to associate or socialize with someone (JG, KC): 2003 *That '70s Show*, Fox-TV series: *Why would I wanna pal around with you?* 2010 *Scrubs*, NBC-TV series: *I'm looking for a work friend, someone to pal around with at the hospital* || since 1879, from *pal* "brother"

palimony *n.* ROMANY money or property awarded when an unmarried couple separate (KC): **2014** *Time*: *The contract was designed to protect Sterling if Castro decided to seek palimony*; **2013** *New York Post*: *Orman will continue to pay palimony to the mother of his four children* || since 1979, from *pal* "brother" and *alimony*

pally (or **pallie**) *n.* ROMANY a friend, especially a close one (JG, KC): **2001** *Heist*, film: *You take care, pally!* **2003** *Cheaper by the Dozen*, film: *Be careful, pally. Slow down on that stuff* || since 1892, from *pal* "brother" and suffix *-y*

palsy-walsy *adj.* ROMANY friendly, often with an undertone of uncertainty (AS, JG, KC): **1995** *Goofy Movie*, film: *Since we're all bein' palsy-walsy here, how 'bout lettin' me hook up the R.V.?* **2015** Huffington Post: *He got palsy walsy with Cameron* || since 1934, from *pal* "brother" and partial reduplication

pandejo *n.* SPANISH *potentially offensive* an irresponsible person who flouts or protests COVID-19 restrictions: **2020** *Los Angeles Times*: *Don't be a pandejo. Take COVID-19 seriously*; **2021** *Atlantic*: *The pandejos who party in their front yard are as bad as the anti-vaxxers and militia types the left rightfully mocks* || since 2020, from *pandemic* and *pendejo* "clumsy or stupid person"

panocha *n.* SPANISH *offensive* the vagina (JG): **2003** *Three Amigos*, film: *Is that a panocha between your legs?* **2005** Soy Chicano: *She can't get impregnated by me if she rubs all my mecos all over her panocha* || dating unknown, from *panocha* "vagina," ultimately from "brown sugar"

papacito *n.* SPANISH a man, especially a young and handsome one: **2013** *New Yorker*: *They called you papacito and followed you everywhere*; **2015** *Latin Times*: *Women are in love with this papacito* || since 1973, from *papacito* "little father"

paper tiger *n.* CHINESE a person or thing that appears threatening but is ineffectual (KC): **2015** *Vallejo Times Herald*: *Over the years the U.S. has shown itself to be a paper tiger, not willing to stand up for itself or its allies*; **2015** *Bloomberg*: *Is Russia a paper tiger?* || since 1952, from *zhǐ lǎohǔ* "paper tiger," popularized by Mao Zedong

papi (or **papí**) *n.* SPANISH a man, especially a Puerto Rican (JG): **2001** *Double Whammy*, film: *You love me! I'm your papi!* **2013** Enjoygram: *She's legal now and ready for all the papís!* || since 2000, from *papí* "little father"

papi chulo (or **papí chulo**) *n.* SPANISH a sexually attractive man, especially if also manipulative: **2010** *Law & Order*, NBC-TV series: *"Who was that?" "Jorge Vargas, papi chulo. Thinks he's a real ladies' man"*; **2015** *Latina Magazine*: *Tell a guy he's a papi chulo, and he'll feel like a million bucks* || dating unknown, from *papí chulo* "attractive man," literally "attractive father"

parlay *v.* [1] ITALIAN to expand or develop, especially by increasing something from a small initial outlay (JG, KC): **2021** *Forbes*: *His first attorney general parlayed this frustration into legal action*; **2022** Cinema Blend: *He eventually* *parlayed that success into a thriving TV career* [2] FRENCH to speak or talk: **2011** *Mr. Popper's Penguins*, film: *I've parlayed with the Tavern people*; **2015** Composite Arts: *We parlayed about her work* || in the first sense since 1890, from *paroli* "cast at dice"; in the second sense since 1830, from *parlez-vous* "do you speak"

parley-voo[1] *v.* FRENCH to speak, especially a foreign language (JG, KC): **2008** Barbara Kipfer and Robert Chapman: *She wondered if he parley-vooed Chinese*; **2015** Be Press: *They parley-vooed with the nuns* || since 1830, from *parlez-vous* "do you speak"

parley-voo[2] *n.* FRENCH the French language (JG): **2009** *Macleans*: *We don't speak the parley-voo around here*; **2015** Bookie Jar: *I can't understand the parley-voo like Captain Marat* || since 1754, from *parlez-vous* "do you speak"

paskudnik *n.* YIDDISH a despicable person: **1997** Joyce Antler: *They were not very different from the shlemiels and paskudniks her mother used to warn her against*; **2018** Just Jared: *You are a racist which makes you, to quote my grandmother, a paskudnik* || since 1960, from *paskudne* "nasty" and suffix *-nik*

pato *n.* SPANISH *potentially offensive* a homosexual male (JG): **2003** *In the Cut*, film: *Hey pato, kiss my ass!* **2013** *News*, ABC-TV program: *La Comay called him a "pato" – a derogatory term for gay men* || since 1967, from *pato* "duck"

peacenik *n.* YIDDISH a member of a peace movement, a pacifist (AS, KC): **2012** *New York Magazine*: *The GOP will try to portray him as some kind of peacenik*; **2012** *Globe and Mail*: *He made headlines around the world as peacenik and vocal advocate of Israeli-Palestinian détente* || since 1963, from *peace* and suffix *-nik*

pedo *n.* SPANISH [1] *potentially offensive* gas expelled from anus: **2014** Twitter: *Every time I hiccup, sneeze, cough and flatulate (a.k.a. cut a pedo), the pain is unbearable*; **2015** UF student: *The old geezer let out a smelly pedo* [2] problem or trouble (TD): **1993** *Bound by Honor*, film: *Oh, he's gonna start some pedo, homes!* **2014** YouTube: *You got pedo with him, you got pedo with me* || since 1974, from *pedo* "fart" and "problem"

pendejo[1] *n.* SPANISH *potentially offensive* [1] a stupid person (TD): **1996** *Escape from L.A.*, film: *Eh, pendejo, you think I'm stupid?* **2014** *OC Weekly*: *Some pendejo thought it funny to throw a burrito at the fasting protestors* [2] a pervert (JG): **2009** Topix: *This pendejo should get an extra special sentence if he did it*; **2014** Twitter: *You are a sick pendejo looking for validation of your abuse* || since 1974 in the first sense, since 2000 in the second, from *pendejo* "clumsy or stupid person," ultimately "pubic hair"

pendejo[2] *adj.* SPANISH *potentially offensive* [1] stupid (TD): **1995** *My Family*, film: *Yeah, well, the law's pendejo!* **2011** *Dallas Observer*: *I know illegals who are more American than your pendejo ass* [2] perverted: **1993** *Full Eclipse*, film: *Clean the fucking pendejo scum!* **2014** Prime Wire: *This movie is very pendejo* || since 1974 in the first sense, since 2000 in the second, from *pendejo* "clumsy or stupid person," ultimately "pubic hair"

perfectamundo *adv.* SPANISH excellent (TD): **2015** *Snow Cake*, film: *"I'll put the garbage out." "Perfectamundo!"*; **2015** Facebook: *The translation is simply perfectamundo* ‖ since 1992, from *perfect* and *-mundo* "world"

perfecto *adj.* SPANISH excellent (JG, TD): **2016** *Texas Monthly*: *Your own response is perfecto for your particular case*; **2015** Mediaite: *Carol is perfecto for CNN* ‖ since 1987, from *perfecto* "perfect"

perico *n.* SPANISH cocaine (JG, TD): **2007** International Sex Guide: *You can buy a kilo of perico in Medellin for 200 dollars, sell it for 24,000 in the United States*; **2014** Twitter: *It's a bathtub full of whiskey, a kilo of perico, and at least six hookers* ‖ since 1975, from *perico* "parakeet"

pero like *adv.* SPANISH however: **2014** *Miami New Times*: *"Suzie, that boy is no good for you." "Pero like, he's super-hot"*; **2015** *Miami Herald*: *Only in Miami are phrases such as "pero like" and "que cute" thrown around* ‖ since 2000, from *pero* "but" and *like*

phony, phoney[1] *adj.* IRISH GAELIC fake or false (AS, JG, KC, TD): **2013** *Wolf of Wall Street*, film: *From the two million shares offered for sale, a million belonged to me held in phony accounts*; **2013** *Last Vegas*, film: *Everything about you is phony: your teeth, your hair, even your tan is phony* ‖ since 1900, from *fáinne* "(fake) ring"

phony, phoney[2] *n.* IRISH GAELIC [1] a fake or false thing (AS, JG, KC, TD): **1990** *Goodfellas*, film: *My Social Security cards and driver's licenses were phonies*; **2013** News, NBC-TV program: *The tickets she purchased from a stranger on Craigslist were phonies* [2] a person who affects some identity or role, an insincere poseur (AS, JG, KC, TD): **1999** *American Beauty*, film: *Well, your mom's the one who's embarrassing. What a phony!* **2005** *Batman Begins*, film: *All of you phonies, all of you two-faced friends . . . please, leave me in peace!* ‖ since 1900, from *fáinne* "(fake) ring"

phony-baloney, phoney-baloney *adj.* IRISH GAELIC fake or false (JG, KC, TD): **2011** *New York Magazine*: *We don't need your kind of manipulation and phony-baloney help*; **2018** *Forbes*: *People can sniff out phony-baloney brands from miles away* ‖ since 1936, from *fáinne* "(fake) ring" and *baloney* "nonsense"

phony up, phoney up *v.* IRISH GAELIC to falsify or fabricate (JG, TD): **2014** *Orlando Sentinel*: *She stabbed herself to phony up evidence and make herself look like a victim*; **2017** Nevada Today: *You can't phony up genuine relationships* ‖ since 1936, from *fáinne* "(fake) ring"

phooey *excl.* YIDDISH [1] what a terrible smell (KC): **1996** *Long Kiss Goodnight*, film: *Oh, phooey! I burned the damned muffins!* **2011** YouTube: *Phooey! That stinks!* [2] I am disgusted (KC): **1990** *Chicago Tribune*: *Reagan said "phooey" to suggestions that he's undermining peace prospects with his insistence on continued aid to the rebels*; **2003** *Girls Will Be Girls*, film: *"I love you!" "Phooey!"* ‖ since 1902, from *fui* "ugh"

phudnik *n.* YIDDISH a boring or annoying person with a Ph.D.: **2000** *Los Angeles Times*: *"I'm a phudnik. That's a nudnik with a Ph.D.," she explained*;

2004 *New Yorker: Legman was disdainful of folklorists with Ph.Ds., whom he called "phudniks"* || dating unknown, from blending *Ph.D.* and *(n)udnik* "boring person"

pickaninny (or **piccaninny**) *n.* SPANISH *offensive* a black child (AS, JG, TD): **2005** *Washington Post: It is a classic "pickaninny," a black child, oafish and with apelike features*; **2015** *New York Post: They referred to Harrison as a "pickaninny" and "the Ethiopian"* || since 1785, from *pequeño* "tiny"

pickney *n.* SPANISH *offensive* a black child (AS, JG, TD): **2010** Bev Clarke: *These ain't days to bring so many pickneys in this world*; **2014** Tumblr: *I'm back in school and have to worry about what to teach these damn pickneys* || since 1799, from *pequeño* "small"

pinche *adj.* SPANISH *offensive* despicable (TD): **2006** *Walkout*, film: *The pinche cops across the street hassled me, man*; **2010** *Our Family Wedding*, film: *Why ask a question when you know the answer, pinche puta?* || since 1974, from *pinche* "fucking," ultimately from "kitchen boy"

pinga *n.* SPANISH *offensive* the penis (JG, TD): **2014** Wordnik: *Sarah got tired of sucking his pinga and told him to finish himself off*; **2014** Alan Holloway: *Papa never played with his pinga* || since 1960, from *pingo* "mischievous" or "naughty"

pinta (or **la pinta**) *n.* SPANISH a prison (JG, TD): **2007** Sandro Meallet: *"If you only knew how it happens in the pinta." Hector's mind drifted back to incarceration for a few seconds*; **2016** *News*, KOB-TV program: *You don't wanna go to la pinta* || since 1971, from *pinta* "penitentiary" and *pinto* "painted black and white," from the color combination of older prisoner uniforms

pinto *n.* SPANISH a convict or ex-convict (JG, TD): **2007** Urban Dictionary: *That pinto was just released from Pelican Bay*; **2009** Manuel G. Gonzales: *Less numerous than their black counterparts, Latino pintos (convicts or ex-convicts) represent a statistically significant population* || since 1978, from *pinta* "penitentiary" and *pinto* "painted black and white," from the color combination of older prisoner uniforms

pisher *n.* YIDDISH [1] an inexperienced young person (KC): **2018** *Kominsky Method*, Netflix-TV series: *Those little pishers, they are making a million dollars a week*; **2022** *Marvelous Mrs. Maisel*, Amazon-TV series: *I knew you when you were a pisher* [2] an insignificant or inconsequential person (AS, JG, KC): **1996** Laurence Goldstein: *In Hollywood, when you're a writer, you're just a pisher*; **2006** Huffington Post: *Did that stop the old kvetch, that pisher? No, never!* || since 1941, from *pisher* "inexperienced or insignificant person," literally "someone who urinates"

pisto *n.* SPANISH an alcoholic beverage, especially beer: **1993** *Bound by Honor*, film: *Relax! Here, have some pisto!* **2005** *Harsh Times*, film: *Well, we got pisto, we got frajos. Only one thing's missin': biyatches!* || dating unknown, from *pisto* "traditional Spanish dish from La Mancha, similar to ratatouille"

placa *n.* SPANISH [1] a nickname, especially an artistic nickname on a public wall (JG, TD): 2011 Samba: *His name is Emilio, but placa is Chuco*; 2013 Los Santos Roleplay: *What set you from on the outside, and what's your placa?* [2] the police or a police officer (JG): 2012 Alfonso Moret: *Let's vamoose. The placa is coming*; 2015 UF student: *The placa showed up almost right away* || since 1974 in the first sense, since 1992 in the second, from *placa* "plaque" or "badge"

plata *n.* SPANISH money: 1993 *Bound by Honor*, film: *Gilbert can smell money from across town. He came to help you spend that plata*; 2011 Yahoo Answers: *I think America has enough plata to buy him* || dating unknown, from *plata* "money," ultimately from *plata* "silver"

plonk *n.* FRENCH cheap and inferior wine (AS, JG, KC): 2009 *New York Times*: *He is an enthusiastic quaffer of plonk*; 2009 *Globe and Mail*: *You'll stand around, have a few laughs, swill some plonk* || since 1960, from *vin blanc* "white wine"

plotz[1] *v.* YIDDISH to lose emotional control, to burst with emotion, especially with anger, irritation, or frustration (AS, JG, KC): 1999 *Angel*, WB-TV series: *Here he comes. He's gonna plotz when he sees us*; 2004 *Meet the Fockers*, film: *"You didn't tell Dad?" "Not yet. He's gonna plotz"* || since 1920, from *platsn* "to burst"

plotz[2] *n.* YIDDISH a stupid person (JG): 2010 Facebook: *The guy's a real plotz. Just look what he did!* 2015 *New York Times*: *He's such a plotz!* || since 1961, from *platsn* "to burst"

plotzed *adj.* YIDDISH drunk (JG, KC): 2005 *Globe and Mail*: *They bring their wives when they'd rather get plotzed and bond*; 2011 Capitol Confidential: *Imagine the arguments we'd have once we got plotzed* || since 1962, from *platsn* "to burst"

plush *adj.* FRENCH luxurious, stylish, and thus expensive (AS, KC): 2003 *Will & Grace*, NBC-TV series: *How would you like to go back to my plush suite at the Palace Hotel?* 2012 *Kitchen Nightmares*, Fox-TV series: *Look at that marble on the bar. That's plush* || since 1927, from *peluche* "soft and costly fabric"

plushy *adj.* FRENCH luxurious, stylish, and thus expensive (KC): 2006 *Battlestar Galactica*, Sci-Fi-TV series: *You're sitting in your plushy little office*; 2013 *Catholic Herald*: *They looked after us well, installing us in the very plushy Jerusalem Hilton* || since 1927, from *peluche* "soft and costly fabric" and suffix -*y*

pocho *n.* SPANISH *potentially offensive* a Mexican American who emulates behavior or values of the non-Hispanic majority (AS, TD): 2014 *Los Angeles Times*: *He was mocked as a pretty boy and a pocho – not a real Mexican*; 2021 LAist: *Many saw me as a pocho because I spoke English and lacked fluency in Spanish* || since 1944, from *pocho* "faded"

Polack[1] *n.* POLISH *offensive* a Pole or a person of Polish descent (AS, JG, KC, TD): 2005 *Angels in America*, HBO-TV series: *Why was the Kosciuszko Bridge* *named after a Polack?* **2012** *Seven Psychopaths*, film: *The Polack married a nigger?* ‖ since 1879, from *Polack* "Pole"

Polack² *adj.* POLISH *offensive* Polish: **2009** *Seattle Weekly*: *I used to frequent a cantina in Chicago where half of the bar was Polack, the other half beaner*; **2016** Persephone Magazine: *It's a Very Polack Christmas* ‖ since 1879, from *Polack* "Pole"

Polacky *adj.* POLISH *offensive* Polish: **2011** Narkive: *The Polacky pedophiles will say and do anything to deflect public reaction*; **2016** Facebook: *He found himself sequestered within seclusion of a Polacky spa* ‖ since 1879, from *Polack* "Pole" and suffix *-y*

politico *n.* SPANISH a politician, especially unscrupulous (AS, TD): **2010** *Ghost Writer*, film: *Look, it's a new ghost writer he needs, not another goddamn politico*; **2014** *Los Angeles Times*: *He takes a moment to marvel at the all-star team of thinkers and policos who gave birth to the United States* ‖ since 1893, from *politico* "politician"

pollo *n.* SPANISH an immigrant smuggled from Mexico to the USA (JG, KC): **2004** *Tucson Weekly*: *Thousands of pollos (smuggled immigrants in border lingo) are out there and headed north*; **2012** *Vice*: *The cartel operates long the Gulf, trafficking coke and Central American illegals called pollos* ‖ since 1980, from *pollo* "chicken"

Polski *n.* POLISH *offensive* a Pole or a person of Polish descent (TD): **2012** Word Press: *Neil and Ola are a Scot and a Polski who like to challenge national stereotypes*; **2011** Chitown Racing: *I've got two races set up with some Polskis* ‖ since 1997, from *polski* "Polish"

poon *n.* FRENCH *offensive* [1] a woman considered as a sex object (AS, JG, KC, TD): **2005** *40 Year Old Virgin*, film: *I need some poon. I need genital to genital connection*; **2016** *Film*: *Daddy's gotta go get me some poon* [2] the vagina (JG, TD): **2013** *Village Voice*: *She lifted up her leg and pushed her poon on the window and started grinding against it*; **2015** Bustle: *Luckily, there are moisturizers you can use to keep your poon happy* ‖ since 1957 in the first sense, since 1968 in the second, from *poontang*, ultimately from *putain* "prostitute"

poontang *n.* FRENCH *offensive* [1] a woman considered as a sex object (AS, JG, KC, TD): **1999** *South Park*, film: *I can't wait for our first shore leave so I can get me some fucking poontang*; **2008** *King of Kong*, film: *I got a gnarly piece of poontang* [2] the vagina (JG, TD): **2003** Urban Dictionary: *Her poontang was the warmest I had ever fucked*; **2010** Blogger: *She showed me her poontang and smiled* ‖ since 1929 in the first sense, since 1947 in the second, from *putain* "prostitute"

poppycock *n.* DUTCH nonsense: **2014** *Los Angeles Times*: *In both cases, the theory has been proved to be poppycock*; **2016** *Alaska Dispatch News*: *It's all poppycock. It's all illusion* ‖ since 1865, from *pappekak* "soft dung"

porfa *adv.* SPANISH please: **2008** Daily Motion: *Vote for me, porfa*; **2014** *Miami New Times*: *You're just more likely to hear the shortened "porfa" down here* ‖ since 2000, from *por favor* "please"

pot *n.* SPANISH marijuana (AS, JG, KC): **2012** *Ted*, film: *All I do is smoke pot and watch movies*; **2018** *Buffalo News*: *Niagara Falls police confiscated the pot but did not arrest Flickner* ‖ since 1938, from *potiguaya* "marijuana leaves"

pothead *n.* SPANISH a user of marijuana, especially a heavy user (AS, JG, KC): **2000** *Meet the Parents*, film: *"Are you a pothead, Focker?" "What? No, Jack. I pass on grass all the time"*; **2018** *Dallas Morning News*: *I hate to break it to the potheads, but marijuana is still illegal in Texas* ‖ since 1955, from *pot(iguaya)* "marijuana leaves" and *head*

potch¹, potsh *n.* YIDDISH a slap or smack (JG): **1991** Leroy Ostransky: *I had to give the punk a potch*; **2009** *Seattle Times*: *He earned a potch in the tuchis* ‖ since 1966, from *patsh* "slap"

potch², potsh *v.* YIDDISH to slap or smack (JG): **2001** Sol Steinmetz: *My mother potched my face*; **2010** *Foreign Policy*: *Go kvetch somewhere else, before you get potched and start crying* ‖ since 1892, from *patshn* "to slap"

pow-wow¹ *n.* ALGONQUIN a meeting or discussion (AS, JG, KC, TD): **1998** *Parent Trap*, film: *I suggest we continue with this little pow-wow inside*; **2012** *American Banker*: *What's the purpose of this unusual executive pow-wow?* ‖ since 1812, from *pow'waw* "medicine man" or "ceremony"

pow-wow² *v.* ALGONQUIN to talk or discuss (AS, JG, KC, TD): **2013** *Duke Chronicle*: *We sort of pow-wowed about it and decided that we had to make it happen*; **2015** *Asheville Citizen-Times*: *Cindy and her mother pow-wowed around the kitchen table* ‖ since 1812, from *pow'waw* "medicine man" or "ceremony"

PR *n.* SPANISH [1] Puerto Rico (AS, JG, TD): **2002** *25ᵗʰ Hour*, film: *You've never been to PR in your life?* **2014** *National Geographic*: *The majority of the Spanish that came to PR during the last 500 years were good people* [2] a Puerto Rican (JG, TD): **2007** Trip Advisor: *Many PR's receive federal assistance*; **2015** *American Interest*: *The PRs are again fleeing the island in droves headed to the US* [3] a potent variety of marijuana, especially if grown in or imported from Panama (JG): **2010** Smoked Meat: *I've only smoked PR once before*; **2014** International Cannagraphic: *he sold his PR for only a $120 a pound* ‖ since 1909 in the first sense, since 1957 in the second, since 1969 in the third, from *Puerto* or *Panama Red* respectively

prima donna *n.* ITALIAN a temperamental person with inflated ego (AS, JG, KC): **1993** *Groundhog Day*, film: *"Rita, I can't stay here!" "Prima donna!"*; **2008** *Tropic Thunder*, film: *I am dealing with a bunch of prima donnas* ‖ since 1936, from *prima donna* "chief female singer in an opera," literally "first lady"

primo (or **el primo**) *adj.* SPANISH the best (JG): **2013** *Shameless*, Showtime-TV series: *"Smells good!" "Yeah, it's primo stuff, twenty bucks a joint"*; **2014** *Austin Chronicle*: *The people's choice taco winner was el primo* ‖ since 1970, from *el primo* "something which is the best"

pronto *adv.* SPANISH immediately or without delay (AS, KC, TD): **1994** *Pulp Fiction*, film: *We got to get off the road pronto*; **2014** *USA Today*: *I'm going to need him to call me pronto* || since 1850, from *pronto* "soon" or "promptly"

puerco *n.* SPANISH a boorish and coarse man, especially if gluttonous: **1993** *Bound by Honor*, film: *I want my fuckin' chop, puerco!* **2014** Meet Up: *I could have made a real purco of myself feeding on the corn cake* || dating unknown, from *puerco* "boor," ultimately from *puerco* "pig" or "pork"

pull an el floppo *phr.* SPANISH to collapse or fail (JG): **1993** *Seattle Times*: *This week, the widely watched Dow, a compendium of 30 blue-chip stocks, pulled an el floppo, tumbling in five straight sessions*; **2012** Boston Online: *You mean the ones who pulled an el floppo last September?* || since 1936, from *flop* and mock Spanish prefix word *el* and suffix *-o*

pull an el foldo *phr.* SPANISH to collapse or fail (JG): **2009** New Jersey Real Estate Report: *It was all about trying to help people get out of debt. What a silly concept! It's smarter to pull an el foldo*; **2011** *Washington Monthly*: *All other candidates would have pulled an el foldo as well* || since 1943, from *fold* and mock Spanish prefix word *el* and suffix *-o*

puss *n.* IRISH GAELIC the face (JG, KC): **2018** *Entertainment Weekly*: *She can be seen without an ounce of makeup on her puss*; **2017** *Chicago Now*: *Is his puss sour because he can't grab any, including Melania's?* || since 1890, from *pus* "mouth"

puta *n.* SPANISH *offensive* [1] a prostitute (AS, JG, KC, TD): **2002** *White Oleander*, film: *It's the puta. She's so ugly now*; **2013** TMZ: *I will pay to see this puta in action* [2] a sexually promiscuous woman (AS, TD): **2007** *Savage Grace*, film: *That's right. That's you I'm talking about, you little puta*; **2009** *Bring It On: Fight to the Finish*, film: *Your sister told you I'm some puta chasing after a rich white boy* [3] a despicable woman (JG): **1995** *Desperado*, film: *You owe me $300, puta*; **2009** Fan Fiction: *I never liked that puta Carina. She is bad for the jefe* || since 1936 in the first two senses, since 1967 in the third, from *puta* "prostitute" or "despicable woman"

puta madre *excl.* SPANISH *offensive* [1] I am irritated: **2002** *Frida*, film: *"The doctor says you should eat more." "Puta madre!"*; **2013** *Dead in Tombstone*, film: *Puta madre, get out of my sight!* [2] I am surprised: **2006** *Dexter*, Showtime-TV series: *"You remember now?" "Puta madre!"*; **2013** UCB student: *Are you his cousin? Puta madre!* || dating unknown, from *puta* "prostitute" or "despicable woman" and *madre* "mother"

puto *n.* SPANISH *offensive* [1] a male prostitute (JG, TD): **2009** *La Mission*, film: *Suck on this, puto!* **2014** Hollywood Reporter: *Did you know this guy is a puto?* [2] a male homosexual (JG, TD): **1993** *Bound by Honor*, film: *Welcome to San Quentin. You want me to rape you, puto?* **2014** *OC Weekly*: *Jump off the nearest bridge, the world will not miss a puto like you* [3] a despicable man (JG): **1990** *Rookie*, film: *Did you hear what that puto said about my car?* **2014** iPhoneogram: *I never liked that puto*

|| since 1972 in the first sense, since 1992 in the second, since 1977 in the third, from *puto* "male prostitute" or "despicable man"

putz[1] *n.* YIDDISH [1] the penis (AS, JG, KC): **1990** *Q & A*, film: *I'm sitting here, pulling my putz*; **1994** *Quiz Show*, film: *That big uncircumcised putz is on the cover of Time magazine* [2] a despicable person, especially stupid or ineffectual (AS, JG, KC): **1993** *Fatal Instinct*, film: *They'll think I'm a putz for passing up a sure thing*; **2016** *New Republic*: *Donald Trump may be a putz, but he's not meshuggener* || since 1934 in the first sense, since 1950s in the second, from *pots* "despicable person," literally "penis"

putz[2] *v.* YIDDISH to waste time doing nothing (AS, JG, KC): **2008** *Deal*, film: *Enough putzing, enough playing!* **2011** *Charleston Gazette*: *James loves putzing around his Charleston house* || since 1953, from *pots* "despicable person," literally "penis"

putz around *v.* YIDDISH to waste time doing nothing (AS, JG, KC): **2012** *Sports*, NBC-TV program: *Every single second you putz around, you are increasing the probability that you will lose*; **2012** *Globe and Mail*: *Dr. Dunn dismissed Dr. Galea's treatments as unscientific and described him as putzing around* || since 1970s, from *pots* "despicable person," literally "penis," and verbal particle *around*

putz around with *v.* YIDDISH [1] to provoke or play with someone: **1994** Kinky Friedman: *Sheriff Frances Kaiser was no one to putz around with; she was a big, tall, no-nonsense type*; **2006** My Space: *He did putz around with me a lot during my shift* [2] to tamper or meddle: **2011** *Examiner*: *Fans will be able to putz around with the customization*; **2011** *Sailing Magazine*: *I can sit below and putz around with charts, plotters and dividers* || since 1970s, from *pots* "despicable person," literally "penis," and verbal particles *around with*

putz with *v.* YIDDISH [1] to provoke or play with someone: **2011** Google Blogs: *He'd putz with me and my friends*; **2011** NYU student: *This guy is crazy, don't putz with him* [2] to tamper or meddle: **2010** *Los Angeles Times*: *You could clearly see him putzing with the guitar and pedals*; **2016** Madison Online: *James was always putzing with something and loved to figure out how things worked* || since 1970s, from *pots* "despicable person," literally "penis," and verbal particle *with*

Q

quack *n.* DUTCH an incompetent or fraudulent doctor (AS, JG, KC, TD): **1994** *Ed Wood*, film: *The surgeon turned out to be a quack*; **2015** *Washington Examiner*: *On Thursday, the famous doctor on television will hit back against charges that he's a quack* || since 1659, from Middle Dutch *quacken* "to prattle"

que[1] (or **qué**) *adv.* SPANISH how: **2003** *Miami New Times*: *As savvy muchachos know, it is the number one show on commercial television, and que nice!* **2013** *Blaze You Out*, film: *Loyalty! Que cute!* || dating unknown, from *qué* "what" or "how"

que² (or **qué**) *pron.* SPANISH what: **2009** *Crank: High Voltage*, film: *"You, Ferret, this ain't Roots, man!" "Que?"*; **2017** *Snowfall*, FX-TV series: *"Do you think it was weird Enrique has this oyster on his wall?" "Que?"* || dating unknown, from *qué* "what" or "how"

que onda (or **qué onda**) *sent.* SPANISH [1] what is going on: **2002** *CSI: Crime Scene Investigation*, CBS-TV series: *Que onda? What's the lab crime want with me?* **2011** *Unforgettable*, NBC-TV series: *Que onda? You need more help with your investigation?* [2] hello: **2010** *Southland*, NBC-TV series: *Que onda, brother! How are you?* **2010** Blogger: *So he comes up to me and says, "Que onda!"* || dating unknown, from *que onda* "how are things," literally "how are waves"

que pasa (or **qué pasa**) *sent.* SPANISH [1] what is going on (JG, KC): **1991** *Terminator 2: Judgment Day*, film: *Que pasa? What's up?* **2014** Vera R. Moreno: *Hey, you two, que pasa? What is all the whispering about?* [2] hello (JG): **2007** *Breakfast with Scott*, film: *Dammy, que pasa? What's up?* **2013** Facebook: *Que pasa guys! When are y'all going on tour again and coming to Dallas?* || since 1996, from *qué pasa?* "what is happening?"

R

rabbi *n.* YIDDISH a benefactor or sponsor (JG, KC, TD): **2008** William Safire: *In political relationships, a rabbi is primarily a sponsor or protector, although there is a second meaning of mentor or teacher*; **2003** *Wire*, HBO-TV series: *I figure when the detail's over, I go back to straight narcotics. Try to get over to Dawson's shift, find a new rabbi* || since 1932, from *rebe* "benefactor or sponsor," literally "rabbi"

-rama (or **-arama, -orama**) *suffix* GREEK a spectacular display or instance of what is indicated (JG, KC, TD): **2010** Metro: *Highlights include "Pornorama," a marathon showing of porn films*; **2016** Abe Books: *Various chapters of this sexorama detail lusty life in the big city* || since 1954, from *panorama*, ultimately from *(h)orama* "sight" or "view"

ranfla *n.* SPANISH a car with a lowered suspension or otherwise customized (JG): **2007** *Riverfront Times*: *It is the same as jacking a ranfla, which involves a nominal knowledge of hot-wiring*; **2013** GTA Forums: *They are hanging out in their driveways in their ranflas kicking loud-ass music* || since 1981, from *ranfla* "ramp"

rapmeister *n.* GERMAN a skillful performer of rap songs (KC): **1992** *Black Enterprise*: *After two minutes the rapmeister readjusts his baseball cap, bids the banker goodbye, and grins*; **2009** *New York Times*: *Tracing his path from baby crack dealer to Broadway rapmeister, Andersen gracefully shimmies in and out of the identities he assumed to survive in a county jail* || dating unknown, from *rap* and *Meister* "master"

Raza or (**La Raza**) *n.* SPANISH [1] an advocacy group for Latin Americans: **2009** Daily Kos: *He told the members of La Raza how proud he was to have Hispanic blood* *in his family*; **2016** *Nashville Scene*: *La Raza is the largest Latino nonprofit organization in the country* [2] Latin American heritage, especially as a source of pride: **2014** Convicted Artist: *I'm a local artist from El Chuco, and I'm just trying to represent for all my raza!* **2015** Huffington Post: *You were the first woman I saw in person, who fought for la raza* || dating unknown, from *la raza* "race"

real-estatenik *n.* YIDDISH a real-estate agent: **2000** Rachel Rubin: *An example is Mickey's description of his mother as a "buttinsky" or Herman's reference to Baruch Goldfarb as a "real-estatenik"*; **2012** Daily Kos: *Now the real estateniks are eager to sell or rent all the new luxury apartments* || dating unknown, from *real-estate* and suffix *-nik*

reefer *n.* SPANISH marijuana or marijuana cigarette (AS, JG, KC, RS, TD): **2000** *Traffic*, film: *If a judge or politician puts a reefer in their mouth, I'll do a story on it*; **2016** *South Florida Reporter*: *It's probably safe to say Poppy Bush never touched a reefer* || since 1923, from *grifa* "marijuana"

refusenik *n.* YIDDISH [1] someone who refuses to cooperate or refuses something (AS): **2011** *New York Magazine*: *But as his time on Twitter has gone by, even this onetime refusenik has shown signs of caving*; **2012** *Globe and Mail*: *The number of refuseniks now encompasses new parts of the political spectrum, including educated professionals* [2] a Jew from the former Soviet Union who was refused permission to leave the country (AS): **2009** *Perestroika*, film: *You're the famous Greenberg, the first physicist refusenik!* **2014** *Americans*, FX-TV series: *He's an eloquent advocate for those Jewish refuseniks still trapped in the Soviet Union* || since 1968, from *refuse* and suffix *-nik*

reshtetle, reshtetl *v.* YIDDISH to move from New York City to Florida, especially from Brooklyn to Boca Raton: **1994** *Newsweek*: *Director David Gordon keeps his spirited cast bopping like a re-shtetled Tommy Tune*; **2002** Payson Stevens: *To reshtetle is to move from Brooklyn to Boca, only to find that the people in your co-op or condo are the same ones you left* || dating unknown, from *re* and *shtetl* "small Jewish town or village in Eastern Europe" and meiotic association with New York City

rican *n.* SPANISH *offensive* a Puerto Rican (JG, TD): **2006** *Departed*, film: *Fucking Ricans think they know everything*; **2015** Philly Voice: *They should build it and add the sign "whites and any people other than black and ricans only"* || since 1967, from *Puerto Rican*

roca (or **la roca**) *n.* SPANISH crack cocaine (TD): **2003** Urban Dictionary: *Hey, you got some roca?* **2013** Blogspot: *Asking the locals where you can score some "roca" (crack)* || since 1994, from *roca* "rock"

rojo flow *n.* SPANISH *offensive* menstruation (TD): **2015** Tumblr: *Rojo flow right now!* **2009** Tom Dalzell: *Rojo flow is the bleed period of the menstrual cycle* || since 2001, from *rojo* "red" and *flow*

ruca *n.* SPANISH [1] a female gang member (JG): **1993** Tey Diana Rebolledo: *It has been captured in Chicana literature as the streetwise, tough ruca seen in poems by*

Hernandez and Vigil; **2006** New Mexico Boxing: *You were so tough. What happened to the tough ruca?* [2] a girlfriend or wife, especially the one of an inmate (TD): **1993** *Bound by Honor*, film: *The rucas got their hearts broke;* **1995** *My Family*, film: *You want me to marry this ruca?* ‖ since 1971 in the first sense, since 1992 in the second, from *ruca* "old and worn-out" or "useless"

ruco *n.* SPANISH a boyfriend or husband (TD): **2006** Urban Dictionary: *Hands off that boy, he's my ruco;* **2011** Gregory Boyle: *What's your ruco got planned for you tonight?* ‖ since 1950, from *ruco* "old and worn-out" or "useless"

running dog *n.* CHINESE a subordinate with little authority (AS, KC, TD): **2012** *New York Review of Books: They say I'm a running dog of the Americans;* **2014** *New York Times: Stockman tried to tar him as a running dog of the left* ‖ since 1937, from *zǒu gǒu* "run dog," a dog that runs at its master's command

Russki (or **Russky**) *n.* RUSSIAN *offensive* a Russian or a person of Russian descent (AS, JG, TD): **2013** *Family*, film: *Boris Godunov, it's a story written by a Russki;* **2019** *Billions*, Showtime-TV series: *With that fucking Russky backing them up, my options are limited* ‖ since 1858, from *Ruskiy* "Russian"

S

Saigon quickstep *n.* VIETNAMESE diarrhea, especially as contracted in a foreign country (TD): **2009** Tom Dalzell: *No matter how bad the combat rations were, none produced the dreaded Saigon quickstep;* **2015** Carol Burke: *None produced the dreaded "Saigon quickstep," as impressively as did the local street food* ‖ since 1970, from *Saigon* and *quickstep* "a type of fast dance"

Saigon tea *n.* VIETNAMESE illegally distilled alcohol (TD): **2015** *Pittsburgh Post-Gazette: Saigon tea was a flavored concoction that was the expensive ticket to a bar girl's company;* **2020** *New Republic: Many Vietnamese women sold glasses of "Saigon tea" to lonely U.S. grunts* ‖ since 1970, from *Saigon* and *tea*

salsa gringa *n.* SPANISH a mild salsa: **2013** Yelp: *They have super-hot salsa, pico de gallo, salsa gringa (mild);* **2016** Facebook: *Pictured here is their burrito, stuffed with guacamole and salsa gringa* ‖ since 1970, from *salsa* and *gringa* "white woman from an English-speaking country"

-san *suffix* JAPANESE someone involved in or characterized by what is indicated: **2010** Blogger: *The boss-san will be very angry;* **2018** *Duluth News Tribune: Bob, like other Marines, was assigned a "mama san" to care for his linen, uniform, and general bunk area* ‖ since 1940, from honorific ending *san*

sans *prep.* FRENCH without: **2004** *Sideways*, film: *She's not married. No rock. She came to the bar sans rock;* **2015** *Albuquerque Journal: She landed parts in school and community plays before moving to New York with her husband sans money or contacts* ‖ dating unknown, from *sans* "without"

sashay *v.* FRENCH to walk in a casual way (AS, JG, KC, TD): **2007** *Day Zero*, film: *I sashayed around the stage*; **2010** *Treme*, HBO-TV series: *I'm watching people sashay* ‖ since 1836, from *chassé* "gliding step in dancing"

sausagefest *n.* GERMAN *potentially offensive* a party or group where the vast majority of the people are males: **2015** Salon: *If there's one thing you can bank on with Samantha Bee's forthcoming TBS show it's that it won't be a sausage fest*; **2017** *New York Magazine*: *The Trump Cabinet Is Shaping Up to Be a Total Sausagefest* ‖ dating unknown, from *sausage* "penis" and *Fest* "festival," and analogy to *sausage party*

savvy[1] *n.* SPANISH intelligence (AS, KC, TD): **2010** *Yale Alumni Magazine*: *These hidden talents include creative abilities, practical savvy, and wisdom*; **2014** *USA Today*: *Beside talent, it takes savvy and steely nerves to handle the pressure* ‖ since 1825, from *saber* "to know"

savvy[2] *adj.* SPANISH intelligent (AS, KC): **2010** *People Magazine*: *He easily broke them down with his good looks and savvy way with words*; **2016** *Wyoming Tribune*: *Foxes are way too savvy to tangle with dogs* ‖ since 1785, from *saber* "to know"

savvy[3] *v.* SPANISH to comprehend (AS, KC, TD): **2007** *Epic Movie*, film: *This isn't even a working pirate ship, savvy?* **2011** *Sniper: Reloaded*, film: *You do not get to use the can till your mission is completed. Savvy?* ‖ since 1785, from *saber* "to know"

sawski, sawsky *n.* YIDDISH a ten-dollar bill (JG): **1984** *Billboard*: *Hurt slipped her two sawskies and a fin to pay off the bets*; **2007** My Space: *We rigged his room with a one-way whorehouse mirror and charged a sawski to watch it* ‖ since 1944, from *saw* "ten dollars" and suffix *-ski*

sayonara *excl.* JAPANESE goodbye (AS, TD): **2013** *Wolverine*, film: *You asked me to come say goodbye. Sayonara!* **2015** *Daily Beast*: *He finished fifth in Iowa with 0.9 percent of the vote and said sayonara* ‖ since 1968, from *sayōnara* "goodbye"

scarol, scarole *n.* ITALIAN money: **2007** Urban Dictionary: *I'm here for the fuckin scarol*; **2021** *Many Saints of Newark*, film: *My grandfather was an associate but he stacked more scarol than any of the made guys* ‖ dating unknown, from *scarola* "endive"

schaygetz *see* shaygetz

schlemazel, shlemazel *n.* YIDDISH [1] an unlucky and gullible person, especially a fool (AS, JG): **2015** *American Thinker*: *They tried to shift blame for their own incompetence to a schlemazel*; **2013** *Bleacher Report*: *The following are the NBA's biggest schlemazels* [2] a difficult and confused situation (KC): **1982** *Jewish Language Review*: *Schlemazel is a confused situation generally*; **2006** Yahoo Groups: *He got in a little schlemazel* ‖ since 1948, from *shlimazl* "someone with a chronic bad luck," literally "bad luck" or "bad constellation"

schlemiel, shlemiel *n.* YIDDISH a stupid, awkward, and clumsy person who is also unlucky (AS, JG): **1991** *Los Angeles Times*: *The father is inept (a schlemiel) and* *the grandfather complains (a kvetch)*; **1999** *Chicago Tribune*: *He will be perceived as a schlemiel for taking the job under the circumstances* ‖ since 1870, from *shlemil* "stupid and unlucky bungler," probably from the name of the main character in Adelbert von Chamisso's German fable *Peter Schlemihls Wundersame Geschichte*

schlep¹, shlep *v.* YIDDISH [1] to drag, carry, or pull, especially with difficulty (AS, JG, KC): **1999** *Entrapment*, film: *I'm astonished that you could do it. All that schlepping at your tender age*; **2011** *Macleans*: *It's good for schlepping crap from Target* [2] to move slowly or with difficulty (AS, JG, KC): **2002** *Get a Clue*, film: *Brooklyn? I'm not schlepping out to Brooklyn*; **2009** *Los Angeles Times*: *They also depict their characters basking in such fair-weather pleasures as hanging out with family, eating waffle cones, playing board games and schlepping across the sand dunes* ‖ since 1930 in the first sense, since 1971 in the second, from *shlepn* "to drag" and *shlepn zikh* "to trudge"

schlep², shlep *n.* YIDDISH [1] a long, slow, or difficult journey (AS, JG, KC): **2005** *Los Angeles Times*: *Because it was such a schlep, I picked up only a couple of bags*; **2006** *Boston Legal*, ABC-TV series: *If I needed surgery, I might consider making the schlep* [2] a stupid, incompetent and clumsy person (AS, JG, KC): **2008** *Kings of South Beach*, film: *Change the way your dress. You look like a schlep*; **2009** Oregon Live: *Her sympathy for the pathetic schlep gets in the way* ‖ since 1958 in the first sense, since 1939 in the second, from *shlepn* "to drag"

schleppable, shleppable *adj.* YIDDISH that can be moved or carried (KC): **2001** *PC World*: *Canon is certainly more schleppable*; **2002** *New Statesman*: *An empty stage, a pipe and a schleppable stool were the only props in evidence for these shows* ‖ since 1990s, from *shlep(n)* "to drag" and adjectival suffix *-able*

schlepper, shlepper *n.* YIDDISH [1] someone who makes a long, slow, or difficult journey or carries heavy things: **1997** *Chicago Sun-Sentinel*: *Christmas brings out the schlepper in millions of air travelers*; **2013** *Roadie*, film: *You're a fucking schlepper carrying other people's shit!* [2] a stupid, incompetent, and clumsy person (AS, KC): **1994** *Chicago Tribune*: *Vincent, forced to resign in 1992, called acting commissioner Bud Selig "small-town schlepper"*; **1999** *Sopranos*, HBO-TV series: *This is for reasons we couldn't comprehend or codify, you pathetic schlepper* [3] an insignificant or inconsequential person (JG): **2010** Blogs: *He's a schlepper with inferiority complex*; **2021** *Hill*: *You feel like a billionaire. But you're just a schlepper* [4] a vehicle designed to transport a family, especially a slow or heavy one: **2011** *Car and Driver*: *The Elantra is the family schlepper*; **2012** America Online Autos: *Hyundai invited us to hop a plane to Seoul to sample their new force-fed family schlepper* ‖ since 1934 in the first two senses, since 1947 in the third, since 1990s in the fourth, from *shlepn* "to drag" or *shleper* "tramp"

schlepper bag, shlepper bag *n.* YIDDISH a tote bag: **2000** *Boca Raton News*: *When you go shopping, would rather see a name on a bus or on a schlepper bag to hold your groceries?* **2009** *South Florida Sun-Sentinel*: *He showed up with a schlepper bag filled with openers* ‖ since 2000, from *shlepn* "to drag" and *bag*

schleppy, shleppy *adj.* YIDDISH [1] moving slowly or with difficulty: **1997** *Baltimore Sun*: *We're usually very schleppy and bedraggled as we roll out of our bus bunks*; **2008** Tennis Forum: *She used to look so schleppy on the court* [2] stupid, incompetent, and clumsy (JG, KC): **2012** *Chicago Tribune*: *The schleppy brother got a D in calculus*; **2012** *New York Daily News*: *Perhaps the TNT NBA analyst was upset over a schleppy coach* ‖ since 1940, from *shlep(n)* "to drag" and adjectival suffix *-y*

schlimazel, shlimazel *n.* YIDDISH [1] an unlucky and gullible person, especially a fool (AS, JG): **2015** Android Community: *You need to help our little schlimazel*; **2015** Monsters and Critics: *It is both drop proof and water resistant, great news for a schlimazel like me* [2] a difficult and confused situation (KC): **2005** *Weeds*, Showtime-TV series: *I apologize, I didn't mean to cause such a schlimazel*; **2016** Gold Seek: *It's not funny if one is caught up in this schlimazel* ‖ since 1948, from *shlimazl* "someone with a chronic bad luck," literally "bad luck" or "bad constellation"

schlock¹, shlock *n.* YIDDISH [1] something that has no value, especially shoddy or inferior merchandise (AS, JG, KC): **2001** *Crocodile Dundee in Los Angeles*, film: *It's unbelievable schlock, I kid you not*; **2010** *Los Angeles Times*: *They are perfectly fine selling their schlock to the public* [2] nonsense (JG): **2012** Fan Fiction: *I don't really want to listen to this schlock right now*; **2022** Reddit: *What kind of idiots believe this schlock?* ‖ since 1915, from *shlak* "inferior merchandise," literally "blow" or "apoplectic stroke"

schlock², shlock *adj.* YIDDISH [1] having no value, shoddy or inferior (JG, KC): **2003** *Two and a Half Men*, CBS-TV series: *Did she say that I'm a lazy-ass schlock jingle writer?* **2010** *Los Angeles Times*: *Sergei was ashamed of his schlock performances* [2] nonsensical: **2008** Lonely Planet: *It's a stupid and schlock thing to say about a fellow competitor*; **2011** *New York Times*: *On the basis of this argument he went on to accuse Christy of shlock economics* ‖ since 1915, from *shlak* "inferior merchandise"

schlock artist, shlock artist *n.* YIDDISH someone making or selling something that has no value, especially shoddy or inferior merchandise: **1997** *Washington Post*: *Does 220,000 hardback copies really mean that you're a schlock artist?* **2012** Huffington Post: *Neiman was what we call a schlock artist in the business* ‖ dating unknown, from *shlak* "inferior merchandise" and *artist*

schlock house, shlock house *n.* YIDDISH a store selling something that has no value, especially shoddy or inferior merchandise: **2004** Word Wizard: *Where did you buy that? In a schlock-house?* **2010** Broadway World: *Before the remodeling, the place looked like a schlock house* ‖ since 1940s, from *shlak* "inferior merchandise" and *house*

schlock joint, shlock joint *n.* YIDDISH [1] a store that selling something that has no value, especially shoddy or inferior merchandise (KC): **2005** Digital Photography Review: *Don't shop the schlock joints that pretend to offer better deals than the legitimate places*; **2012** Journal Home: *Go to a schlock joint and you will find* *plenty of normal t-shirts* [2] an inferior restaurant (KC): 2011 Yahoo: *There are a lot of all-you-can-eat Chinese schlock joints in town*; 2012 City Search: *You're going to put this schlock joint ahead of the class places* ‖ since 1940s, from *shlak* "inferior merchandise" and *joint*

schlockmeister, shlockmeister *n.* YIDDISH someone making or selling something that has no value, especially shoddy or inferior merchandise (JG, KC): 2008 *Vanity Fair*: *Levine was known as an enormously successful schlockmeister. He would buy junky films, have an aggressive ad campaign, and make a lot of money*; 2015 Hollywood Reporter: *There are gross-out plot devices which wouldn't be out of place in the work of schlockmeister Wong Jing* ‖ since 1965, from *shlak* "inferior merchandise" and *mayster* "master"

schlock shop, shlock shop *n.* YIDDISH a store that selling something that has no value, especially shoddy or inferior merchandise (JG, KC): 2009 *Canyon News*: *The first indicator of a schlock shop is their merchandise*; 2012 Yelp: *Conway is a giant schlock shop, jammed full of cheap clothing and housewares* ‖ since 1940s, from *shlak* "inferior merchandise" and *shop*

schlock store, shlock store *n.* YIDDISH a store that selling something that has no value, especially shoddy or inferior merchandise (JG): 1996 *New York Times*: *Benjamin Fox described it as a schlock store out of step with the neighborhood's upscale trends*; 2017 *Cambridge Day*: *We had one more schlock store in Harvard Square now* ‖ since 1915, from *shlak* "inferior merchandise" and *store*

schlockudrama, shlockudrama *n.* YIDDISH a movie or television play that has no value, is shoddy or inferior (KC): 2006 Daily Kos: *It implies that the ABC schlockudrama doesn't meet high standards either*; 2013 News Busters: *It was no surprise HBO's schlockudrama "Game Change" won best TV movie at Sunday's Golden Glove Awards* ‖ since 1990s, from *shlak* "inferior merchandise" and *drama*

schlocky, shlocky *adj.* YIDDISH [1] having no value, shoddy, or inferior (AS, JG, KC): 2006 *Boston Legal*, ABC-TV series: *We've become such a dumb, fat, bubblegum nation, schlocky and superficial*; 2012 Apartment Ratings: *Luckily the leak happened in my bathroom over the tub but the repair job on the leak was very schlocky* [2] nonsensical: 2004 *Pittsburgh Post-Gazette*: *I hope we don't have schlocky ideas, unless it is on purpose*; 2010 *Los Angeles Times*: *I've spent most of my career taking pretty schlocky ideas and turning them into something a little original* ‖ since 1968, from *shlak* "inferior merchandise" and adjectival suffix *-y*

schlong¹, shlong *n.* YIDDISH [1] the penis (JG, KC): 1996 *Foxfire*, film: *How do you know if a guy's got a really big schlong?* 2005 *Matador*, film: *I'll tell you a joke about a fifteen-inch schlong* [2] a despicable person, especially an idiot (JG): 1998 *Like It Is*, film: *I seem to recall he was a bit of a schlong*; 2012 Yahoo Finance: *I'm CEO material, you stupid schlong!* ‖ since 1865 in the first sense, since 1978 in the second, from *shlang* "penis," literally "snake"

schlong², **shlong** *v.* YIDDISH to defeat or victimize: **2015** *Washington Monthly*: *This poll shows he'd schlong the current Republican front-runner*; **2016** *Miami Sun Times*: *Hillary is going to schlong him in the general election* ‖ since 2015, from *shlang* "penis," literally "snake," and *get schlonged* "to be cheated or victimized"

schlontz, **shlontz** *n.* YIDDISH the penis (KC): **2008** Health Knowledge: *All he'd have to do was dip his schlontz*; **2014** UCB student: *She's in love with his big schlontz* ‖ since 1970s, from blending *shlang* and *shvants*, both meaning "penis"

schlub, **shlub** *n.* YIDDISH [1] a boorish and ill-mannered person, especially from the country (AS, KC, JG, KC): **2002** *Monk*, USA-TV series: *Come on, you're treating me like another schlub. This is family!* **2012** *Village Voice*: *Louise turns a camera on the pointless, shapeless, everyday life of a New York schlub* [2] a sloppy, slovenly, or poorly dressed person: **2012** *New York Post*: *Leelee Sobieski shlepped around a white floor-length evening gown while Judd Apatow dressed like a schlub*; **2012** *Globe and Mail*: *Craig looks like an everyday schlub in his plaid cargo shorts* ‖ since 1964, from *zshlob* "coarse or boorish person"

schlubby, **shlubby** *n.* YIDDISH [1] boorish and ill-mannered, especially from the country (JG, KC): **2011** *Wall Street Journal*: *Miernik is schlubby, irritating, untrustworthy, and obstinately undecipherable*; **2012** *New York Times*: *They are young, smart-looking, very schlubby* [2] sloppy, slovenly, or poorly dressed: **1994** *Crumb*, film: *She put him on a diet, and put him in safari outfits, but he was still shlubby*; **2012** *Minneapolis Star Tribune*: *Mitch is played by schlubby-looking Damon* ‖ since 1968, from *zshlob* "coarse or boorish person" and adjectival suffix *-y*

schlump¹, **shlump** *n.* YIDDISH [1] a sloppy, slovenly, or poorly dressed person (AS): **1999** *New York Times*: *I would never trust a designer who looks like a schlump*; **2006** *Cincinnati Magazine*: *I should note that I'm not exactly a schlump: I only go out in sweats if I'm headed to the gym* [2] a stupid, inept, or dull person (KC): **2012** *Boston Globe*: *Screenwriter Jason Segel stars as a schlump who loses his TV star girlfriend to a preening British rocker*; **2012** *South Florida Sun-Sentinel*: *They don't think I belong. They think I'm a schlump* ‖ since 1948, from *shlump* "slovenly or unfashionable person"

schlump², **shlump** *v.* YIDDISH [1] to waste time doing nothing (KC): **2000** Kathleen Taylor: *Alanna schlumped around the cafe*; **2010** Spark People: *I have schlumped for weeks now. I just cannot seem to pull it together* [2] to move slowly or with difficulty: **2006** Liz Ireland: *I schlumped back to my office, feeling defeated*; **2010** Campaign Site Builder: *They schlumped out of their seats slowly* ‖ since 1948, from *shlump* "slovenly or unfashionable person"

schlump around, **shlump around** *v.* YIDDISH to waste time doing nothing (KC): (KC): **2012** Neuro Talk: *Today I mostly schlumped around and recuperated*; **2019** UCB student: *Last summer I just schlumped around at the beach* ‖ since 1948, from *shlump* "slovenly or unfashionable person" and verbal particle *around*

schlumpy, shlumpy *n.* YIDDISH [1] sloppy, slovenly, or poorly dressed: **2007** *Glamour: If you wear something schlumpy, you'll feel schlumpy and less motivated*; **2012** *New York Times: For one thing, he was dressed in schlumpy clothes* [2] stupid, inept, or dull: **1993** *New York Magazine: As a teenager, Regan had the requisite schlumpy jobs*; **1994** *Spin Magazine: Meanwhile, he writes perfectly schlumpy rock anthems for people who take nothing seriously except their careers* || since 1948, from *shlump* "slovenly or unfashionable person" and adjectival suffix *-y*

schmaltz, shmaltz, shmalts *n.* YIDDISH excessive sentimentality, especially in music or film (AS, JG, KC): **2012** *Chicago Tribune: It added a degree of schmaltz that demeaned the original*; **2012** *New York Times: Barnamoff plans on expanding out from the core repertoire and upping the schmaltz quotient* || since 1935, from *shmalts* "sentimentality," literally "lard," and association with something too greasy to be easily digested

schmaltzed up, shmaltzed up, shmaltsed up *adj.* YIDDISH excessively sentimental, especially in music or film: **2003** *Piano World: I became curious about classical music listening to Mantovani playing a schmaltzed-up version of Claire de Lune*; **2011** *Los Angeles Times: It's a schmaltzed-up melodrama* || dating unknown, from *shmalts* "sentimentality," literally "lard," and verbal particle *up*

schmaltz up, shmaltz up, shmalts up *v.* YIDDISH to add excessive sentimentality, especially in music or film (KC): **1996** *New York Times: It's easy to imagine how Hollywood might have schmaltzed up this story*; **2004** *Texas Monthly: The author really schmaltzed it up* || dating unknown, from *shmalts* "sentimentality," literally "lard," and verbal particle *up*

schmaltzy, shmaltzy, shmaltsy *adj.* YIDDISH excessively sentimental, especially in music or film (AS, JG, KC): **2012** *Los Angeles Times: The singer also did "In the Heart of a Woman," a schmaltzy power ballad from 1993*; **2013** *Canadian Living: In honour of Saint Valentine, forget the cutesy tins and schmaltzy heart-shaped boxes – treat your sweetie to a batch of favourite brownies* || since 1935, from *shmalts* "sentimentality," literally "lard," and adjectival suffix *-y*

schmatte, shmatte, shmate, shmotte *n.* YIDDISH [1] a shabby or unstylish garment (AS, JG, KC): **1996** *New York Times: Food snobs, for example, regress to eating Campbell's tomato soup, while fashion compulsives are reduced to wearing schmattes like sweatshirts and drawstring pants*; **2008** *New Yorker: All of Sarah's schmattes cost less* [2] any garment: **2002** *New York Observer: Expensive fragrances, like expensive schmattes, often seem louche and tarty while cheaper merch has gone all subtle and organic*; **2010** *New York Times: It's a very nice schmatte, actually* [3] a despicable and untrustworthy person, especially if sycophantic: **1990** *Miller's Crossing*, film: *The shmatte steals from me*; **2001** Leo Rosten: *As a girl, she was decent; now she's a schmatte* || since 1972, from *shmate* "shabby or unstylish garment," literally "rag"

schmear¹, shmear, schmeer *v.* YIDDISH [1] to bribe (JG, KC): **1992** *Mad About You*, NBC-TV series: *"Schmear him? How much?" "Fifty"*; **2011** *New York Post: Jurors* *were schmeared!* [2] to flatter or cajole (AS, KC): **2011** Google Blogs: *To schmear or not to schmear?* **2012** Twitter: *Wow, Allie, you really know how to schmear!* [3] to slander or describe negatively in public (JG, KC): **2009** *Business Insider*: *The press has schmeared him*; **2010** *New York Times*: *Don't Schmear Me, Ford Warns* || since 1930, from *shmirn* "to grease"

schmear², shmear, schmeer *n.* YIDDISH [1] a bribe (JG, KC): **1985** *New York Magazine*: *It's a system in which a schmear is nothing so crass as money, simply a favor, but where favors are as tangible as gold bricks*; **2010** Yahoo Finance: *Be sure to give him a schmear* [2] a slander or negative public description of someone (JG, KC): **2008** Topix: *Before you attempt any more slimes and schmears of Senator Obama, you should check your own candidate's background*; **2011** Populist: *Stop the schmear against Palin!* [3] everything or totality: **2008** *Toronto Life*: *Efforts to put the whole schmear in context valiantly miss the point*; **2012** *New York Post*: *I used to work in marketing, handling big accounts, dining at fancy restaurants, traveling abroad, staying at luxurious hotels – the whole schmear* || since 1958, from *shmir* "grease" or "smudge"

schmeck, shmeck *n.* YIDDISH [1] heroin (JG, KC): **1986** Richard Condon: *Charlie was in Miami to handle a problem with a schmeck producer*; **2014** UCLA student: *She was addicted to schmeck* [2] a bit: **2008** *St. Augustinian*: *Let's throw 'em a real curve ball and opt for a schmeck of Lao Tze*; **2010** Topix: *They don't have a schmeck of common sense* || since 1932 in the first sense, since 1968 in the second, from *shmek* "sniff" and *shmekn* "to smell"

schmeer *see* schmear

schmegegge, shmegegge *n.* YIDDISH [1] an incompetent and stupid person (JG, KC): **1998** *Baltimore Sun*: *Only a schmegegge would ever bet on a nebbish*; **2007** Jordan Sonnenblick: *Don't just stumble around like a schmegegge!* [2] nonsense (JG, KC): **2001** *What's the Worst That Could Happen*, film: *What I want to know is what are you doing about this schmegegge?* **2006** Israel Forum: *However, all this schmegegge of yours doesn't matter anyway* || since 1964, from *shmegege* "stupid person"

schmendrick, shmendrick *n.* YIDDISH [1] a weak, naive, or cowardly person (JG): **1994** *Esquire*: *A schmendrick trusts other people simply because they are sitting close by*; **2012** *East Valley Tribune*: *It is high time to stop being a schmendrick living in a Spielberg movie and deal with reality* [2] an insignificant person: **2009** *New York Magazine*: *Justin Timberlake said he was just some schmendrick from a goy band*; **2014** UCLA student: *Don't pay attention to him. He's just a shmendrick* [3] a stupid, awkward, or inept person (KC): **1990** *Look Who's Talking*, film: *You can't wait for this schmendrick to get his act together*; **2006** *Evidence*, ABC-TV series: *Let this go to trial with the schmendrick here trying to remember what you name is* || since 1944, from *shmendrik* "weak or stupid person," from the name of a character in Abraham Goldfaden's operetta *Shmendrik Oder Di Komishe Khasene*

schmo, shmo, shmoe, schmoe *n.* YIDDISH [1] a naive, gullible, or stupid person (JG, KC): **1994** *Hudsucker Proxy*, film: *I don't think they promoted me because they* *thought I was a schmo*; 2008 *Los Angeles Times*: *President Bush tries to say l'ichayim, ends up looking like a schmo* [2] an average or mediocre person (AS, KC): 1991 *Hudson Hawk*, film: *Every schmoe has a fantasy that the planet revolves around them*; 2002 *Guys*, film: *He's just an ordinary guy. He's a schmo* || since 1938 in the first sense, since 1948 in the second, alteration of *schmuck* which itself comes from *shmok* "penis" or "despicable person," literally "jewel"

schmooze¹, shmooze, shmues *n.* YIDDISH [1] idle or gossipy conversation (AS, JG, KC): 1998 *Sex and the City*, HBO-TV series: *I gotta go back out there to do a schmooze at the Capri restaurant*; 2000 Joan Connor: *Hey, let's you and me have a little schmooze* [2] ability to talk persuasively, especially by using flattery (JG, KC): 2004 *Laws of Attraction*, film: *Oh please, save the L.A. schmooze for Judge Judy*; 2012 Lonely Planet: *I wouldn't have the schmooze and confidence to be a salesman* || since 1939, from *shmues* "talk" or "chat"

schmooze², shmooze, shmues *v.* YIDDISH [1] to converse idly or to gossip (AS, JG, KC): 2006 *Boston Legal*, ABC-TV series: *I love having a drink with you, schmoozing*; 2013 *Big Bang Theory*, CBS-TV series: *You have some nerve to show here to schmooze with the tenure committee* [2] to talk persuasively to someone, especially by using flattery (AS, JG, KC): 1995 *Dunston Checks In*, film: *I gotta go schmooze the guests*; 2021 *Arkansas Democrat-Gazette*: *They schmooze clients and lobby government officials* || since 1897, from *shmuesn* "to talk" or "to chat"

schmooze and cruise, shmooze and cruise *phr.* YIDDISH to mingle socially, and especially converse idly or gossip: 2002 *Los Angeles Weekly*: *He showed up early, schmoozed and cruised for a few minutes, and then hastily decamped*; 2012 *Zagat*: *You can schmooze and cruise but not dine well upstairs* || dating unknown, from *shmuesn* "to talk" or "to chat" and *cruise*

schmoozefest, shmoozefest *n.* YIDDISH AND GERMAN an idle or gossipy conversation session (JG, KC): 1998 *Dawson's Creek*, WB-TV series: *I just got sucked into this nightmare academic schmoozefest. I have, like, two more profound things to say and I'm out of here*; 2002 *New York Times*: *Money pumped into New York's economy by bigwigs on a spree at the schmoozefest called the World Economic Forum: $13 million* || since 1990s, from *shmues* "talk" or "chat" and *Fest* "festival"

schmoozer, shmoozer *n.* YIDDISH [1] a gossipy or talkative person (AS, KC): 2009 *Washington Monthly*: *He is an antsy and incorrigible schmoozer*; 2012 *New York Times*: *He is also a schmoozer who has had lunch with Donald Trump* [2] someone who talks persuasively, especially by using flattery (AS, JG): 2012 Huffington Post: *He always had confidence and was a schmoozer*; 2012 *Seattle Times*: *His greatest asset as a schmoozer is something that can't be taught* || since 1909, from *shmuesn* "to talk" or "to chat" and suffix *-er*

schmoozy, shmoozy *adj.* YIDDISH [1] gossipy or talkative (AS): 1996 *Fear*, film: *Come on! Not even a nice, schmoozy conference call? Please!* 2011 *Dallas Observer*: *I'm not a schmoozy person* [2] able to talk persuasively, especially by using flattery (AS): 2004 Christian Forums: *They just look like a coupla schmoozy* *politicians to me*; **2010** *Stamford Advocate*: *The phone rings and a schmoozy person talks them into making a donation* ‖ since 1954, from *shmues* "talk" or "chat" and adjectival suffix *-y*

schmuck, shmuck *n.* YIDDISH [1] the penis (JG): **1998** Elizabeth Claire: *Maybe he has a big schmuck*; **2015** *Forbes*: *When you're in the locker room you could say, "look at his schmuck"* [2] a despicable person (AS, JG, KC): **2005** *Match Point*, film: *He's another schmuck who cheated on his wife*; **2021** *Vanity Fair*: *You're a schmuck for not wearing a mask* ‖ since 1892, from *shmok* "penis" or "despicable person," literally "jewel"

schmucky, shmucky *adj.* YIDDISH despicable (JG, KC): **2010** *Chicago Tribune*: *The character played by Rudd is a little schmucky*; **2016** Gothamist: *It was a schmucky thing to do, he shouldn't have done it* ‖ since 1952, from *shmok* "penis" or "despicable person," literally "jewel," and adjectival suffix *-y*

schmutz, shmutz *n.* YIDDISH [1] dirt: **1999** *Play It to the Bone*, film: *You got schmutz all over the phone*; **2021** *The Mitchells vs. The Machines*, film: *You've got some schmutz all over the screen* [2] something immoral, filthy, or obscene (KC): **2003** Harold Bloom: *Why all the schmutz? The story is the schmutz*; **2010** *South Florida Sun-Sentinel*: *Why don't we clean out the schmutz from Congress, once and for all* ‖ since 1959, from *shmuts* "dirt" or "filth"

schmutzy, shmutzy *adj.* YIDDISH [1] dirty: **2010** Yelp: *The tables and counters are a schmutzy mess and are not routinely wiped down*; **2010** *Time Out New York*: *Despite decor that Jewish mothers might call "schmutzy," this legendary deli is a madhouse at breakfast and brunch* [2] immoral, filthy, or obscene: **2007** Word Press: *This isn't just a schmutzy pickup line*; **2014** *Time*: *It's a schmutzy comedy with an adorable new star* ‖ dating unknown, from *shmuts* "dirt" or "filth" and adjectival suffix *-y*

schneider, shneider *v.* YIDDISH [1] to win before one's opponent has scored (KC): **1989** *Los Angeles Times*: *Nothing can be more embarrassing in a World Series than getting schneidered*; **2011** *Sports Illustrated*: *Defending the Cup, the U.S. schneidered the Rumanians* [2] to defeat decisively or spectacularly (KC): **2001** Richard G. Stern: *I'm schneidered. You win*; **2008** Working Class Conservative: *Obama, as they used to say in the Catskills, schneidered her* ‖ dating unknown, from *shnayder* "clean sweep in a card game," literally "tailor"

schnockered, shnockered *adj.* YIDDISH drunk (JG, KC): **1998** *That '70s Show*, Fox-TV series: *It sounds like he was as schnockered as you were on St. Patrick's Day*; **1998** *Parent Trap*, film: *May I offer you some bubbly, in the hope that you'll get schnockered?* ‖ since 1955, from *(far)shnoshket* "drunk"

schnook, shnook *n.* YIDDISH [1] a timid, passive, and unassertive person (JG, KC): **2001** *New York Times*: *Bloch was such a schnook. I almost hated protecting him, but then he was your friend*; **2001** *Curse of the Jade Scorpion*, film: *You're being too rough on him. He's just kind of schnook who's more insecure than anything else* [2] a stupid, incompetent, or ineffectual person (AS, JG, KC): **2005** *Producers*, film: *I'm a schnook, bottom line is I stink*; **2009** Thinking Pharma: *I'm savvier than that schnook* [3] an unimportant, average, or mediocre person: **1990** *Simpsons*, Fox-TV series: *I gotta ride the bus like a schnook*; **2015** *Washington Free Beacon*: *He's now a schnook, just like everyone else, eating catsup and egg noodles and waiting in line* || since 1948, from *shnuk* "elephant trunk"

schnooky, shnooky *adj.* YIDDISH [1] timid, passive, and unassertive: **1995** *Variety*: *A schnooky kid is transported to days of yore to revivify the glory of Camelot*; **2005** Live Journal: *Don't let his name fool you, he's not as schnooky as he sounds* [2] stupid, incompetent, or ineffectual (AS): **2010** *Boston Magazine*: *Ben Stiller plays the schnooky new guard, but the fun is in the supporting cast*; **2012** *New York Times*: *The last is Woody Allen's "Oedipus Wrecks," wherein a schnooky lawyer (guess who?) inadvertently "creates" the Jewish Mother From Hell* [3] unimportant, average, or mediocre: **1998** *Entertainment Weekly*: *It's an extremely sweet story of a schnooky wedding singer (Adam Sandler) who falls in love*; **2009** Price Scope: *It's really too bad that such a master craftsman has such a schnooky personality image* || since 1948, from *shnuk* "elephant trunk" and adjectival suffix *-y*

schnor¹, shnor, schnorr, shnorr *v.* YIDDISH to beg or obtain something without paying: **2011** *Clanton Park Bulletin*: *He has been schnorring meals for twenty years*; **2012** *New York Magazine*: *She cut to the chase, she need a job. It was her first valuable lesson in schmoozing and schnorring* || since 1968, from *shnorn* "to beg"

schnor², shnor, schnorr, shnorr *n.* YIDDISH [1] a beggar or parasitic person, especially if audacious: **2009** Baby Center: *I had a roomie that was such a schnor I had to put my initials on my individual eggs*; **2013** UCB student: *Quit being such a shnorr and get a job!* [2] a cheapskate: **2007** *Californication*, Showtime-TV series: *"I left my wallet at home!" "Don't be such a fucking schnorr, Runkle!"*; **2010** Live Journal: *I hate feeling like a shnorr* || since 1948, from *shnorn* "to beg" and *shnorer* "beggar"

schnorrer, shnorrer *n.* YIDDISH [1] a beggar or parasitic person, especially if audacious (AS, JG, KC): **1999** *Sopranos*, HBO-TV series: *You do think I'm a schnorrer? A parasite?* **2012** *Globe and Mail*: *I lent you that money out of the goodness of my heart, now you treat me like a punk, a putz, a schnorrer?* [2] a cheapskate (AS, JG, KC): **1990** *Law & Order*, NBC-TV series: *I haven't seen or heard from him since, lousy shnorrer*; **2012** Huffington Post: *Lucy likes the option of wearing a dress to an event then returning it afterwards. Lucy is a schnorrer* || since 1884 in the first sense, since 1951 in the second, from *shnorn* "to beg" and *shnorer* "beggar"

schnoz, shnoz, schnozz, shnozz *n.* YIDDISH the nose, especially if very long or big (AS, KC): **1995** *Chicago Tribune*: *He was more than a bit awkward, with a big schnoz and a somewhat obnoxious manner*; **2001** *Man Who Wasn't There*, film: *You can't know the reality of what would have happened if you hadn't stuck in your goddamn schnozz* || since 1942, from *shnoyts* "snuff of a candle"

schnozzle, shnozzle, snozzle *n.* YIDDISH the nose, especially if very long or big (KC): **2003** *Jungle Book 2*, film: *Attacking? I'm the one socked in the schnozzle!* **2006** *Village Voice*: *This time a bad cold and a schnozzle full of snot are not the reasons* || since 1930, from *shnoytsl* "small snuff of a candle"

schnozzola, shnozzola *n.* YIDDISH the nose, especially if very long or big (AS, KC): **2012** TMZ: *I'd be forced to punch that person in the shnozzola*; **2014** *Washington Post*: *"Botched," in which two plastic surgeons fix failed plastic surgeries, has made me feel better about my schnozzola* || since 1930, from *shnoytsl* "small snuff of a candle"

schpilkes *see* shpilkes

schtark, shtark *adj.* YIDDISH strong: **2009** Society Rants: *Eitan is a very shtark boy*; **2011** Yeshiva World: *I don't know what they teach you in high school but guys are very interested in looks, even the very shtark ones* || dating unknown, from *shtark* "strong"

schtarker, shtarker *n.* YIDDISH [1] a physically strong person, especially if muscular (JG, KC): **1991** *New Yorker*: *You have to be a real shtarker to lift those things*; **1999** *Bone Collector*, film: *Your mother? God bless her. It's Morris the Shtarker I'm worried about. He's 79 with a tricky ticker and active pecker* [2] a mentally tough person (JG, KC): **1991** *Spy Magazine*: *She was such a shtarker with that mouth, she could have been a lawyer*; **2000** *New York Times*: *D'Amato learned his lesson during his 1998 re-election campaign when he tried to be a shtarker* [3] a powerful and important person (JG): **2000** *New York Times*: *We could be losing money, but now I'm a bit of a shtarker, you know, a Jewish word for a big shot*; **2002** *South Florida Sun-Sentinel*: *They will choose as their candidate one or two shtarkers* [4] an enforcer or hired thug (JG): **2010** *Seattle Post Intelligencer*: *He supplemented his income working as a schtarker – muscle – for John D. Hertz*; **2016** *Tablet Magazine*: *Because he was tough and a good fighter, he worked as a shtarker, and for a price would beat up someone who owed money* || since 1934 in the first three senses, since 1952 in the fourth, from *shtarker* "strong person"

schtick, shtick *n.* YIDDISH [1] an act or play or entertainer's stage routine (AS, JG, KC): **2012** *New Yorker*: *He worked in the Catskills and did his shtick on New York stages*; **2016** *Tampa Bay Times*: *Today, Letterman, Leno and Stewart are gone, and Colbert has toned down his political schtick on CBS* [2] a characteristic mannerism or style (AS, JG, KC): **2001** *Ghost World*, film: *"I was just joking around with the customers. It's my shtick." "Well, lose it"*; **2006** *Garfield: A Tail of Two Kitties*, film: *You can drop that shtick, boy!* [3] one's special area of interest or specialization (AS, JG, KC): **2010** *Undercover Boss*, CBS-TV series: *This may not be your shtick*; **2011** *Jewish Daily Forward*: *Ballroom dancing is not my shtick* || since 1960s, from *shtik* "piece"

schtinker, shtinker *n.* YIDDISH [1] a despicable, disgusting, or untrustworthy person: **2009** *Jewish Chronicle*: *Bring back Borat! Brüno is a shtinker!* **2011** *Wall Street Journal*: *Every shtinker was granted one without exception* [2] an informant or informer: 2006 Haruth: *A shtinker is a rat or the one who sings to the cops*; 2007 *America Magazine*: *Shtinker was prison slang for a rat, freier or patsy* [3] the anus or buttocks: 2002 *Da Ali G Show*, HBO-TV series: *You can take me up the schtinker*; 2009 *Village Voice*: *What if I put up a flute up my shtinker?* || dating unknown, from *shtinken* "to stink" and *shtinker* "someone who stinks"

schtunk, shtunk *n.* YIDDISH [1] a scandal: 2011 Yahoo Answers: *How do you put up with the schtunk?* 2012 Blogspot: *Why make such a shtunk over an opinion?* [2] a despicable, disgusting, or stupid person (KC): 2006 Free Republic: *Now we see how a schtunk like Lieberman got elected in the first place*; 2011 Daily Kos: *Stop being such a shtunk!* || since 1968, from *(ge)shtank* "stinking"

schtup¹, shtup *v.* YIDDISH [1] to have sex with (AS, JG, KC): 1998 *Price Above Rubies*, film: *I was lying on a desk getting shtupped by my brother-in-law*; 2005 *Thing About My Folks*, film: *He shtupped everything that moved between Baltimore and Syracuse* [2] to have sex (AS, JG, KC): 2009 *Taking Woodstock*, film: *No shtupping in the bushes!* 2009 *My Life in Ruins*, film: *I mean, look at porn stars. They get to schtup all day. They should be happy* [3] to cheat, swindle, or victimize (JG): 2006 Cafe Hayek: *Bush and his ilk are oil men and they're going to keep shtupping us until we can't take it anymore*; 2011 Cigar Family: *Bush shtupped us!* || since 1965 in the first two senses, since 1952 in the third, from *shtupn* "to push" or "to shove"

schtup², shtup *n.* YIDDISH [1] sexual intercourse (AS, JG, KC): 2003 *Two and a Half Men*, CBS-TV series: *I'm seeing someone new, you ask if I'm paying her by the hour or per schtup!* 2007 My Space: *That night, while they're having a great shtup, Talia suddenly turns on the bedside lamp and sees Jonathan with a vibrator in his hand* [2] a sex partner (KC): 1999 *New York Press*: *You're such a good shtup*; 1999 Weekly Wire: *She's looking for a good shtup* || since 1968, from *shtup* "push" or "shove"

schtupfest, shtupfest *n.* YIDDISH AND GERMAN [1] intense or lengthy sexual activity: 2010 Blogs: *The shtupfest lasted all night long*; 2011 Millions: *It is our own private allegorical code for yet another imminent schtupfest* [2] a sexual orgy: 2006 Free Republic: *There were many randy men and women back then, it was one big shtupfest*; 2007 *Washington Post*: *Joel, did you have help writing this? I only ask because the celebrity schtupfest part of it looks a little like Liz's Celebritology* || dating unknown, from *shtup* "push" or "shove" and *Fest* "festival"

schtuppable, shtuppable *adj.* YIDDISH [1] ready and willing to have sex (KC): 2009 Bimmer Fest: *It's nice to see that Valerie is still schtuppable*; 2010 OK Cupid: *I think you are shtuppable. Look at this fucking love connection!* [2] highly desirable as a sex partner (KC): 2007 Minx: *Jessica Alba is so shtuppable!* 2012 DVD Empire: *Rebecca Linares, a stunningly sexy brunette, is still very shtuppable* || dating unknown, from *shtup* "push" or "shove" and adjectival suffix *-able*

schvantz, shvantz *n.* YIDDISH the penis (JG, KC): 2006 *Funny Money*, film: *Change! That's what keeps your schvantz growing*; 2009 Free Republic: *I hope this kid cuts his shvantz off* || since 1954, from *shvants* "penis," literally "tail"

schvartze, shvartze *n.* YIDDISH *offensive* a black-skinned person (JG, KC): 2010 *New York Magazine*: *He was a racist, using the term "schvartzes" to describe black people*; 2012 *Tablet Magazine*: *Vanessa, please do not tell me you date the schvartzes* || since 1961, from *shvarts* "black"

schvartzer, shvartzer *n.* YIDDISH *offensive* a black-skinned person (JG, KC): 1996 *Get on the Bus*, film: *I bet you'd like to call me a nigger or, what do you call it? A schvartzer*; 2011 *Boardwalk Empire*, HBO-TV series: *This show needs some girl dancing like a shvartser* || since 1961, from *shvartser* "black-skinned person" and *shvarts* "black"

schvitz¹, shvitz, shvits *v.* YIDDISH to sweat: 2012 *Toronto Life*: *I haven't shvitzed that intensely since I was at a Russian banya*; 2013 *Style at Home*: *Do you schvitz much during the summer?* || since 1992, from *shvitsn* "to perspire"

schvitz², shvitz, shvits *n.* YIDDISH [1] sweat: 2011 *Daily Beast*: *If it can clean up and get rid of the smell of baby poop, then it can certainly get rid of the smell of schvitz for me*; 2016 *New York Post*: *The cabbie is helping New Yorkers beat the heat by rigging his front air conditioner with duct tubing to funnel cold air directly, to schvitz-soaked passengers in the back* [2] a session in a steam bath: 2004 *Suzie Gold*, film: *Can't I have a shvitz in my own sauna?* 2013 *Whole Health Chicago*: *Someone will bring you a beer, a beverage that tastes astonishingly good after a schvitz* || since 1992, from *shvitsn* "to perspire"

schvitzer, shvitzer *n.* YIDDISH [1] someone who sweats excessively: 2009 *Fashion Binge*: *Make sure he wears V-neck T-shirt underneath if he's a schvitzer*; 2010 *Word Press*: *I'm not a shvitzer, I'm a walker. I walk everyday. It really opens your pores, you know* [2] a braggart: 2009 *New York Times*: *Others call AIPAC an overrated bunch of shvitzers (showoffs)*; 2010 *Jewish Daily Forward*: *A shvitzer is a braggart, and the term is definitely derogatory, though not in the extreme* | from *shvitsn* "to perspire" and suffix *-er*

semper fi *excl.* LATIN greetings to a fellow Marine (TD): 2004 *Librarian*, film: *"Semper fi!" "You were a Marine?"*; 2010 *Maiden Heist*, film: *I'm really proud to have served with you. Semper fi!* || since 1951, from shortened version of the US Marine Corps creed *semper fidelis*, ultimately from *semper fidelis* "always faithful"

sexfest *n.* GERMAN a prolonged sex session, especially an orgy: 2004 *TV Guide*: *They invite four local Italian men for a party and a sexfest ensues*; 2012 *New York Times*: *Marriage is not a sexfest with a flawless best friend but something that takes enormous investment* || dating unknown, from *sex* and *Fest* "festival"

Shabbes goy *n.* YIDDISH a gentile asked on the Sabbath by Orthodox Jews to perform duties forbidden for them: 2006 *Shortbus*, film: *Nice to meet you, I'm shabbes goy, and if you're Jewish, I can help you turn on your lights*; 2007 *Company*, TNT-TV series: *He's my shabbes goy* || dating unknown, from *shabes-goy*, literally "Sabbath goy"

shamus *n.* IRISH GAELIC a private detective (AS, JG, KC, TD): 2013 *NCSI: Los Angeles*, CBS-TV series: *"The guy's a private eye." "A little help?" "Gumshoe,* *a shamus, a bird dog"*; 2013 *Broken City*, film: *"You a shamus?" "No, security"* || since 1934, from the Irish name *Seamus*, on account of many American police detectives being of Irish descent

shaygetz, schaygetz *n.* YIDDISH [1] a gentile boy or young man (JG): 2005 *Cinderella Man*, film: *You lousy shaygetz! That's a warning!* 2012 *Albany Times Union*: *She took a job teaching at the law school and wound up marrying a shaygetz who thinks "Hava Nagila" is means "have a tequila"* [2] a charming mischievous rascal (JG): 2010 Blogs: *She called him a naughty shaygetz!* 2015 Shamash: *Shaygetz is sometimes used to refer to a misbehaving child* || since 1919 in the first sense, since 1965 in the second, from *sheygets* "young gentile man"

shekels *n.* YIDDISH money (AS, JG, KC): 2009 *I Love You, Man*, film: *I was wondering if you would consider loaning me a few shekels?* 2015 *PC Magazine*: *If you're willing to shell out a few more shekels, the Acer TravelMate is still budget-friendly at a list price of $379* || since 1883, from *shekel* "ancient Jewish coin" and plural suffix *-s*

shicker¹, shikker *n.* YIDDISH a drunk or drunkard (AS): 2004 *Naples Daily News*: *That shicker had too much to drink*; 2007 *Mad Men*, AMC-TV series: *He's a shikker. Daddy will hate him* || since 1898, from *shiker* "drunk"

shicker², shikker *adj.* YIDDISH drunk (AS, JG, KC): 2006 Joyce Eisenberg and Ellen Scolnic: *Jews are allowed to get shikker during the feast of Purim*; 2010 Surfcasting: *El Presidente got so shicker he couldn't see, think or walk* || since 1898, from *shiker* "drunk"

shickered, shikkered *adj.* YIDDISH drunk (AS, JG): 2009 *Harvard Crimson*: *I thought Passover was the Jewish holiday to get shickered on Manischevitz*; 2010 *New York Times*: *I arrived at work completely shickered* || since 1898, from *shiker* "drunk" and suffix *-ed*

shiksa, shikse *n.* YIDDISH *offensive* [1] a non-Jewish woman, especially a young and attractive one (AS, JG): 2004 *Connie and Carla*, film: *She falls for this guy still living at home with his mother who's never gonna accept a shiksa with a past for a daughter-in-law*; 2009 *New Yorker*: *It's contingent upon eating hamburgers and shacking up with shikses* [2] (used especially by Orthodox Jews) a Jewish woman who is not Orthodox, pious, or observant: 2003 *Joan of Arcadia*, CBS-TV series: *Now he thinks I'm being tainted by the heathen shiksa*; 2012 *New Jersey Jewish News*: *She looked like a shiksa. She changed her name to Mary* || since 1892, from *shikse* "gentile woman"

shitski, shitsky *n.* YIDDISH [1] excrement: 2005 Buzz House: *You have never seen her take a shitski?* 2014 UCLA student: *Hey, dude, you got shitski on your shoes*; [2] something worthless or of inferior quality: 2010 Blogger: *How can your read this shitski?* 2011 NYU student: *How much did you pay for this shitsky?* [3] nonsense: 2010 Free Republic: *What a piece of shitsky!* 2014 UCLA student: *Quit talking shitski!* [4] nothing: 2007 Talk Sox: *Good reading on your part, guys, but frankly* *none of this means shitsky to me*; **2008** Topix: *All of the above means shitski* [5] a despicable person: **2011** Muscular Development: *That guy sounds like a total piece of shitski*; **2011** Yahoo Answers: *I'm not trying to be a shitski, but why here?* ‖ dating unknown, from *shit* and suffix *-ski*

shittoir (or **le shittoir**) *n.* PSEUDO-FRENCH *potentially offensive* a toilet or bathroom with a toilet: **2012** Forum: *Flush the toilet when you're leaving the shittoir*; **2015** Travelpod: *The bug got into my guts and I've been chained to the shittoir for the last three days* ‖ dating unknown, from *shit* "excrement" and suffix *-oir*

shiv[1] *n.* ROMANY a knife or knife-like weapon (AS, JG, KC, TD): **2008** *Big Stan*, film: *You want that shiv, don't you?* **2011** *Change-Up*, film: *You know how to make a shiv?* ‖ since 1897, from *chiv* "blade"

shiv[2] *v.* ROMANY to stab (JG, TD): **1995** *Usual Suspects*, film: *Too bad he got shivved*; **2013** *Identity Thief*, film: *I will shiv you in the yard* ‖ since 1931, from *chiv* "blade"

shlemazel *see* schlemazel

shlemiel *see* schlemiel

shlep *see* schlep

shleppable *see* schleppable

shlepper bag *see* schlepper bag

shlepper *see* schlepper

shleppy *see* schleppy

shlimazel *see* schlimazel

shlock *see* schlock

shlock artist *see* schlock artist

shlock house *see* schlock house

shlock joint *see* schlock joint

shlockmeister *see* schlockmeister

shlock shop *see* schlock shop

shlockudrama *see* schlockudrama

shlocky *see* schlocky

shlong *see* schlong

shlub *see* schlub

shlump *see* schlump

shlumpy *see* schlumpy

shmalts *see* schmaltz

shmaltsed up *see* schmaltzed up

shmalts up *see* schmaltz up

shmaltsy *see* schmaltzy

shmaltz *see* schmaltz

shmaltzed up *see* schmaltzed up

shmaltz up *see* schmaltz up

shmaltzy *see* schmaltzy

shmate *see* schmatte

shmatte *see* schmatte

shmear *see* schmear

shmeck *see* schmeck

shmegegge *see* schmegegge

shmendrick *see* schmendrick

shmo *see* schmo

shmoe *see* schmo

shmooze *see* schmooze

shmoozer *see* schmoozer

shmotte *see* schmatte

shmuck *see* schmuck

shmucky *see* schmucky

shmues *see* schmooze

shmutz *see* schmutz

shmutzy *see* schmutzy

shneider *see* schneider

shnockered *see* schnockered

shnook *see* schnook

shnooky *see* schnooky

shnor *see* schnorr

shnorrer *see* schnorrer

shnoz *see* schnozz

shnozz *see* schnozz

shnozzle *see* schnozzle

shnozzola *see* schnozzola

shoot off one's bazoo *n.* DUTCH to boast or brag (JG, KC): **1994** James Thorpe: *I've had to keep my trap shut for the last few weeks but now that he has gone I can shoot off my bazoo occasionally*; **2008** Kurt Vonnegut: *I heard Ma was shooting off her bazoo to everybody about how her boy was in a time-screen company* || since 1882, from *bazuin* "trumpet" and analogy to *blow off one's mouth*

shoot one's burritos *phr.* SPANISH to vomit: **2013** Blogs: *It's gonna make you shoot your burritos*; **2014** Facebook: *I ended up in the bathroom shooting my burritos* || dating unknown, from *shoot* and *burrito* "cornflour tortilla with savory filling," and analogy to *shoot one's cookies* or *shoot one's lunch*

shoot one's tacos *phr.* SPANISH to vomit: **2013** Blogs: *This practically guarantees you're gonna shoot your tacos*; **2014** UNM student: *She drank way too much and shot her tacos* || dating unknown, from *shoot* and *taco* "type of tortilla stuffed with various ingredients," and analogy to *shoot one's cookies* or *shoot one's lunch*

shpilkes, schpilkes *n.* YIDDISH [1] nervousness or anxiety (JG): **2010** *You Don't Know Jack*, film: *Would you save me the schpilkes and stay retired for crying out loud?* **2011** Huffington Post: *They are having schpilkes because they can't get to their cell phone during class time* [2] impatience or overabundance of energy: **2011** NYU Tisch Online: *She calls it schpilkes, she's always got to do something*; **2021** *Buffalo News: Your kids have schpilkes and can't sit still* || since 1982, from *shpilkes* "nervousness" or "impatience," literally "pins," and *zitsn oyf shpilkes* "to be nervous or impatient," literally "to sit on pin and needles"

shpritz[1] *n.* YIDDISH a bit or dose (KC, TD): **2012** *Sessions*, film: *Want a shpritz?* **2013** *New York Daily News: Parishioners are invited to bring in their pets for a prayer and a shpritz of holy water* || since 1970, from *shprits* "squirt"

shpritz[2] *v.* YIDDISH to squirt or spray (TD): **2008** *Big Bang Theory*, CBS-TV series: *Don't schpritz him with that body spray!* **2011** *New Yorker: They interrupted, teased, and shpritzed each other* || since 1967, from *shprits* "squirt"

shtark *see* schtark

shtarker *see* schtarker

shtick *see* schtick

shtinker *see* schtinker

shtunk *see* schtunk

shtup *see* schtup

shtuppable *see* schtuppable

shvantz *see* schvantz

shvartzer *see* schvartzer

shvits *see* schvitz

shvitz *see* schvitz

shvitzer *see* schvitzer

shyster[1] *n.* GERMAN a dishonest or unscrupulous person, especially a lawyer (AS, JG, KC): **1998** *Enemy of the State*, film: *Actually, I believe the slur "shyster" is generally reserved for Jewish attorneys*; **2018** Hollywood Reporter: *Uncle Shimmy was a shyster. He had a supply store, and he ripped off black people* ‖ since 1843, from *Scheisser* "despicable or stupid person" and *Scheisse* "feces" and *-ster*

shyster[2] *adj.* GERMAN dishonest or unscrupulous (JG): **2016** *Lexington Herald Leader*: *They should have known better than to hire a shyster lawyer*; **2018** *Toledo Blade*: *One of the things I cannot forgive my hometown for is that it allowed the local country club to be torn down by a shyster developer* ‖ since 1843, from *Scheisser* "despicable or stupid person" and *Scheisse* "feces" and *-ster*

si (or **sí**) *part.* yes: **2001** *Blow*, film: *"Our business here today is cocaine, yes?" "Si. Yes. It is"*; **2006** *Employee of the Month*, film: *"Do you know the plan?" "Si, got it"* ‖ dating unknown, from *sí* "yes"

sicknik *n.* YIDDISH [1] a hypochondriac or someone who is constantly sick: **1989** Leo Rosten: *She is such a sicknik they should bury her next to her doctor*; **2006** *National Review*: *Maybe we will call them "sickniks," maybe we will call them "toddies" for the hot lemonade and whiskey they take for double pneumonia* [2] someone who likes black humor: **1989** *Time*: *Adams does a take-off on a sicknik who is telling jokes about a plane crash*; **2012** *Los Angeles Times*: *"Nightmares of Bunker Hill" is a bus tour for those who revel in the murders, suicides, brothels, gambling places and opium dens of 19th century L.A. Oh, you delightful sickniks!* ‖ since 1959, from *sick* and suffix *-nik*

simpatico[1] (or **simpático**) *adj.* SPANISH nice or affable (AS, KC): **2015** *Washington Post*: *They might find more simpatico audiences outside of Alabama*; **2015** *Chicago Tribune*: *He and Mayor Rahm Emanuel have become more simpatico* ‖ since 1864, from *simpático* "nice" or "sympathetic"

simpatico[2] (or **simpático**) *n.* SPANISH niceness or affability (KC): **1999** *Story of Us*, film: *It's hard to explain. There was an instant connection, this simpatico*; **2010** *Last Play at Shea*, film: *We were always good friends. We had this good simpatico between us* ‖ since 1864, from *simpático* "nice" or "sympathetic"

sitzfleisch (or **Sitzfleisch**) *n.* GERMAN [1] the buttocks (JG): **1997** *New York Times*: *Having Ochs stabbed in his Sitzfleisch instead of pinked on the arm was perhaps crasser than necessary*; **2014** Word Press: *That doesn't mean that you should be sitting on your sitzfleisch the whole time* [2] stamina or staying power (JG): **2014** *New York Times*: *His students all have the sitzfleisch to get into graduate school*; **2015** Chronicle of Higher Education: *I didn't have the Sitzfleisch to be a scholar* || since 1840, from *Sitzfleisch*, ultimately from *sitzen* "to sit" and *Fleisch* "flesh"

skeeve[1] *v.* ITALIAN to be disgusted by something or someone (TD, JG): **1999** *Sopranos*, HBO-TV series: *"Sometimes I think you skeeve me." "Skeeve you? You're the mother of my children. How could I?"*; **2013** *Staten Island Advance*: *Yuck, I skeeve that!* || since 1976, from *schifo* "disgust" or *schifare* "to disgust"

skeeve[2] *n.* ITALIAN a disgusting person (TD, JG): **2021** *Orlando Weekly*: *All possibility of criminality aside, Florida House representative Matt Gaetz does appear to be a real skeeve*; **2022** Facebook: *Weinstein? What a skeeve* || since 1976, from *schifo* "disgust" or *schifare* "to disgust"

skeeve out *v.* ITALIAN to disgust (TD, JG): **2005** *Today Show*, NBC-TV program: *Oysters kind of skeeve me out*; **2021** *New York Magazine*: *Hotel sheets skeeve me out, so I travel with this sleep sack* || since 1976, from *schifo* "disgust" or *schifare* "to disgust" and *out*

skeevy *adj.* ITALIAN disgusting (KC, TD, JG): **2015** *Entertainment Weekly*: *She sneaks off to skeevy motel rooms with her history teacher*; **2021** *Paste Magazine*: *I lived with two 26-year-old guys who were friends with my skeevy boyfriend* || since 1976, from *schifo* "disgust" or *schifare* "to disgust" and suffix *-y*

-ski (or **-sky**) *suffix* YIDDISH AND POLISH (someone or something) involved in or characterized by what is indicated (JG, KC, TD): **2018** *Forbes*: *The brewski is only available at these three restaurants*; **2018** *Pittsburgh Post-Gazette*: *She's a buttinski; he's perpetually annoyed with her* || since 1830, from *-ski*

skosh[1] *n.* JAPANESE a small amount (AS, JG, KC, TD): **2010** *CSI: Miami*, CBS-TV series: *This day and age with all the technology at our fingertips, we're still referring to things in smidges and skoshes*; **2015** *Suburban Gothic*, film: *I gave the bitch a skosh of chloroform* || since 1961, from *sukoshi* "a little"

skosh[2] *adv.* JAPANESE a little: **2010** *Sons of Tucson*, Fox-TV series: *Could you tilt left a bit? Just a skosh more*; **2016** *New Yorker*: *The next three episodes are a skosh better than HBO's "Vinyl"* || since 1961, from *sukoshi* "a little"

slap someone some skin *phr.* MANDINKA to slap hands in greeting or congratulation (JG): **2000** *Dawson's Creek*, WB-TV series: *All right, slap me some skin. That was good work*; **2006** *Creatures from the Pink Lagoon*, film: *What's up, my brother? Slap me some skin!* || since 1939, from *i golo don n bolo* "place your skin in my hand"

slew *n.* IRISH GAELIC a large number (AS, JG, KC): **2016** *Northwest Arkansas News*: *We have been exposed to a slew of slurs*; **2016** Digital Spy: *Sony revealed a slew of communication accessories alongside its Xperia X handsets at MWC* || since 1839, from *sluagh* "multitude"

slugfest *n.* GERMAN a fight, especially a fistfight (AS, JG, KC): **2010** *Pawn Wars*, History-TV series: *It was a fifteen-round slugfest*; **2016** *Time*: *It's unlikely that Trump swayed many swing voters during the 90-minute slugfest at Washington University in St. Louis* || since 1908, from *slug* "hard hit" and *Fest* "festival"

smithereens *n.* IRISH GAELIC small pieces or fragments (AS, JG, KC): **2016** *New York Sun*: *They would blow the GOP to smithereens*; **2016** Bleacher Report: *That man will pick up your soul and crush it, obliterate it into a million tiny smithereens* || since 1810, from *smidirín* "small fragments"

snoop *v.* DUTCH to pry (AS, JG, KC): **2015** *Topeka Capital Journal*: *The bomber was snooping for information*; **2016** *New York Post*: *Obama's NSA was snooping on Congress* || since 1832, from *snoepen* "to pry"

snoop around *v.* DUTCH to go around in a prying manner (AS, JG, KC): **2015** *News*, CBS-TV program: *It's not unusual for children to sometimes snoop around to see what they're getting for Christmas*; **2016** *Examiner*: *Desperate for answers, she asks Jett to snoop around* || since 1832, from *snoepen* "to pry" and *around*

snozzle *see* schnozzle

soixante-neuf *n.* FRENCH sexual activity between two people involving mutual oral stimulation of each other's genitals (AS, JG): **2011** *Codebreaker*, film: *I told them we were engaged in mutual masturbation, soixante-neuf*; **2013** *New Yorker*: *The camera rises over the pair of them, locked and prostrated by the eager geometry of soixante-neuf* || since 1883, from *soixante-neuf* "sixty-nine," which suggests reciprocally inverse positions

someone should be so lucky *sent.* YIDDISH someone's expectations are unlikely to be fulfilled, especially because they are unrealistic (JG): **2013** UCB student: *"She may get a raise." "She should be so lucky!"*; **2015** Blogs: *"Planning to move in?" "You should be so lucky"* || since 1957, from *zol emetser azoy mazldik zayn* "someone should be so lucky"

someone should live so long *sent.* YIDDISH someone should live long to see something so unrealistic: **2009** *New York Times*: *Can you imagine it? I should live so long*; **2013** *Dallas Morning News*: *"Legal gambling in Texas? I should live so long"* || since 1960, from *zol emetser azoy lang lebn* "someone should live so long"

songfest *n.* GERMAN a song festival or singing session: **2012** *Richmond Daily News*: *After dinner, a songfest was led by Rotarian Price Collier*; **2015** *Hillsboro Times Gazette*: *A songfest will be held at the New Market Community Church on August 15* || dating unknown, from *song* and *Fest* "festival"

son of puta *n.* SPANISH *offensive* a despicable person: **2006** *Scanner Darkly*, film: *Son of puta! He did it on purpose!* **2013** *National Review*: *His name basically means* *"son of puta"* ‖ dating unknown, from *son (of a bitch)* and *puta* "prostitute" or "despicable woman"

sourpuss *n.* IRISH GAELIC a bad-tempered or habitually sullen person (AS, JG, KC): **2011** *Help*, film: *Remember, no gentleman wants to spend the evening with a sourpuss*; **2012** *Justified*, FX-TV series: *"Goodnight!" "Oh come on, don't be a sourpuss!"* ‖ since 1934, from *sour* and *pus* "mouth"

spaghetti *n.* ITALIAN *offensive* an Italian or person of Italian descent (JG, KC, TD): **1985** *Montreal Gazette*: *He'd tease me about being Italian and he'd call me spaghetti*; **2015** Twitter: *I would call him spaghetti and he'd get all defensive* ‖ since 1915, from *spaghetti* "type of pasta"

spaghetti bender *n.* ITALIAN *offensive* an Italian or person of Italian descent (JG, TD): **1986** *Chicago Tribune*: *I've been called everything from a dago to a wop to a spaghetti bender*; **2009** Mental Floss: *He regularly referred to him as a "spaghetti bender"* ‖ since 1967, from *spaghetti* "type of pasta" and *eater*

spaghetti eater *n.* ITALIAN *offensive* an Italian or person of Italian descent (JG, TD): **2012** NYU student: *The bitch called me a spaghetti eater!* **2007** Yahoo Answers: *His name ends in a vowel, which automatically makes him a spaghetti eater* ‖ since 1918, from *spaghetti* "type of pasta" and *eater*

spaghetti western *n.* ITALIAN a cowboy film made in Europe by Italian directors (AS, JG, KC, TD): **2009** *CSI: Crime Scene Investigation*, CBS-TV series: *Well, this was more like a spaghetti western*; **2015** *Washington Post*: *I felt as though I had come across some dreadful scene in a spaghetti western* ‖ since 1967, from *spaghetti* "type of pasta" and *western*

Spanglish *n.* SPANISH [1] a variety of American English that contains many Spanish expressions, often modified (AS, KC): **2012** *Law & Order: Special Victims Unit*, NBC-TV series: *"Were they speaking English or Spanish?" "Spanglish"*; **2018** Hollywood Reporter: *The characters often speak in Spanglish, peppering their majority-English sentences with Spanish words and phrases* [2] a variety of American slang that contains many Spanish expressions, often modified: **1992** *Tablet Magazine*: *He sprinkles in Spanglish and hip-hop slang*; **2001** *Tortilla Soup*, film: *Please cut the Spanglish!* ‖ since 1954, from blending *Spanish* and *English*

Speedy Gonzales *n.* SPANISH [1] a person who is very fast (JG): **1997** *Career Girls*, film: *Who the fuck do you think I am? Speedy Gonzales?* **2016** Facebook: *If you're a Speedy Gonzales and finish sooner, then you get to enroll in any of their other classes* [2] *potentially offensive* a man who ejaculates prematurely: **2003** *Smallville*, WB-TV series: *"Did you see the look on her face?" "Speedy Gonzales!"*; **2013** *Dads*, Fox-TV series: *She's doing Speedy Gonzales* ‖ since 1977, from the name *Speedy Gonzales*, a character in the Warner Brothers series of cartoons

spic (or **spick**) *n.* PSEUDO-SPANISH *offensive* [1] a Spanish-speaking person (AS, JG, TD): **1995** *Empire Records*, film: *Go to the white neighborhood all you want, you'll always be a spic*; **2015** *News*, Fox-TV program: *She was hostile to Latinos and called* *them spics and illegals* [2] the Spanish language (JG, TD): **2011** Mary Monroe: *Well, them other spics, they speak spic*; **2012** YouTube: *In reply to Gustavo, I don't understand spic* || since 1913 in the first sense, since 1933 in the second, from an imitation of a Spanish speaker pronouncing "speak"

spico (or **spicko**) *n.* PSEUDO-SPANISH *offensive* a Spanish-speaking person (TD): **2007** Storm Front: *The spickos all want to go to the States*; **2012** Topix: *I hate chinkies, japies, and spickos, too* || since 1967, from an imitation of a Spanish speaker pronouncing "speak" and mock Spanish suffix *-o*

Spictown (or **Spic Town**) *n.* PSEUDO-SPANISH *offensive* a Spanish-speaking neighborhood (JG, TD): **2010** Phora: *Every night I hear the sirens heading towards Spictown*; **2011** Ben Zeller: *Solomon's mother had been born across the tracks in Spic Town* || since 1953, from an imitation of a Spanish speaker pronouncing "speak" and *town*

spiel[1] *n.* YIDDISH [1] persuasive or eloquent talk (AS, JG, KC): **2003** *Nip/Tuck*, FX-TV series: *Save the spiel. The lady in your waiting room convinced me you weren't worth my time*; **2010** *Miss Nobody*, film: *Sarah Jane delivers the powerpoint presentation and the big spiel* [2] an advertising monologue or salesperson's speech intended to attract customers (AS, JG, KC): **1998** *Buffy the Vampire Slayer*, WB-TV series: *You're in the trade! Sorry about the spiel, but around Valentine's Day I get a lot of tourists shopping for love potions*; **2007** Word Press: *She had quite a spiel and sold several of her "regularly $400 but for this show only, $200" irons* || since 1894, from *shpil* "play"

spiel[2] *v.* YIDDISH [1] to talk in a persuasive or eloquent way (AS, JG): **2002** *Max*, film: *Don't spiel me. Where's your wife?* **2012** Tumblr: *I sat there and spieled about the evils of marriage* [2] (of a salesperson) to make an advertising monologue or a speech intended to attract customers (JG): **2011** Huffington Post: *The charming waiter spieled about artisanal cheese*; **2011** Marketing Power: *Every person I've met doesn't walk in and start spieling* || since 1894, from *shpiln* "to play"

spieler *n.* YIDDISH [1] a persuasive or eloquent talker (AS, JG, KC): **1995** *Los Angeles Times*: *Both are good listeners and even spielers, both know how resonating a good, hard fact can be*; **2011** *Time*: *She clapped me on the shoulder and exclaimed, "Boy, you are some spieler!"* [2] a salesperson who makes advertising monologues or speeches intended to attract customers: **1995** *Chicago Tribune*: *A spieler is a person who attracts customers by a voluble line of extravagant claims and skillful persuasion*; **2012** Wikipedia: *He reminisces about Fane's struggle to the top, beginning as a spieler for his stripper girlfriend Laurel* || since 1894, from *shpiler* "player"

spig *n.* PSEUDO-SPANISH *offensive* a Spanish-speaking person (JG, TD): **2005** Urban Dictionary: *It suggests they are all spigs*; **2013** Topix: *You just mad because of what I said about your fellow spigs* || since 1969, a corrupted version of *spic*

spinmeister *n.* GERMAN an influential spokesperson employed to give a favorable interpretation of events to the news media, especially on behalf of a political party

(AS, KC): **2007** *Los Angeles Times*: *He kept his job as a spinmeister for the State Department*; **2009** *Tulsa World*: *Asking people questions will also change a conversation quicker than a spinmeister deflecting questions about Obama's stimulus plan* || since 1980s, from *spin* and *Meister* "master"

splatterfest *n.* GERMAN an event when a lot of people die, especially one depicted in a movie (KC): **2009** *New York Times*: *It's a splatterfest so exuberantly goofy that you can't help laughing*; **2012** DVD Talk: *I wouldn't characterize "Halloween 4" as a splatterfest, but it does pack a hefty body count* || dating unknown, from *splatter* and *Fest* "festival"

spookerican *n.* SPANISH *offensive* a person of African American and Puerto Rican descent: **1996** Word Wizard: *"Spill" and "spookerican" describe a Puerto Rican/Black mix*; **2014** Tumblr: *He was not afraid to be as Luciano said a "Spookerican"* || dating unknown, from *spook* "African American" and *Puerto Rican*

supremo (or **el supremo**) *adj.* SPANISH excellent (TD): **1993** *Teenage Mutant Ninja Turtles*, CBS-TV series: *Not only that, we're getting a supremo sauna!* **2014** Car Blaze: *Toyota is a supremo car producer* [2] extreme (TD): **2007** Blogspot: *I made a supremo effort*; **2013** Facebook: *He didn't do you any favor with that supremo screwup* || since 1979, from *supremo* "supreme"

Sureños (or **Surenos**) *n.* SPANISH the Mexican mafia from Southern California: **2005** *San Francisco Gate*: *There are few statistics on the number of crimes committed by Sureños*; **2016** *Santa Barbara Independent*: *Hundreds associated with the Sureños are booked each year* || dating unknown, from *sureños* "southerners"

T

tabla *n.* SPANISH a surfboard (TD): **2005** *Trav Buddy*: *Once I saw a guy that was surfing with his dog in his tabla!* **2012** Word Press: *Closer inspection showed that their tablas were posher* || since 1977, from *tabla* "board"

taco *n.* SPANISH *offensive* [1] a Mexican or person of Mexican descent (JG, KC): **1995** *Bad Boys*, film: *The goddamn taco is gonna kill me*; **2008** *Milk*, film: *Don't let Cesar Chavez hear you calling him "taco!"* [2] the penis: **2013** YouTube: *It looks like he's jerking his taco*; **2014** *Two and a Half Men*, CBS-TV series: *We had sex. I ate his taco* [3] the vagina: **2013** Puffy Network: *She can't keep her hands off of herself, which is understandable given that she has a big taco*; **2014** XXX Bunker: *A babe is pleasing her taco with kinky toys* || since 1969 in the first sense, since 2001 in the second and third, from *taco* "type of tortilla stuffed with various ingredients"

taco belle *n.* SPANISH AND FRENCH *offensive* a Latin American woman, especially if attractive (JG): **1993** *Washington Post*: *She is a taco belle who has already won the heart of a handsome rancher*; **2016** *New York Daily News*: *Marla* *used to be Donald Trump's taco belle* || since 1989, from *taco* "type of tortilla stuffed with various ingredients" and *belle*, modeled on *Southern belle*

taco bender *n.* SPANISH *offensive* a Mexican or person of Mexican descent (JG, TD): **2007** *John from Cincinnati*, HBO-TV series: *Goddamn taco benders just ran past me like I was Homeland Security!* **2013** *News*, NBC-TV program: *Juan was being called things like a taco bender* || since 1969, from *taco* "type of tortilla stuffed with various ingredients"

taco breath *n.* SPANISH *offensive* a Mexican or person of Mexican descent (JG): **2000** Luis Gabriel Aguilera: *Hey, taco breaths! Go back to Mexico!* **2013** MMA Weekly: *Okay, taco breath, swim south back to Mexico!* || since 1978, from *taco* "type of tortilla stuffed with various ingredients" and *breath*

taco eater *n.* SPANISH *offensive* a Mexican or person of Mexican descent (JG): **2007** *New York Times*: *And so the migration of the taco eaters begins*; **2008** City Data: *If I say, "Them damn Taco Eaters are invading our country," that is likely to be found offensive* || since 1978, from *taco* "type of tortilla stuffed with various ingredients" and *eater*

taco head *n.* SPANISH *offensive* a Mexican or person of Mexican descent (JG): **1997** *Retroactive*, film: *I'll take care of you later, taco head!* **2014** Instagram: *If you really wanna make him mad, call him a taco head* || since 1977, from *taco* "type of tortilla stuffed with various ingredients" and *head*

Taco Hell *n.* SPANISH a Taco Bell fast-food restaurant (TD): **2013** Chowhound: *I haven't been back to Taco Hell ever since*; **2016** *People Magazine*: *I would have picked Taco Hell over this gross place. I grew up in SoCal, and I love the Mexican food* || since 1985, from *taco* "type of tortilla stuffed with various ingredients" and phonetic similarity with *Taco Bell*

tacoland (or **taco land**) *n.* SPANISH a Mexican or Mexican American neighborhood (JG, TD): **2010** Fan Fiction: *You were born in tacoland, that makes you a spic*; **2014** Facebook: *Sanchez, go back to Tacoland where you belong!* || since 1968, from *taco* "Mexican or person of Mexican descent" and *land*

taco queen *n.* SPANISH *offensive* a white gay person who prefers Hispanic partners (JG): **2004** Word Press: *You're just Hispanic-looking enough to appeal to some of the taco queens I know*; **2007** Urban Dictionary: *He's such a taco queen, he travels to Mexico just to hang out in gay bars there* || since 1972, from *taco* "Mexican or person of Mexican descent" and *queen*

Taco Town *n.* SPANISH [1] a Mexican or Mexican American neighborhood: **2009** Urban Dictionary: *"Where you live?" "I live next to Walmart, you know, in Taco Town"*; **2016** LA Downtown News: *Initially I was a little scared because this is such a big taco town* [2] San Jose, California (JG): **2007** First Nations: *I catch the bus every morning in Taco Town*; **2014** Yelp: *Although I live in Taco Town I love*

Taco Bell ‖ since 1986, from *taco* "Mexican or person of Mexican descent" and *Town*

taco wagon *n.* SPANISH a car with its rear end lowered (JG): **2011** Urban Dictionary: *Why do wetbacks drive taco wagons?* **2013** Garage Journal: *I wonder if it would be ok to have this painted on my taco wagon?* ‖ since 1969, from *taco* "Mexican or person of Mexican descent" and *wagon*

take a bath *phr.* YIDDISH [1] to go bankrupt or lose a lot of money (KC): **2011** *InSecurity*, CBC-TV series: *Thank God I got my shares out before he went to jail. A lot of losers took a bath*; **2011** *Good Wife*, CBS-TV series: *When I shorted CEMEX on the Caracas Exchange, I took a bath* [2] to lose or be ruined (KC): **2008** *Carolina Journal*: *Two years later, the party took a bath*; **2019** *USA Today*: *Republicans took a bath after President Richard Nixon resigned in 1974 in the face of near-certain impeachment and conviction* ‖ since 1935, from *araynfirn in bod* "to lead to a bath"

tali *n.* ARABIC a Taliban, member of a fundamentalist Muslim movement in Afghanistan, especially its militia fighters: **2013** Robert Murrhee: *They would try and draw fire from the Taliban in the village and see if the Talis wanted to come out and play*; **2017** *Shooter*, USA-Network-TV series: *Three talis on the north road! Move, move, move!* ‖ since 1990, from *tālib* "student"

talkfest *n.* GERMAN a lengthy, gossipy, or idle conversation session (AS): **2015** *Akron Beacon Journal*: *Carman garnered an extremely loyal following for this talkfest*; **2015** *Los Angeles Times*: *He seized control of the floor for a ten-hour talk fest* ‖ dating unknown, from *talk* and *Fest* "festival"

talkmeister *n.* GERMAN a radio or television program commentator, interviewer, or host: **2003** *Chicago Tribune*: *Friedman is a pugnacious talkmeister, known for his ability to elicit from his guests rage, humor and much else on live TV*; **2009** *Boston Herald*: *CNN talkmeister Larry King has bought a condo at Los Angeles' exclusive new Carlyle Residences, reportedly paying some $4 million* ‖ dating unknown, from *talk* and *Meister* "master"

tang *n.* FRENCH *offensive* the vagina (JG, KC, TD): **2004** Adult DVD Talk: *She had a need for the dang in her tang, and this guy delivered*; **2015** USA Sex Guide: *I was preoccupied with her tang and her ass* ‖ since 1969, from *poontang*, ultimately from *putain* "prostitute"

tatas *n.* SPANISH *potentially offensive* female breasts (JG, KC, TD): **2008** *Grizzly Park*, film: *Are your tatas silicone?* **2015** *Life & Style Weekly*: *She had her tatas on full display in a cleavage-baring black dress* ‖ since 1982, from *tetas* "female breasts"

tchotchke *n.* YIDDISH [1] a plaything or trinket (AS, JG, KC): **2007** *Damages*, film: *Patty doesn't want family photographs, tchotchkes, knicknacks*; **2009** *Two and a Half Men*, CBS-TV series: *He still gives me handmade tchotchkes for Christmas* [2] a cute and adorable person, especially a child (JG, KC): **2007** *Metropolis Magazine*: *I would say my tchotchke is Jenny*; **2021** YouTube: *Just look at my little tchotchke growing up!* ‖ since 1964, from *tshatshke* "bauble" or "trinket," variant of *tsatske*

tecata *n.* SPANISH [1] heroin (JG): 2010 Castaño Pérez: *This type of heroin is called tecata*; 2012 David Montejano: *He had not given up the tecata (heroin)* [2] a female heroin addict: 1993 *Los Angeles Times*: *I lost my mother, she was a tecata (heroin addict)*; 2012 Johnny M. Sanchez: *The back trailers were abandoned, that's where we would let the tecatos and tecatas shoot up* ‖ since 1967, from place in Mexico

tecato *n.* SPANISH a heroin addict (JG): 2012 *Los Angeles Times*: *Monica doubted that such advances would ever benefit the tecatos in northern New Mexico*; 2015 *News*, KRQE-TV program: *The tecato that hit them is a lowlife* ‖ since 1970, from place in Mexico

Tejana *n.* SPANISH a female Texan of Mexican origin or descent: 2005 *Deseret News*: *She's originally from Texas, so she's a Tejana*; 2015 *Village Voice*: *Paredez is a Tejana from San Antonio* ‖ dating unknown, from *Tejana* "female inhabitant of Tejas," ultimately from *Tejas* "former Northern Mexican state, now Texas"

Tejano *n.* SPANISH a Texan of Mexican origin or descent (AS, KC): 1997 *Selena*, film: *Nobody'll kick us out of this joint. They're Tejanos, like us*; 2016 *News*, NBC-TV series: *The Tejanos and other Latinos that vote for Republicans are not voting against their interests* ‖ dating unknown, from *Tejano* "inhabitant of Tejas," ultimately from *Tejas* "former Northern Mexican state, now Texas"

tetas *n.* SPANISH *potentially offensive* female breasts: 2003 *Washington Heights*, film: *These are the hugest tetas I've ever seen in my life*; 2014 *Americans*, FX-TV series: *I want to rub my tetas all over the Congressman's desk* ‖ since 1982, from *tetas* "female breasts"

tetona *n.* SPANISH *potentially offensive* a big-breasted woman: 2012 Twitter: *What a tetona! Yummy!* 2014 International Sex Guide: *Send me some info on that tetona you posted here* ‖ dating unknown, from *tetona* "big-breasted woman," ultimately from *tetas* "female breasts"

that's the way the cookie crumbles *sent.* YIDDISH such is life: 2015 *Fresno Bee*: *If Southeast gets a little extra, well, that's the way the cookie crumbles*; 2015 Enterprise News: *That's the way the cookie crumbles, especially in this game* ‖ since 1956, from *azoy vert dos kikhl tsebrokhn* "a cookie crumbles in this way"

Tia Juana (or **Tía Juana**) *n.* SPANISH Tijuana, Mexico: 2012 *Motorcyclist Magazine*: *He rode at a 30 miles an hour clip over the highway from Tia Juana to San Diego*; 2015 *Chicago Tribune*: *U.S. travelers heading from the airport to the U.S. can avoid the 15-minute drive to the congested border crossing in Tia Juana-San Ysidro* ‖ dating unknown, from *Tía* "aunt" and *Juana*, popular first name

Tijuana Bible *n.* SPANISH a small pornographic comic book (JG, KC, TD): 2008 Richard Price: *There were assorted fetish magazines and reproduced Tijuana bibles*; 2016 Motherboard: *This was the era of the "Tijuana Bible," the handheld pornographic comic books* ‖ since 1966, from *Tijuana* and *bible*

Tio Taco (or **Tío Taco**) *n.* SPANISH *offensive* a Mexican American who emulates behavior or values of the non-Hispanic majority (JG, TD): **2008** Nancy Maclean: *Hector Garcia found himself scorned as a "Tio Taco," a Mexican Uncle Tom*; **2012** *Phoenix New Times*: *He'll be condemned to be the Tio Taco of El Paso* ‖ since 1969, from *Tío Taco* "Uncle Taco," modeled on *Uncle Tom* "African American who emulates behavior or values of the white majority"

Tio Tomas (or **Tío Tomás**) *n.* SPANISH *offensive* a Mexican American who emulates behavior or values of the non-Hispanic majority (JG): **2007** Real Clear Politics: *It inspired one reader on the Latino left to recently label me a "Tio Tomas" (a Hispanic Uncle Tom)*; **2015** Twitter: *I'm sick of being called Tio Tomas* ‖ since 1971, from *Tío Tomás* "Uncle Tomas," modeled on *Uncle Tom* "African American who emulates behavior or values of the white majority"

tipo *n.* SPANISH (used especially as a term of address) a man: **2004** Urban Dictionary: *Oye, tipo, are we going to the movies tonight?* **2015** UF student: *Yo, tipo, get away from my car!* ‖ dating unknown, from *tipo* "man," literally "type"

TJ *n.* SPANISH Tijuana, Mexico (JG, TD): **2007** *Prison Break*, Fox-TV series: *"What's it going to take for you to forget you ever found us?" "There ain't enough pesos in TJ"*; **2016** Digital Journal: *One can reach the San Diego airport and from there easily reach our clinic in TJ* ‖ since 1963, from *TiJuana*

T.L. *n.* YIDDISH an insincere flatterer, a sycophant (JG): **1996** Leo Rosten: *He's the worst T.L. you ever saw!* **2012** Alternate History: *I would like to know what people would think about such a TL* ‖ since 1972, from *toches-leker* "sycophant," literally "someone who licks buttocks"

tofu *n.* CHINESE an empty box shown in place of an undisplayed character in computer encoding: **2015** Photoshop: *Photoshop swaps the font for another that does not have those missing glyphs in order to avoid displaying "tofu" or missing glyph icons*; **2016** *Christian Science Monitor*: *When your computer doesn't recognize a language, a blank box is displayed on the screen, commonly known as a tofu* ‖ since 2000, from *dòufu* "curd made from mashed soybeans, used in Asian cooking"

tokus, tochus *n.* YIDDISH buttocks (AS, JG, KC): **2004** *House, M.D.*, Fox-TV series: *She's good looking, you saw that tokus*; **2012** *Austin Chronicle*: *Oy, this child, if I'm not wiping her tokus, it's her schnoz!* ‖ since 1914, from *toches* "buttocks," literally "underneath"

tokus licker, tochus licker, tokus leker, tochus leker *n.* YIDDISH an insincere flatterer, a sycophant (JG): **2009** *Wall Street Examiner*: *De Graaf is a tochus licker tonight*; **2012** Blogger: *They are insincere, they are tokus lickers* ‖ since 1952, from *toches-leker* "sycophant," literally "someone who licks buttocks"

tonto *n.* SPANISH *offensive* a stupid or silly person (JG): **1982** *48 Hours*, film: *Maybe you should've stolen a better truck, tonto!* **2014** *OC Weekly*: *These tontos have* *allowed the opposition to pit them against their only ally* || since 1999, from tonto "silly" or "stupid"

tortilla eater *n.* SPANISH *offensive* a Mexican: **1991** *New York Times*: *He called Vargas a tortilla-eater*; **2008** Marta Acosta: *That's as demeaning as calling me a "tortilla eater"* || dating unknown, from *tortilla* and *eater*

toss one's burritos *phr.* SPANISH to vomit: **2003** Deviant Art: *I think I'm gonna toss my burritos*; **2007** Free Republic: *Bill Richardson is about to toss his burritos!* || dating unknown, from *toss* and *burrito* "cornflour tortilla with savory filling," and analogy to *toss one's cookies* or *toss one's lunch*

toss one's tacos *phr.* SPANISH *offensive* to vomit (JG): **2007** Blogspot: *Marta is no longer dancing in that corner, but rather, tossing her tacos all over the floor*; **2010** Date Hookup: *My nephew tossed his tacos in a tennis ball can. Now that's talent!* || since 1941, from *toss one's cookies* and *taco* "type of tortilla stuffed with various ingredients," and analogy to *toss one's cookies* or *toss one's lunch*

tough shitski *excl.* YIDDISH it is very unfortunate and there is nothing you can do about it (JG, TD): **2008** Urban Dictionary: *You have a problem with me? Tough shitski!* **2015** YouTube: *For those who may complain, tough shitski!* || since 1959, from *tough* and *shitski*, and analogy to *tough shit, tough titty*, or similar expressions denoting unfortunate situation

tough tokus, tough tochus *excl.* YIDDISH it is very unfortunate and there is nothing you can do about it: **2001** *Scrubs*, NBC-TV series: *"Don't give me that!" "And secondly, I'm the attending, so tough tochus!"*; **2012** Huffington Post: *Either way, Obama will be elected to a second term. Tough tochus, Gipper!* || dating unknown, from *tough* and *toches* "buttocks," literally "underneath," and analogy to *tough shit, tough titty*, or similar expressions denoting unfortunate situation

touristas *n.* SPANISH [1] diarrhea, especially as contracted in a foreign country (JG): **2002** Tom Clark: *I got the touristas, which is a highly advanced case of diarrhea*; **2003** Film Wise: *Harrison Ford had a bad case of the touristas* [2] foreign tourists, especially in Mexico: **2009** *Spokane Spokesman-Review*: *This time of year, Cancum, Mexico is typically bustling with touristas*; **2014** Ed Hat: *Do these touristas purchase more than a T-shirt?* || since 1960, from *turistas* "tourists"

traficante *n.* SPANISH a drug trafficker: **2009** Word Press: *I was introduced to some traficantes although not much conversation took place*; **2015** Vice News: *She had been shot by a stray bullet during a shootout between police and traficantes a few hours earlier* || dating unknown, from *traficante* "trafficker"

trashmeister *n.* GERMAN someone making or selling something that has no value, especially shoddy or inferior merchandise: **2000** *National Post*: *Have the years of shame finally caught up with the trashmeister?* **2013** New Republic: *I worry* *about the power of the trashmeisters who now dominate so many of our galleries* ‖ dating unknown, from *trash* and *Meister* "master"

trayf *see* treyf

tres (or **très**) *adv.* FRENCH extremely (JG): **2007** *Game Plan*, film: *You look très gorgeous!* **2018** Susan Cushman: *There are plenty of tres sophisticated Mensa society folks who fear to fly* ‖ since 1920, from *très* "very"

treyf, treif, trayf *adj.* YIDDISH objectionable or suspicious: **1996** David G. Roskies: *On the other side of the Polish-Soviet border, Manger was so treyf that all mention of him was forbidden*; **2012** Zeta Boards: *The "but" usage here is grammatically very treyf* ‖ dating unknown, from *treyf* "ritually impure or unfit to eat" and hence "objectionable"

tsatske, tsatskeh *n.* YIDDISH [1] a plaything or trinket (AS, JG, KC): **1990** *New York Times*: *The apartment was filled with antiques and tsatskes*; **1997** *Chicago Tribune*: *What they have created is a strip of restaurants, clothing stores and tsatske shops* [2] a cute and adorable person, especially a child (JG, KC): **2012** *Gettysburg Review*: *She used to call me a tsatske – how lovingly she said it – my tsatske*; **2012** UCLA student: *Who's that sexy tsatske in the second row?* ‖ since 1964, from *tsatske* "bauble" or "trinket," variant of *tchotchke*

tsimmes *n.* YIDDISH great outrage, fuss, or complaining, especially over a trivial matter (AS): **2009** Word Press: *After a great tsimmes over some disobedient technology and a dozen of kibitzers offering solutions, we got rolling*; **2009** Bike Forums: *What is all the tsimmes with the Honda?* ‖ since 1968, from *tsimes* "fuss and confusion," literally "stew of sweetened vegetables or fruit"

tsunami *n.* JAPANESE an arrival or occurrence of something in overwhelming amounts (AS): **2016** Front Page Magazine: *Today, the reoccurring tsunami of bullshit preempts any attempt to understand what's going on*; **2016** *Christian Science Monitor*: *It's been partly obscured by a tsunami of Donald Trump-related coverage* ‖ since 1950, from *tsunami* "a very high, large wave, especially if caused by an earthquake"

tsuris *n.* YIDDISH troubles, worries, or woes (AS, JG, KC): **2008** *New York Times*: *He seems too young for all this tsuris*; **2011** *Los Angeles Times*: *He is on the verge of resigning, he doesn't need the tsuris* ‖ since 1901, from *tsores* "troubles" or "woes"

tummel[1] *n.* YIDDISH [1] commotion or burst of energy: **2008** Carole S. Kessner: *His appearances are being greeted with the usual tummel (much commotion)*; **2010** *Seattle Post Intelligencer*: *Of course, all this tummel would have global implications* [2] a comedy act or entertainment with audience participation, especially in a summer resort: **1989** *New York Times*: *Jackie Mason has defined his successful Broadway show as the ultimate tummel*; **2013** Blogspot: *They were a tummel team long before Martin and Lewis and just as funny* ‖ dating unknown, from *tuml* "commotion"

tummel [2] *v.* YIDDISH [1] to make a commotion or burst with energy: **2006** Jeffrey Shandler: *Can there be a better date to tummel and to celebrate?* **2011** Amazon Music: *To "tummel" means to make a joyful noise* [2] to work as a comedian or entertainer and to encourage audience participation, in a summer resort: **1999** *Spin Magazine*: *He danced, tummeled, he did pantomime, the audience loved him*; **2004** *New York Times*: *At our meeting celebrating his 90th birthday, he danced, joked and tummeled with the heart of a showman* || dating unknown, from *tumlen* "to cause a commotion"

tummler *n.* YIDDISH [1] someone creates a commotion or bursts with energy (JG): **2010** *Los Angeles Times*: *She's a striver, she's a tummler (Yiddish for someone who shakes things up)*; **2014** UCLA student: *He's a "tummler," a ball of fire* [2] a comedian or entertainer whose job is to encourage audience participation, in a summer resort (AS): **2010** Hollywood USA: *He learned his trade in his teen as a tummler in the Catskills*; **2012** *Boston Globe*: *Lou Goldstein was the consummate tummler, one of a zany species of entertainer who kept them laughing, or tried to, long time ago in the borscht belt hotels of the Catskills* || since 1938, from *tumler* "someone who makes a commotion"

turistas *n.* SPANISH [1] diarrhea, especially as contracted in a foreign country (AS, JG): **2007** Protein Power: *This strange E. coli then causes what we all know as the Turistas or traveler's diarrhea*; **2010** Manuel Medrano: *I woke up with a terrible stomach ache and a case of the turistas (diarrhea)* [2] foreign tourists, especially in Mexico (AS): **1996** *Texas Monthly*: *Some turistas find sour cream or plain tortillas more apt to soothe the burn*; **2008** *Minneapolis-St. Paul Star Tribune*: *The roads are rough and signs are few, but some turistas brave them in rental cars* || since 1960, from *turistas* "tourists"

tush *n.* YIDDISH [1] buttocks (AS, JG, KC): **2001** *Shrek*, film: *When an ogre in the bush grabs a lady by the tush, that's bad*; **2006** *Gray Matters*, film: *I asked to see her husband's tattoo on his tush* [2] a sexually attractive woman: **2007** *Portland Tribune*: *It's a good place to look for some tush*; **2011** Yahoo Answers: *I see as many tushes hanging out here as I do in a more mixed neighborhood* [3] self: **1999** *Runaway Bride*, film: *Meet me. I'll save your tush*; **2002** *Just a Dream*, film: *Get your tush over to the set!* || since 1962, from *toches* "buttocks," literally "underneath"

tushie, tushy *n.* YIDDISH [1] buttocks (JG, KC): **2005** *Pretty Persuasion*, film: *You wiggle your little tushy in front of the audience, and presto! A star is born*; **2011** *Rio*, film: *Linda! You've got to shake your tushie!* [2] a sexually attractive woman: **1990** *Married with Children*, Fox-TV series: *I was entrapped by a middle-aged librarian who saw a hot little tushie and wanted more*; **2012** Wrap: *Demi pushes Peres again on his inappropriate exploitation of underage tushies, threatening legal action* [3] self: **2009** *Rampage*, film: *You guys kicked my little tushie out the door*; **2009** *Examiner*: *If you haven't gotten the vaccine, get your tushies over to the nearest pharmacy doctor's office and get it!* || since 1962, from *toches* "buttocks," literally "underneath," and suffixes *-ie* or *-y*

two tacos short of a combination plate *phr.* SPANISH *potentially offensive* [1] not very intelligent (JG): **1989** *Washington Post*: *Their reporting is about two tacos short of* *a combination plate*; **2005** Free Republic: *I don't care how physically adult they seem – they are two tacos short of a combination plate, judgment-wise* [2] eccentric or odd (JG): **1997** *Santa Fe New Mexican*: *There are definite signs when someone becomes two tacos short of a combination plate*; **2014** Democratic Underground: *"That guy is really certifiable." "Exactly. He's two tacos short of a combination plate"* || since 1986, from *taco* "type of tortilla stuffed with various ingredients"

tzimmes *n.* YIDDISH great outrage, fuss, or complaining, especially over a trivial matter (AS): **2015** Twitter: *Despite all the tzimmes, queries work!* **2015** UNF student: *Such a tzimmes over such bullshit?* || since 1968, from *tsimes* "fuss and confusion," literally "stew of sweetened vegetables or fruit"

tzuris *n.* YIDDISH troubles, worries, or woes (JG, KC): **2009** Spiked: *His cushy life is shredded to pieces as his tzuris mount*; **2011** *Jewish Week*: *I was still healing from the tzuris* || since 1901, from *tsores* "troubles" or "woes"

U

uber- (or **über-**) *prefix.* GERMAN supreme or extreme (AS): **2009** Lifehacker: *Got your own ubergeeky method for navigating around your operating system with the keyboard?* **2009** Blogspot: *My dad, an uberfeminist, forbid me from trying out to be a cheerleader* || dating unknown, from *über* "over"

ubercool *adj.* GERMAN totally superior or excellent: **2014** *Houston Chronicle*: *What was uncool in the hall was ubercool in her class*; **2014** *News*, NBC-TV program: *I feel ubercool to have met him* || dating unknown, from *über* "over" and *cool* "excellent"

ubercrazy *adj.* GERMAN totally crazy: **2012** Word Press: *I'm revving up for an ubercrazy weekend*; **2012** YouTube: *This is an ubercrazy metal tune* || dating unknown, from *über* "over" and *crazy*

ubersexy *adj.* GERMAN totally sexy: **2013** *USA Today*: *We share a love of ubersexy alpha male characters*; **2008** *News*, Fox-TV program: *The ubersexy screen siren was sporting a few more much-needed curves* || dating unknown, from *über* "over" and *sexy*

Uncle Tomahawk *n.* ALGONQUIN *offensive* a Native American who emulates behavior or values of the white majority (JG): **1993** *Chicago Tribune*: *Haney called an Indian student who supports the Seminoles' nickname an "Uncle Tomahawk"*; **2014** *Globe and Mail*: *It led to his being called an "Uncle Tomahawk" by a rival aboriginal leader* || since 1970, from *uncle* and *tomahawk,* analogous to *Uncle Tom* "African American who emulates behavior or values of the white majority"

up the ying-yang *n.* CHINESE to the extreme, to excess (JG, TD): **2000** *Little Nicky*, film: *I got energy up the ying-yang*; **2009** *Race to Witch Mountain*, film: *I say this place is fortified up the ying-yang* || since 1965, from *ying-yang* "rectum" (ultimately from *yīng-yáng* "Chinese philosophy yin-yang") and analogy to *up to one's ass* "to the extreme"

V

vafangool *excl.* ITALIAN *offensive* I hold you in contempt: **2000** *Sopranos*, HBO-TV series: *Maybe it's this, maybe it's that, maybe it's . . . vafangool!* **2000** Uproxx: *We hope you enjoy the episode as much as we enjoyed making it. And if you don't, va fangool* || dating unknown, from dialectal pronunciation of *vaffanculo* "go do it in the ass"

vaffanculo *excl.* ITALIAN *offensive* I hold you in contempt: **2006** *Nation*: *Justice Antonin Scalia responded to protesters by raising the five fingers of his right hand in front of his chin and saying "Vaffanculo"*; **2007** *Shoot 'Em Up*, film: *"You know I'm a good Girl Scout." "So you'll do it!" "Vaffanculo! Screw yourself, Smith!"* || dating unknown, from *va' a fare in culo* "go do it in the ass"

vam *v.* SPANISH to leave or depart, especially hastily (JG): **2007** Urban Dictionary: *C'mon man, this party is lame, let's vam*; **2010** Blogger: *It's getting late. We'd better vam outta this place* || since 1840, from *vamos* "let's go"

vamoose *v.* SPANISH to leave or depart, especially hastily (AS, JG, KC, TD): **2008** *Scooby-Doo and the Goblin King*, film: *Right now is our chance to vamoose*; **2016** *Military Times*: *They can be elusive and have a tendency to vamoose quickly once spotted* || since 1834, from *vamos* "let's go"

vamoose the ranch *phr.* SPANISH to leave or depart, especially hastily: **2012** *Fort Scott Tribune*: *A larger number of slaves vamoose the ranch, and those that remain refuse to work*; **2014** Spell Check: *I reckon I had better vamoose the ranch* || since 1840, from *vamos* "let's go" and *the ranch*

vato *n.* SPANISH [1] any person of Latin American descent (JG): **2011** Flickr: *I know some vatos on the Eastside*; **2018** *Narcos: Mexico*, Netflix-TV series: *"I want a hundred!" "Not now, vato!"* [2] a person (TD): **2001** *Bubble Boy*, film: *She left me for some vato*; **2014** *Phoenix New Times*: *It was five years ago but he does remember the face of one vato in the crowd* || since 1950 in the first sense, since 1971 in the second, from *bato* "simpleton" or "man," ultimately from *chivato* "small goat"

vato loco *n.* SPANISH [1] a crazy person, especially of Latin American descent (JG, TD): **2013** *San Diego Free Press*: *You better talk to Tony before some vato loco does something stupid*; **2018** *Albuquerque Journal*: *I'll show them what being a vato loco is really about* [2] a mentally unbalanced and violent member of a Mexican gang (JG): **2005** Urban Dictionary: *Vato loco is a crazy gangster*; **2012** Tumblr: *I find 40's, 50's subculture living interesting. I'm attracted to vato locos* || since 1965, from *vato loco* "crazy person"

veeno *n.* ITALIAN wine, especially cheap (JG, KC): **2011** Blogspot: *This is to the guys who are sitting around drinking veeno*; **2014** ASU student: *He had too much veeno and passed out* || since 1919, from *vino* "wine"

vendido *n.* SPANISH *offensive* a Mexican American who emulates behavior or values of the non-Hispanic majority: **1993** *Bound by Honor*, film: *"You owe me, vendido!" "Who's the sellout?"*; **2014** *San Jose Mercury News*: *Chicano militants call him a vendido, Spanish for sellout* || since 1944, from *vendido* "sellout"

verboten *adj.* GERMAN forbidden (AS): **2000** *Bring It On*, film: *Tattoos are strictly verboten*; **2007** *Mad Men*, AMC-TV series: *All I have to talk about is work, which is verboten* || dating unknown, from *verboten* "forbidden"

verklemt, verklempt *adj.* YIDDISH overcome with emotion: **2015** *New York Times*: *I'm getting all verklempt just thinking about it*; **2022** *Entertainment Weekly*: *He has more confidence and wasn't going to get verklempt about things* || dating unknown, from *farklemt* "emotionally disturbed"

veterano *n.* SPANISH an experienced, respected gang member (JG, TD): **2005** *Harsh Times*, film: *He's old school. Veterano named Eddie*; **2009** *Boondock Saints II*, film: *My Uncle Cesar is a veterano. Out the game, but still got his name* || since 1975, from *veterano* "veteran"

vieja *n.* SPANISH [1] old woman: **2008** Fan Fiction: *She wants to borrow a phone, vieja, can you bring it?* **2013** UCB student: *Let me help you, vieja* [2] one's wife or girlfriend: **2014** *Gang Related*, Fox-TV series: *What's this I hear about some mysterious vieja of yours?* **2015** *Miami New Times*: *He'd call her his vieja, or "old lady," in front of other workers and grab her butt on the work line* || dating unknown, from *vieja* "old one" or "oldtimer"

viejo *n.* SPANISH [1] old man: **1990** *Hard to Kill*, film: *Remember me, viejo?* **2003** *Washington Heights*, film: *Viejo, you know she ain't gonna pay you, right?* [2] one's husband or boyfriend: **2007** Soy Chicano: *Her viejo is much ugly*; **2014** Facebook: *Your viejo is on the phone with mine* || dating unknown, from *viejo* "old one" or "oldtimer"

Viet *n.* VIETNAMESE *offensive* a Vietnamese or a person of Vietnamese descent (TD): **2006** Storm Front: *The losses sustained by the Viets have never been verified*; **2008** JCVD, film: *In the 70s, it was the Viets, now the Arabs* || since 1966, from *Vietnam*

Vietnik *n.* VIETNAMESE AND YIDDISH someone who opposed the Vietnam war (JG): **2005** *Leatherneck Magazine*: *He will be an anti-war hero to aging Vietniks*; **2007** Free Republic: *Here for example is an excerpt from Time, it's about Vietniks' anti-war demonstration* || since 1966, from blending *Viet(nam)* and suffix *-nik*

Viet shits *n.* VIETNAMESE *offensive* diarrhea, especially as contracted in a foreign country (TD): **2014** Tom Dalzell: *Viet shits is diarrhea*; **2015** Tripod: *The kid here has dysentery. The Viet shits. If you don't want him dead, you better do something* || since 1984, from *Vietnam* and *shits*, and analogy to *G.I. shits* "diarrhea contracted by American soldiers"

vig *n.* YIDDISH interest on a loan or debt, profits of a bookmaker, usurer, or criminal conspirator (AS, JG, KC): **1995** *Get Shorty*, film: *"He's three weeks over on the vig. That's the interest." "I know what vig is"*; **2012** *New York Times*: *Vig, or vigorish, is a gambling term, meaning the money a bookmaker collects on every bet taken – a kind of dependable handling fee* || since 1968, from *vigrish* "interest from winnings"

vigorish *n.* YIDDISH interest on a loan or debt, profits of a bookmaker, usurer, or criminal conspirator (AS, JG, KC): **1990** *Goodfellas*, film: *I never had to pay the vigorish he demands*; **2022** *News*, Fox-TV program: *That way, the oddsmakers are guaranteed a profit through a cut of the action, called the vigorish* || since 1912, from *vigrish* "interest from winnings"

vino *n.* ITALIAN wine, especially cheap (AS, JG, KC): **1992** *Scent of a Woman*, film: *I meant to pick up some vino on my way, but I blew it*; **1998** *Object of My Affection*, film: *Would you like a glass of vino?* || since 1919, from *vino* "wine"

viva *excl.* ITALIAN long live (AS): **2018** *Santa Cruz Sentinel*: *The children pumped their fists while shouting, "Viva!"*; **2018** Jewish News: *About five hecklers shouted "Viva Palestine" while waving the Tunisian flag* || since 1960, from *viva* "long live"

W

waitroid *n.* GREEK a waiter or waitress: **2003** Democratic Underground: *Those who have been a waitroid know what I mean*; **2008** Plentyoffish: *I worked my way through college as a waitroid* || dating unknown, from *wait* and suffix *-oid*

waitron *n.* GREEK a waiter or waitress: **1991** *Los Angeles Times*: *A waitron sounds like a robot and a waitperson sounds sexless*; **2007** *Washington Monthly*: *I used to work as a waitron in the lounge of the Hilton* || dating unknown, from *wait* and suffix *-on*

wastoid *n.* GREEK [1] a worthless person (TD): **2008** Blue Light: *I got fed up with being a total wastoid so I finally just started a job this week for the first time*; **2015** Tumblr: *The boy wants to be a rock star but he's a wastoid* [2] an alcohol or drug addict (TD): **2012** *Spring Breakdown*, film: *They're burnouts, wastoids and sluts*; **2014** *Blue Bloods*, CBS-TV series: *It's one wastoid wasting another* || since 1985, from *waste* and suffix *-oid*

webnik *n.* YIDDISH someone obsessed with the Internet: **2001** *Washington Post*: *Greetings, Webniks, from North Central College in Naperville, Illinois!* **2003** *Boston Globe*: *Stock options and assorted other carrots are luring webniks to job after job* || since 1990s, from *web* and suffix *-nik*

weenie *n.* GERMAN *offensive* [1] the penis (AS, JG, KC, TD): **2009** *Hangover*, film: *He's jacking his little weenie*; **2012** *American Reunion*, film: *You'll be teaching him about masturbation and all the do's and don'ts that have to do with the little guy's weenie* [2] an ineffectual or weak person (AS KC): **1995** *Home for the Holidays*, film:

Go back to your own goddamn holidays! Weenie! **1996** *Pinky and the Brain*, WB-TV series: *We'll see who's a weenie!* || since 1960, from *Wienerwurst* "Vienna sausage"

weiner *n.* GERMAN *offensive* [1] the penis (JG, TD): **2006** *South Park*, Comedy Central-TV series: *You pull on your weiner until the white stuff comes out*; **2009** *Shut Up and Sing*, film: *Ted is like an ATM machine with legs and a weiner* [2] an ineffectual or weak person (KC): **2013** *So This Is Christmas*, film: *Jason can be a real weiner at times*; **2015** Facebook: *Reading is for weiners* || since 1960, from *Wienerwurst* "Vienna sausage"

wet job *n.* RUSSIAN a murder or assassination: **2018** *Washington Post*: *These are throwbacks to earlier KGB active measure, "wet jobs" on dissidents like Markov*; **2018** *Globe and Mail*: *It consisted of local agents stationed all over the world in preparation for killings, known as "wet jobs"* || dating unknown, from *mokroye delo* "wet work"

what gives *sent.* YIDDISH [1] what is going on (JG, KC): **1995** *While You Were Sleeping*, film: *Who is it? What gives?* **2009** *Boondock Saints II*, film: *George, what gives here?* [2] hello (JG, KC): **2003** *Cooler*, film: *What gives? Is it McGann?* **2015** Tumblr: *What gives? I haven't seen you around* || since 1940, from *vos gibt's* "how are things"

what's cooking *sent.* YIDDISH what is going on: **1996** *Big Night*, film: *You're good looking, but you don't know what's cooking*; **2010** *Burning Palms*, film: *"Hey, babe, what's cooking?" "Nothing, I'm just shopping"* || since 1926, from *vos kokht zikh in tepl* "what is cooking in the pot"

what's to lose *sent.* YIDDISH it is worth trying: **2007** *New York Times*: *His massage therapy makes him feel better. What's to lose?* **2007** *Spin Magazine*: *Give everything a go because, frankly, what's to lose?* || dating unknown, from *vos iz tsu farlirn* "what is to lose"

what's with someone *sent.* YIDDISH why is someone behaving in this particular way (KC): **2014** *Ottawa Citizen*: *What's with you? You get laid last night?* **2015** *Los Angeles Times*: *What's with you people? Who cares what you think?* || since 1930, from *vos iz mit emetser* "what is with someone"

what's with something *sent.* YIDDISH why this particular thing (KC): **2003** *Shanghai Knights*, film: *What's with the personal attacks?* **2002** *Pianist*, film: *"What's with the coat?" "It's cold"* || since 1930, from *vos iz mit epes* "what is with something"

whole caboodle *phr.* DUTCH everything entirely (AS, JG, KC): **2018** *Time Out*: *Vic's sale of the whole caboodle is interrupted by the surprise appearance of his brother*; **2019** *Stylist Magazine*: *But Anne says it's more than that: she wants to take sacrament together, exchange holy vows and wear rings, the whole caboodle* || since 1848, from *whole,* prefix *ka-* and *boedel* "property"

whole enchilada *n.* SPANISH everything or totality (KC, TD): **1998** *Parent Trap*, film: *"What do you mean getting married?" "Tie, gown, the whole enchilada"*; **2005**

Chicken Little, film: *He's going for the whole enchilada* || since 1966, from *whole* and *enchilada* "tortilla with meat and chili sauce"

whole megillah *n.* YIDDISH [1] anything very long or complicated (AS, KC): 2000 *Los Angeles Times*: *He got shot with a tranquilizer dart. The zookeepers took care of him, and that ended the whole megillah*; 2012 *Austin Chronicle*: *Items 93–98 will be public hearings on the general funds budget, including the discussion of the whole megillah (Item 95) as well as the proposed property tax rate (Item 97)* [2] everything or totality (AS, KC): 1990 *Simpsons*, Fox-TV series: *We've got archery, wallet-making, the whole megillah*; 2005 *Romance and Cigarettes*, film: *"She's a redhead." "Au naturel?" "The whole megillah"* [3] great outrage, fuss, or complaining, especially over a trivial matter: 1984 *Miami Vice*, NBC-TV series: *I'm sure Sonny will take the blame for the whole megillah*; 2007 Wyoming Network: *Valerie Plame was not a covert overseas agent at the time the whole megillah about her erupted* || since 1909 in the first sense, since 1954 in the second and third, from *whole* and *megile* "scroll" or "volume," especially the Book of Esther read aloud in its entirety at Purim celebrations

Whorez *n.* SPANISH *potentially offensive* Ciudad Juárez, Mexico (TD): 2010 Topix: *She was getting it for her relatives in Whorez*; 2010 Free Republic: *I went to Whorez about 35 years ago and had a tremendous time* || since 1970, from *(Ciudad) Juárez,* a city in Mexico (ultimately from *Benito Juárez,* former president of Mexico) and its reputation for prostitutes

wiener *n.* GERMAN *offensive* [1] the penis (AS, JG, KC, TD): 2009 *17 Again*, film: *Stan has a small wiener*; 2008 *Step Brothers*, film: *And she grabs me by the wiener!* [2] an ineffectual or week person (AS): 1996 *Twister*, film: *Turn him off! What a wiener!* 2022 Screen Rant: *He's a wiener and no one likes him* || since 1960, from *Wienerwurst* "Vienna sausage"

wiener dog *n.* GERMAN a dachshund (KC): 2017 *Vancouver Sun*: *His dad would get him a wiener dog*; 2021 *News*, WBAY-TV program: *Thursday, an officer noticed a woman walking a wiener dog on a leash downtown* || since 1922, from *Wienerwurst* "Vienna sausage" and *dog*

wisenheimer *n.* YIDDISH an irritating person who behaves as if they know everything (JG, KC): 2005 *Ringer*, film: *Watch out for this wisenheimer, Jeffy! He can be trouble*; 2012 *Washington Post*: *One becomes a wisenheimer because it feels good, at first* || since 1902, from *wise* or *visn* "to know" and name-forming suffix *-heymer*

wooden kimono *n.* JAPANESE a coffin, especially a cheap one (JG, KC): 1991 *Come See the Paradise*, film: *You'll be in the army or end up being sent home in a wooden kimono*; 2005 Urban Dictionary: *Jimmy's in a wooden kimono, six feet under* || since 1911, from *wooden* and *kimono* "loose traditional Japanese robe"

wop *n.* ITALIAN *offensive* an Italian or a person of Italian descent (AS, JG, KC): 2013 *Blood Ties*, film: *There's a nigger, a kike and a wop*; 2008 *Righteous Kill*, film:

The wop is Joe Scianci from Bensonhurst. He's a mid-level guy ‖ since 1912, from Southern Italian dialect *guappo* "showy"

wordnik *n.* YIDDISH someone obsessed with words: **2009** Wordnik: *Erin is a wordnik because she has spent so much time working with words*; **2016** Meet Up: *It's a meetup for wordniks and people interested in dictionaries* ‖ dating unknown, from *word* and suffix *-nik*

wow[1] *n.* SCOTTISH GAELIC [1] exclamation meaning "I am impressed and excited" (AS): **2018** *Chicago Tribune*: *The pass traveled only three yards but it elicited many wows*; **2018** *Grand Island Independent*: *He verbalized his excitement with a "wow" as he continued* [2] something impressive and exciting (AS): **2016** *Edmonton Journal*: *There are so many wows in the show*; **2018** *Chicago Daily Herald*: *By doing one large fashion show a year, we can give it 100 percent of our energy to that one show and make it a wow* ‖ since 1920, from *wow*

wow[2] *v.* SCOTTISH GAELIC to impress and excite (AS): **2012** *Desperate Housewives*, ABC-TV series: *I have to wow them with a Power Point presentation*; **2012** *Glee*, Fox-TV series: *This is our chance to wow them* ‖ since 1920, from *wow*

wow[3] *adj.* SCOTTISH GAELIC impressive and exciting (AS): **2016** Hollywood Reporter: *This was a wow speech*; **2018** *Shreveport Times*: *In those days, being a heart surgeon was a wow thing* ‖ since 1920, from *wow*

wow factor *n.* SCOTTISH GAELIC an impressive and exciting quality or feature: **2009** *One Week*, film: *What our city needs is something with a big wow factor*; **2018** *Vogue*: *It was so clean and simple, but still, there was a wow factor* ‖ dating unknown, from *wow* and *factor*

wow moment *n.* SCOTTISH GAELIC a moment when one is impressed and excited: **2018** *Arizona Daily Star*: *For those who understand how difficult it is, it was a wow moment*; **2018** *Economic Times*: *They had a "wow" moment at a chance meeting with Hollywood star Robert De Niro* ‖ dating unknown, from *wow* and *moment*

Y

yalla *excl.* ARABIC hurry up (JG, KC, TD): **2014** *Bordering on Bad Behavior*, film: *Alright, yalla man! Let's eat!* **2006** *Dead End*, film: *Vamos, amigos! Yalla!* ‖ since 2000, from *yalla* "hurry up" and *ya Allāh* "Oh God"

yalla yalla *excl.* ARABIC hurry up (JG, KC, TD): **2013** *Hunting Elephants*, film: *Yalla yalla! Let's go hunt those elephants!* **2018** E! Online: *This is wrong . . . let them go, yalla yalla* ‖ since 2000, from *yalla* "hurry up" and *ya Allāh* "Oh God"

yang *n.* CHINESE the penis (JG, KC, TD): **2014** Blogspot: *Michael has a big yang*; **2015** Urban Dictionary: *Suck my yang!* ‖ since 1965, from *yáng* "masculine principle in the Chinese philosophy yin-yang"

Yank¹ *n.* DUTCH an American (AS, JG, KC): **2001** *Mummy Returns,* film: *I heard the Yanks who found it nine years ago all died;* **2018** *Air & Space Magazine: How did the Yanks get along with their counterparts in the Royal Air Force?* ‖ since 1778, from Yankee, itself perhaps from *Janke,* diminutive of *Jan* "John"

Yank² *adj.* DUTCH American (AS, JG, KC): **2004** Tweak Town Forums: *You have a Yank mentality; kick it because the rest of the world is different;* **2005** Blogger: *Do you understand the Yank talk?* ‖ since 1778, from Yankee, itself perhaps from *Janke,* diminutive of *Jan* "John"

yayo *n.* SPANISH cocaine (JG, TD): **2018** Hip-Hop Wired: *The authorities found the yayo after he sold undercover cops heroin;* **2018** *OC Weekly: Maybe you should lay off the yayo, Kevin* ‖ since 1985, from *llello* "cocaine"

yen *n.* CHINESE an intense craving (JG, KC): **2016** *Austin Chronicle: Russell is an ex-con with pop-star aspirations and a yen for underage female runaways;* **2016** *Modesto Bee: Coaches and anyone else with a yen for sports medicine are welcome to attend* ‖ since 1906, from *yuàn* "desire" or "wish"

yen for something *v.* CHINESE to have an intense craving (JG, KC): **2006** *New York Times: Alexander yens for it hungrily;* **2010** Tech Gadgets: *The steady rise in the number of home office users yenning for superior performance at an affordable price has led to this* ‖ since 1919, from *yuàn* "desire" or "wish"

yenta, yente *n.* YIDDISH a gossipy and annoying person, especially a woman (AS, JG, KC): **1993** *Nanny,* CBS-TV series: *I was on the phone with my mother, and she can be such a yenta;* **2009** Gothamist: *He raises the stakes by calling the mayor a yenta, "a female motormouth"* ‖ since 1923, from *yente* "gossipy woman," popularized by a female character Yente Telebente in a regular column of the New York newspaper the *Jewish Daily Forward*

yents *see* yentz

yentser *see* yentzer

yentz, yents *v.* YIDDISH [1] to have sex with (JG, KC): **2004** Soccer 24–7: *I remember yentzing her from behind;* **2006** Literotica: *To get yentzed is to get screwed, either literally or figuratively* [2] to have sex (JG, KC): **2011** Steve Stern: *Stop kvetching and start yentzing (having sex)!* **2014** UCLA student: *She likes to yentz in any position* [3] to cheat, swindle, or victimize (JG, KC): **2008** Magic Cafe: *They will think you yentzed them out of their money;* **2011** Urban Dictionary: *I really got yentzed when I bought that Yugo from Gotti's Used Cars* ‖ since 1939 in the first two senses, since 1931 in the third, from *yentsn* "to have sex," literally "to do it"

yentzer, yentser *n.* YIDDISH [1] a sex partner: **1996** Leo Rosten: *Yentzer is one who copulates;* **2011** NYU student: *Is he a good yentzer?* [2] a sexually insatiable or proficient person: **1982** John E. Gardner: *"You know what a yentzer is?" "A sexual performer, I guess";* **2011** NYU student: *He's such a yentzer! We did it all night long*

[3] a crook or swindler (JG): **1984** *Once Upon a Time in America*, film: *Bugsy's coming! Yentzer! Schmuck!* **2010** *San Diego Reader*: *Suppose your neighbor is a gonif (crook) or a yentzer (a philanderer and a crook). Then what? Can you trust your neighbors?* ‖ since 1930s, from *yentsn* "to have sex," literally "to do it"

yerba *n.* SPANISH marijuana (JG): **2010** Blue Light: *What sort of "effects" were you hoping to yield from smoking yerba?* **2013** Facebook: *We better smoke yerba and have group sex!* ‖ since 1967, from *yerba* "herb"

yerba buena *n.* SPANISH marijuana (JG): **2007** Soy Chicano: *I smoked some yerba buena earlier*; **2014** *Okay Magazine*: *What happens if you smoke yerba buena?* ‖ since 1967, from *yerba buena* "mint"

yesca *n.* SPANISH marijuana (JG, KC, TD): **2005** *Harsh Times*, film: *"Yesca?" "Bingo! I need to feel some reefer madness"*; **2011** *OC Weekly*: *On this day, the world's counterculture gather and pay a hazy homage to yesca* ‖ since late 1940s, from *yesca* "tinder"

yeyo *n.* SPANISH cocaine (JG, TD): **2013** *Miami New Times*: *It might also give you a few bad habits – and we're not talking about hookers and yeyo*; **2016** *Orlando Weekly*: *An off-duty deputy found 50 pounds of uncut yeyo off the coast of Englewood Beach, Florida* ‖ since 1982, from *llello* "cocaine"

Yid *n.* YIDDISH (*offensive* when used by non-Jews) a Jew (AS, JG, KC): **1999** *New York Times*: *She'd even gone so far, in one of her early novels, as to call him a "yid," but her husband crossed out the insult and replaced it with "boy"*; **2012** *New York Observer*: *He was a badass of the Hebrew persuasion, a yid with an id* ‖ since 1874, from *yid* "Jew"

yiddishe kop, yiddisher kop *n.* YIDDISH [1] Jewish way of thinking, especially being smart: **2007** *New Yorker*: *My rabbis told me I had a yiddishe kop, which meant I was smart*; **2011** Charley Rosen: *I was fed up with the whole concept of yiddisher kop, the notion that Jewish brainpower is so superior* [2] someone who thinks in a Jewish way, especially in a smart way: **2010** Forward: *Despite any aspersions, Perelman may just be a Yiddishe kop pressured past the point of endurance*; **2012** *San Diego Reader*: *I don't think Dick was a Yiddishe kop* ‖ dating unknown, from *yidisher kop*, literally "Jewish head"

Yiddish highway *n.* YIDDISH US 301 between New York and Miami, where traditionally many Jews travel for retirement (JG): **2009** Tom Dalzell: *Yiddish highway is US 301*; **2015** Dawg Shed: *I'm not gonna be stuck on the Yiddish Highway for four hours!* ‖ since 1979, from *yidish* "Jewish" and *highway*

yideneh, yidene *n.* YIDDISH [1] (*offensive* when used by non-Jews) a Jewish woman: **1995** Robert Eisenberg: *She is the archetypal yideneh, an iron-willed Jewess*; **2012** East European Food: *There wasn't a Jewish bone in her body, yet she cooked like a yidene* [2] any gossipy person, especially a woman: **1996** Leo Rosten: *Two yidenehs were talking about their children*; **2000** James Atlas: *He defines a yideneh as a gossipy woman* ‖ dating unknown, from *yidene* "Jewess"

yidentify *v.* YIDDISH to be able to spot a fellow Jew in a large group: **2011** *Jewish Magazine*: *Yidentify is to be able to determine Jewish origins*; **2011** Tumbler: *This is what Steven Pinker called the ability to yidentify. You see someone and think they might be Jewish* || since 1990s, from blending *yid* "Jew" and *identify*

Yinglish *n.* YIDDISH [1] a variety of English that contains many Yiddish expressions, often modified: **1994** Mendele: *Other relatives spoke to me in Yinglish*; **2004** *New York Times*: *An English translation should be in English, not in Yinglish* [2] a variety of English slang that contains many Yiddish expressions, often modified: **1992** *New York Times*: *It is surely the most often lampooned locution in Yinglish*; **1998** *Chicago Tribune*: *He demonstrated that he's a complete shmo. That's short but effective Yinglish* || since 1951, from blending *Yiddish* and *English*

ying-yang (or **yin-yang**) *n.* CHINESE [1] the rectum (JG, KC, TD): **2009** Urban Dictionary: *The drug smuggler stuffed it up his yin yang*; **2010** *Rookie Blue*, Global-TV series: *She's got drugs up the ying-yang* [2] the penis (JG, KC, TD): **2009** *Lesbian Vampire Killers*, film: *You think his ying-yang is big?* **2015** UNF student: *That pervert started pulling his ying-yang* || since 1968 in the first sense, since 1981 in the second, from *yīng-yáng* "Chinese philosophy yin-yang"

yold *n.* YIDDISH [1] a stupid person: **1990** Howard Simons: *You were always being told you were a yold in school*; **2019** *Tablet Magazine*: *Her goyfriend is made out to be a yold* [2] a naive or gullible person: **1996** Leo Rosten: *I acted like a real yold*; **2007** *New York Times*: *A yold believes the shmendrick's claim that it wasn't his fault* || dating unknown, from *yold* "stupid or naive person"

Yugo *n.* CROATIAN *offensive* a person from the former Yugoslavia or a person of Yugoslavian descent (JG): **1988** *Little Nikita*, film: *"I like your new helper." "Yeah, he's Joe, Yugo out of Vancouver"*; **2005** *Angela*, film: *If you fail, I'm sending two Yugos on your ass* || dating unknown, from *yugo* "south," *slav* "Slavic person," and *Yugoslavia*

yutz *n.* YIDDISH [1] the penis (JG): **2011** Democratic Underground: *If the guy was proven guilty he would vote to hang him by his yutz*; **2012** Twitter: *You can tell how big his yutz is* [2] a despicable and stupid person (JG, KC): **1993** *Dave*, film: *Let's hope this yutz can pull it off*; **2022** *Marvelous Mrs. Maisel*, Amazon-TV series: *You gotta pay them. Not the rent, you yutz, payola! Give 'em a taste* || since 1980s, from blending *yold* "stupid or naive person" and *putz* "despicable naive person"

Z

zaftig, zaftik, zoftig, zoftik *adj.* YIDDISH curvaceous (AS, JG, KC, TD): **2007** *Californication*, Showtime-TV series: *Most of my girlfriends were somewhat zaftig*; **2016** Huffington Post: *I am watching my weight now that I live in Honolulu. I don't want to get zaftig* || since 1929, from *zaftik* "juicy"

zany *adj.* ITALIAN amusingly or ridiculously strange: **2011** *Futurama*, Fox-TV series: *Hermes, is this one of your zany practical jokes?* **2015** *San Diego Union-Tribune*: *Without* *proper context, the announcements can seem zany* ‖ since 1918, from earlier sense "buffoon-like," from dialectal *Zanni*, variant of *Gianni* and nickname for *Giovanni* "John," name of servants acting as clowns in the *commedia dell'arte*

zetz¹, zets *n.* YIDDISH a blow or punch (JG): **2003** *Looney Tunes: Back in Action*, film: *Give him a zets every once in a while*; **2011** *Examiner: Watch out, because Tracy will give you a zetz* ‖ since 1979, from *zets* "blow" or "hit"

zetz², zets *v.* YIDDISH to blow or punch: **2000** *Vanity Fair: I was zetzing them all the time*; **2009** *News*, Fox-TV program: *Garfunkel made one crack about Simon's missing toupee, and Simon zetzed him back* ‖ since 1979, from *zetsn* "to blow" or "to hit"

zhlub *n.* YIDDISH [1] a boorish and ill-mannered person, especially from the country (JG, KC): **2001** *New York Times: What can you expect from such a zhlub?* **2015** UNF student: *I can tell a zhlub a mile away* [2] a sloppy, slovenly, or poorly dressed person: **1992** *New York Magazine: He was known as a zhlub. He was overweight, and he didn't care about haircuts*; **2006** *San Francisco Chronicle: Andy lives a schizophrenic existence, working at the center of the couture world, while dressing like a zhlub* [3] a stupid person (JG): **2011** NYU student: *What a zhlub? How many times do I have to tell him?* **2014** Facebook: *What a zhlub! So stupid!* ‖ since 1964 in the first two senses, since 1950 in the third, from *zshlob* "coarse or boorish person"

zoftig *see* zaftig

zoftik *see* zaftig

zombie *n.* KIKONGO [1] an apathetic or dull person (AS, JG, KC, TD): **2018** Elite Daily: *Personally, I feel like a zombie when I don't clock in closer to eight or nine hours of rest*; **2018** Moms: *With so much on their plate, it's no wonder that many moms look like zombies, with very little sleep at night* [2] a strange or bizarre person (JG, KC, TD): **2008** *Step Brothers*, film: *Don't you touch my drums, zombie!* **2012** Twitter: *That fucking zombie freaks me out* ‖ since 1930, from *zumbi* "fetish"

zombie out *v.* KIKONGO to make someone look like a zombie (JG, KC, TD): **2015** Vibe: *I didn't take it during the day because it zombied me out*; **2018** *News*, Fox-TV program: *He was taking 13–14 prescription drugs per day and described the feeling "zombied out"* ‖ since 1930, from *zumbi* "fetish" and *out*

zombie weed *n.* KIKONGO phencyclidine, the recreational drug known as PCP (JG, TD): **2015** Oregon Live: *The pain goes away because you're thinking about other stuff. I don't want the zombie weed. I'm a functional stoner*; **2017** *News*, WMTV-TV program: *Zombie weed is a synthetic narcotic that people smoke that could be made from a number of different chemical compounds* ‖ since 1970, from *zumbi* "fetish" and *weed*

zorro belly *n.* SPANISH *potentially offensive* someone who has an abdomen with post-operation scars: **1998** *Hartford Courant: Zorro belly is someone with many surgical scars on the abdomen*; **2010** Ralph Keyes: *Zorro belly refers to a patient whose abdomen has many scars from previous surgeries* ‖ dating unknown, from the fictional, sword-wielding character *Zorro*, itself from Spanish zorro "fox" and *belly*

Sources

Conversation

ASU students (Arizona State University, Tempe, AZ); CUNY students (City University of New York, New York, NY); FSU students (Florida State University, Tallahassee, FL); NYU students (New York University, New York, NY); SU students (Stanford University, Stanford, CA); UA students (University of Arizona, Tucson, AZ); UCB students (University of California at Berkeley, Berkeley, CA); UCLA students (University of California at Los Angeles, Los Angeles, CA); UCSD students (University of California at San Diego, San Diego, CA); UF students (University of Florida, Gainesville, FL); UM students (University of Miami, Miami, FL); UNF students (University of North Florida, Jacksonville, FL); UNM students (University of New Mexico, Albuquerque, NM); USF students (University of South Florida, Tampa, FL).

Film

8 Mile (2002); *10 Items or Less* (2006); *17 Again* (2009); *25th Hour* (2002); *40 Year Old Virgin* (2005); *48 Hours* (1982); *88 Minutes* (2007); *1408* (2007); *Abandon* (2002); *Above the Rim* (1994); *Aces: Iron Eagle III* (1992); *Adventures of Tintin* (1991); *After School Special* (2006); *Against the Wall* (1994); *Air America* (1990); *Airheads* (1994); *All the Pretty Horses* (2000); *Amazing Spider-Man* (2012); *American Beauty* (1999); *American Gangster* (2007); *American Me* (1992); *American Pie 2* (2001); *American Pie Presents: Band Camp* (2005); *American Pie Presents: Beta House* (2007); *American Psycho* (2000); *American Reunion* (2012); *American Sniper* (2014); *American Splendor* (2003); *American Wedding* (2003); *America's Sweethearts* (2001); *Angela* (2005); *Anger Management* (2003); *Another Day in Paradise* (1999); *Another Stakeout* (1993); *Ant Bully* (2006); *Anything Else* (2003); *Armageddon* (1998); *Assassins Run* (2013); *At First Sight* (1999); *Avatar*

(2007); *Bachelor Party* (1984); *Bad Boys* (1995); *Bad Boys II* (2003); *Bandits* (2001); *Barton Fink* (1991); *Basketball Diaries* (1995); *Batman Begins* (2005); *Batman Forever* (1995); *Be Careful* (2011); *Before Night Falls* (2000); *Behind the Mask* (2006); *Besties* (2012); *Beverly Hills Chihuahua* (2008); *Beverly Hills Cop III* (1994); *Big Daddy* (1999); *Big Fat Liar* (2002); *Big Lebowski* (1998); *Big Momma's House 2* (2006); *Big Night* (1996); *Big Stan* (2008); *Black Snake Woman* (2006); *Blade II* (2002); *Blaze You Out* (2013); *Blood Ties* (2013); *Blow* (2001); *Blue in the Face* (1995); *Body and Soul* (2000); *Bone Collector* (1999); *Boondock Saints II* (2009); *Bordering on Bad Behavior* (2014); *Borderland* (2007); *Bound by Honor* (1993); *Boyz n the Hood* (1991); *Breakfast with Scott* (2007); *Bring It On* (2000); *Bring It On: All or Nothing* (2006); *Bring It On: Fight to the Finish* (2009); *Broadcast News* (1987); *Brokeback Mountain* (2005); *Broken City* (2013); *Broken Hill* (2009); *Bubble Boy* (2001); *Bulletproof* (1996); *Burning Palms* (2010); *Butler* (2013); *Capturing the Friedmans* (2003); *Career Girls* (1997); *Carlito's Way* (1993); *Carlito's Way: Rise to Power* (2005); *Casino* (1995); *Cats & Dogs* (2001); *Change-Up* (2011); *Charlie Wilson's War* (2007); *Chasing Amy* (1997); *Chasing Ice* (2012); *Cheaper by the Dozen* (2003); *Chicago* (2002); *Chicken Little* (2005); *Children of Men* (2006); *Choke* (2008); *Chosen One* (2010); *Christmas Cottage* (2008); *Cinderella Man* (2005); *Click* (2006); *Clueless* (1995); *Codebreaker* (2011); *Collateral* (2004); *Come See the Paradise* (1991); *Con Air* (1997); *Confessions of an American Bride* (2005); *Connie and Carla* (2004); *Conspiracy Theory* (1997); *Constantine* (2005); *Contact* (1997); *Contract* (2006); *Conversations with Other Women* (2005); *Cooler* (2003); *Courage Under Fire* (1996); *Crank: High Voltage* (2009); *Crazy Beautiful* (2001); *Creatures from the Pink Lagoon* (2006); *Criminal* (2004); *Crocodile Dundee in Los Angeles* (2001); *Crossing Guard* (1995); *Crumb* (1994); *Curse of the Jade Scorpion* (2001); *Cut Runs Deep* (2000); *Cutting Edge: The Magic of Movie Editing* (2004); *Dallas Buyers Club* (2013); *Damages* (2007); *Dance with the Devil* (1997); *Dante's Peak* (1997); *Dark Knight* (2008); *Dave* (1993); *Day Without a Mexican* (2004); *Day Zero* (2007); *Dead End* (2006); *Dead in Tombstone* (2013); *Dead Presidents* (1995); *Dead Silence* (1997); *Deal* (2008); *Deconstructing Harry* (1997); *Defiance* (2009); *Delirious* (1991); *Departed* (2006); *Desperado* (1995); *Die Hard 2* (1990); *Diggstown* (1992); *Dirty* (2005); *Distinguished Gentleman* (1992); *Django Unchained* (2012); *Dogma* (1999); *Donnie Brasco* (1997); *Don't Drink the Water* (1994); *Double Take* (2001); *Double Whammy* (2001); *Down with Love* (2003); *Due Date* (2010); *Dumb and Dumber* (1994); *Dunston Checks In* (1995); *Eastern Promises* (2007); *Easy A* (2010); *EDtv* (1999); *Education of Charlie Banks* (2009); *Ed Wood* (1994); *El Cantante* (2006); *Elvis Has Left* the Building (2004); *Empire Records* (1995); *Employee of the Month* (2006); *Encino Man* (1992); *Enemy of the State* (1998); *Entrapment* (1999); *Epic Movie* (2007); *Escape from L.A.* (1996); *Ex Drummer* (2007); *Eye of the Storm* (2011); *Face/Off* (1997); *Family* (2013); *Far and Away* (1992); *Fargo* (1996); *Fatal Instinct* (1993); *Fear* (1996); *Fear and Loathing in Las Vegas* (1998); *Felon* (2008); *Filthy Rich* (1982); *Five Dollars a Day* (2008); *Flight of the Intruder* (1991); *Flintstones* (1994); *Forger* (2012); *Forrest Gump* (1994); *For Your Consideration* (2006); *Foxfire* (1996); *Freeway Killer* (2010); *Fresh* (1994); *Frida* (2002); *Friday* (1995); *From Dusk till Dawn* (1996); *Fugitive* (1993); *Full Eclipse* (1993); *Funny Money* (2006); *Fun with Dick and Jane* (2005); *Game* (1997); *Game Plan* (2007); *Garfield: A Tail of Two Kitties* (2006); *Gas, Food, Lodging* (1992); *Get a Clue* (2002); *Get on the Bus* (1996); *Get Shorty* (1995); *Ghost World* (2001); *Ghost Writer* (2010); *Gift* (2000); *Girls Will Be Girls* (2003); *Glass House* (2001); *Glengarry Glen Ross* (1992); *Goats* (2012); *Godzilla* (1998); *Gone Baby Gone* (2007); *Goodfellas* (1990); *Good Luck Chuck* (2007); *Good Morning Vietnam* (1987); *Goofy Movie* (1995); *Gotti* (1996); *Gray Matters* (2006); *Green Mile* (1999); *Grindhouse* (2007); *Grizzly Man* (2007); *Grizzly Park* (2008); *Grosse Pointe Blank* (1997); *Groundhog Day* (1993); *Grumpier Old Men* (1995); *Guys* (2002); *Gypsies, Tramps and Thieves* (2006); *Half Baked* (1998); *Half Past Dead 2* (2007); *Hamburger Hill* (1987); *Hangover* (2009); *Hannibal* (2001); *Hard Candy* (2005); *Hard to Kill* (1990); *Harsh Times* (2005); *Havana* (1990); *Havoc* (2005); *Headspace* (2005); *He Got Game* (1998); *Heist* (2001); *Held Up* (1999); *Help* (2011); *Hercules* (1997); *Hoffa* (1992); *Holiday* (2006); *Home Alone* (1990); *Home for the Holidays* (1995); *Homeward Bound* (1993); *Honeydipper* (2008); *Horrible Bosses 2* (2014); *Hottie and Nottie* (2008); *How the Grinch Stole Christmas* (2000); *Hudson Hawk* (1991); *Hudsucker Proxy* (1994); *Hunting Elephants* (2013); *Hustle* (2004); *Identity Thief* (2013); *Ides of March* (2011); *In Good Company* (2004); *I Love You, Man* (2009); *In Plain Sight* (2008); *Internship* (2013); *In the Cut* (2003); *Inspector Gadget* (1999); *It's Complicated* (2009); *I Want Candy* (2007); *Jackie Brown* (1997); *JCVD* (2008); *Jersey Shore Massacre* (2014); *Jesse Stone: Sea Change* (2007); *JFK* (1991); *Jimmy Show* (2001); *Judge Dredd* (1995); *Jungle Book 2* (2003); *Jungle 2 Jungle* (1997); *Just a Dream* (2002); *Just Friends* (2005); *Kate and Leopold* (2001); *Kick-Ass* (2010); *Kill Bill: Vol. 2* (2004); *Kill the Irishman* (2012); *Kill the Poor* (2003); *Kill Your Darlings* (2013); *Kindergarten Cop* (1990); *King of Kong* (2008); *King of the Hill* (1993); *Kings of South Beach* (2008); *Kiss Me, Guido* (1997); *Knockaround Guys* (2001); *Kung Fu Panda* (2008); *L.A. Confidential* (1997); *Ladykillers* (2004); *La Mission* (2009); *Land of the Dead* (2005); *Last Boy Scout* (1991);

Last Dragon (1985); *Last Man Standing* (1996); *Last Play at Shea* (2010); *Last Seduction* (1994); *Last Vegas* (2013); *Laws of Attraction* (2004); *Lay the Favorite* (2012); *Legally Blonde 2* (2003); *Leningrad* (2007); *Léon* (1994); *Lesbian Vampire Killers* (2009); *Librarian* (2004); *Licence to Kill* (1989); *Life* (1999); *Life As We Know It* (2010); *Life of Pi* (2012); *Like It Is* (1998); *Line of Duty* (2013); *Little Nicky* (2000); *Little Nikita* (1988); *Little Secrets* (2002); *Lone Star* (1996); *Lone Survivor* (2014); *Long Kiss Goodnight* (1996); *Longest Yard* (2005); *Look Who's Talking* (1990); *Looney Tunes: Back in Action* (2003); *Loss of Sexual Innocence* (2000); *Lost Highway* (1997); *Lost World: Jurassic Park* (1997); *Love Ranch* (2011); *Love, Wedding, Marriage* (2011); *Love Wrecked* (2006); *Madagascar* (2005); *Madagascar 3* (2012); *Maiden Heist* (2010); *Main Street* (2010); *Mambo Kings* (1992); *Man in the Car* (2007); *Man on the Moon* (1999); *Man Who Knew Too Little* (1997); *Man Who Wasn't There* (2001); *Many Saints of Newark* (2021); *Married to the Mob* (1988); *Matador* (2005); *Match Point* (2005); *Max* (2002); *Me and the Kid* (1993); *Meet the Fockers* (2004); *Meet the Parents* (2000); *Memorial Day* (2012); *Men in Black* (1997); *Men in Black 3* (2012); *Men of Honor* (2000); *Miami Trail* (2003); *Milk* (2008); *Miller's Crossing* (1990); *Million Dollar Baby* (2005); *Minority Report* (2002); *Miss Congeniality* (2000); *Miss March* (2009); *Miss Nobody* (2010); *Models* (1999); *Monument Men* (2014); *Morning Glory* (2010); *Mr. Magoo* (1997); *Mr. Popper's Penguins* (2011); *Mulan II* (2005); *Mummy Returns* (2001); *Munich* (2005); *Muppets from Space* (1999); *Muppets' Wizard of Oz* (2005); *My Best Friend's Girl* (2008); *My Family* (1995); *My Life in Ruins* (2009); *Neighbors* (2014); *New York City Serenade* (2007); *New York, I Love You* (2009); *Next Friday* (2000); *Nixon* (1995); *Nobody's Perfect* (1990); *Object of My Affection* (1998); *O Brother, Where Art Thou?* (2000); *Obsessed* (2009); *Ocean's Twelve* (2004); *Off the Map* (2011); *Old Dogs* (2009); *Once Upon a Time in America* (1984); *One, Two, Many* (2008); *One Week* (2009); *Only the Lonely* (1991); *Oscar* (1991); *Our Family Wedding* (2010); *Out Cold* (2001); *Out For Justice* (1991); *Painted House* (2003); *Paranormal Activity* (2014); *Parent Trap* (1998); *Pathology* (2008); *Pearl Harbor* (2001); *People I Know* (2002); *Perdita Durango* (1997); *Perestroika* (2009); *Perrier's County* (2010); *Pianist* (2002); *Piñero* (2002); *Pit Fighter* (2005); *Platoon* (1987); *Play It to the Bone* (1999); *Porno* (2000); *Powder Blue* (2009); *Pretty Persuasion* (2005); *Price Above Rubies* (1998); *Prime* (2005); *Prince of the City* (1981); *Private Parts* (1997); *Producers* (2005); *Pulp Fiction* (1994); *Punisher* (1989); *Q & A* (1990); *Queer Duck: The Movie* (2006); *Quiz Show* (1994); *Race to Space* (2001); *Race to Witch Mountain* (2009); *Raising Cain* (1992); *Rambo* (2008); *Rampage* (2009); *Ray* (2004); *Red Hook Summer* (2013); *Requiem for a Dream* (2000); *Retroactive* (1997); *Righteous Kill* (2008); *Ringer* (2005); *Rio* (2011); *R.I.P.D.* (2013); *Rise of the Footsoldier* (2007); *River's Edge* (1987); *Roadie* (2013); *Road of No Return* (2009); *Road to Perdition* (2002); *Robin Williams: Weapons of Self Destruction* (2009); *Rockaway* (2007); *Romance and Cigarettes* (2005); *Romeo Must Die* (2000); *Rookie* (1990); *Rose Red* (2002); *Rounders* (1998); *Royal Tenenbaums* (2001); *Runaway Bride* (1999); *Rundown* (2003); *Running Man* (1987); *Running Scared* (2006); *Safe Men* (1998); *Savage Grace* (2007); *Savages* (2012); *Saving Private Ryan* (1998); *Say It Isn't So* (2001); *Scanner Darkly* (2006); *Scarface* (1983); *Scary Movie* (2000); *Scent of a Woman* (1992); *School Dance* (2014); *Scooby-Doo and the Goblin King* (2008); *Scooby-Doo and the Monster of Mexico* (2003); *Scoop* (2006); *Scott Pilgrim vs. the World* (2010); *Scream 2* (1997); *See Spot Run* (2001); *Selena* (1997); *Selma* (2015); *Sessions* (2012); *Seven Psychopaths* (2012); *Sex and the City* (2008); *Shall We Dance* (2004); *Shanghai Ghetto* (2002); *Shanghai Knights* (2003); *Shark Attack 3* (2002); *Shark Bait* (2006); *Sharktopus* (2010); *She's the One* (1996); *Shoot 'Em Up* (2007); *Shortbus* (2006); *Short Cuts* (1993); *Shrek* (2001); *Shrek 2* (2004); *Shut Up and Sing* (2009); *Sideways* (2004); *Silver City* (2004); *Simpsons* (2007); *Sin City* (2005); *Sitter* (2011); *Sixth Sense* (1999); *Sixty Six* (2006); *Skills* (2010); *Skulls II* (2002); *Sliding Doors* (1998); *Slight Case of Murder* (1999); *Smokin' Aces* (2007); *Sniper: Reloaded* (2011); *Snow Cake* (2015); *Snow on Tha Bluff* (2012); *So This Is Christmas* (2013); *Soul Plane* (2004); *Source Code* (2011); *South Park* (1999); *Space Cowboys* (2000); *Spanglish* (2004); *Speed* (1994); *Spirit* (2008); *Spring Breakdown* (2012); *Stand and Deliver* (1988); *Starsky and Hutch* (2004); *Step Brothers* (2008); *Stick* (1985); *Stiletto* (2008); *Story of Us* (1999); *Stranger Than Fiction* (2006); *Straw Dogs* (2011); *Streets of Laredo* (1995); *Striptease* (1996); *Suburban Gothic* (2015); *Superbad* (2007); *Super Troopers* (2001); *Surf School* (2006); *Suzie Gold* (2004); *Switch* (1991); *Sydney White* (2007); *Taking Care of Business* (1990); *Taking Woodstock* (2009); *Talented Mr. Ripley* (1999); *Tango and Cash* (1989); *Ted* (2012); *Terminator 2: Judgment Day* (1991); *That Thing You Do* (1996); *The Mitchells vs. The Machines* (2021); *There's Something about Mary* (1998); *Thing About My Folks* (2005); *Third Wish* (2005); *This Is the End* (2013); *This Means War* (2012); *Thousand Words* (2012); *Three Amigos* (2003); *Three Kings* (1999); *Top Five* (2014); *Tortilla Soup* (2001); *Toy Story* (1999); *Traffic* (2000); *Transformers* (2007); *Transformers: Revenge of the Fallen* (2009); *Tremors 3: Back to Perfection* (2001); *Triggerman* (2009); *Tropic Thunder* (2008); *True Stories* (1986); *Truman Show* (1998); *Tune in Tomorrow* (1990); *Tutor* (1983); *Twelve Monkeys* (1996); *Twister* (1996); *Ugly Truth* (2009); *Undocumented* (2010); *Unforgiven* (2009); *U-Turn*

(1997); *Under the Volcano* (1984); *Usual Suspects* (1995); *Virginity Hit* (2010); *Viva Cuba* (2005); *Voice* (2015); *Walkout* (2006); *Walk to Remember* (2002); *Wall Street* (1987); *War* (2007); *Washington Heights* (2003); *Wedding Crashers* (2005); *We Own the Night* (2007); *We're the Millers* (2013); *What's the Worst That Could Happen* (2001); *What Women Want* (2000); *While You Were Sleeping* (1995); *Whiplash* (2014); *White Chicks* (2004); *White Oleander* (2002); *Who's Your Daddy?* (2005); *Windtalkers* (2002); *Witness to the Mob* (1998); *Wolf of Wall Street* (2013); *Wolverine* (2013); *Wrong Side of Town* (2010); *Wyvern* (2009); *You Don't Know Jack* (2010); *You Don't Mess with the Zohan* (2008); *Zombieland* (2009); *Zoolander* (2001); *Zoom* (2006).

Internet

4Plebs; Abe Books; Absolute Write; Academia; Addiction Blog; Adult DVD Talk; Aging Rebel; Air Talk; Alcoholism; Alternate History; Amateur Album; Amazon Music; American History; American Thinker; America Online Autos; Amoeba; Android Community; Angelfire; Anime Source; Apartment Ratings; Apple Discussions; Arizona Sports Fans; Arkansas Online; Ars Technica; Asheville Clicks; Atlas Tales; Autoblog; Auto Evolution; Baby Center; Baby Gaga; Battle On; Beacon; Bear Insider; Bebo; Bedbug King; Be Press; Berkeleyside; Big Brother Network; Big Soccer; Bike Forums; Bimmer Fest; BioWorld; Black Agenda Report; Black Planet; Bladesmith's Forum; Blaze; Bleacher Report; Blip; Blogger; Blogs; Blogspot; Blogster; Bloomberg; Blue Light; Bookie Jar; Borderland Beat; Borderzine; Bossip; Boston Online; Boxing Scene; Box Rec; Boyz Tube; Break; Bright Hub; Broadway World; Brooklyn Daily; Brooklyn Vegan; Brown Pride; Brush Beat; Bustle; BuzzFeed; Buzz House; Cafe Hayek; Cafe Mom; Cafe Press; Campaign Outsider; Campaign Site Builder; Cannabis Culture; Cannabis News; Capitol Confidential; Car Blaze; Car Lounge; Catholic Philly; Celebitchy; Cheeky Chicago; Chicago Syndicate; Chitown Racing; Chowhound; Christian Forums; Chronicle of Higher Education; Cigar Chronicles; Cigar Family; Cinema Blend; Citizen of the Month; City Data; City Search; City X Guide; Cleveland Online; Community Baby Center; Complex; Composite Arts; Coney Island Online; Consumerist; Conversation; Convicted Artist; Cool Tweets; Core77; Cowboy Job; Creators Syndicate; Crown Heights; Curious Girlfriend; Daily Beast; Daily Caller; Daily Kos; Daily Motion; Daily Strength; Daily XY; Dallas Entree Journal; Date Hookup; Daviant Art; Dawg Shed; Deadline; Dead

Mule; Deadspin; Death and Taxes; Deep Politics Forum; Democratic Underground; Denver Hypnosis; Deviant Art; Diary Land; Digital Digest; Digital Journal; Digital Photography Review; Digital Spy; Dining Chicago; Diplomacy World; Direct Marketing News; Discovery Gaming; Dodgers Nation; Down Trend; Drinks Mixer; Drive; Drug Library; Drug Test; Drug War Chronicle; DVD Empire; DVD Talk; DVX User; Earthlink; East European Food; East Village; Eater; E-Cigarettes; Ecoustics; Ed Hat; Elite Daily; El Paso Online; Enjoygram; Enterprise News; E! Online; E-Poetry; E-Reading Club; Escapist Magazine; Etymonline; Express Milwaukee; Extra; Facebook; Fan Fiction; Fark; Fashion Binge; Fashion Spot; Fiction Press; Film Wise; First Nations; Flavorwire; Flickr; Florida Politics; Forum Mazda Miata; Forums; Freak Angels; Free Gay Pix; Freeones; Free Republic; Frisky; Front Page Magazine; Fulton History; Gaia Online; Gamefaqs; Game Forge; Garage Journal; Gate World; Gay Speak; Gear Page; Geek Hack; Geo Cities; Georgia Outside News; Gizmodo; Global News; Gold Eagle; Gold Seek; Golf News Now; Google Blogs; Google Groups; Got Poetry; Gothamist; Grass City; Grease Car; Greenwich Time; Groove Shark; GTA Forums; Guestbook; Harmony Central; Haruth; Health 24; Health Knowledge; Heeb Magazine; Hip-Hop Wired; Hipster Jew; Hispanic Post; Hollywood Billboard; Hollywood Life; Hollywood Reporter; Hollywood USA; Home Spring; Homo Sex Info; Homosexual Tube; Honolulu Civil Beat; Hood Up; Hot New Hip Hop; Houston Culture; Houston Salsa Congress; Huddle; Huffington Post; Idaho Gangs; IGN Boards; In Character; Indeed; Indy Bay; Inquisitr; Inside Higher Ed; Inspirational Stories; Instagram; International Cannagraphic; International Sex Guide; Investor Village; Investors Hub; iPhoneogram; Israel Forum; Jab Comix; Jalopnik; Jewish Baltimore; Jewish Holiday; Journal Home; Just Jared; Katz's Delicatessen Online; Kickstarter; Kscapeowners; LA Downtown News; LA Eastside; LAist; Latin Life; Legends of America; Leland Report; Lifehacker; Lipstick Alley; Literotica; Live Journal; Live Leak; Lively Arts; Lolly Dream; Lonely Planet; Los Santos Roleplay; Lubbock Online; Mac Forums; Madison Online; Magic Cafe; Market Watch; Marketing Power; Mashable; Mayan Heritage; Medi Lexicon; Mediaite; Meet Up; Megalomaniac; Meme Generator; Men Stuff; Mental Floss; Meta Filter; Mexican Cupid; Miami Online; Mike Online; Millions; Military; Minx; Missouri Whitetails; MMA Junkie; MMA Weekly; Moe Lane; Moms; Monsters and Critics; Mormon Discussions; Motherboard; Motley Fool; Motorcycle USA; Mr. Conservative; Mr. Skin; MSF High; Mugshots; Muppet Central; Mustang World; My Diary; My San Antonio;

My Space; Naira Land; Narkive; National; National Board of Review of Motion Pictures; National Public Radio; Neuro Talk; Nevada Today; New Jersey Real Estate Report; New Mexico Boxing; News Busters; Newser; Newsmax; Newsworks; New World News; NJOP; NOLA; NYU Tisch Online; Ocean Beach Rag; Ocean Breeze Recovery; Officer; OK Cupid; Old Jews Telling Jokes; OpEd News; Open Writing; Opiophile; Oregon Live; Paleo Owl; Parenting Teens; Patch; PB Nation; PC Gamer Magazine; Penny Arcade; Perez Hilton; Persephone Magazine; Philly; Philly Voice; Phora; Pinterest; Planet Ice; Planet Love; Plentyoffish; Politico; Pop Crush; Popculture Reviewed; Populist; Pornhub; Porno4Portable; Prelude Power; Price Scope; Prime Wire; Protein Power; Puerto Rico Online; Puffy Network; Queerty; Questia; Quizlet; Quora; Radical Riders; Railroad Forum; Rational Wiki; Real Clear Politics; Reality Mod; Reckoning; Red Bubble; Reddit; Red Tape; Red Tube; Reuters; Ripoff Report; Roadbike Review; Road Route Map; Roominate; Roots Web; Salon; Samba; Screen Rant; Seibertron; Serious Seats; SF Gate; Shamash; She Knows; Shesaurus; Short Shots; Shroomery; Silicon Investor; Smoked Meat; Smoking Gun; Smut Post; Soap Opera Network; Soccer 24–7; Social Contract; Society Rants; Soda Head; Sound Cloud; Sox Talk; Soy Chicano; Spark People; Spell Check; Spiked; Spinning Globe; Sport Bikes; St. Augustine Online; Steam Community; St. Louis Racing; Storm Front; Straight Dope; Stranger; Street Advisor; Street Gangs; Stripes; Style Rookie; Subway Surf; Surfcasting; Talker Bill; Talk Sox; Tarheel Sack; Tech Gadgets; Teen Spot; Tennis Forum; Tennis Planet; That's Poppycock; Thinking Pharma; Time Zone; TMZ; Tom Collins; Topix; Toronto City Feeds; Toronto Real Estate; Townhall; TPM Election Central; Trance Addict; Trav Buddy; Travelpod; Tribesone; Trip Advisor; Tripod; Tropical Fish; True News USA; Tube Porn Classic; Tumbler; Tumblr; TVLine; Tweak Town Forums; Tweet Tunnel; Twicsy; Twin Turbo; Twisting Nether Gazette; Twitpic; Twitter; Type Pad; uKnowLingo; Uproxx; Urban Dictionary; Urban Spoon; USA Sex Guide; Velocity Reviews; Verbotomy; Vulture; Washington Scene; Wattpad; Weapon Evolution; Webstagram; Weebly; Weekly Wire; Weight Watchers; Whole Health Chicago; Why Eat; Wicked Local; Wikipedia; Wiki Spaces; Wiktionary; Word Mavens; Word Meaning; Wordnik; Word Press; Word Wizard; Working Class Conservative; World Heritage; World Sex Guide; World Wide Words; Wrap; Wyoming Network; Xbox 360; XXX Bunker; Yahoo; Yahoo Answers; Yahoo Finance; Yahoo Groups; Yahoo Movies; Yahoo Travel; Yahoo Voices; Yelp; Yeshiva World; Yiddishslangdictionary; You Be Mom; Your Houston News; Your Tango; YouTube; Zeta Boards.

Literature

Ilana Abramovitch and Seán Galvin, *Jews of Brooklyn* (2002); Marta Acosta, *Happy Hour at Casa Dracula* (2008); Luis Gabriel Aguilera, *Gabriel's Fire* (2000); Irving L. Allen, *The City in Slang* (1995); Michael Anderson, *The Presence of the Past* (2018); Christine Andreae, *Smoke Eaters: A Thriller* (2000); Joyce Antler, *The Journey Home: Jewish Women and the American Century* (1997); Rudy Apodaca, *A Rare Thing* (2011); Alberto Arcia, *Cut and Run: The Misadventures of Alex Perez* (2013); James Atlas, *Bellow: A Biography* (2000); Sylvia Barack Fishman, *Follow My Footprints: Changing Images of Women in American Jewish Fiction* (2000); Jeanne Barrack, *Bend in the Road* (2009); Gary Lee Berry, *A Handicapped Cowboy's Story* (2010); Harold Bloom, *Philip Roth* (2003); Gregory Boyle, *Tattoos on the Heart* (2011); Maurice Broaddus, *Pimp My Airship* (2019); Cecil Brown, *I, Stagoalee* (2011); Tim Bugansky, *Anywhere but Here* (2007); Carol Burke, *Camp All-American* (2015); Greg Caldwell, *Blood Lotto* (2006); Philip Caputo, *Del Corso's Gallery* (2012); Jim Carlton, *Conversations with Great Jazz and Studio Guitarists* (2009); Grace Carol, *Eye to Eye* (2012); José Casas, *Offering* (2006); Denise Chavez, *Loving Pedro Infante* (2002); Elise Chenier, *Strangers in Our Midst: Sexual Deviancy in Post-War Ontario* (2008); Ercille Christmas, *Thoughts of a Proud American* (2006); Elizabeth Claire, *Dangerous English* (1998); Tom Clark, *Edward Dorn: A World of Difference* (2002); Bev Clarke, *Beneath the Flowering Flamboyants* (2010); Carrie Cobb, *A Day in the Life of Becky the Unfortunate* (2009); Tom Coffey, *Miami Twilight* (2003); Len Cohen, *The Race of Her Life: A Political Suspense Thriller* (2005); Sharleen Cohen, *The Day after Tomorrow* (2006); Paul Collins, *Trust Me!* (2011); Fred C. Collom, *The Dumb Gringo* (2004); Richard Condon, *Prizzi's Family* (1986); Joan Connor, *We Who Live Apart: Stories* (2000); Catherine Coulter, *Wild Star* (2002); David T. Courtwright, *Addicts Who Survived* (2013); Nicholas A. Cummings, *Focused Psychotherapy* (1995); Susan Cushman, *Southern Writers on Writing* (2018); Tom Dalzell, *The Routledge Dictionary of Modern American Slang and Unconventional English* (2009); Tom Dalzell, *Vietnam War Slang* (2014); Don DeLillo, *Libra* (1988); Junot Díaz, *The Brief Wondrous Life of Oscar Wao* (2007); Junot Díaz, *This Is How You Lose Her* (2012); David Dobson, *Trust* (2013); Dennis Doph, *Manflower* (2015); Sam Dworkis, *ExTension* (1994); Connie Eble, *Slang and Sociability* (1996); Joyce Eisenberg and Ellen Scolnic, *Dictionary of Jewish Words* (2006); Robert Eisenberg, *Boychiks in the Hood: Travels in the Hasidic Underground* (1995); Lawrence Jeffrey Epstein, *At the Edge of a Dream: the Story of Jewish Immigrants in New York's Lower East Side 1880–1920* (2007); Ed Falco, *Toughs* (2014); Henry L. Feingold, *Zion in America* (2002); Ralph M. Flores, *The Horse in the Kitchen: Stories of a Mexican-American Family* (2004); Laurie Fox, *My Sister from the Black Lagoon: A Novel of My Life* (2010); Kinky Friedman, *Armadillos and Old Lace* (1994); Emmanuel Frost, *The Complete Drug Slang Dictionary* (2004); Rómulo Gallegos, *Doña Barbara: A Novel* (2012); Laura E. Garcia et al., *Teatro Chicana: A Collective Memoir and Selected Plays* (2010); Ricardo L. Garcia, *Brother Bill's Bait Bites Back and Other Tales from the Raton* (2004); John E. Gardner, *Every Night's a Festival* (1982); James Alex Garza, *The Imagined Underworld: Sex, Crime, and Vice in Porfirian Mexico City* (2007); Linda Glasser, *Bridge to America* (2005); Laurence Goldstein, *The Movies: Texts, Receptions, Exposures* (1996); Manuel G. Gonzales, *Mexicanos: A History of Mexicans in the United States* (2009); Hilda González-Angiulo, *Las Señoras: From Funds of Knowledge to Self Discovery* (1998); Charles Henderson, *Jungle Rules: A True Story of Marine Justice in Vietnam* (2007); Robert Hendrickson, *The Facts on File Dictionary of American Regionalisms* (2000); Mary Hoffman, *David* (2011); Alan Holloway, *Daddy's Little Boy* (2014); Keith Huff, *A Steady Rain* (2013); Harry Hunsicker, *The Next Time You Die* (2007); Liz Ireland, *The Pink Ghetto* (2006); Harvey Jacobs, *The Juror: A Novel* (1980); Susan Johnson, *Wine, Tarts, & Sex* (2008); Erica Jong, *Inventing Memory: A Novel of Mothers and Daughters* (1997); Michio Kaku, *Beyond Einstein: The Cosmic Quest for the Theory of the Universe* (1997); Michelle Kane, *Confessions of a Catholic Schoolgirl* (2007); Michael Kearney, *Changing Fields of Anthropology: From Local to Global* (2004); Carole S. Kessner, *Marie Syrkin: Values Beyond the Self* (2008); Ralph Keyes, *Euphemania: Our Love Affair with Euphemisms* (2010); Barbara Kipfer and Robert Chapman, *Dictionary of American Slang* (2008); Melvin Lasky, *Media Warfare: The Americanization of Language* (2011); Monique Layton, *Street Women and the Art of Bullshitting* (2010); Laura Lee Cummings, *Pachucas and Pachucos in Tucson* (2009); Peter Lehman, *Close Viewings: An Anthology of New Film Criticism* (1990); Elmore Leonard, *Glitz* (1985); Jimmy Lerner, *You Got Nothing Coming* (2002); Rachel Levine, *Cyberyenta's Oldfashioned Wisdom for Newfangled Times* (2000); John MacDonald, *Crime Is a Business* (2014); Nancy Maclean, *Freedom Is Not Enough* (2008); Curtis Marez, *Drug Wars: The Political Economy of Narcotics* (2004); Samuelin Martínez, *AmeriCaCa* (2013); James A. Matisoff, *Blessings, Curses, Hopes, Fears: Psycho-Ostensive Expressions in Yiddish* (2000); Virginia McConnell, *Sympathy for the Devil* (2001); Marco

McPeek Villatoro, *The Holy Spirit of My Uncle's Cojones* (1999); Sandro Meallet, *Edgewater Angels* (2007); Pablo Medina, *The Cigar Roller* (2007); Manuel Medrano, *Américo Paredes* (2010); Johnny Miles, *A Stroke at Midnight* (2008); Jim Miller, *Counter Intelligence* (2010); Ayisha Monroe, *Doin' It* (2012); Mary Monroe, *The Upper Room* (2011); David Montejano, *Quixote's Soldiers* (2010); David Montejano, *Sancho's Journal* (2012); Patricia M. Montilla, *Latinos and Latinas in Popular Culture* (2013); Edmundo Morales, *Cocaine: The Gold Rush in Peru* (1989); Vera R. Moreno, *Big Dreams and Heartaches* (2014); Alfonso Moret, *Hearts in Jeopardy* (2012); Timothy Morrisroe, *Ace Minus One* (2006); Robert Murrhee, *Virgins of Kandahar* (2013); Armando Navarro, *The Immigration Crisis: Nativism, Armed Vigilantism, and the Rise of a Countervailing Movement* (2008); Thomas Nordegren, *The A-Z Encyclopedia of Alcohol and Drug Abuse* (2002); Robert Olen Butler, *The Star of Istanbul* (2015); Jerry Oppenheimer, *Madoff with the Money* (2010); Leroy Ostransky, *Sharkey's Kid: A Memoir* (1991); Gail Parent, *David Meyer Is a Mother* (1990); Castaño Pérez, *Patterns of Heroin Use* (2010); Leon Pettiway, *Honey, Honey, Miss Thang* (1996); Jeffrey Prather, *Chase: Terror on the Border* (2013); Richard Price, *Lush Life* (2008); Reyes Ramos, *An Ethnographic Comparison of the Mexican American Drug Culture in El Paso, Texas: 1987 to 1997* (1998); Tey Diana Rebolledo, *Infinite Divisions: An Anthology of Chicana Literature* (1993); Tamis Hoover Renteria, *Chicanos Professionals: Culture, Conflict, and Identity* (2013); Mordechai Richler, *Belling the Cat: Essays, Reports, and Opinions* (1998); Cole Riley, *Little White Lies* (2013); Raquel Z. Rivera, *New York Ricans from the Hip Hop Zone* (2003); Deborah Rodriguez, *Margarita Wednesdays* (2014); Luis J. Rodriguez, *Always Running: La Vida Loca: Gang Days in L.A.* (2012); Esther Romeyn, *Street Scenes* (2008); Charley Rosen, *The House of Moses All-Stars: A Novel* (2011); David G. Roskies, *A Bridge of Longing: The Lost Art of Yiddish Storytelling* (1996); Leo Rosten, *Leo Rosten's Giant Book of Laughter* (1989); Leo Rosten, *Joys of Yiddish* (1996); Leo Rosten, *The New Joys of Yiddish* (2001); Rachel Rubin, *Jewish Gangsters of Modern Literature* (2000); William Safire, *Safire's Political Dictionary* (2008); Johnny M. Sanchez, *Imprisoned by a Memory* (2012); Richard Sand, *Hell's Reunion* (2006); Ilene Schneider, *Talk Dirty Yiddish* (2008); Mordechai Schreiber, *Rabbi and the Nun* (1991); Jeffrey Shandler, *Adventures in Yiddishland: Postvernacular Language and Culture* (2006); Shirley Shapiro, *The Convent* (2002); Gini Sikes, *8 Ball Chicks* (1997); Howard Simons, *Jewish Times: Voices of the American Jewish Experience* (1990); Jordan Sonnenblick, *Notes from the Midnight Driver* (2007); Sol

Steinmetz, *Yiddish and English: The Story of Yiddish in America* (2001); Howard Stern, *Miss America* (1995); Richard G. Stern, *Pacific Tremors* (2001); Steve Stern, *Lazar Malkin Enters Heaven* (2011); Payson Stevens, *Meshuggenary: Celebrating the World of Yiddish* (2002); Kathleen Taylor, *Cold Front: A Tory Bauer Mystery* (2000); James Thorpe, *Henry Edwards Huntington: A Biography* (1994); Harry Turtledove, *Armistice: The Hot War* (2017); Luis Valdez, *Zoot Suit and Other Plays* (1992); James Diego Vigil, *Barrio Gangs: Srteet Life and Identity in Southern California* (1988); Kurt Vonnegut, *Armageddon in Retrospect* (2008); Diane Whiteside, *Bond of Darkness* (2008); Robert A. Wilson, *Schrodinger's Cat Trilogy* (2009); Ben Zeller, *Secrets of Beaver Creek* (2011).

Press

Advocate; Ad Week; Air & Space Magazine; Akron Beacon Journal; Alaska Dispatch; Albany Times Union; Albuquerque Journal; Allentown Morning Call; America Magazine; American Banker; American Conservative; American Interest; American Spectator; Arab American News; Arizona Daily Star; Arizona Daily Sun; Arizona Republic; Arizona State University News; Arkansas Democrat-Gazette; Arkansas Times; Asheville Citizen-Times; Atlanta Journal Constitution; Atlantic Monthly; Augusta Chronicle; Austin American-Statesman; Austin Chronicle; Autocar; Auto Week; Avery Journal Times; Baltimore City Paper; Baltimore Sun; Bay Area Reporter; Beacon Magazine; Billboard Magazine; Black Enterprise; Boca Raton News; Body Building; Bookmarks Magazine; Boston Globe; Boston Herald; Boston Magazine; Boulder Weekly; Bradenton Times; Brooklyn Daily; Brooklyn Newspaper; Brooklyn Rail; Buffalo News; Burlington Times News; Business Insider; Businessweek; Calgary Sun; Cambridge Day; Canadian Living; Canyon News; Capitol Weekly; Car and Driver; Carolina Journal; Catholic Herald; Charleston Gazette; Charlotte Observer; Cherry Hill Courier Post; Chicago Daily Herald; Chicago Magazine; Chicago Now; Chicago Reader; Chicago Sun-Sentinel; Chicago Sun-Times; Chicago Tribune; Christian Science Monitor; Cigar Aficionado; Cincinnati Magazine; City Journal; Clanton Park Bulletin; Columbus Dispatch; Computer; Computer World; Connecticut Magazine; Contra Costa Times; Cornell Daily Sun; Corpus Christi Caller; Cosmopolitan; Curve Magazine; Cycling Weekly; Daily Californian; Daily Nebraskan; Dallas Morning News; Dallas Observer; Dallas Voice; Dalles Chronicle; Denver Post; Deseret News; Desert Sun; Des Moines Register; Detroit Times; Duke Chronicle; Duluth News Tribune; East Bay Express; East Valley Tribune; Ebony; Ebony Magazine; Economic Times; Edmonton

Journal; Elle; El Paso Times; English Today; Entertainment Tonight; Entertainment Weekly; Esquire; Eugene Weekly; Evansville Courier & Press; Examiner; Fairfield Daily Republic; Fashion Magazine; Film; Financial Times; Florida Sun Sentinel; Florida Today; Fodor's; Forbes; Foreign Policy; Fort Scott Tribune; Fortune; Forward; Fresno Bee; Gay Times Magazine; Gettysburg Review; Glamour; Globe and Mail; Good Housekeeping; GQ Magazine; Grand Island Independent; Halifax Chronicle Herald; Hamilton Spectator; Harper's Magazine; Hartford Courant; Harvard Business Review; Harvard Crimson; Harvard Magazine; Henderson Daily Dispatch; High Times; Highline Times; Hill; Hillsboro Times Gazette; Hilton Head Island Pocket; Honolulu Advertiser; Houston Chronicle; Houston Press; Huntington Herald-Dispatch; Indianapolis Star; InformationWeek; InfoWorld; Inquirer; Instyle; International Living; Jackson Hole News & Guide; Jewish Chronicle; Jewish Daily Forward; Jewish Journal; Jewish Journal of Greater Los Angeles; Jewish Language Review; Jewish Magazine; Jewish Week; Johnsonville Press; Kansas City Star; Kelowna Daily Courier; Knoxville News-Sentinel; LA Sentinel; Las Vegas Review-Journal; Las Vegas Sun; Las Vegas Weekly; Latina; Latina Magazine; Latin Times; LA Weekly; Leatherneck Magazine; Life & Style Weekly; Life Magazine; Lincoln Journal Star; Los Angeles Daily News; Los Angeles Magazine; Los Angeles Review of Books; Los Angeles Times; Los Angeles Times Magazine; Los Angeles Weekly; Lowrider Magazine; Macleans; Maledicta; Management Today; Marijuana Magazine; Maxim; Mediaweek; Mendele; Men's Health; Men's Journal; Metro Weekly; Metropolis Magazine; Miami Herald; Miami News; Miami New Times; Miami Sun Times; Michigan Daily; Military Times; Milwaukee Journal Sentinel; Minneapolis Star Tribune; Minneapolis-St. Paul Star Tribune; Missoulian; Mobile Spokesman-Review; Modern Jewish Studies; Modesto Bee; Monterey County Weekly; Montreal Gazette; Mother Jones; Motor Trend; Motorcyclist Magazine; Mountain Eagle; Muscular Development; Napa Valley Register; Naples Daily News; Naples News; Nashville Scene; Nation; National Enquirer; National Geographic; National Post; National Review; National Spectator; Newark Star-Ledger; New Jersey Jewish News; New Orleans Review; New Orleans Tribune; New Republic; News of the Day; New Statesman; Newsweek; New York Daily News; New York Magazine; New York Newsday; New York Observer; New York Post; New York Press; New York Review of Books; New York Stage; New York Sun; New York Times; New Yorker; North Shore News; Northwest Arkansas News; OC Weekly; Okay Magazine; Omaha World-Herald; Orange County Register; Orlando Sentinel; Orlando Weekly; Ottawa Citizen; Out Magazine; Outside; Overdrive Magazine; Palm Beach Post; Paste Magazine; PC Magazine; PC World; People Magazine; Philadelphia City

Paper; *Philadelphia Inquirer*; *Philadelphia Weekly*; *Phoenix New Times*; *Piano World*; *Pine Island Eagle*; *Pittsburgh Post-Gazette*; *Popular Science*; *Portland Tribune*; *Princeton Union Eagle*; *Psychology Today*; *Reno News & Review*; *Richmond Daily News*; *Riverfront Times*; *Rochester Democrat and Chronicle*; *Rocky Mountain News*; *Rolling Stone*; *Sacramento Bee*; *Sailing Magazine*; *Salem News*; *Salinas Californian*; *Salt Lake Tribune*; San *Antonio Current*; *San Diego Downtown News*; *San Diego Free Press*; *San Diego Jewish Journal*; *San Diego Magazine*; *San Diego Reader*; *San Diego Union-Tribune*; *San Francisco Business Times*; *San Francisco Chronicle*; *San Francisco Examiner*; *San Francisco Gate*; *San Francisco Weekly*; *San Jose Mercury News*; *Santa Barbara Independent*; *Santa Cruz Sentinel*; *Santa Fe New Mexican*; *Seattle Post Intelligencer*; *Seattle Times*; *Seattle Weekly*; *Shreveport Times*; *Silicon Valley's Metro*; *Slate Magazine*; *South Florida Gay News*; *South Florida Reporter*; *South Florida Sun-Sentinel*; *Spartanburg Herald Journal*; *Spine Health*; *Spin Magazine*; *Spokane Spokesman-Review*; *Sports Illustrated*; *Spy Magazine*; *Stamford Advocate*; *Stanford Daily*; *State*; *Staten Island Advance*; *St. Augustinian*; *St. Louis Post-Dispatch*; *St. Louis Today*; *Style at Home*; *Stylist Magazine*; *Surfer Magazine*; *Tablet Magazine*; *Tampa Bay Times*; *Tennessean*; *Texas Magazine*; *Texas Monthly*; *Time*; *Time Out*; *Time Out Chicago*; *Time Out New York*; *Toledo Blade*; *Topeka Capital Journal*; *Torontoist*; *Toronto Life*; *Toronto Star*; *Toronto Sun*; *Townhall*; *Tribe Magazine*; *Tri-City Herald*; *Tucson Sentinel*; *Tucson Weekly*; *Tulsa World*; *TV Guide*; *Twin Falls Times-News*; *USA Today*; *Us Magazine*; *U.S. News & World Report*; *Us Weekly*; *Vallejo Times Herald*; *Vancouver Sun*; *Vanity Fair*; *Variety*; *Ventura County Star*; *Vibe*; *Vice News*; *Vicksburg Daily News*; *Villager*; *Village Voice*; *Vogue*; *Voice of San Diego*; *Waco Tribune-Herald*; *Wall Street Examiner*; *Wall Street Journal*; *Washington Blade*; *Washington Examiner*; *Washington Free Beacon*; *Washingtonian*; *Washington Monthly*; *Washington Post*; *Washington Times*; *Willamette Week*; *Winnipeg Free Press*; *Winnipeg Sun*; *Wired*; *Wyoming Tribune*; *Yale Alumni Magazine*; *Zagat*.

Television

3rd Rock from the Sun (NBC-TV series); *7th Heaven* (WB-TV series); *ALF* (NBC-TV series); *American Dad!* (Fox-TV series); *Americans* (FX-TV series); *Angel* (WB-TV series); *Angels in America* (HBO-TV series); *Arrested Development* (Fox-TV series); *Battlestar Galactica* (Sci-Fi-TV series); *Being Erica* (CBS-TV series); *Big Bang Theory* (CBS-TV series); *Billable Hours* (Showcase-TV series); *Billions* (Showtime-TV series); *Bionic Woman* (NBC-TV series); *Blue Bloods* (CBS-TV series); *Boardwalk Empire*

(HBO-TV series); *Bones* (Fox-TV series); *Boston Legal* (ABC-TV series); *Breaking Bad* (AMC-TV series); *Buffy the Vampire Slayer* (WB-TV series); *Californication* (Showtime-TV series); *Cheers* (NBC-TV series); *Chicago Fire* (NBC-TV series); *Chuck* (NBC-TV series); *Cold Case* (CBS-TV series); *Combat Hospital* (ABC-TV series); *Community* (NBC-TV series); Company (TNT-TV series); *CSI: Crime Scene Investigation* (CBS-TV series); *CSI: Miami* (CBS-TV series); *Da Ali G Show* (HBO-TV series); *Dads* (Fox-TV series); *Dawson's Creek* (WB-TV series); *Day Break* (ABC-TV series); *Deadwood* (HBO-TV series); *Desperate Housewives* (ABC-TV series); *Deuce* (HBO-TV series); *Dexter* (Showtime-TV series); *Eastbound & Down* (HBO-TV series); *Entourage* (HBO-TV series); *ER* (NBC-TV series); *Everwood* (WB-TV series); *Everybody Hates Chris* (UPN-TV series); *Everybody Loves Raymond* (CBS-TV series); *Evidence* (ABC-TV series); *Family Guy* (Fox-TV series); *Fargo* (FX-TV series); *Felicity* (WB-TV series); *Frasier* (NBC-TV series); *Freaks and Geeks* (NBC-TV series); *Fresh Prince of Bel-Air* (NBC-TV series); *Friends* (NBC-TV series); *Futurama* (Fox-TV series); *Gang Related* (Fox-TV series); *Gilmore Girls* (WB-TV series); *Glee* (Fox-TV series); *Glee Project* (Oxygen-TV program); *Good Guys* (Fox-TV series); *Good Wife* (CBS-TV series); *Grey's Anatomy* (ABC-TV series); *Grimm* (NBC-TV series); *Hawaii Five-O* (CBS-TV series); *Hawthorne* (TNT-TV series); *Hill Street Blues* (NBC-TV series); *Homeland* (Showtime-TV series); *House M.D.* (Fox-TV series); *House of Lies* (Showtime-TV series); *How I Met Your Mother* (CBS-TV series); *InSecurity* (CBC-TV series); *Intelligence* (CBS-TV series); *Joan of Arcadia* (CBS-TV series); *John from Cincinnati* (HBO-TV series); *Justified* (FX-TV series); *Killing* (AMC-TV series); *Kitchen Confidential* (Fox-TV series); *Kitchen Nightmares* (Fox-TV series); *Kominsky Method* (Netflix-TV series); *Larry King Live* (CNN-TV program); *Las Vegas* (NBC-TV series); *Law & Order* (NBC-TV series); *Law & Order: Special Victims Unit* (NBC-TV); *Lie to Me* (Fox-TV series); *Lost Girl* (Showcase-TV series); *Mad About You* (NBC-TV series); *Mad Men* (AMC-TV series); *Married with Children* (Fox-TV series); *Marvelous Mrs. Maisel* (Amazon-TV series); *Mentalist* (CBS-TV series); *Miami Vice* (NBC-TV series); *Millennium* (Fox-TV series); *Modern Family* (ABC-TV series); *Monk* (USA-TV series); *Moonlighting* (ABC-TV series); *Nanny* (CBS-TV series); *Narcos: Mexico* (Netflix-TV series); *NCSI: Los Angeles* (CBS-TV series); *News* (ABC-TV program); *News* (CBC-TV program); *News* (CBS-TV program); *News* (CNBC-TV program); *News* (CNN-TV program); *News* (Fox-TV program); *News* (KCET-TV program); *News* (KOB-TV program); *News* (KQED-TV program); *News* (KRQE-TV program); *News* (KWQC-TV program); *News* (MTV-TV program); *News* (NBC-TV program); *News* (NJTV-TV program); *News* (WBAY-TV program); *News* (WFTV-TV program); *News* (WGME-TV program); *Nip/Tuck* (FX-TV series); *Northern Exposure* (CBS-TV series); *Nurse Jackie* (Showtime-TV series); *NYPD Blue* (ABC-TV series); *O.C.* (Fox-TV series); *Office* (NBC-TV series); *Orange Is the New Black* (Netflix-TV series); *Parenthood* (NBC-TV series); *Parks and Recreation* (NBC-TV series); *Pawn Wars* (History-TV series); *Pinky and the Brain* (WB-TV series); *Prison Break* (Fox-TV series); *Quantum Leap* (NBC-TV series); *Queer As Folk* (Showtime-TV series); *Ray Donovan* (Showtime-TV series); *Real L Word* (Showtime-TV series); *Rescue Me* (FX-TV series); *Rookie Blue* (Global-TV series); *Scrubs* (NBC-TV series); *Seinfeld* (NBC-TV series); *Sex and the City* (HBO-TV series); *Shameless* (Showtime-TV series); *Shield* (FX-TV series); *Shooter* (USA-Network-TV series); *Simpsons* (Fox-TV series); *Six Feet Under* (HBO-TV series); *Smallville* (WB-TV series); *Snowfall* (FX-TV series); *Sons of Anarchy* (FX-TV series); *Sons of Tucson* (Fox-TV series); *Sopranos* (HBO-TV series); *Southland* (NBC-TV series); *South Park* (Comedy Central-TV series); *Sports*, CBS-TV program; *Sports* (Fox-TV program); *Sports* (NBC-TV program); *Stranger Things* (Netflix-TV series); *Taxi Brooklyn* (NBC-TV series); *Teenage Mutant Ninja Turtles* (CBS-TV series); *That '70s Show* (Fox-TV series); *Today Show* (NBC-TV program); *Tour of Duty* (CBS-TV series); *Travel* (CNN-TV program); *Treme* (HBO-TV series); *Twin Peaks* (ABC-TV series); *Two and a Half Men* (CBS-TV series); *Undercover Boss* (CBS-TV series); *Unforgettable* (NBC-TV series); *Universe* (History-TV series); *Up All Night* (NBC-TV series); *Weeds* (Showtime-TV series); *Will & Grace* (NBC-TV series); *Wire* (HBO-TV series).

Bibliography

Adams, Michael. 2009. *Slang: The People's Poetry*. New York: Oxford University Press

Adeleye, Gabriel G. with Kofi Acquah-Dadzie. 1999. *World Dictionary of Foreign Expressions: A Resource for Readers and Writers*. Ed. Thomas J. Sienkiewicz with James T. McDonough, Jr. Wauconda, IL: Bolchazy-Carducci Publishers

Agius Vallejo, Jody. 2012. *Barrios to Burbs: The Making of the Mexican American Middle Class*. Stanford, CA: Stanford University Press

Akmajian, Adrian. 2001. *An Introduction to Language and Communication*. Cambridge, MA: MIT Press

Algeo, John. 1991. *Fifty Years among New Words: A Dictionary of Neologisms*. New York: Cambridge University Press

Algeo, John (ed.). 2001. *The Cambridge History of the English Language, Vol. VI: English in North America*. Cambridge: Cambridge University Press

Algeo, John and Thomas Pyles. [1964] 2005. *The Origins and Development of the English Language*. Boston, MA: Thomson Wadsworth

Allen, Irving Lewis. 1993. *The City in Slang*. New York: Oxford University Press

Ayto, John. 1998. *The Oxford Dictionary of Slang*. Oxford: Oxford University Press

Ayto, John. 1999. *Twentieth Century Words*. Oxford: Oxford University Press

Ayto, John and John Simpson. 1992. *The Oxford Dictionary of Modern Slang*. Oxford: Oxford University Press

Bauer, Laurie. 2002. *An Introduction to International Varieties of English*. Edinburgh: Edinburgh University Press

Bell, Allan. 2014. *The Guidebook to Sociolinguistics*. Malden, MA: Wiley Blackwell Publishing

Bentley, Harold W. 1973. *A Dictionary of Spanish Terms in English with Special Reference to the American Southwest*. New York: Octagon Books

Bloomfield, Leonard. 1933. *Language*. Chicago: The University of Chicago Press

Bluestein, Gene. 1998. *Anglish/Yinglish: Yiddish in American Life and Literature*. Lincoln: University of Nebraska Press

Bryson, Bill. 1994. *Made in America*. New York: Secker and Warburg Publishing

Bucholtz, Mary. 2011. *White Kids: Language, Race and Styles of Youth Identity*. Cambridge: Cambridge University Press

Bühler, Karl. 1990. *The Theory of Language* [translation of *Sprachtheorie* from 1934]. Amsterdam: John Benjamins

Chambers, Jack, Peter Trudgill, and Natalie Schillin-Estes (eds.) [2002] 2004. *The Handbook of Language Variation and Change*. Oxford: Blackwell Publishing

Chambers, Jack. 2003. *Sociolinguistic Theory*. Oxford: Blackwell Publishing

Chapman, Robert L. 1986. *New Dictionary of American Slang*. New York: Harper and Row Publishers

Chapman, Robert L. and Barbara Ann Kipfer. 1995. *Dictionary of American Slang*. New York: Harper Collins

Clyne, Michael. 2004. *Dynamics of Language Contact*. Cambridge: Cambridge University Press

Coleman, Julie. 2004. *A History of Cant and Slang Dictionaries, Vol. 1: 1567–1785*. Oxford: Oxford University Press

Coleman, Julie. 2005. *A History of Cant and Slang Dictionaries, Vol. 2: 1785–1858*. Oxford: Oxford University Press

Coleman, Julie. 2008. *A History of Cant and Slang Dictionaries, Vol. 3: 1858–1936*. Oxford: Oxford University Press

Coleman, Julie. 2010. *A History of Cant and Slang Dictionaries, Vol. 4: 1936–1984*. Oxford: Oxford University Press

Coleman, Julie. 2012. *The Life of Slang*. New York: Oxford University Press

Coleman, Julie (ed.). 2014. *Global English Slang: Methodologies and Perspectives*. Abingdon: Routledge

Crowther, Jonathan. 1999. *Oxford Guide to British and American Culture*. Oxford: Oxford University Press

Crystal, David. [1980] 1991. *A Dictionary of Linguistics and Phonetics*. Fourth Edition. Oxford: Blackwell Publishing

Crystal, David. 1987. *The Cambridge Encyclopedia of Language*. Cambridge: Cambridge University Press

Crystal, David. [1995] 1999. *The Cambridge Encyclopedia of the English Language*. Second Edition. Cambridge: Cambridge University Press

Crystal, David. 2004. *The Stories of English*. New York: Overlook Press

Crystal, David. 2005. *How Language Works*. New York: Avery and Penguin Group

Culpeper, Jonathan. [1997] 2005. *History of English*. Abingdon: Routledge

Dalzell, Tom. 1996. *Flappers 2 Rappers*. New York: Merriam Webster

Dalzell, Tom. [2009] 2018. *The Routledge Dictionary of Modern American Slang and Unconventional English*. Abingdon: Routledge

Dalzell, Tom. 2010. *Damn the Man! Slang of the Oppressed in America*. Mineola, NY: Dover Publications

Dalzell, Tom and Terry Victor. 2008. *Vice Slang*. Abingdon: Routledge

De Mente, Boye. 1996. *NTC's Dictionary of Mexican Culture Words*. New York: McGraw Hill

Dickson, Paul. 1994. *War Slang: American Fighting Words and Phrases from the Civil War to the Gulf War*. New York: Pocket Books

Donaldson, Bruce. 2016. *Colloquial Dutch: The Complete Course for Beginners*. Third Edition. Abingdon: Routledge

Dumas, Bethany and Jonathan Lighter. 1978. "Is *Slang* a Word for Linguists?" *American Speech*. Vol. 53, 5–17

Dunkling, Leslie. 1990. *A Dictionary of Epithets and Terms of Address*. New York: Routledge

Durkin, Philip. 2014. *Borrowed Words: A History of Loanwords in English*. Oxford: Oxford University Press

Eble, Connie. 1996. *Slang and Sociability*. Chapel Hill: University of North Carolina Press

Eble, Connie. 2004. "Slang." In Edward Finegan and John R. Rickford (eds.). *Language in the USA: Themes for the Twenty-First Century*. Cambridge: Cambridge University Press, 375–386

Fasold, Ralph. 1984. *The Sociolinguistics of Society*. New York: Basil Blackwell Publishing

Fernandez, Roberto G. 1983. "English Loanwords in Spanish." *American Speech*. *Vol. 58*, 16

Field, Frederic. 2002. *Linguistic Borrowing in Bilingual Contexts*. Philadelphia: John Benjamins

Finegan, Edward and John R. Rickford (eds.). 2004. *Language in the USA: Themes for the Twenty-First Century*. Cambridge: Cambridge University Press

Fishman, Joshua. 1970. *Sociolinguistics: A Brief Introduction*. Rowley, MA: Newbury House

Fisiak, Jacek. 1961. 'Zapożyczenia angielskie w języku polskim. Analiza interferencji leksykalnej.' Unpublished Ph.D. dissertation. University of Łódź

Fisiak, Jacek. 2000. *An Outline of History of English*. Poznań: Wydawnictwo Poznańskie

Fought, Carmen. 2003. *Chicano English in Context*. New York: Palgrave Macmillan

Fromkin, Victoria, Robert Rodman, and Nina Hyams. 2014. *An Introduction to Language*. Boston, MA: Wadsworth

Galvan, Roberto and Richard Teschner. 2001. *Dictionary of Chicano Spanish*. New York: McGraw Hill

Garcarz, Michał. 2013. *African American Hip Hop Slang: A Sociolinguistic Study of Street Speech*. Wrocław: Atut

Geller, Ewa. 1994. *Jidysz – język Żydów polskich*. Warsaw: PWN

Görlach, Manfred (ed.). 2001. *A Dictionary of European Anglicisms: A Usage Dictionary of Anglicisms in Sixteen European Languages*. Oxford: Oxford University Press

Görlach, Manfred (ed.). 2002. *An Annotated Bibliography of Anglicisms*. Oxford: Oxford University Press

Görlach, Manfred. 2003. *English Words Abroad*. Philadelphia: John Benjamins Publishing

Graddol, David, Dick Leith, and Joan Swann. 1996. *English: History, Diversity and Change*. London: Routledge

Gramley, Stephan and Kurt-Michael Pätzold. 2004. *A Survey of Modern English*. London: Routledge

Green, Jonathon. 1994. *Slang Down the Ages*. London: Kyle Kathie

Green, Jonathon. 2010. *Green's Dictionary of Slang, Vols. 1–3*. London: Chambers Harrap

Green, Jonathon. 2015. *Vulgar Tongue: Green's History of Slang*. Oxford: Oxford University Press

Green, Jonathon. 2016. *Slang: A Very Short Introduction*. Oxford: Oxford University Press

Green, Lisa. 2002. *African American English: A Linguistic Introduction*. Cambridge: Cambridge University Press

Grosjean, François. 1982. *Life with Two Languages: An Introduction to Bilingualism*. Cambridge, MA: Harvard University Press

Halliday, Michael. 1978. *Language As a Social Semiotic*. London: Edward Arnold

Haspelmath, Martin and Uri Tadmoor (eds.). 2009. *Loanwords in the World's Languages: A Comparative Handbook*. Berlin: De Gruyter Mouton

Haugen, Einar. 1950. "The Analysis of Linguistic Borrowing." *Lingua*. Vol. 2, 210–231

Hayard, Napoléon. 2015. *Dictionnaire Argot Français*. Seattle: Amazon Kindle Edition

Hitchins, Henry. 2009. *The Secret Life of Words: How English Became English*. New York: Macmillan

Hoffman, Paul and Matt Freedman. 1983. *Dictionary Shmictionary! A Yiddish and Yinglish Dictionary*. New York: Quill Publications

Holmes, Janet. [1992] 2013. *An Introduction to Sociolinguistics*. London: Routledge

Jakobson, Roman. 1960. "Closing Statement: Linguistics and Poetics." In Thomas A. Sebeok (ed.), *Style in Language*. Cambridge, MA: MIT Press, 350, 377

Johanson, Lars. 2002. *Structural Factors in Turkic Language Contacts*. London: Routledge

Jones-Reid, M.F., Charlene Lopez, and Linton H. Robinson. 2000. *Mexican Slang plus Graffiti*. Round Rock, TX: One Ear Publications

Kan Qian. 2021. *Colloquial Chinese: The Complete Course for Beginners*. Third Edition. London: Routledge

Kany, Charles Emil. 1960. *American-Spanish Euphemisms*. Berkeley: University of California Press

Katamba, Francis. 2005. *English Words: Structure, History, Usage*. Second Edition. New York: Routledge

Kipfer, Barbara. 1984. *Workbook on Lexicography*. Exeter: University of Exeter Press

Kipfer, Barbara and Robert L. Chapman. 2007. *Dictionary of American Slang*. New York: Harper Collins

Knapp, Robbin D. 2005. *German English Words*. Raleigh, NC: Lulu Press

Kövecses, Zoltán. 2000. *American English: An Introduction*. Orchard Park, NY: Broadview Press

Kowalczyk, Małgorzata. 2010. "Slavic-Yiddish Lexical Borrowings in American Slang." *Kwartalnik Neofilologiczny*. Vol. LVII 1/2010, 14, 16, 19

Kowalczyk, Małgorzata. 2011. "The Applications of News Generators in Dictionary Making." *Kwartalnik Neofilologiczny*. Vol. LVIII 4/2011, 457–471

Kowalczyk, Małgorzata. 2013. *Americanisms*. Gdańsk: Wydawnictwo Uniwersytetu Gdańskiego

Kowalczyk, Małgorzata. 2014. *Bazinga! A Dictionary of Colloquial English Interjections*. Gdańsk: Wydawnictwo Uniwersytetu Gdańskiego

Kowalczyk, Małgorzata. 2015. "Ay Caramba! Functions of Spanish Borrowings in American Slang." *Kwartalnik Neofilologiczny*. Vol. 1/2015, 46–47

Kowalczyk, Małgorzata. 2016. "Zapożyczenia z języków Azji Wschodniej w angielszczyźnie potocznej." *Gdańskie Studia Azji Wschodniej*. Vol. 8, 158, 163

Kowalczyk, Małgorzata. 2017. "Colloquial Interjections in English and Polish: A Functional Classification." *On the Verge Between Language and Translation*. Vol. 1, 25–34

Kowalczyk, Małgorzata and Maciej Widawski. 2017. *Czarny slang. Słownik slangu afroamerykańskiego*. Bydgoszcz: Wydawnictwo UKW

Kowalczyk, Małgorzata and Maciej Widawski. 2019a. "Spanish Borrowings in American Slang and Their Semantic Fields." In Michał Borodo, Jacek Mianowski and Paweł Schreiber (eds.) *Memory, Identity, Cognition: Exploration in Culture and Communication*. Berlin: Springer, 17–28

Kowalczyk, Małgorzata and Maciej Widawski. 2019b. *The Dictionary of English Loanwords in Informal Polish*. Bydgoszcz: Wydawnictwo UKW

Kuźniak, Marek. 2009. *Foreign Words and Phrases in English: Metaphoric Astrophysical Concepts in Lexicogical Study*. Wrocław: Wydawnictwo Uniwersytetu Wrocławskiego

Labov, William. [1972] 1991. *Sociolinguistic Patterns*. Philadelphia: University of Pennsylvania Press

Lakoff, George and Mark Johnson. 1980. *Metaphors We Live By*. Chicago: University of Chicago Press

Lea, Diana and Jennifer Bradbery (eds.). 2020. *Oxford Advanced Learner's Dictionary*. Tenth Edition. Oxford: Oxford University Press

Lieber, Rochelle. 2010. *Introducing Morphology*. Cambridge: Cambridge University Press

Lighter, Jonathan E. 1994. *Historical Dictionary of American Slang, Vol. A-G*. New York: Random House

Lighter, Jonathan E. 1997. *Historical Dictionary of American Slang, Vol. H-O*. New York: Random House

Lighter, Jonathan. 2001. "American Slang." In John Algeo (ed.). *The Cambridge History of the English Language, Vol. VI: English in North America*. Cambridge: Cambridge University Press, 219–253

Lipski, John M. 2008. *Varieties of Spanish in the United States*. Washington, DC: Georgetown University Press

Llamas, Carmen, Louise Mullany, and Peter Stockwell (eds.). 2007. *The Routledge Companion to Sociolinguistics*. London: Routledge

Mallinson, Christine, Becky Childs, and Gerard Van Herk (eds.). 2013. *Data Collection in Sociolinguistics: Methods and Applications*. London: Routledge

Malmkjaer, Kirsten (ed.). 2009. *The Routledge Linguistics Encyclopedia*. London: Routledge

Mańczak-Wohlfeld, Elżbieta. 1994. *Angielskie elementy leksykalne w języku polskim*. Kraków: Universitas

Mańczak-Wohlfeld, Elżbieta. 1995. *Tendencje rozwojowe zapożyczeń angielskich w języku polskim.* Kraków: Universitas

Mańczak-Wohlfeld, Elżbieta. 2006. *Angielsko-polskie kontakty językowe.* Kraków: Wydawnictwo Uniwersytetu Jagiellońskiego

Mańczak-Wohlfeld, Elżbieta. 2010. *Słownik zapożyczeń angielskich w polszczyźnie.* Warsaw: PWN

Matras, Yaron. 2009. *Language Contact.* Cambridge: Cambridge University Press

Matthews, P.H. 2007. *The Concise Oxford Dictionary of Linguistics.* Oxford: Oxford University Press

Mauk, David and John Oakland. [1995] 2005. *American Civilization: An Introduction.* New York: Routledge

McArthur, Tom. 1992. *Oxford Companion to the English Language.* Oxford: Oxford University Press

McArthur, Tom. 2003. *Oxford Guide to World English.* Oxford: Oxford University Press

McCrum, Robert, Robert MacNeil, and William Cran. 2003. *The Story of English.* London: Penguin Books

McIntosh, Colin. 2013. *Cambridge Advanced Learner's Dictionary.* Fourth Edition. Cambridge: Cambridge University Press

Mencken, H.L. 1919. *The American Language: A Preliminary Inquiry into the Development of English in the United States.* New York: Alfred A. Knopf

Mesthrie, Rajend. 2001. *Concise Encyclopedia of Sociolinguistics.* Amsterdam: Elsevier

Meyerhoff, Miriam. [2006] 2011. *Introducing Sociolinguistics.* London: Routledge

Munro, Pamela. 1989. *Slang U.* Los Angeles: University of California Los Angeles Press

Murray, Thomas. 1996. "Spanish Loanwords in Contemporary American Slang." In Félix Rodríguez González. *Spanish Loanwords in the English Language: A Tendency Toward Hegemony Reversal.* Berlin: Walter de Gruyter, 105–137

Muysken, Pieter. 2000. *Bilingual Speech: A Typology of Code-Mixing.* Cambridge: Cambridge University Press

Myers-Scotton, Carol. 1993. *Social Motivation for Codeswitching.* Oxford: Clarendon Press

Myers-Scotton, Carol. 2006. *Multiple Voices: An Introduction to Bilingualism.* Malden, MA: Blackwell Publishing

Neufeldt, Victoria. 1999. "Informality in Language." *Dictionaries: Journal of the Dictionary Society of North America. Number 20/1999*, 1–22

Olivares, Rafael A. 1998. *NTC's Dictionary of Latin American Spanish.* New York: McGraw Hill

Ostler, Rosemarie. 2003. *Dewdroppers, Waldos, and Slackers: A Decade-by-Decade Guide to the Vanishing Vocabulary of the Twentieth Century.* New York: Oxford University Press

Partridge, Eric. 1933. *Slang To-Day and Yesterday.* London: Routledge & Kegan Paul

Pearce, Michael. 2007. *The Routledge Dictionary of English Language Studies.* New York: Routledge

Pfeffer, Alan J. and Garland Cannon. 2010. *German Loanwords in English: A Historical Dictionary.* Cambridge: Cambridge University Press

Polański, Kazimierz (ed.). 1993. *Encyklopedia językoznawstwa ogólnego.* Wrocław: Ossolineum

Poplack, Shana. 2018. *Borrowing: Loanwords in the Speech Community.* Oxford: Oxford University Press

Ramondino, Salvatore. 1996. *The New World Spanish/English, English/Spanish Dictionary.* New York: Signet Books

Reid, Elizabeth. 2003. *Spanish Lingo for the Savvy Gringo.* El Cajon, CA: Sunbelt Publications

Rodríguez González, Félix. 1996. *Spanish Loanwords in the English Language: A Tendency Toward Hegemony Reversal.* Berlin: Walter de Gruyter

Romaine, Suzanne. [1994] 2000. *Language in Society: An Introduction to Sociolinguistics.* New York: Cambridge University Press

Room, Adrian. 2000. *Cassell Dictionary of Word Histories.* London: Cassell

Rosten, Leo. [1968] 1996. *The Joys of Yiddish.* New York: Simon and Schuster

Rundell, Michael (ed.). 2002. *Macmillan English Dictionary for Advanced Learners.* Oxford: Macmillan Education

Sakel, Jeanette and Daniel Everett. 2012. *Linguistic Fieldwork.* Cambridge: Cambridge University Press

Schneider, Edgar. 2007. *Postcolonial English: Varieties around the World.* Cambridge: Cambridge University Press

Schultz, Julia. 2018. *The Influence of Spanish on the English Language since 1801.* Newcastle upon Tyne: Cambridge Scholars Publishing

Simpson, John and Edmund Weiner. 1989. *The Oxford English Dictionary.* Second Edition. Oxford: Oxford University Press

Smallman, C. Shawn and Kimberley Brown. 2015. *Introduction to International and Global Studies.* Chapel Hill: University of North Carolina Press

Smitherman, Geneva. 2000. *Black Talk: Words and Phrases from the Hood to the Amen Corner.* Boston, MA: Houghton Mifflin

Soukhanov, Anne. 1999. *Encarta World English Dictionary.* New York: St. Martin's Press

Soukhanov, Anne and Stuart Berg Flexner. 1997. *Speaking Freely.* New York: Oxford University Press

Spears, Richard A. 1981. *Slang and Euphemism.* New York: Signet Books

Spears, Richard A. 1990. *NTC's Dictionary of American Slang and Colloquial Expressions.* Lincolnwood, IL: NTC

Spears, Richard A. 1998. *NTC's Thematic Dictionary of American Slang and Colloquial Expressions.* Lincolnwood, IL: NTC

Spolsky, Bernard. [1998] 2007. *Sociolinguistics.* New York: Oxford University Press

Stefanowitsch, Anatol and Stefan Th. Gries. 2007. *Corpus-Based Approaches to Metaphor and Metonymy.* Berlin: Mouton Gruyter

Steinmetz, Sol. 2010. *There's a Word for It: The Explosion of the American Language since 1900*. New York: Harmony Books

Steinmetz, Sol and Barbara Ann Kipfer. 2006. *The Life of Language*. New York: Random House

Stevens, Payton R., Charles M. Levine, and Sol Steinmetz. 2002. *Meshuggenary: Celebrating the World of Yiddish*. New York: Simon & Schuster

Stevenson, Angus. 2010. *Oxford Dictionary of English*. Oxford: Oxford University Press

Stockwell, Robert. 2002. *Sociolinguistics: A Resource Book for Students*. London: Routledge

Stockwell, Robert and Donka Minkova. 2001. *English Words: History and Structure*. Cambridge: Cambridge University Press

Swan, Michael. 2003. *Practical English Usage*. Oxford: Oxford University Press

Tagliamonte, Sali. 2012. *Variationist Sociolinguistics: Change, Observation, Interpretation*. Malden, MA: Wiley Blackwell

Thomason, Sarah. 2001. *Language Contact*. Washington, DC: Georgetown University Press

Thomason, Sarah and Terrence Kaufman. 1988. *Language Contact, Creolization, and Genetic Linguistics*. Berkeley: University of California Press

Thorne, Tony. 1990. *Bloomsbury Dictionary of Contemporary Slang*. London: Bloomsbury Publishing

Thorne, Tony. 2009. *Dictionary of Contemporary Slang*. London: A & C Black

Titelman, Gregory. 1996. *Random House Dictionary of Popular Proverbs & Sayings*. New York: Random House

Trudgill, Peter. [1974] 2000. *Sociolinguistics: An Introduction to Language and Society*. London: Penguin Books

Urdang, Lawrence and Frank R. Abate. 1988. *Loanwords Dictionary*. New York: Gale Research

Van Herk, Gerard. 2012. *What Is Sociolinguistics?* Malden, MA: Wiley Blackwell

Von Polenz, Peter. 1967. "Fremdwort und Lehnwort Sprachwissenschaftlich Betrachtet." *Muttersprache. Vol. 77*, 65–80

Wardhaugh, Ronald. 1986. *An Introduction to Sociolinguistics*. Oxford: Blackwell

Weinreich, Uriel. [1953] 1968. *Languages in Contact: Findings and Problems*. The Hague: Mouton

Wentworth, Harold and Stuart Berg Flexner. [1960] 1975. *Dictionary of American Slang*. New York: Thomas Crowell

Wex, Michael. 2005. *Born to Kvetch: Yiddish Language and Culture in All Its Moods*. New York: St. Martin's Press

Widawski, Maciej. 1997. *Nowy słownik slangu i potocznej angielszczyzny*. Gdańsk: L & L

Widawski, Maciej. 2001. "Digging the Lingo of European Teens." *American Speech. Vol. 76.* 1, 104–108

Widawski, Maciej. 2008. "On Universality of Slang Usage: Motives for Using Slang in English and Polish." *Kwartalnik Neofilologiczny*. Vol. LV *2/2008*, 284–289

Widawski, Maciej. 2011. "Compounding in African American Slang." *Kwartalnik Neofilologiczny. Vol.* LVIII 4/2011, 441

Widawski, Maciej. 2012. *Yinglish*. Gdańsk: Wydawnictwo Uniwersytetu Gdańskiego

Widawski, Maciej. 2013. "Semantic Change in African American Slang." *Studia Anglica Posnaniensia. Vol. 48/1,* 69

Widawski, Maciej. [2015] 2019. *African American Slang: A Linguistic Description.* Cambridge: Cambridge University Press

Widawski, Maciej and Małgorzata Kowalczyk. 2011. *The Dictionary of City Names in American Slang.* Frankfurt: Peter Lang Verlag

Widawski, Maciej and Małgorzata Kowalczyk. 2012a. "Celebrating Five Years of the UG Student Slang Project." *Beyond Philology. Vol. 9,* 200

Widawski, Maciej and Małgorzata Kowalczyk. 2012b. *Black Lexicon.* Gdańsk: Wydawnictwo Uniwersytetu Gdańskiego

Widawski, Maciej and Małgorzata Kowalczyk. 2015. *The Dictionary of Spanish Loanwords in American Slang.* Gdańsk: Wydawnictwo Uniwersytetu Gdańskiego

Winford, Donald. 2003. *An Introduction to Contact Linguistics.* Oxford: Blackwell Publishing

Winn, Peter. 2006. *Americas: The Changing Face of Latin American and the Caribbean.* Berkeley: University of California Press

Witalisz, Alicja. 2007. *Anglosemantyzmy w języku polskim.* Kraków: Wydawnictwo Tertium

Wohlgemuth, Jan. 2009. *A Typology of Verbal Borrowings.* Berlin: Walter de Gruyter

Yule, George. [1985] 2014. *The Study of Language.* Cambridge: Cambridge University Press

Zuckerman, Ghil'ad. 2003. *Language Contact and Lexical Enrichment in Israeli Hebrew.* New York: Palgrave Macmillan

Index

Abate, Frank, 7
abbreviation, 93–94, 114
accentuation, 79, 81, 104, 143
acronym, 93, 94, 105, 144
Adams, Michael, 8, 32, 35, 40, 110, 116
adaptation, 26, 28, 70, 73, 79
Adeleye, Gabriel, 7
adjective, 63, 64, 78, 143
adjectivization, 101, 105, 144
adverb, 63, 66, 78, 143
affix, 66, 78, 86, 143
affix word, 85–87
affixation, 84, 90, 104, 144
Africa, 56
African American English, 37, 56, 57, 118
African American Vernacular, 10, 11, 38, 57
African Americans, 39
African languages, 56, 57
Akmajian, Adrian, 24
alcohol, 122, 128–130
Algeo, John, 6, 7, 8, 24, 62, 84, 112
Allen, Irving Lewis, 2, 113
alteration, 70
amalgamation, 94
amelioration, 100
American English, 1, 10–11, 35–36, 80, 81, 82, 104, 117, 141, 142, 143, 144, 145, 146
American society, 1, 14, 34, 39, 48, 61, 69, 80, 118, 120, 141, 145, 146
appropriation, 3, 9, 118
Arabic, 56, 58, 83, 142
argot, 40
Arizona, 13
article, 89
assimilation, 2, 3, 17, 60, 67–70, 78, 101, 118, 143
Austria, 83
Ayto, John, 1, 33, 35, 42, 135

back clipping, 93
bad English, 37
Bauer, Laurie, 35

Belarusian, 49
Bell, Allan, 8
Bentley, Harold, 6
binomial, 92
binomial phrase, 92
blend, 94
blending, 94–95, 105, 144
Bloomfield, Leonard, 60, 117
Bluestein, Gene, 7
books on borrowing, 5–7, 20
books on informal language, 7–10, 20
borrowing, 2, 3, 5, 11, 22–27, 43, 61–63, 141, 146
borrowing proper, 25, 78, 142
broadening, 99
Brown, Kimberley, 22
Bucholtz, Mary, 118
Bühler, Karl, 106

cacophemism, 42
California, 13
caló, 47
calque, 25
cannibal borrowing, 109
Cannon, Garland, 7
cant, 40
Cantonese, 53
Chambers, Jack, 8
changes overview, 143–144
Chapman, Robert, 9, 10, 12, 13, 18, 32, 33, 75, 110, 119, 126, 129
Chinese, 20, 26, 53–54, 58, 62, 78, 83, 104, 142, 143
circumfix, 88
citation borrowing, 27, 68
citations, 1, 2, 3, 12, 15, 16–17, 19, 20, 141, 145, 146
classical languages, 54
cliché, 92
clipped compound, 93
clipped phrase, 94
clipping, 93–94, 104, 114, 144
Clyne, Michael, 24
code switch, 27, 28, 44, 141

327

Milton Keynes UK
Ingram Content Group UK Ltd.
UKHW051446100923
428198UK00028B/49